THE 68000 MICROPROCESSOR

ARCHITECTURE, SOFTWARE, AND INTERFACING TECHNIQUES

THE 68000 MICROPROCESSOR

ARCHITECTURE, SOFTWARE, AND INTERFACING TECHNIQUES

Walter A. Triebel

Avtar Singh, Ph.D.

PRENTICE-HALL, Englewood Cliffs, New Jersey 07632

Library of Congress Cataloging-in-Publication Data

Triebel, Walter A.
  The 68000 microprocessor.

  Bibliography: p.
  Includes index.
  1. Motorola 68000 (Microprocessor) I. Singh,
Avtar.   . II. Title.
QA76.8.M67T75 1986   004.165   85-25607
ISBN 0-13-811357-2

Editorial/production supervision and
interior design: **Kathryn Pavelec**
Cover design: **Joe Curcio**
Manufacturing buyer: **Gordon Osbourne**

Portions of this text were previously published as
16-BIT MICROPROCESSORS: Architecture, Software, and Interface Techniques
by Triebel and Singh (Prentice-Hall, 1985).

Printed in the United States of America

10 9 8 7 6 5 4 3 2 1

ISBN 0-13-811357-2 025

PRENTICE-HALL INTERNATIONAL (UK) LIMITED, *London*
PRENTICE-HALL OF AUSTRALIA PTY. LIMITED, *Sydney*
PRENTICE-HALL CANADA INC., *Toronto*
PRENTICE-HALL HISPANOAMERICANA, S.A., *Mexico*
PRENTICE-HALL OF INDIA PRIVATE LIMITED, *New Delhi*
PRENTICE-HALL OF JAPAN, INC., *Tokyo*
PRENTICE-HALL OF SOUTHEAST ASIA PTE. LTD., *Singapore*
EDITORA PRENTICE-HALL DO BRASIL, LTDA., *Rio de Janeiro*
WHITEHALL BOOKS LIMITED, *Wellington, New Zealand*

Walter A. Triebel
To my wife, Frieda

Avtar Singh
*To my parents, Amar Kaur
and Lal Singh*

CONTENTS

PREFACE

Today, the 68000 family is one of the more widely used families of 16-bit microprocessors in modern microcomputer-based products. The 68000 is the microprocessor employed in the popular Macintosh personal computer, as well as in a wide variety of other electronic equipment. Individuals involved in the design of microprocessor-based equipment need a *systems-level* understanding of the 68000 microcomputer system. That is, a thorough knowledge of its software, hardware, and interfacing is required.

This book represents an extensive study of the architecture, software, and interfacing techniques used in the design of 68000-based microcomputers. This material is developed in the following five chapters: Chapter 2, The 68000 Microprocessor; Chapter 3, 68000 Microprocessor Programming 1; Chapter 4, 68000 Microprocessor Programming 2; Chapter 6, Memory and Input/Output Interfaces of the 68000 Microprocessor; Chapter 7, Exception Processing of the 68000 Microprocessor.

With the first of these chapters we develop a thorough understanding of the internal architecture of the 68000 microprocessor. This includes material on its instruction execution control.

Chapters 3 and 4 present in detail software issues such as addressing modes, the instruction set, and the analysis and writing of assembly-language programs. A large number of practical applications are illustrated through example programs.

The latter two, Chapters 6 and 7, are concerned with hardware and introduce architectural features and circuit design techniques for the memory, input/output, and interrupt interfaces of the 68000 microcomputer. Extensive coverage of bus cycles, address maps, program storage memory subsystems, data storage memory subsystems, input/output interface circuits, and interrupt interface circuits is included. A number of large-scale integrated (LSI) peripheral controllers, such as the 6821 peripheral interface adapter, the 6850 asynchronous communication adapter, and the 68230 parallel interface/timer, are also studied in depth.

Two additional chapters are included that introduce Motorola's MC68000 Educational Microcomputer Board. This board is an educational microcomputer system that can be used to execute and debug assembly-language programs written for the 68000 microprocessor. Chapter 5 introduces the educational microcomputer and the commands that can be issued to the microcomputer. Moreover, examples are used to demonstrate how programs are assembled, verified, executed, and debugged.

Chapter 8 is a study of the circuitry in the MC68000 educational microcomputer. This chapter illustrates a practical application of the material on interfacing techniques presented in Chapters 6 and 7. The architecture and circuit design of the 68000-based microcomputer is described in detail.

This book is written for use as a textbook in the electronic engineering technology curricula offered at universities and community colleges. Use of the book does require prior knowledge of basic digital electronics. This background is at a level consistent with, but not necessarily as extensive as, the material presented in two earlier Prentice-Hall books: *Integrated Digital Electronics, 2nd ed.,* Walter A. Triebel, 1985; and *Handbook of Semiconductor and Bubble Memories,* Walter A. Triebel and Alfred E. Chu, 1982. Since this book includes a large amount of practical information on 68000 microcomputer architecture, assembly-language programming, and interface circuit design, it is also a valuable reference for practicing engineers and technicians.

WALTER A. TRIEBEL

AVTAR SINGH

THE 68000 MICROPROCESSOR

Architecture, Software, and Interfacing Techniques

1
INTRODUCTION TO MICROPROCESSORS AND MICROCOMPUTERS

1.1 INTRODUCTION

The most recent advances in computer system technology have been closely related to the development of high-performance 16-bit microprocessors and their microcomputer systems. During the last three years, the 16-bit microprocessor market has matured significantly. Today, several complete 16-bit microprocessor families are available. They include support products such as large-scale integrated (LSI) peripheral devices, development systems, emulators, and high-level software languages. Over the same period of time, these higher-performance microprocessors have become more widely used in the design of new electronic equipment and computers.

This book presents a detailed study of one of the more popular 16-bit microprocessors, the 68000 by Motorola Incorporated. Included is material on the internal architecture of the 68000 microprocessor, its assembly language programming, and the interface techniques used in the design of 68000-based microcomputer systems. In this chapter we begin our study of 16-bit microprocessors and microcomputers. The following topics are discussed:

1. The digital computer
2. Mainframe computers, minicomputers, and microcomputers
3. Hardware elements of the digital computer system
4. General architecture of a microcomputer system
5. Types of microprocessors and single-chip microcomputers

1.2 THE DIGITAL COMPUTER

As a starting point, let us consider what a *computer* is, what it can do, and how it does it. A computer is a digital electronic data processing system. Data are input to the computer in one form, processed within the computer, and the information that results is either output or stored for later use. Figure 1.1 shows a modern computer system.

Computers cannot think about how to process the data that were input. Instead, the user must tell the computer exactly what to do. The procedure by which a computer is told how to work is called *programming* and the person who writes programs for a computer is known as a *programmer*. The result of the programmer's work is a set of instructions for the computer to follow. This is the computer's *program*. When the computer is operating, the instructions of the program guide it step by step through the task that is to be performed.

For example, a large department store can use a computer to take care of bookkeeping for its customer charge accounts. In this application, data about items purchased by the customers, such as price and department, are entered into the computer by an operator. These data are stored in the computer under the customer's account number. On the next billing date, the data are processed and a tabular record of each customer's account is output by the computer. These statements are mailed to the customers as a bill.

In a computer, the program controls the operation of a large amount of electronic circuitry. It is this circuitry that actually does the processing of data. Electronic computers first became available in the 1940s. These early computers were built with vacuum-tube electronic circuits. In the 1950s, a second generation of computers was built. During this period, transistor electronic circuitry, instead of tubes, was used to produce more compact and more reliable computer systems. When the *integrated circuit* (IC) came into the electronic market during the 1960s, a third generation of computers appeared. With ICs, industry could manufacture more complex, higher-speed, and very reliable computers.

Today, the computer industry is continuing to be revolutionized by the advances made in integrated-circuit technology. It is now possible to manufacture *large-scale integrated circuits* (LSI) that can form a computer with just a small group of ICs. In fact, in some cases, a single IC can be used. These new technologies are rapidly advancing the low-performance, low-cost part of the computer marketplace by permitting simpler and more cost-effective designs.

1.3 MAINFRAME COMPUTERS, MINICOMPUTERS, AND MICROCOMPUTERS

For many years the computer manufacturers' aim was to develop larger and more powerful computer systems. These are what we call *large-scale* or *mainframe computers*. Mainframes are always *general-purpose computers*. That is, they are

Figure 1-1 Modern large-scale computer (International Business Machine Corp).

designed with the ability to run a large number of different types of programs. For this reason, they can solve a wide variety of problems.

For instance, one user can apply the computer in an assortment of scientific applications where the primary function of the computer is to solve complex mathematical problems. A second user can apply the same basic computer system to perform business tasks such as accounting and inventory control. The only difference between the computer systems used in these two applications could be their programs. In fact, today many companies use a single general-purpose computer to resolve both their scientific and business needs.

Figure 1.1 is an example of a mainframe computer manufactured by International Business Machine Corporation (IBM). Because of their high cost, mainframes find use only in central computing facilities of large businesses and institutions.

The many advances that have taken place in the field of electronics over the past two decades have led to rapid advances in computer system technology. For instance, the introduction of *small-scale integrated* (SSI) *circuits,* followed by *medium-scale integrated* (MSI) *circuits,* and *large-scale integrated* (LSI) *circuits,* has led the way in expanding the capacity and performance of the large mainframe computers. But at the same time, these advances have also permitted the introduction of smaller, lower-performance, and lower-cost computer systems.

Figure 1-2 Minicomputer system (Digital Equipment Corp.).

As computer use grew, it was recognized that the powerful computing capability of a mainframe was not needed by many customers. Instead, they desired easier access to a machine with smaller capacity. It was to satisfy this requirement that the *minicomputer* was developed. Minicomputers, such as that shown in Fig. 1.2, are also digital computers and are capable of performing the same basic operations as the earlier, larger systems. However, they are designed to provide a smaller functional capability. The processor section of this type of computer is typically manufactured using SSI and MSI electronic circuitry.

Minicomputers have found wide use as general-purpose computers, but their lower cost also allows their use in dedicated applications. A computer used in a dedicated application represents what is known as a *special-purpose computer.* By "special-purpose computer" we mean a system that has been tailored to meet the needs of a specific application. Examples are process control computers for industrial facilities, data processing systems for retail stores, and medical analysis systems for patient care. Figure 1.3 shows a minicomputer-based retail store data processing system.

Figure 1-3 Retail store data processing system (Sweda International Incorporated).

The newest development in the computer industry is the *microcomputer.* Today, the microcomputer represents the next step in the evolution of the computer world. It is a computer that has been designed to provide reduced size and capability from that of a minicomputer, with a much lower cost.

The heart of the microcomputer system is the *microprocessor.* A microprocessor is a general-purpose processor built into a single IC. It is an example of an LSI device. Together with the use of LSI circuitry in the microcomputer have come the benefits of smaller size, lighter weight, lower cost, reduced power requirements, and higher reliability.

The low cost of microprocessors, which can be as low as $1, has opened the use of computer electronics to a much broader range of products. Figures 1.4 and 1.5 show some typical systems in which a microcomputer is used as a special-purpose computer.

Figure 1-4 Calculator (Texas Instruments, Incorporated).

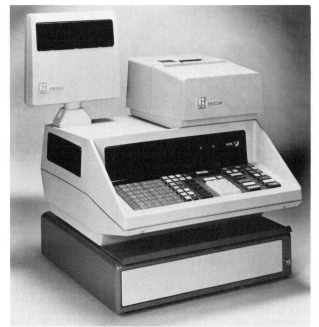

Figure 1-5 Point-of-sale terminal (Sweda International Incorporated).

Microcomputers are also finding wide use as general-purpose computers. Figures 1.6 and 1.7 are examples of personal computer systems. In fact, microcomputer systems designed for the high-performance end of the microcomputer market are rivaling the performance of the lower-performance minicomputers and at a much lower cost to the user.

Figure 1-6 Personal computer (AT&T Information Systems).

Figure 1-7 Personal computer (Apple Computer Inc.).

1.4 HARDWARE ELEMENTS OF THE DIGITAL COMPUTER SYSTEM

The hardware of a digital computer system is divided into four functional sections. The block diagram of Fig. 1.8 shows the four basic units of a simplified computer: the *input unit, central processing unit, memory unit,* and *output unit.* Each section has a special function in terms of overall computer operation.

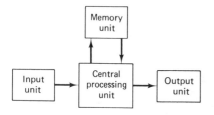

Figure 1-8 Block diagram of a digital computer (Walter A. Triebel, Integrated Digital Electronics, © 1979. Adapted by permission of Prentice-Hall, Inc., Englewood Cliffs, N.J.).

The *central processing unit* (CPU) is the heart of the computer system. It is responsible for performing all arithmetic operations and logic decisions initiated by the program. In addition to arithmetic and logic functions, the CPU controls overall system operation.

On the other hand, the input and output units are the means by which the CPU communicates with the outside world. The *input unit* is used to input information and commands to the CPU for processing. For instance, a Teletype terminal can be used by the programmer to input a new program.

After processing, the information that results must be output. This output of data from the system is performed under control of the *output unit*. Examples of ways of outputting information are as printed pages produced by a high-speed printer or displayed on the screen of a video display terminal.

The *memory unit* of the computer is used to store information such as numbers, names, and addresses. By "store," we mean that memory has the ability to hold this information for processing or for outputting at a later time. The programs that define how the computer is to process data also reside in memory.

In computer systems, memory is divided into two different sections, known as *primary storage* and *secondary storage*. They are also sometimes called *internal memory* and *external memory*, respectively. *External memory* is used for long-term storage of information that is not in use. For instance, it holds programs, files of data, and files of information. In most computers, this part of memory employs storage on magnetic media such as magnetic tapes, magnetic disks, and magnetic drums. This is because they have the ability to store large amounts of data.

Internal memory is a smaller segment of memory used for temporary storage of programs, data, and information. For instance, when a program is to be executed, its instructions are first brought from external memory into internal memory together with the files of data and information that it will affect. After this, the program is executed and its files updated while they are held in internal memory. When the processing defined by the program is complete, the updated files are returned to external memory. Here the program and files are retained for use at a later time.

The internal memory of a computer system uses electronic memory devices instead of storage on a magnetic media memory. In most modern computer systems, semiconductor read-only memory (ROM) and random access read/write memory (RAM) are in use. These devices make internal memory much faster-operating than external memory.

Neither semiconductor memory nor magnetic media memory alone can satisfy the requirements of most general-purpose computer systems. Because of this fact, both types are normally present in the system. For instance, in a personal computer system, working storage is typically provided with RAM, while long-term storage is provided with floppy disk memory. On the other hand, in special-purpose computer systems, such as a video game, semiconductor memory is used. That is, the program that determines how the game is played is stored in ROM, and data storage, such as for graphic patterns, is in RAM.

1.5 GENERAL ARCHITECTURE OF A MICROCOMPUTER SYSTEM

Now that we have introduced the *general architecture* of a digital computer, let us look at how a microcomputer fits this model. Looking at Fig. 1.9, we find that the architecture of the microcomputer is essentially the same as that of the digital computer in Fig. 1.8. It has the same function elements: input unit, output unit, memory unit, and in place of the CPU, a *microprocessor unit* (MPU). Moreover, each element serves the same basic function relative to overall system operation.

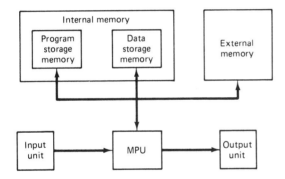

Figure 1-9 General microcomputer system architecture.

The difference between minicomputers, mainframe computers, and microcomputers does not lie in the fundamental blocks used to build the computer; instead, it relates to the capacity and performance of the electronics used to implement their blocks and the resulting overall system capacity and performance. As indicated earlier, microcomputers are designed with smaller capacity and lower performance than either minicomputers or mainframes.

Unlike mainframes and minicomputers, a microcomputer can be implemented with a small group of components. Again the heart of the computer system is the MPU (CPU) and it performs all arithmetic, logic, and control operations. However, in a microcomputer the MPU is implemented with a single microprocessor chip instead of a large assortment of SSI and MSI logic functions such as in minicomputers and mainframes. Notice that correct use of the term "microprocessor" restricts its use to the central processing unit in a microcomputer system.

Notice that we have partitioned the memory unit into an internal memory section for storage of active data and instructions and an external memory section for long-term storage. As in minicomputers, the long-term storage medium in a

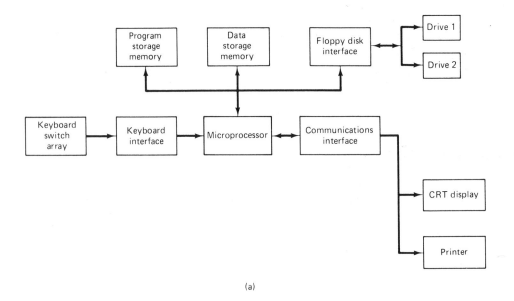

(a)

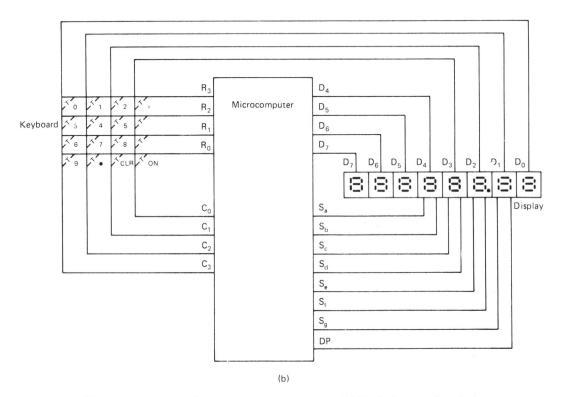

(b)

Figure 1-10 (a) Block diagram of a personal computer; (b) block diagram of a calculator.

microcomputer is frequently a floppy disk. However, Winchester rigid disk drives are becoming popular when storage requirements are higher than those provided by floppy disks. In industrial applications, where the environment for the equipment is rugged, bubble memories are also employed as long-term storage devices.

Internal memory of the microcomputer is further subdivided into *program storage memory* and *data storage memory.* Typically, internal memory is implemented with both ROM and RAM ICs. Data, whether they are to be interpreted as numbers, characters, or instructions, can be stored in either ROM or RAM. But in most microcomputer systems, instructions of the program and data such as lookup tables are stored in ROM. This is because this type of information does not normally change. By using ROM, its storage is made *nonvolatile*. That is, if power is lost, the information is retained.

On the other hand, the numerical and character data that are to be processed by the microprocessor change frequently. These data must be stored in a type of memory from which they can be read by the microprocessor, modified through processing, and written back for storage. For this reason, they are stored in RAM instead of ROM.

Depending on the application, the input and output sections can be implemented with something as simple as a few switches for inputs and a few light-emitting diodes (LEDs) for outputs. In other applications, for example in a personal computer, the input/output (I/O) devices can be more sophisticated, such as video display terminals and printers, just like those employed in minicomputer systems.

Up to this point, we have been discussing what is known as a *multichip microcomputer system,* that is, a system implemented with a microprocessor and an assortment of support circuits, such as ROMs, RAMs, and I/O peripherals. This architecture makes for a very flexible system design. Its ROM, RAM, and I/O capacity can be easily expanded by just adding more devices. This is the circuit configuration used in most larger microcomputer systems. An example is the personal computer system shown in Fig. 1.10(a).

Devices are now being made that include all the functional blocks of a microcomputer in a single IC. This is called a *single-chip microcomputer.* Unlike the multichip microcomputer, single-chip microcomputers are limited in capacity and not as easy to expand. For example, a microcomputer device can have 4K bytes of ROM, 128 bytes of RAM, and 32 lines for use as inputs or outputs. Because of this limited capability, single-chip microcomputers find wide use in special-purpose computer applications. A block diagram of a calculator implemented with a single-chip microcomputer is shown in Fig. 1.10(b).

1.6 TYPES OF MICROPROCESSORS AND SINGLE-CHIP MICROCOMPUTERS

The principal way in which microprocessors and microcomputers are categorized is in terms of the number of binary bits in the data they process, that is, their word length. Figure 1.11 shows that the three standard organizations used in the design

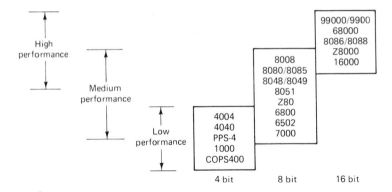

Figure 1-11 Microprocessor and single-chip microcomputer categories and relative performance.

of microprocessors and microcomputers are 4-bit, 8-bit, and 16-bit data words.

The first microprocessors and microcomputers, which were introduced in the early 1970s, were all designed to process data that were arranged 4 bits wide. This organization is frequently referred to as a *nibble* of data. Many of the early 4-bit devices, such as the PPS-4 microprocessor made by Rockwell International Incorporated and the TMS1000 single-chip microcomputer made by Texas Instruments Incorporated, are still in wide use today.

The low performance and limited system capabilities of 4-bit microcomputers limits their use to simpler, special-purpose applications. Some common uses are in calculators and electronic toys. In this type of equipment, low cost, not high performance, is the overriding requirement in the selection of a processor.

In the 1973–1974 period, second-generation microprocessors were introduced. These devices, such as Intel Corporation's 8008 and 8080, were 8-bit microprocessors. That is, they were designed to process 8-bit (one-byte-wide) data instead of 4-bit data.

The newer 8-bit microprocessors exhibited higher-performance operation, larger system capabilities, and greater ease of programming. They were able to provide the system requirements for many applications that could not be satisfied by 4-bit microcomputers. These extended capabilities led to widespread acceptance of multichip 8-bit microcomputers for special-purpose system designs. Examples of some of these dedicated applications are electronic instruments, cash registers, and printers.

Somewhat later, 8-bit microprocessors began to migrate into general-purpose microcomputer systems. In fact, the Z-80A is still the host MPU in a number of personal computers.

Late in the 1970s, 8-bit single-chip microcomputers, such as Intel's 8048, became available. The full microcomputer capability of this single chip further reduces the cost of implementing designs for smaller, dedicated digital sytems. In fact, 8-bit microcomputers are still being designed for introduction into the marketplace. An example is Intel's new 8051 family of 8-bit microcomputers. Newer devices, such as the 8051, offer a one-order-of-magnitude-higher performance, more powerful instruction sets, and special on-chip functions such as interval/event timers and universal asynchronous receiver/transmitters (UARTs).

The plans for development of third-generation 16-bit microprocessors were announced by many of the leading semiconductor manufacturers in the mid-1970s. The 9900 was introduced in 1977, followed by a number of other key devices, such as the 9981, 8086, 8088, Z8000, 68000, 99000, and 16000. These devices all provide high performance and have the ability to satisfy a broad scope of special-purpose and general-purpose microcomputer applications. All of the devices have the ability to handle 8-bit as well as 16-bit data words. Some can even process data organized as 32-bit words. Moreover, their powerful instruction sets are more in line with those provided by minicomputers instead of those of 8-bit microprocessors.

In terms of special-purpose applications, 16-bit microprocessors are replacing 8-bit processors in applications that require very high performance: for example, certain types of electronic instruments. A single-chip 16-bit microcomputer, the 8096, is also available for use in this type of application.

16-bit microprocessors are also being used in applications that can benefit from some of their extended system capabilities. For instance, they are beginning to be used in word-processing systems. This type of system requires a large amount of character data to be temporarily active; therefore, it can benefit from the ability of a 16-bit microprocessor to access a much larger amount of data storage memory.

Most new personal computers are being designed with 16-bit microprocessors. For instance, Apple, in its personal computer, the McIntosh, uses the 68000 microprocessor to implement the microcomputer.

ASSIGNMENT

Section 1.2

1. What guides the computer as to how it is to process data?
2. What type of electronic devices are revolutionizing the low-performance, low-cost computer market today?

Section 1.3

3. What is the key difference between mainframe, mini-, and microcomputers?
4. What is meant by "general-purpose computer"?
5. What is meant by "special-purpose computer"?

Section 1.4

6. What are the building blocks of a general computer system?
7. What is the difference between primary and secondary storage?

Section 1.5

8. What are the basic building blocks of a microcomputer system?

9. What is the difference between program storage and data storage memory in a microcomputer?

10. What is the difference between internal and external storage memory in a microcomputer?

Section 1.6

11. What are the standard data word lengths of microprocessors and microcomputers available today?

12. What is the difference between a multichip microcomputer and a single-chip microcomputer?

13. Name five 16-bit microprocessor families.

2 | THE 68000 MICROPROCESSOR

2.1 INTRODUCTION

In Chapter 1, some general aspects of microprocessors and microcomputers were introduced. With the present chapter, we begin our study of Motorola's 68000 microprocessor. In this chapter we describe the general architecture of the 68000. The six chapters that follow are devoted to other aspects such as instruction set, programming, and hardware interfacing. The following topics are discussed in this chapter:

1. The 68000 microprocessor
2. Interface signals of the 68000
3. Internal architecture of the 68000
4. Instruction execution control

2.2 THE 68000 MICROPROCESSOR

16 bit data bus - word - 2 bytes

The 68000 is a very powerful 16-bit microprocessor whose development was announced by Motorola, Inc., in 1979. Since then Motorola has concentrated on bringing the device up to production, providing tools to support hardware and software development, and initiating development of a new family of LSI support peripherals. With apparent success in these areas, they have continued the growth of the product family by introducing other microprocessors, such as the 68008, 68010, and 68020.

The 68000 is manufactured using HMOS (high-density N-channel MOS) technology. The present-day advances in circuit design, process technology, and chip fabrication techniques have enabled Motorola, Inc. to implement very high performance operation and complex functions for the 68000. The circuitry within the 68000 is equivalent to approximately 68000 MOS transistors.

The 68000 microprocessor is packaged into a 64-pin package. This package is shown together with its pin assignments in Fig. 2.1. Notice that use of this large package eliminates the need for multifunction pins. For instance, the address bus and data bus are not multiplexed. The fact that each lead serves just one electrical function simplifies design of the external hardware interfaces in a 68000 microcomputer system.

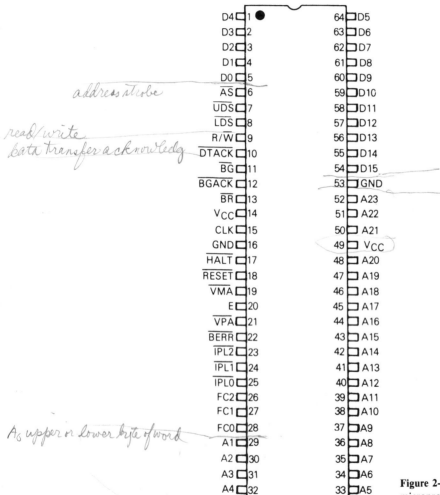

address strobe

read/write
data transfer acknowledg

A₀ upper or lower byte of word

Figure 2-1 Pin layout of the 68000 microprocessor (Motorola, Inc.).

The 68000 employs a very powerful 32-bit general-purpose internal architecture. It has 16 internal general-purpose registers that are all 32 bits in length. Eight of these registers are *data registers* and the other eight are *address registers*.

The architecture of the 68000 was planned to permit all types of data and address operations to be performed from its data registers and address registers, respectively. That is, none of its data registers have dedicated functions such as for use as an accumulator or for input/output. Therefore, instructions can be written such that their operands reside in any of the data registers or storage locations in memory. Moreover, data processed by the 68000 can be expressed in five different types. They are *bit, BCD (4-bit), byte, word,* and *long word (32-bit).*

The address registers are also designed for general use and do not have dedicated functions. For instance, if the MOVE instruction was to have its source operand located in memory instead of in one of the internal registers, any one of the address registers can be specified to contain this address.

The architecture of the 68000 includes a number of powerful hardware and software functions. From a hardware point of view, we see that the 68000 has a large 23-bit external address bus. This gives it a very large 16M-byte logical address space. A software function that has been included in the architecture is the ability to create a *user/supervisor environment* for the 68000 microcomputer system. This feature helps the programmer to protect the software operating system and provides support for *multiprocessing* and *multitasking* applications.

2.3 INTERFACES OF THE 68000 MICROPROCESSOR

Now that we have briefly introduced the 68000 microprocessor, let us look at its electrical interfaces. From the block diagram in Fig. 2.2, we see that the signal lines can be grouped into seven interfaces: the *address/data bus, asynchronous bus control, processor status lines, system control bus, interrupt control bus, bus arbitration control bus,* and *synchronous control bus.* It is through these buses and lines that the 68000 is connected to external circuitry such as memory and input/output peripherals.

Address and Data Bus

Earlier we pointed out that the 68000 microprocessor has independent address and data buses. This simplifies the design of the memory and I/O interfaces because the address and data signals, need not be demultiplexed with external circuitry. Moreover, the address bus, data bus, and memory address space are used to interface to input/output devices in addition to interface to the memory subsystem. That is, all I/O devices in the 68000 microcomputer system are memory-mapped.

Earlier we indicated that the 68000 has a 23-bit *unidirectional address bus.* The function of the signals at these lines, A_{23} through A_1, is to supply addresses to the memory and input/output subsystems. A_{23} represents the most significant bit of the address and A_1 the least significant bit. Bit A_0, which is maintained internal to the

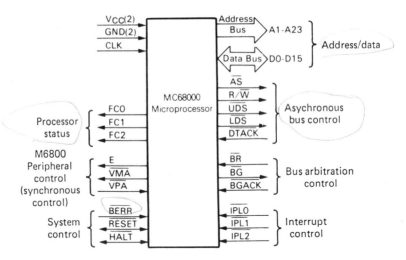

Figure 2-2 Block diagram of the 68000 microprocessor (Motorola, Inc.).

68000, indicates whether the upper or lower byte of a word is to be used when processing byte data.

The 16 *bidirectional data lines* are labeled D_{15} through D_0. They either carry read/write data between microprocessor and memory or input/output data between the microprocessor and I/O peripherals.

Asynchronous Control Bus

The control of the 68000's bus is *asynchronous*. By this we mean that once a bus cycle is initiated, it is not completed until a signal is returned from external circuitry. The signals that are provided to control address and data transfers are *address strobe* (AS), *read/write* (R/W), *upper data strobe* (UDS), *lower data strobe* (LDS), and *data transfer acknowledge* (DTACK).

The 68000 must signal external circuitry when an address is available, and whether a read or write operation is to take place over the bus. It does this with the signals AS and R/W, respectively. At the moment a valid address is present on the address bus, the 68000 produces the address strobe (AS) control signal. The pulse to logic 0 that is output as AS is used to signal memory or I/O devices that an address is available.

Read/write (R/W) signals which type of data transfer is to take place over the data bus. During a read or input bus cycle, when the microprocessor reads data from bus lines D_0 through D_{16}, the R/W output is switched to logic 1. Similarly, when data are written or output to memory or I/O devices, the 68000 indicates this condition by a logic 0 on this line.

Since the bus cycle is asynchronous, external circuitry must signal the 68000 when the bus cycle can be completed. Data transfer acknowledge (DTACK) is an input to the microprocessor which indicates the status of the current bus cycle. During a read or input cycle, logic 0 at $\overline{\text{DTACK}}$ signals the microprocessor that valid data are on the data bus. In response, it reads and latches the data internally and completes the bus cycle. On the other hand, during a write or output operation, $\overline{\text{DTACK}}$ informs the microprocessor that the data have been written to memory or a peripheral device. Thus we see that in both cases $\overline{\text{DTACK}}$ is used to terminate the bus cycle.

Two other control outputs provided on the 68000 are upper data strobe ($\overline{\text{UDS}}$) and lower data strobe ($\overline{\text{LDS}}$). These two signals act as an extension of the address bus and signal whether a byte or word of data is being transferred over the data bus. In the case of a byte transfer, they also indicate if the data will be carried over the upper eight or lower eight data lines. Logic 0 at $\overline{\text{UDS}}$ signals that a byte of data is to be transferred across upper data lines D_{15} through D_8 and logic 0 at $\overline{\text{LDS}}$ signals that a byte of data is to be transferred over lower data lines D_7 through D_0.

Figure 2.3 shows the logic levels of $\overline{\text{UDS}}$, $\overline{\text{LDS}}$, and R/$\overline{\text{W}}$ for each type of data transfer operation. For instance, if $\overline{\text{UDS}} = 0$, $\overline{\text{LDS}} = 0$, and R/$\overline{\text{W}} = 1$, a read operation is taking place over the complete data bus.

Example 2.1

Specify the address and control signals that occur to read the lower byte from the word stored at address $001B36_{16}$.

Solution. The address lines A_{23} through A_1 directly specify an even (upper) byte address. The odd (lower) byte address is obtained by $\overline{\text{LDS}}$ being active. Thus we get

$$A_{23}A_{22} \cdots A_1A_0 = 001B37_{16}$$
$$= 0000000000011011001101111_2$$

and

$$\overline{\text{LDS}} = 0$$

$$\overline{\text{UDS}} = 1$$

Since a byte of data is to be read,

$$\text{R/}\overline{\text{W}} = 1$$

and the data are supplied to the 68000 on the lower data lines D_0 through D_7.

$\overline{\text{UDS}}$	$\overline{\text{LDS}}$	R/$\overline{\text{W}}$	Operation
0	0	0	Word → memory/IO
0	1	0	High byte → memory/IO
1	0	0	Low byte → memory/IO
1	1	0	Invalid data
0	0	1	Word → microprocessor
0	1	1	High byte → microprocessor
1	0	1	Low byte → microprocessor
1	1	1	Invalid data

Figure 2-3 Memory access relationships for $\overline{\text{UDS}}$, $\overline{\text{LDS}}$, and R/$\overline{\text{W}}$ (Motorola, Inc.).

Processor Status Bus and the Function Codes

During every bus cycle executed by the 68000, it outputs a 3-bit processor status code. These status codes are also known as *function codes* and are output on lines FC_0 through FC_2. They tell external circuitry which type of bus cycle is in progress: That is, whether data or program is being accessed and if the microprocessor is in the *user* or *supervisor state*.

The table in Fig. 2.4(a) shows the implemented function codes and also the ones that are reserved for future expansion. For instance, the code 110_2 on $FC_2FC_1FC_0$ indicates that an instruction or immediate operand aquisition bus cycle is in progress from *supervisor program memory*. Notice that 111_2 has a special function. It is the *interrupt acknowledge code*.

These codes are output by the 68000 at the beginning of each read or write cycle and remain valid until the beginning of the next read or write cycle. The timing relationship between the function code lines, the clock, and $\overline{AS}$ is shown in Fig. 2.4(b). Notice that the function code outputs are valid during the address strobe $\overline{AS}$

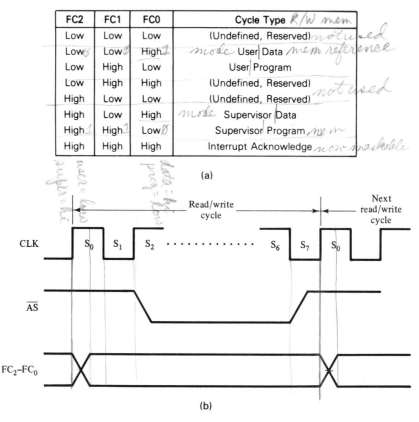

FC2	FC1	FC0	Cycle Type
Low	Low	Low	(Undefined, Reserved)
Low	Low	High	User Data
Low	High	Low	User Program
Low	High	High	(Undefined, Reserved)
High	Low	Low	(Undefined, Reserved)
High	Low	High	Supervisor Data
High	High	Low	Supervisor Program
High	High	High	Interrupt Acknowledge

(a)

(b)

Figure 2-4 (a) Function code table (Motorola, Inc.); (b) relationship between FC_2 FC_1FC_0, CLK, and $\overline{AS}$.

pulse. Therefore, they can be combined with $\overline{AS}$ to generate device or memory select signals. As an example, the function code 001_2 can be used to gate $\overline{AS}$ to the user data section of memory.

System Control Bus

The group of control signals that are labeled as the system control bus in Fig. 2.2 are used either to control the function of the 68000 microprocessor or to indicate its operating state. There are three system control signals: *bus error* ($\overline{BERR}$), *halt* ($\overline{HALT}$), and *reset* ($\overline{RESET}$).

The control line bus error ($\overline{BERR}$) is an input that is used to inform the 68000 of a problem with the bus cycle currently in progress. For instance, it could be used to signal that the bus cycle has not been completed even after a set period of time has elapsed.

On the other hand, $\overline{HALT}$ can be used to implement a hardware mechanism for stopping the processing of the 68000. An external signal applied to the $\overline{HALT}$ input stops the microprocessor at completion of the current bus cycle. In this state all of its buses and control signals are inactive. $\overline{HALT}$ is actually a bidirectional line; that is, it has both an input and output function. When the processor stops instruction execution due to a halt condition, it informs external devices by producing an output signal at the same $\overline{HALT}$ pin.

The $\overline{RESET}$ input can be used to initiate initialization of the 68000 based on the occurrence of a signal generated in external hardware. Typically, this is done at the time of power-up. When an external reset signal is applied, the processor initiates a system initialization sequence.

The $\overline{RESET}$ line is also bidirectional, but unlike $\overline{HALT}$, its output function is initiated through software. This $\overline{RESET}$ output is used to initialize external devices such as LSI peripherals. To reset external devices connected to the $\overline{RESET}$ line, the 68000 must execute the RESET instruction. Execution of this instruction does not affect the internal state of the processor; instead, it just causes a pulse to be output at $\overline{RESET}$.

Interrupt Control Bus

In a 68000 microcomputer system, external devices request interrupt service by applying a 3-bit *interrupt request code* to the $\overline{IPL_2}$ through $\overline{IPL_0}$ inputs. This code is supplied to the microprocessor from the interrupting device to indicate its priority level. The value of $\overline{IPL_2IPL_1IPL_0}$ is compared to the interrupt mask value in the 68000's status register. If the encoded priority is higher than the mask, the interrupting device is serviced; otherwise, it is ignored.

Bus Arbitration Control Bus

The bus arbitration control signals provide a handshake mechanism by which control of the 68000's system bus can be transferred between devices. The device that has control of the system bus is known as the *bus master*. It controls the system address, data, and control buses. Other devices are attached to the bus but are not active. Examples of devices that can be used as masters are host processors or external devices such as *DMA controllers* or *attached processors.*

As shown in Fig. 2.2, the 68000 microprocessor has three control lines for this purpose. They are *bus request* ($\overline{\text{BR}}$), *bus grant* ($\overline{\text{BG}}$), and *bus grant acknowledge* ($\overline{\text{BGACK}}$). A device requests control of the bus by asserting the bus request ($\overline{\text{BR}}$) input. After synchronization, the 68000 responds by switching the bus grant ($\overline{\text{BG}}$) control output to its active low level. This means that it will give up control of the bus at completion of the current bus cycle.

At this point, the requesting device waits for the 68000 to complete its bus cycle. The fact that the bus cycle is complete is indicated by address strobe ($\overline{\text{AS}}$) and data transfer acknowledge ($\overline{\text{DTACK}}$) returning to their inactive levels. After this happens, the requesting device asserts bus grant acknowledge ($\overline{\text{BGACK}}$) and also removes bus grant request ($\overline{\text{BR}}$). The 68000 responds by removing the bus grant ($\overline{\text{BG}}$) signal. This completes the bus arbitration handshake. The requesting device has now taken over control of the bus and assumes the role of bus master. When the device has completed its function, it releases control of the bus by negating $\overline{\text{BGACK}}$ for rearbitration or return of bus mastership to the 68000.

Synchronous Control Bus

The 68000 microprocessor also has control signals that can make data transfers over its system bus occur in a synchronous fashion. There are three control signals provided for this purpose. In Fig. 2.2, we see that they are *enable* (E), *valid peripheral address* ($\overline{\text{VPA}}$), and *valid memory address* ($\overline{\text{VMA}}$). These signals provide for simple interface between, say, a 10-MHz 68000 microprocessor and 1-MHz synchronous LSI peripheral devices such as those available for use in 6800 microcomputer systems.

Let us now look at the function of each of these signals. The enable (E) output of the 68000 is used by 6800 peripherals to synchronize its data read/write operations. It is a free-running clock with a frequency equal to one-tenth of that of the 68000 clock frequency. This signal allows 1-MHz LSI peripheral ICs to be used with the 10-MHz 68000. It is applied to the $\overline{\text{E}}$ or PHI$_2$ input of a 6800 family peripheral.

The valid peripheral address ($\overline{\text{VPA}}$) line is an input to the 68000 which is used to tell it to perform a synchronous transfer over its asynchronous system bus. When the address output on the address bus is decoded and found to correspond to an external 6800 peripheral, $\overline{\text{VPA}}$ must be switched to logic 0. This tells the microprocessor to synchronize the next data transfer with the enable (E) signal.

The valid memory address ($\overline{\text{VMA}}$) output is supplied by the 68000 in response to an active $\overline{\text{VPA}}$ input. It indicates to external circuitry that a valid address is on the address bus and that the next data transfer over the data bus will by synchronized with enable (E).

2.4 CLOCK INPUT AND WAVEFORM

Looking at Fig. 2.2, we find that the 68000 has a single *clock input* which is labeled CLK. The clock generator circuitry is not provided on the chip. Instead, the CLK signal must be generated in external circuitry and fed to the 68000. Internally, this signal is used to produce additional clock signals that synchronize the operation of the 68000's circuitry.

The 68000 is available with clock frequencies over the range from as low as 4MHz to as high as 12.5 MHz. Figure 2.5 shows the CLK waveform. For 10-MHz operation, the cycle time (t_{CYC}) is 100 ns. The corresponding maximum pulse width low (t_{CL}) and pulse width high (t_{CH}) are both equal to 45 ns. The maximum rise and fall times of its edges, t_{Cr} and t_{Cf}, are both 10 ns. CLK is at TTL-compatible voltage levels.

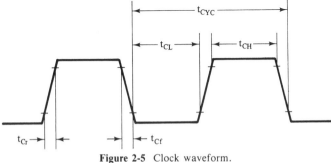

Figure 2-5 Clock waveform.

2.5 INTERNAL REGISTERS OF THE 68000 MICROPROCESSOR

Internal to the 68000 microprocessor are eighteen 32-bit registers and one 16-bit register. Figure 2.6 shows these registers. Notice that they include *eight data registers, seven address registers, two stack pointers, a program counter,* and *the status register.* The status register is the 16-bit register.

Data Registers

There are eight user-accessible data registers within the 68000. As shown in Fig. 2.6, they are called D_0 through D_7. Each register is 32 bits long and its bits are labeled 0 (least significant bit) through 31 (most significant bit). We will refer to these bits as B_0 through B_{31}, respectively.

The data registers are used to store data temporarily for use in processing. For example, they could hold the source and destination operands of an arithmetic or logic instruction. Each register can be accessed for byte operands, for word operands, or for long-word operands. Byte data are always held in the 8 least significant bits of a data register: that is, B_0 through B_7. On the other hand, words of data always reside in the lower 16 bits, B_0 through B_{15}, and long words take up all 32 bits of the register.

The size of data to be used during the execution of an instruction is generally specified in the instruction. For example, a byte move instruction could be written with register D_0 as the location of the source operand and D_7 as the location of the destination operand. Executing the instruction causes the contents of bits B_0 through B_7 of D_0 to be copied into bits B_0 through B_7 of register D_7. Alternatively, the instruction could be set up to process words of data. This time, executing the instruction would cause bits B_0 through B_{15} of D_0 to be copied into B_0 through B_{15} of D_7.

The 68000 can also use the data registers as index registers. In this case the value in the register represents an offset address which when combined with the contents of another register points to the location of data in the memory subsystem.

These registers are said to be truly general purpose. That is, they do not have dedicated functions. For this reason, most instructions can perform their operations on source and destination operands that reside in any of these registers.

Address Registers

The next seven registers, which are labeled A_0 through A_6 in Fig. 2.6, are the address registers. They are also 32 bits in length. These registers are not provided for storage of data for processing. Instead, they are meant to store address information such as base addresses and pointer addresses. Moreover, they can also act as index registers.

Just like the data registers, the address registers are general purpose. That is, an instruction can reference any of them as a base or pointer address for its source or destination operands.

The values of the addresses are loaded into the address registers under software control. When used as a source register, an address register can be accessed as a long-word operand using the complete register or for word operands using the lower 16 bits. On the other hand, when used as a destination register, all 32 bits are always affected.

Stack Pointers

Two other internal registers are used to hold address information. They are called the *user stack pointer* (USP) and the *supervisor stack pointer* (SSP). Only one of these two stack pointers is active at a time. For this reason, they are shown as a single register, A_7 in Fig. 2.6.

Unlike the address registers discussed earlier, these two registers have dedicated functions. The user stack pointer is active whenever the 68000 is operating in a mode known as the user state. When in this mode, the supervisor stack pointer is inactive. The address held in the user stack pointer identifies the top of the user stack in the user part of system memory. This *user stack* is the place where return addresses, register data, and other parameters are saved during operations such as the call to a subroutine.

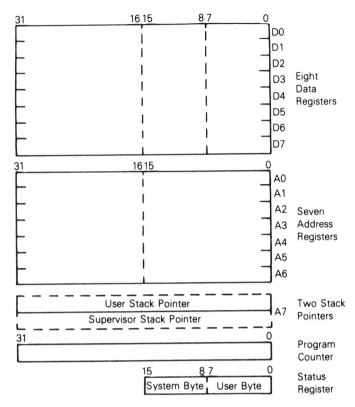

Figure 2-6 Internal registers of the 68000 microprocessor (Motorola, Inc.).

The 68000 can be switched to a second mode, known as the supervisor state. This causes the supervisor stack pointer to become active and the user stack pointer to become inactive. The address in the supervisor stack pointer register points to the top of a second stack. It is called the *supervisor stack* and resides in the supervisor part of memory. The supervisor stack is used for the same purposes as the user stack, but it is also used by *supervisory calls* such as *software exceptions, interrupts*, and *internal exceptions*.

The address values in USP and SSP can be modified through software. However, they can be modified only when the 68000 is set to operate in the supervisor mode.

Program Counter

The program counter (PC) register holds an address that typically points to the next instruction that is to be executed. It is automatically incremented by 2 with the fetch of the instruction. In this way, it points to the next word of a multiword instruction, an immediate source operand, or the next sequential instruction in the program. Instructions for the 68000 can take up from one to five words of program storage memory.

In Fig. 2.6 PC is shown as a 32-bit register; however, only the lower 24 bits are actually used in currently available 68000 devices. These 24 bits can generate 16M unique memory addresses for accessing bytes of data. But instructions are always stored at word boundaries. Therefore, the address space can also be considered to represent an 8M-word address space. The range of word addresses is even addresses from 000000_{16} through $FFFFFE_{16}$. In this way we see that program storage memory can reside anywhere in the 8M-word address space.

Status Register

Figure 2.6 also shows the 16-bit status register (SR) of the 68000 microprocessor. Here we see that this register is subdivided into two parts, called the *user byte* and the *system byte*.

The status register is shown in more detail in Fig. 2.7. Here we see that the bits implemented in the user byte are *flags* that indicate the processor state resulting from the execution of an instruction. The five conditions represented by the implemented bits are: *carry* (C), *overflow* (V), *zero* (Z), *negative* (N), and *extended carry* (X). Let us now look at each of these condition flags in more detail.

1. *Carry* (C): The carry flag, bit 0, is set if an add operation generates a carryout or a subtract (or compare) operation needs a borrow. Otherwise, it is reset. During shift or rotate operations, it holds the bit that is rotated or shifted out of a register or memory location.

2. *Overflow* (V): If an arithmetic operation on signed numbers produces an incorrect result, the overflow flag (bit 1) is set; otherwise, it is reset. During an arithmetic shift operation, this flag gets set as the result of a change in the most significant bit; otherwise, it gets reset.

3. *Zero* (Z): If an operation produces a zero as its result, the zero flag (bit 2) of SR is set. A nonzero result clears Z.

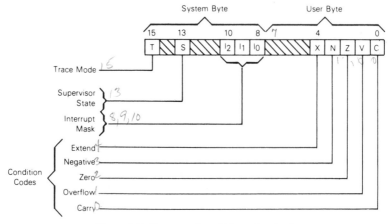

Figure 2-7 Status register (Motorola, Inc.).

4. *Negative* (N): The content of bit 3 is a copy of the most significant bit (sign bit) of the result during arithmetic, logic, shift, or rotate operations. In other words, a negative result sets the N bit and a positive result clears it.

5. *Extend* (X): During arithmetic, shift, or rotate operations, the extend flag, bit 4, receives the carry status. It is used as the carry bit in multiprecision operations.

These user bits of the status register can be tested through software to determine whether or not certain events have occurred. Typically, the occurrence of an event indicates that a change in program environment should be initiated. For instance, the overflow bit could be tested and if it is set program control is passed to an overflow service routine.

The system byte of SR contains bits that control operational options available on the 68000 microprocessor and also contains the *interrupt mask*. The implemented bits in this byte and their functions are identified in Fig. 2.7. Let us now look at these functions.

1. *Interrupt mask* ($I_2I_1I_0$): Bits 8 through 10 of SR are the interrupt mask of the 68000. This 3-bit code determines which interrupts can be serviced and which are to be ignored. Interrupting devices with priority higher than the binary value of $I_2I_1I_0$ will be accepted and those with lower or the same priority will be ignored. For example, if $I_2I_1I_0$ equals 011_2, then levels 4 through 7 are able to be active, while levels 1 through 3 are masked out.

2. *Supervisor* (S): Bit 13 of SR is used to select between the *user* and *supervisor* *states* of operation. A logic 1 in this bit indicates that the 68000 is operating in the supervisory state. If it is logic 0, the 68000 operates in the user state.

3. *Trace mode* (T): The T status bit is used to enable or disable *trace (single-step)* *mode* of operation. To activate the single-step mode, bit 15 must be set. When set in this way, the microprocessor executes an instruction, then enters the supervisor state, and vectors to a trace service routine. The service routine may pass control to a mechanism that permits initiation of execution of the next instruction or debug mode of operations for displaying the contents of the various internal registers.

The contents of the complete status register can be read at any time through software. Unimplemented bits are always read as logic 0. However, the system byte can be modified only when the 68000 is in the supervisor state.

2.6 INSTRUCTION EXECUTION CONTROL

Now that we have introduced the 68000 microprocessor, its external interfaces, and internal registers, we continue by examining how it performs the internal operations required during the execution of an instruction. Figure 2.8 shows the internal execution

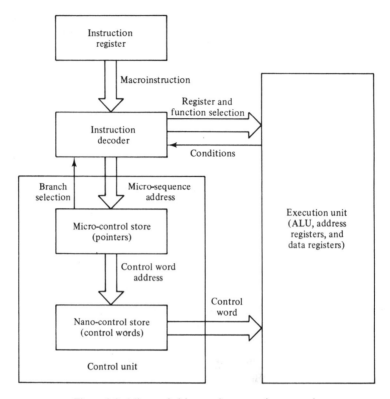

Figure 2-8 Microcoded instruction execution control.

skip til end of course

control architecture. It includes the *instruction register, instruction decoder, control unit,* and *execution unit.*

Let us begin by overviewing the operation of the execution control section. The instruction register accepts an instruction as it is fetched into the microprocessor for execution. Looking at this block, we see that its outputs supply the inputs of the instruction decoder. Here the instruction is decoded to determine which type of operation is to be performed. Based on the result of this decoding, it produces outputs for input to both the control unit and execution unit. The information passed to the execution unit is called *macroinstruction static* because it does not depend on timing of the execution of the instruction. For example, the registers that are to be used and the operation that is to be performed are macroinstruction static information. Moreover, the decoder supplies a *microsequence starting address* to the control unit. The control unit is responsible for sequencing the operations performed by the execution unit in a way that causes it to perform the operation specified by the instruction.

The 68000 microprocessor employs a *microprogrammed control unit* similar to that used in minicomputers and mainframe computers. That is, the instructions in the instruction set of the 68000 are actually *macroinstructions* and they are emulated by the execution control unit by performing a series of lower-level micro-operations called *microinstructions*. Actually, the control unit contains a series of control words for each instruction. These series of control words are used to tell the execution unit how to perform the macro-operations. They are coded into the *control store* part of the control unit.

In this way we see that the control unit itself does not perform the operation specified by the instruction. Instead, it must interact with the instruction decoder to determine which macro-operation is to be performed, with the execution unit, which contains the data registers, address registers, and arithmetic logic unit, to perform the processing, and possibly the bus interface to control accessing of operands.

Let us now look more closely at the control unit. From Fig. 2.8 we see that the 68000 employs a two-level control store structure. The first level, which is identified as the *micro-control store*, stores a sequence of addresses for each instruction. These addresses are pointers to the micro-operations that need to be performed to emulate the macro-operation. Each address is 9 bits wide and about 625 addresses are needed to implement the complete instruction set. The second level, *nano-control store,* contains a set of about 300 control words. It is these control words that define the unique micro-operations that can be performed by the 68000's execution unit. Each control word is 70 bits in length.

During instruction execution, the macroinstruction decoder outputs to the micro-control store the starting address of the emulation routine for the instruction that is to be performed. In response, the micro-control store starts by outputting the 9-bit address of the first micro-operation that is to be performed. This address is input by the nano-control store and causes the nano-control store to output the 70-bit control word for this operation to the execution unit. This control word is further decoded within the execution unit to produce as many as 180 control signals. At completion of this first micro-operation, the micro-control store outputs the address of the next micro-operation and the nano-control store causes it to be performed. This sequence continues until the complete microcode emulation routine is performed and at its completion another instruction is input to the instruction decoder.

To improve performance, the 68000 overlaps the fetch, decode, and execution phases. For instance, when one instruction is being executed, the next one may be getting decoded, and the one following it may be getting fetched. However, many macroinstructions take more than one machine cycle to execute. For this reason, if the current instruction is not yet complete, the decode or fetch of additional instructions may not take place.

The key benefits derived from use of microcoding are decreased development time and increased flexibility. This is because the development of the instruction set is easier to manage. For instance, modification of the operation of an instruction or implementation of a new instruction does not require any circuit changes; instead, it simply requires changes of the microcode in the control store.

ASSIGNMENT

Section 2.2

1. Name the technology used to fabricate the 68000 microprocessor.
2. In what size package is the 68000 housed?
3. How many general-purpose registers does the 68000 have?
   What are they called? Specify the size of each register.
4. What basic data types is the 68000 able to process directly?

Section 2.3

5. How many address lines are on the 68000 IC? How many unique memory or I/O addresses can be generated using these lines?
6. How many data lines does the 68000 have?
7. What is meant by "asynchronous bus"?
8. What function is served by $\overline{\text{DTACK}}$ during read/write operations?
9. How is byte addressing accomplished by the 68000?
10. Specify the address and asynchronous bus control signals that occur to write a word of data to memory address $A000_{16}$.
11. What function code is output by the 68000 when it fetches an instruction while in the supervisor state?
12. Describe briefly the function of system control lines $\overline{\text{BERR}}$, $\overline{\text{RESET}}$, and $\overline{\text{HALT}}$.
13. How does the 68000 prioritize interrupts?
14. Why are the bus arbitration control signals provided on the 68000?
15. Why is synchronous bus operation also provided for the 68000?

Section 2.4

16. What is the duration of the clock cycle of a 68000 that is operating at 8 MHz?

Section 2.5

17. What is the difference between the functions of the 68000's address and data registers?
18. Define what is meant by a stack. Why are there two stack pointer registers?
19. What function is served by the program counter?
20. Distinguish between the user byte and the system byte of the status register.

Section 2.6

21. What is the difference between a macroinstruction and a microinstruction?
22. What is the difference in the information stored in the micro-control store and the nano-control store?
23. Give a brief description of how instruction execution is implemented in a two-level micro-programmed control unit.

3 | 68000 MICROPROCESSOR PROGRAMMING 1

3.1 INTRODUCTION

Chapter 2 was devoted to the general architectural aspects of the 68000 microprocessor. In this chapter we introduce a large part of its instruction set. These instructions provide the ability to write simple straight-line programs. Chapter 4 covers the rest of the instruction set and some more sophisticated programming concepts. The following topics are presented in this chapter:

1. Software model of the 68000 microprocessor
2. Assembly language and machine language
3. Operand addressing modes
4. The 68000 instruction set
5. Data transfer instructions
6. Binary and decimal arithmetic instructions
7. Logic instructions
8. Shift and rotate instructions

3.2 SOFTWARE MODEL OF THE 68000 MICROPROCESSOR

The purpose of developing a *software model* is to aid the programmer in understanding the operation of the microcomputer system from a software point of view. To be able to program a microprocessor, one does not need to know all of its hardware features. For instance, we do not necessarily need to know the function of the signals at its various pins, their electrical connections, or their switching characteristics. Moreover, the function, interconnection, and operation of the internal circuits of the microprocessor also need not normally be considered.

What is important to the programmer is to know the various registers within the device and to understand their purpose, functions, and operating capabilities and limitations. Furthermore, it is essential to know how external memory is organized and how it is addressed to obtain instructions and data.

The *software model* of the 68000 microprocessor is shown in Fig. 3.1. This model specifies the resources available to programmers for implementing their program requirements. Here we see that the 68000 is represented by eight data registers, seven address registers, two stack pointers, a program counter, and a status register. We discussed each of these registers as part of our study of the 68000's architecture in Chapter 2. However, our concern here is with what can be done with this architecture and how to do it through software. For this purpose, let us review briefly the elements of the model. Moreover, this time we concentrate on their relationship to software.

During normal operation, the 68000 fetches one instruction after the other from memory and executes them. The address held in program counter PC points to the next instruction that is to be fetched. After the instruction is fetched, it is decoded by the 68000 and, if necessary, data operands are read from either the internal registers or memory. Then the operation specified in the instruction is performed on the operands and the results are written to either an internal register or storage location in memory. The 68000 is now ready to execute the next instruction.

Every time an instruction is fetched from memory, the value held in PC is incremented such that it points to the next sequential instruction of the program. In this way, the 68000 is ready to fetch the next instruction of the program for execution.

The programmer has the ability to change the value in PC under software control. For instance, execution of a jump instruction changes the value in PC. When this is done, instructions are no longer executed sequentially.

Data registers D_0 through D_7 are provided for temporary storage of working data. For instance, the instruction

$$\text{ADD.W} \quad \text{D0,D1}$$

employs data registers D_0 and D_1 for storage of its source and destination operands, respectively. The sum that results from executing this instruction is saved in destination register D_1. One nice feature of the architecture of the 68000 is that its internal registers do not have dedicated functions. Instead, they can be employed in a very general way. For instance, the add instruction we just introduced could be written with any combination of these seven data registers as the locations of its source and destination operands.

These data registers also support processing of data in a variety of different data types. For example, most instructions can access the data registers for processing of byte, word, or long-word operands. A few instructions also permit processing of

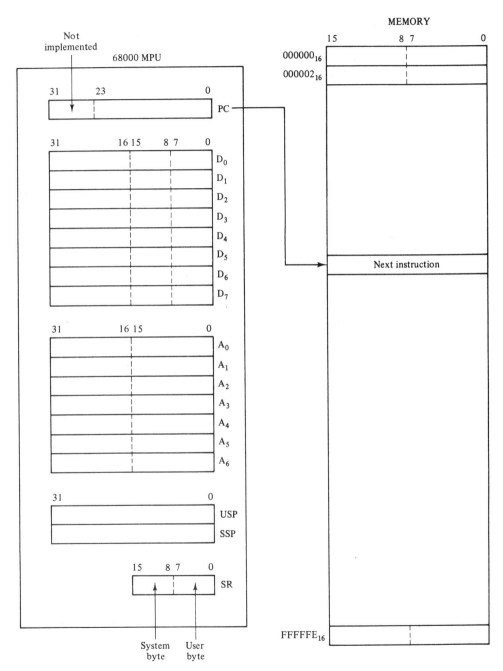

Figure 3-1 Software model of the 68000 microprocessor.

individual bits or data expressed as BCD numbers. The data registers can also be used as *index registers* for generating memory addresses.

Address registers A_0 through A_6 are not used to hold data for processing. Instead, they contain *address pointers* and are used to access source or destination operands that are stored in memory. For example, the instruction

ADD.W   (A0),D1

uses the contents of A_0 to access a source operand that resides in memory. Just as for the data registers, the 68000 permits general use of the address registers. That is, any of the seven address registers could be specified as the pointer to the location of the source operand in the addition instruction.

In Fig. 3.1 we find that there are two stack pointer registers in the software model, called the *user stack pointer* register (USP) and the *supervisor stack pointer* register (SSP). The stack is a special part of the memory subsystem that is used for temporary storage of data. Since the 68000 has two stack pointer registers, there can be two stacks in its microcomputer system, a user stack and a supervisor stack. However, only one of these stacks can be active at a time. The address in USP points to the next storage location that is to be accessed in the user stack. This location is called the top of the stack. Moreover, the value in SSP points to the top of the supervisor stack.

During a subroutine call operation, the contents of specific internal registers of the 68000 typically are pushed onto the stack. Here they are maintained temporarily. At completion of the subroutine, these values are popped off the stack and put back into the same internal register from which they originally resided. For example, if a jump to subroutine (JSR) instruction is executed, the current value in PC is automatically pushed onto the active stack. Moreover, as part of the subroutine, instructions can be executed that cause the contents of other registers to be saved on the stack.

The status register (SR) also is important when programming the 68000. The logic state of the carry (C), overflow (V), zero (Z), negative (N), and extend (X) bits in its user byte are status flags that indicate conditions that are produced as the result of executing an instruction. That is, specific flags are set (logic 1) or reset (logic 0) at the completion of execution of the instruction.

The instruction set of the 68000 includes instructions that can be used either to save the contents of the status register or to load it with new data. Moreover, it contains instructions that are able to use these flags to alter the sequence in which the program executes. For instance, an instruction can be used to test the state of the carry flag and, if it is set, to initiate a jump to another part of the program.

The bits in the system byte of SR control options available on the 68000. For instance, it contains the supervisor (S) bit. This bit can be set or reset under software control to put the 68000 into either the supervisor or user state, respectively.

Also represented in the model is the 68000's *memory address space*. The 68000 supports a very large 16M-byte address space that has few limitations on its use. That is, program memory, data memory, and stack can be located almost at any address and are not limited in size. It also may be important for the programmer to know how memory is organized, how the various data types are stored in memory, what restrictions exist on its use, and the ways in which it can be accessed through addressing modes.

3.3 ASSEMBLY LANGUAGE AND MACHINE LANGUAGE

Now that we have introduced the software model of the 68000, let us continue with the concepts of *assembly language* and *machine language* instructions and programs. It is essential to become familiar with these ideas before attempting to learn the functions of the instructions in the instruction set and their use in writing programs.

Assembly Language Instructions

Assembly language instructions are provided to describe each of the basic operations that can be performed by a microprocessor. They are written using *alphanumeric symbols* instead of the 0s and 1s of the microprocessor's machine code. An example of a short assembly language program is shown in Fig. 3.2(a). The assembly language statements are located on the left. Frequently, comments describing the statements are included on the right. This type of documentation makes it easier for programmers to write, read, and debug code. By the term *code* we mean programs written in the

```
        LEA.L     $1000,A1       SOURCE BLOCK STARTS AT $1000
        LEA.L     $2000,A2       DESTINATION BLOCK STARTS AT $2000
        MOVE.L    #16,D0         BLOCK LENGTH EQUALS 16 WORDS
NXTPT   MOVE.W    (A1)+,(A2)+    MOVE WORD AND POINT TO NEXT WORD
        SUBQ.L    #1,D0          UPDATE COUNT
        BNE.S     NXTPT          REPEAT FOR NEXT WORD
HERE    BRA.S     HERE
```

(a)

```
003000  43F81000      LEA.L     $00001000,A1   SOURCE BLOCK STARTS AT $1000
003004  45F82000      LEA.L     $00002000,A2   DESTINATION BLOCK STARTS AT $2000
003008  203C00000010  MOVE.L    #16,D0         BLOCK LENGTH EQUALS 16 WORDS
00300E  34D9          MOVE.W    (A1)+,(A2)+    MOVE WORD AND POINT TO NEXT WORD
003010  5380          SUBQ.L    #1,D0          UPDATE COUNT
003012  66FA          BNE.S     $00300E        REPEAT FOR NEXT WORD
003014  60FE          BRA.S     $003014
```

(b)

Figure 3-2 (a) Typical 68000 assembly language program; (b) assembled machine code.

language of the microprocessor. Programs written in assembly language are called *source code*.

Each instruction in the source program corresponds to one assembly language statement. The statement must specify which operation is to be performed and what data operands are to be processed. For this reason, an instruction can be divided into two separate parts: its *opcode* and its *operands*. The opcode is the part of the instruction that identifies the operation that is to be performed. For example, typical operations are add, subtract, and move.

In assembly language, we assign a unique letter combination to each operation. This letter combination is referred to as a *mnemonic* for the instruction. For instance, the 68000 assembly language mnemonics for add, subtract, and move are ADD, SUB, and MOVE, respectively.

Operands identify the data that are to be processed by the microprocessor as it carries out the operation specified by the opcode. For instance, an instruction can add the contents of address register A_0 to the contents of A_1. An assembly language description of this instruction is

$$ADD\ A0,A1$$

In this example, the contents of A0 and A1 are added together and their sum is put in A1. Therefore, A0 is considered to be the *source operand* and A1 the *destination operand*.

Here is another example of an assembly language statement:

$$LOOP\ MOVE\ D0,A0\ ;COPY\ D0\ INTO\ A0$$

This instruction statement starts with the word LOOP. It is an address identifier for the instruction MOVE D0,A0. This type of identifier is called a *label* or *tag*. The instruction is followed by "COPY D0 INTO A0." This part of the statement is called a *comment*. Thus a general format for writing an assembly language statement is

$$LABEL\quad INSTRUCTION\quad ;COMMENT$$

Machine Language Instructions

Before a source program can be executed by the microprocessor, it must first be run through a process known as *assembling*. This is normally done on a minicomputer or microcomputer with a program called an *assembler*. The result produced by this step is an equivalent program expressed in the *machine code* that is executed by the microprocessor. That is, it is the equivalent of the source program but now written in 0s and 1s. This program is also referred to as *object code*.

Figure 3.2(b) is a listing that includes the machine language program for the assembly language program in Fig. 3.2(a). It was produced by a 68000 assembler. Reading from left to right, this listing contains addresses of memory locations, followed by the machine code instructions, the original assembly language statements, and comments. Notice that for simplicity the machine code instructions are expressed in hexadecimal notation and not as binary numbers.

3.4 THE OPERAND ADDRESSING MODES OF THE 68000 MICROPROCESSOR

The operands processed by the 68000 as it executes an instruction may be specified as part of the instruction in program memory, may reside in internal registers, or may be stored in data memory. The 68000 has 14 different addressing modes. They are shown in Fig. 3.3. The objective of these addressing modes is to supply different ways for the programmer to generate an *effective address* (EA) that identifies the location of an operand. In general, operands referenced by an effective address reside either in one of the 68000's internal registers or in external data memory.

Mode	Generation
Register Direct Addressing	
Data Register Direct	EA = Dn
Address Register Direct	EA = An
Absolute Data Addressing	
Absolute Short	EA = (Next Word)
Absolute Long	EA = (Next Two Words)
Program Counter Relative Addressing	
Relative with Offset	EA = (PC) + d_{16}
Relative with Index and Offset	EA = (PC) + (Xn) + d_8
Register Indirect Addressing	
Register Indirect	EA = (An)
Postincrement Register Indirect	EA = (An), An ← An + N
Predecrement Register Indirect	An ← An − N, EA = (An)
Register Indirect with Offset	EA = (An) + d_{16}
Indexed Register Indirect with Offset	EA = (An) + (Xn) + d_8
Immediate Data Addressing	
Immediate	DATA = Next Word(s)
Quick Immediate	Inherent Data
Implied Addressing	
Implied Register	EA = SR, USP, SP, PC

NOTES:
EA = Effective Address
An = Address Register
Dn = Data Register
Xn = Address or Data Register
　　 used as Index Register
SR = Status Register
PC = Program Counter
( ) = Contents of

d_8 = 8-bit Offset
　　 (displacement)
d_{16} = 16-bit Offset
　　 (displacement)
N = 1 for Byte, 2 for
　　 Words, and 4 for Long
　　 Words.
← = Replaces

Figure 3-3 Operand addressing modes of the 68000 microprocessor (Motorola, Inc.).

Looking at Fig. 3.3, we see that the 14 addressing modes have been subdivided into six groups based on how they generate an effective address. These groups are: *register direct addressing, absolute data addressing, program counter relative addressing, register indirect addressing, immediate data addressing,* and *implied addressing.* Notice that the addressing modes in all groups other than immediate data addressing produce an effective address. Let us now look into each of these modes in detail.

Register Direct Addressing Modes

Register direct addressing modes are used when one of the data or address registers within the 68000 contains the operand that is to be processed by the instruction. In

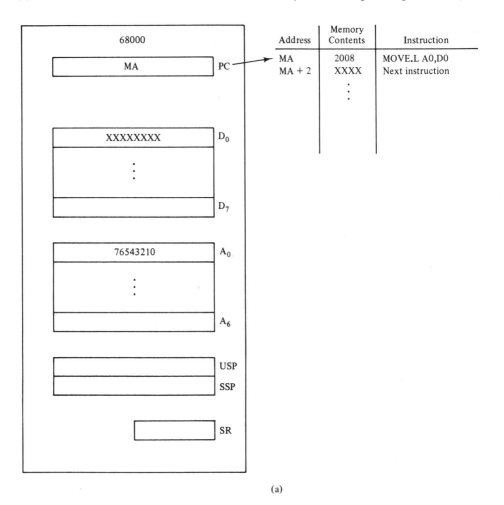

Address	Memory Contents	Instruction
MA	2008	MOVE.L A0,D0
MA + 2	XXXX	Next instruction

(a)

Figure 3-4 Instruction using register direct addressing (a) before execution.

Fig. 3.3, we see that if the specified register is a data register, the addressing mode is called *data register direct addressing*. On the other hand, if an address register is used, it is known as *address register direct addressing*.

Here is an example that employs both data register direct addressing and address register direct addressing.

MOVE.L   A0,D0

MOVE.L is how we write the move instruction to process long-word (32-bit) data. Notice that address register A_0 is specified to contain the source operand. This is an example of address register direct addressing. On the other hand, the destination operand uses data register direct addressing and is specified as the contents of data register D_0. In this example, neither operand is located in memory.

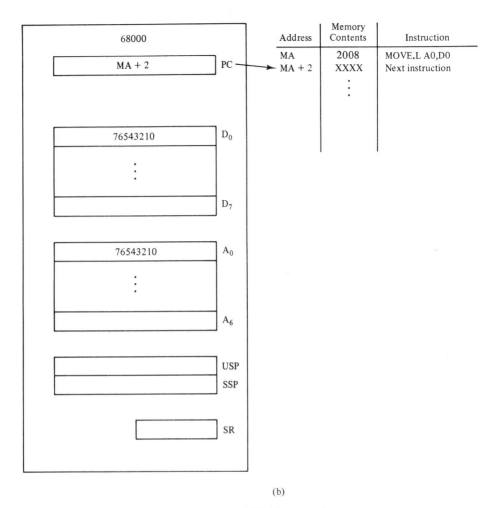

(b)

Figure 3-4   *(cont.)* (b) After execution.

Execution of this instruction causes the long word in address register A_0 to be copied into data register D_0. This operation can also be expressed as

$$A0 \longrightarrow D0$$

In Fig. 3.4(a) we see that before executing the instruction A_0 contains \$76543210 and the contents of D_0 are a don't-care state. The symbol \$ stands for hexadecimal number. At the conclusion of execution of the instruction, both A_0 and D_0 contain \$76543210. This result is shown in Fig. 3.4(b).

Absolute Data Addressing Modes

When the effective address of an operand is included in the instruction, we are using what is called absolute data addressing mode. There are two such modes for the 68000.

They are known as *absolute short addressing* and *absolute long addressing*. These addressing modes are used to access operands that reside in memory.

If an instruction uses absolute short data addressing to specify the location of an operand, a 16-bit absolute address must be included as the second word of the instruction. This word is the effective address of the storage location for the operand in memory. (4 hex places)

As an example, let us consider the instruction

MOVE.L $1234,D0

It stands for move the long word starting at address $1234 in memory into data register D_0. Notice that the instruction is written with $1234 in the location for the source operand. This is the absolute address of the source operand and it is encoded by the

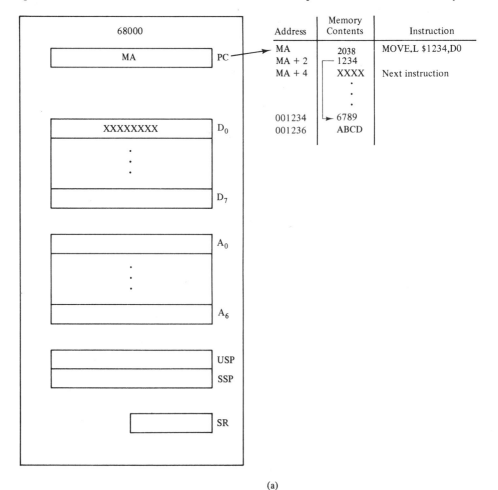

(a)

Figure 3-5 Instruction using absolute data addressing (a) before execution.

assembler into the instruction as shown in Fig. 3.5(a). Notice that the address of the source operand is the next word after the instruction opcode in program memory.

The 68000 automatically does a sign extension based on the MSB of the absolute short address to give a 32-bit address (actually only 24 bits are used). For our example, the sign bit is 0; therefore extending it gives the address 001234_{16}. Since only 16 bits can be used in absolute short data addressing it always generates a memory address either in the range 000000_{16} through $007FFF_{16}$ or $FF8000_{16}$ through $FFFFFF_{16}$. These ranges correspond to the first 32K bytes and the last 32K bytes of the 68000's address space, respectively. Other parts of the 68000's address space cannot be accessed with this addressing mode.

The result of executing this instruction is shown in Fig. 3.5(b). Notice that the long word starting at address 001234_{16}, which equals $6789ABCD_{16}$, is copied into

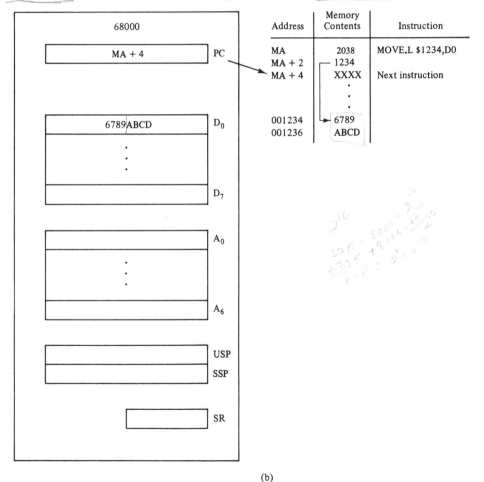

(b)

Figure 3-5 *(cont.)* (b) After execution.

D_0. Here we see that the word at the lower address, 001234_{16}, is copied into the upper 16 bits of D_0 and the word at the higher address 001236_{16} is copied into the lower 16 bits.

Absolute long data addressing permits use of a full 32-bit quantity as the absolute address data. This type of operand is specified in the same way except that its absolute address is written with more than four hexadecimal digits.

For instance, the instruction

MOVE.L $01234,D0

has the same effect as the previous instruction, but the address of the source operand is encoded by the assembler as an absolute long data address. That is, the quantity $01234 is encoded as a 32-bit number instead of a 16-bit number. This means that the instruction now takes up three words of memory instead of two.

Since all 24 bits are used, the operand specified with absolute long addressing can reside anywhere in the address space of the 68000.

Program Counter Relative Addressing Modes

It is possible to specify the location of an operand relative to the address of the instruction that is currently being processed. Program counter relative addressing is provided for this purpose. With it, the effective address of the operand to be accessed is calculated relative to the updated value held in program counter (PC). There are two types of program counter relative addressing: *program counter relative with offset* and *program counter relative with index and offset*.

Let us begin with program counter relative with offset addressing. In this case, a 16-bit quantity identifies the number of bytes the data to be accessed are offset from the updated value in PC. The offset, which is also known as the *displacement*, immediately follows the instruction word in memory. When the instruction is fetched and executed, the 68000 sign-extends the offset to 32 bits and then adds it to the updated contents of the program counter.

EA = PC + d16

The sum that results is the effective address of the operand in memory.

An example of an instruction that employs this addressing mode is as follows:

MOVE.L   TAG,D0

This means "move the long word starting at the memory location with TAG as its label into D_0." The question arises: Where is the label TAG in memory? The answer lies with the assembler. It computes the number of bytes the displacement word in the move instruction is offset from the memory location corresponding to label TAG. This offset is expressed as a signed 16-bit binary number and is encoded as the displacement word of the instruction.

Since the 16-bit quantity specifies the offset in bytes, the operand must reside within + or − 32K (+ 32767 to − 32768) bytes with respect to the updated value in PC.

$$32 = 2^5$$
$$K = 2^{10}$$

$$= 2^{15} = 8000_{16}$$

The second type of program counter relative addressing employs both an index and an offset. In this addressing mode, both the contents of an index register and an 8-bit displacement are combined with the updated PC to obtain the operand's memory address. That is, the effective address is given by

$$EA = PC + Xn + d8$$

The index register, which is identified by X_n, can be any of the 68000's data or address registers. The signed 8-bit displacement is specified by d_8.

Consider this instruction:

MOVE.L   TABLE(A0.L),D0

Here the source operand is written such that TABLE represents the displacement and A_0 is the index register. This instruction says to copy the long word starting at the memory location in TABLE indexed by A_0 into D_0.

In this case, the assembler computes the offset between the updated value in PC and the address of label TABLE. The value of the displacement is encoded as the least significant byte in the second word of the instruction.

The use of program counter relative addressing with offset and index to access a table in memory is illustrated in Fig. 3.6. The starting point of the table in memory is identified by the label TABLE. Since just 8 bits are provided for the offset, the table must begin within $+127$ or -128 bytes of the extension word of the instruction. The size of the table is determined by the index. The ability to specify up to a 32-bit index permits addressing of very long tables. Actually, the size of the data table is limited by the number of address lines on the 68000, which is 23.

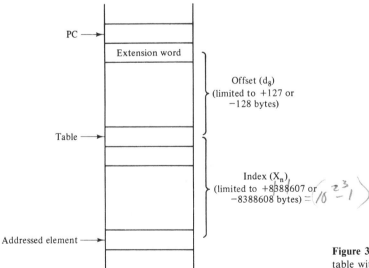

PC →

Extension word

Offset (d_8)
(limited to $+127$ or
-128 bytes)

Table →

Index (X_n)
(limited to $+8388607$ or
-8388608 bytes)

Addressed element →

Figure 3-6 Accessing elements of a table with program counter relative with index and offset addressing.

Address Register Indirect Addressing Modes

Address register indirect addressing is similar to the register direct addressing we discussed earlier in that an internal register is specified when writing the instruction. However, in this case, only address registers A_0 through A_6 can be used. Moreover, the register does not represent the location of the operand; instead, it contains the effective address of the operand in memory. Notice that register indirect addressing enables the 68000 to access information that resides in external memory.

There are five different kinds of register indirect addressing supported by the 68000. As shown in Fig. 3.3, they are called: *register indirect addressing, postincrement register indirect addressing, predecrement register indirect addressing, register indirect with offset addressing*, and *indexed register indirect with offset addressing*. We shall

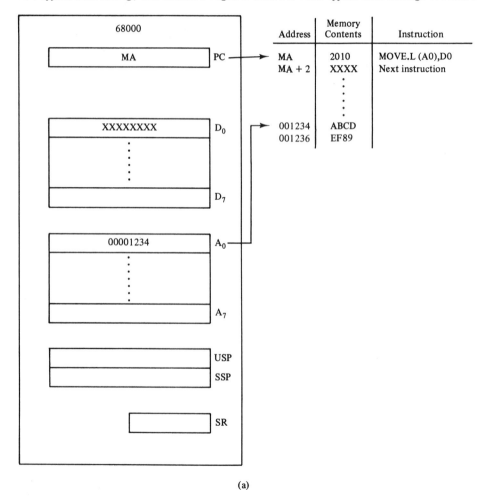

(a)

Figure 3-7 Instruction using address register indirect addressing (a) before execution.

now look at each of these types in more detail.

Register indirect is the simplest form of address register indirect addressing. When it is specified, one of the address registers contains the address of the source or destination operand. For instance, in the instruction

MOVE.L   (A0),D0

the source operand employs register indirect addressing. Notice that this type of addressing is specified by enclosing the name of the address register, which in our example is A_0, with parentheses. The destination operand is specified as D_0 using register direct addressing.

Figure 3.7 illustrates the result of using this addressing mode. In Fig. 3.7(a) we see that the contents of A_0 are $1234. Moreover, we see that the long word stored

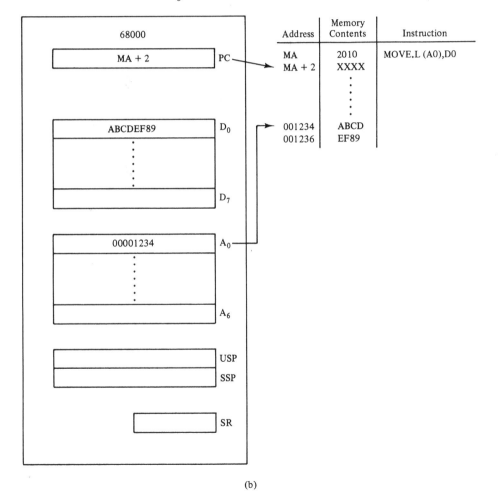

(b)

Figure 3-7   *(cont.)* (b) After execution.

at address $1234 through $1237 is $ABCDEF89. As shown in Fig. 3.7(b), execution of the instruction causes this value to be copied into destination register D_0.

Postincrement register indirect addressing works essentially the same as the register indirect addressing we just demonstrated. However, there is one difference. This is that after the operation specified by the instruction is completed the contents of the address register are automatically incremented by 1, 2, or 4, depending on whether byte, word, or long-word data are processed. In this way, the address points to the next sequential element of data.

Our earlier example can be rewritten to use postincrement register indirect addressing. This gives

$$\text{MOVE.L} \quad (A0)+,D0$$

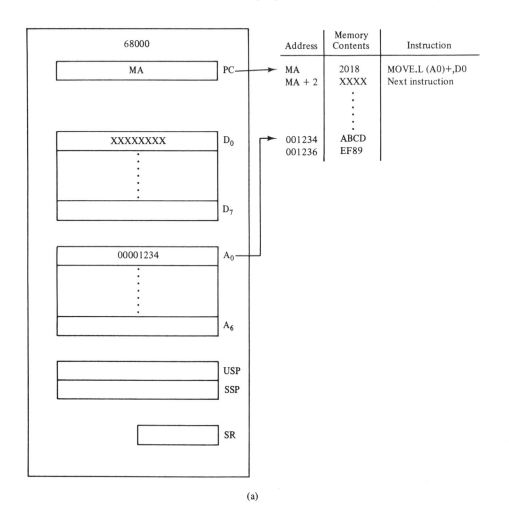

(a)

Figure 3-8 Instruction using postincrement register indirect addressing (a) before execution.

Here we see that including a + symbol after the operand specifies the postincrement operation.

If we assume that the state of the 68000 just prior to execution of this instruction is as shown in Fig. 3.8(a), the results are similar to those shown in Fig. 3.7(b) for register indirect addressing. Again $ABCDEF89 is copied into D_0. But this time the contents of A_0 are also incremented by 4 to give $1238, as shown in Fig. 3.8(b). Therefore, it points to the start of the next long word in data memory.

Predecrement register indirect addressing is the same as postdecrement register indirect addressing except that the contents of the selected address register are decremented instead of incremented. Moreover, the decrement operation takes place prior to performing the operation specified in the instruction.

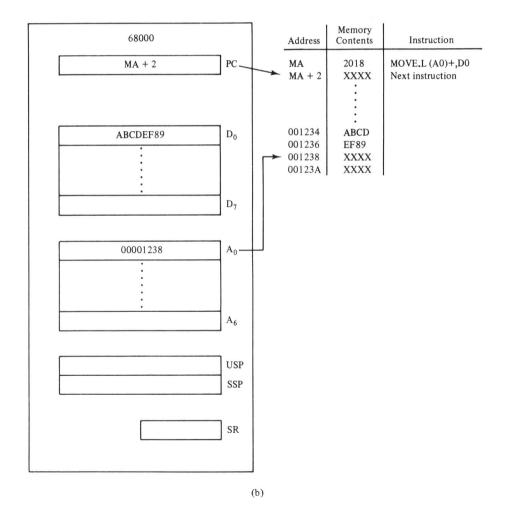

(b)

Figure 3-8 *(cont.)* (b) After execution.

For instance, in the instruction

MOVE.L − (A0),D0

the − symbol identifies predecrement indirect addressing. If this instruction is executed with the 68000 in the state shown in Fig. 3.9(a), the address in A_0 is first decremented by 4 and equals $1230. Therefore, the contents of memory locations $1230 through $1233 are copied into D_0. This result is illustrated by Fig. 3.9(b).

Postincrement and predecrement indirect addressing allow a programmer to implement memory scanning operations without the need to update the address pointer with additional instructions. This type of addressing is useful for performing data processing operations such as block transfer and string searches.

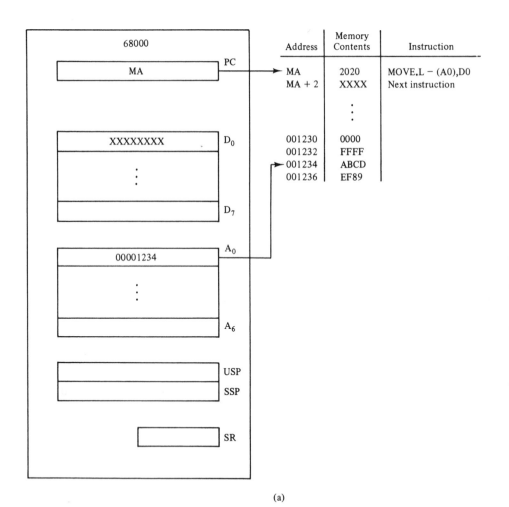

(a)

Figure 3-9 Instruction using predecrement register indirect addressing (a) before execution.

In the address register indirect with offset addressing mode, a sign-extended 16-bit offset value and an address register are specified in the instruction. The effective address of the operand is generated by adding the offset to the contents of the selected address register; that is,

$$EA = An + d16$$

The value of offset d_{16} specifies the number of bytes the storage location to be accessed is offset from the address in A_n. It is encoded as the second word of the instruction.

Let us now consider the instruction

MOVE.W   16(A0),D0

Here we find that an offset of 16 (sixteen bytes) is specified for the source operand.

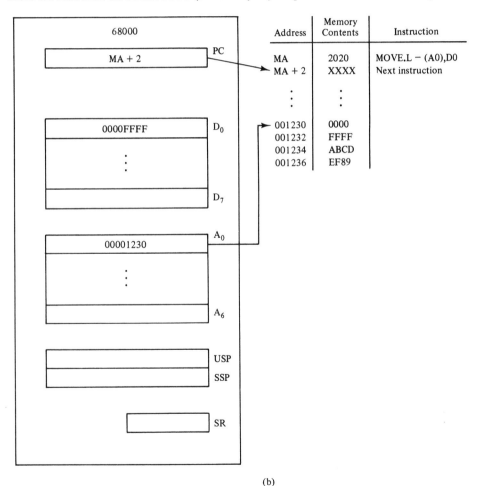

(b)

Figure 3-9 *(cont.)* (b) After execution.

Execution of this instruction for the conditions in Fig. 3.10(a) produces the effective address

$$EA = 1234_{16} + 16_{10} = 1244_{16}$$

As shown in Fig. 3.10(b), the word contents of address \$1244, which equals \$ABCD, are copied into the least significant 16 bits of D_0.

Since the offset is a signed 16-bit integer number, the operand to be accessed must be within $+32767$ or -32768 bytes of the storage location pointed to by the contents of the address register.

The last register indirect addressing mode, indexed register indirect with offset addressing, allows specification of an address register, an offset, and an index register for formation of the effective address. The offset value is limited to a signed 8-bit quantity. On the other hand, the index register can be the contents of any of the

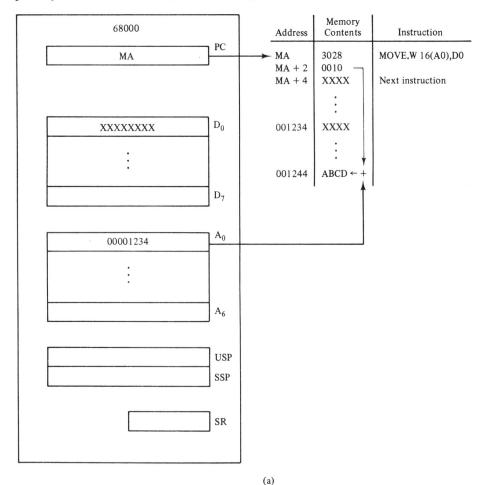

(a)

Figure 3-10 Instruction using register indirect addressing with offset (a) before execution.

68000's data or address registers. The effective address is computed by adding the contents of the address register, the contents of the index register, and the offset. That is,

$$EA = An + Xn + d8$$

Here is an instruction that uses this addressing mode for its source operand.

$$\text{MOVE.W}\quad 16(\text{A0,A1.L}),\text{D0}$$

The offset equals 16_{10}, A_0 is the address register, and A_1 is the index register. Figure 3.11(a) shows that A_0 contains \$1234 and A_1 contains \$2344. In this case, the address of the source operand is obtained as

$$EA = A0 + A1 + 16_{10} = 1234_{16} + 2344_{16} + 10_{16}$$

$$= 3588_{16}$$

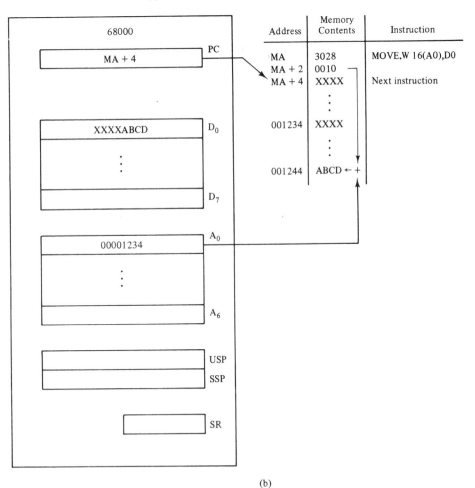

(b)

Figure 3-10 *(cont.)* (b) After execution.

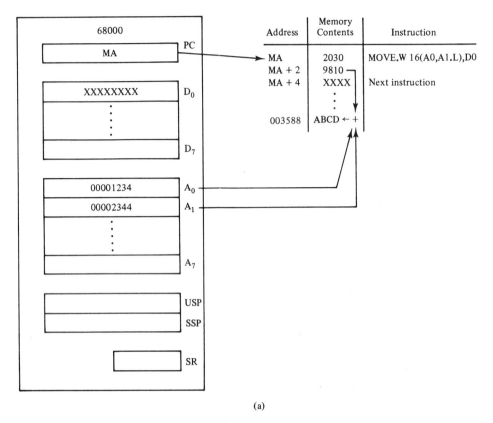

(a)

Figure 3-11 Instruction using indexed register indirect with offset addressing (a) before execution.

Figure 3.11(b) shows that the word contents at this memory location are $ABCD_{16}$. This value is copied into the least significant word of D_0.

Since the offset value is an 8-bit signed integer, the address offset is limited to $+127$ or -128 bytes relative to the location specified by the sum of the contents of the address register and the index register.

Address register indirect with index and offset addressing is very useful when accessing elements of an array in memory. For example, the two-dimensional array of Fig. 3.12(a), which has a size of $m + 1$ rows by $l + 1$ columns can be stored in memory as shown in Fig. 3.12(b). Notice that the first $l + 1$ addresses, with starting address at $00F000_{16}$, contain the elements of row 0 of the array, that is, the elements located at columns 0 through l of row 0. In both figures, these are identified as $E(0,0)$ through $E(0,l)$. The elements of row 0 are followed in memory by those for rows 1 through m.

Let us look at how to access the element located at column j of row i ($E(i,j)$). In order to access this element, the first address register A_0 can be loaded with the beginning address, $00F000$, of the array in memory. In this way, it points to the

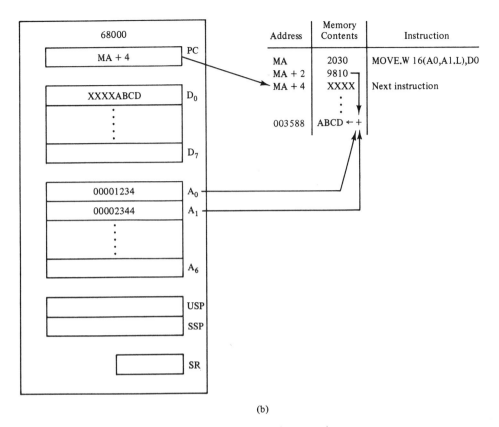

(b)

Figure 3-11 *(cont.)* (b) After execution.

first element in the first row of the array. A_1 can be used as the index register and loaded with an index number such that it points to row i in the array. Assuming that each element uses a word for storage, the value required in index register A_1 in order to access row i is computed as $2i\,(l + 1)$. Finally, the offset can be used to select the appropriate column. For element j, it should be made equal to 2j. In this way, the effective address computed as

$$EA = A0 + 2i\,(l + 1) + 2j$$

points to element E(i,j). Notice that the 8-bit offset limits the number of columns in the array to a maximum of 128.

For instance, let us determine the effective address needed to copy the word in element E(5,6) of the array in Fig. 3.12 with $m = 8$ into D_0. Assume that the array of words is stored starting at address \$00F000. First we must load registers A_0 and A_1 as follows:

$$A0 = 00F000_{16}$$
$$A1 = 2i(l + 1) = 2(5)(8 + 1) = 90_{10} = 5A_{16}$$

Column Row	0	1	$\cdots\cdots\cdots\cdots\cdots\cdots$	l
0	E(0, 0)	E(0, 1)	$\cdots\cdots\cdots\cdots\cdots$	E(0, l)
1	E(1, 0)	E(1, 1)	$\cdots\cdots\cdots\cdots\cdots$	E(1, l)
.	.	.		.
m	E(m, 0)	E(m, 1)	$\cdots\cdots\cdots\cdots\cdots$	E(m, l)

(a)

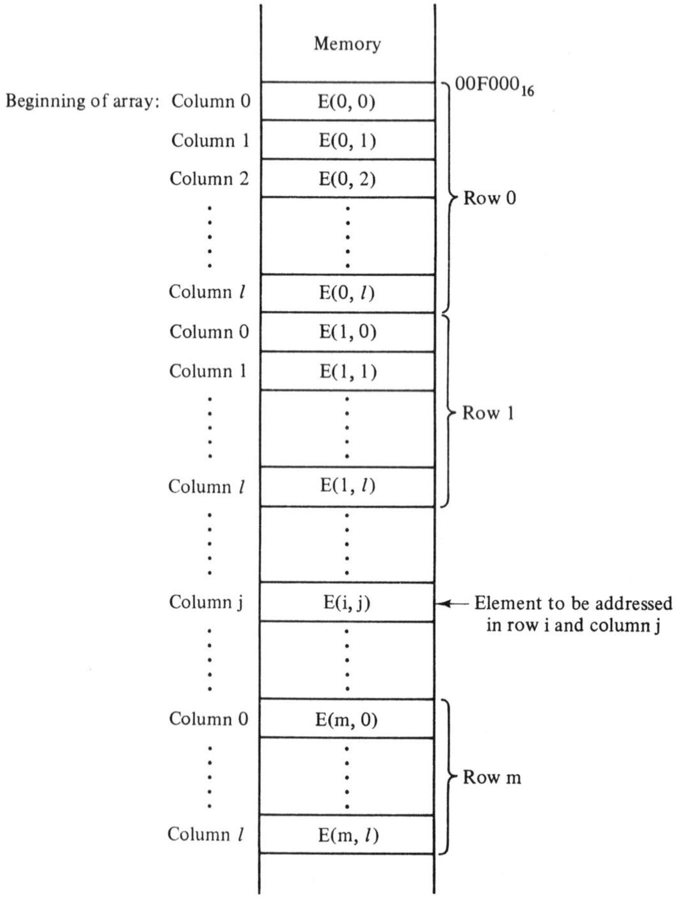

	Memory	
Beginning of array: Column 0	E(0, 0)	$00F000_{16}$
Column 1	E(0, 1)	
Column 2	E(0, 2)	Row 0
Column l	E(0, l)	
Column 0	E(1, 0)	
Column 1	E(1, 1)	
Column l	E(1, l)	Row 1
Column j	E(i, j)	← Element to be addressed in row i and column j
Column 0	E(m, 0)	
Column l	E(m, l)	Row m

(b)

Figure 3-12 (a) An $(m + 1) \times (l + 1)$ two-dimensional array; (b) storage of the array in memory.

54

Then the offset is obtained by multiplying the column dimension of the array element by 2. This gives

$$d8 = 2j = 2(6) = 12_{10} = C_{16}$$

Therefore, the effective address of the element is

$$EA = A0 + A1 + d8 = 00F000_{16} + 5A_{16} + C_{16}$$
$$= 00F066_{16}$$

This element can be copied into D_0 by executing the instruction

$$MOVE.W \quad 12(A0,A1.L),D0$$

Immediate Data Addressing Modes

With immediate data addressing mode, the operand to be processed during the execution of the instruction is supplied in the instruction itself. In general, the data are encoded and stored in the word locations that follow the instruction in program memory. If the instruction processes bytes of data, a special form of immediate addressing can be used. This is known as *quick immediate addressing*. In this case, the data are encoded directly into the instruction's operation word. For this reason, using quick immediate addressing takes up less memory and executes faster.

Here are two examples of instructions that employ immediate data addressing for their source operands.

$$MOVEQ \qquad \#\$C5,D0$$
$$MOVE.W \qquad \#\$1234,D0$$

Notice that the # symbol written before the operand indicates that immediate data addressing is employed. The first instruction, move quick (MOVEQ), illustrates quick immediate addressing. In this instruction, the immediate source operand is $C5_{16}$. As shown in Fig. 3.13(a), it gets encoded as $70C5, where the least significant byte of the instruction word is the immediate operand. Executing this instruction loads D_0 with the sign-extended long-word value of $C5; that is,

$$\$FFFFFFC5 \rightarrow D0$$

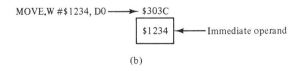

MOVEQ #$C5, D0 ⟶ $70|C5|

⎿ Quick immediate operand

(a)

MOVE.W #$1234, D0 ⟶ $303C

|$1234| ⟵ Immediate operand

(b)

Figure 3-13 (a) Coding of a move instruction with quick immediate operand; (b) coding of a move instruction with general immediate operand.

Looking at the second instruction, we see that its immediate source operand is the word 1234_{16}. Figure 3.13(b) illustrates how its immediate operand gets encoded into the second word of the instruction. When the instruction is executed, sign extension is not performed; instead, the value $1234 is loaded into the least significant 16 bits of D_0. That is,

$$\$1234 \rightarrow \text{Least significant 16 bits of } D_0$$

The most significant 16 bits of D_0 are not affected.

Implied Addressing Mode

Some of the 68000's instructions do not make direct reference to operands. Instead, inherent to their execution is an automatic reference to one or more of its internal registers. Typically, these registers are the stack pointers, the program counter, or the status register.

An example is the instruction

BSR   SUBRTN

It stands for branch to the subroutine at label SUBRTN. Both the contents of the program counter and active stack pointer are always referenced during the execution of this instruction.

Functional Addressing Categories

The addressing modes that we have discussed in this section can be divided into four categories based on the manner in which they are used. These functional categories are: *data addressing, memory addressing, control addressing*, and *alterable addressing*. The relationship between the addressing modes and these four categories is summarized by the table in Fig. 3.14.

Addressing Mode	Mode	Register	Addressing Categories				Assembler Syntax
			Data	Mem	Cont	Alter	
Data Reg Dir	000	reg no.	X	—	—	X	Dn
Addr Reg Dir	001	reg no.	—	—	—	X	An
Addr Reg Ind	010	reg no.	X	X	X	X	(An)
Addr Reg Ind w/Postinc	011	reg no.	X	X	—	X	(An)+
Addr Reg Ind w/Predec	100	reg no.	X	X	—	X	-(An)
Addr Reg Ind w/Disp	101	reg no.	X	X	X	X	d(An)
Addr Reg Ind w/Index	110	reg no.	X	X	X	X	d(An, Ri)
Absolute Short	111	000	X	X	X	X	XXX
Absolute Long	111	001	X	X	X	X	XXXXXX
Prog Ctr w/Disp	111	010	X	X	X	—	d(PC)
Prog Ctr w/Index	111	011	X	X	X	—	d(PC, Ri)
Immediate	111	100	X	X	—	—	#XXX

Figure 3-14 Effective addressing mode categories (Motorola, Inc.).

If an addressing mode can be used to reference data operands, it is categorized as data addressing. Looking at Fig. 3.14, we see that all addressing modes other than address register direct are classified as data addressing. Address register direct is not included because it only allows access to address information.

Similarly, if an addressing mode provides the ability to reference operands in memory, it is classified as memory addressing. Notice in Fig. 3.14 that just the data register direct and address register direct addressing modes are not classified in this way. This is because their use is restricted to accessing information that resides in the internal registers of the 68000.

An addressing mode is considered control addressing if it can be used to reference an operand in memory without specification of the size of the operand. Notice in Fig. 3.14 that all direct addressing modes, indirect addressing modes with either predecrement or postincrement, and the immediate addressing modes are not included in this category.

Moreover, if an addressing mode permits reference to operands that are being written into, it is called an *alterable addressing mode*. That is, alterable addressing modes can be used in conjunction with destination operands. Looking at Fig. 3.14, we see that immediate data addressing is an example of an addressing mode that cannot be used to specify a destination operand. It only can be used to reference source operands.

3.5 INSTRUCTION SET

Now that we have introduced the software model of the 68000 and its addressing modes, we are ready to begin our study of its instructions. Motorola, Inc. has applied *orthogonality* in the design of the instruction set of the 68000. That is, instead of having a large number of instructions that include many special-purpose instructions, they have included a smaller number of general-purpose instructions. But the 68000 is equipped with more powerful addressing modes and most of the instructions can use all of the addressing modes. This makes its general instructions very versatile. Moreover, it results in fewer instruction mnemonics for the programmer to remember and less restrictions on how operands can be accessed during instruction execution.

The 68000 microprocessor provides a very powerful minicomputer-like instruction set. It has 56 basic instruction types. A summary of the instructions is shown in Fig. 3.15. These basic instruction types coupled with their variations, shown in Fig. 3.16, the 14 addressing modes, and five data types produce a large number of executable instructions at the machine code level.

For ease of learning, we will divide the instructions of the 68000's instruction set into functionally related groups. In this chapter the groups covered are: the *data movement instructions*, the *integer arithmetic instructions*, the *decimal arithmetic instructions*, the *logic instructions*, and the *shift and rotate instructions*. The rest of the instruction set will be presented in Chapter 4.

3.6 DATA TRANSFER INSTRUCTIONS

The instruction set of the 68000 provides instructions to transfer data between its internal registers, between an internal register and a storage location in memory, or between two locations in memory. The basic instructions in the data transfer group

Mnemonic	Description
ABCD	Add Decimal with Extend
ADD	Add
AND	Logical And
ASL	Arithmetic Shift Left
ASR	Arithmetic Shift Right
Bcc	Branch Conditionally
BCHG	Bit Test and Change
BCLR	Bit Test and Clear
BRA *lways*	Branch Always
BSET	Bit Test and Set
BSR	Branch to Subroutine
BTST	Bit Test
CHK	Check Register Against Bounds
CLR	Clear Operand
CMP	Compare
DBcc	Test Condition, Decrement and Branch
DIVS	Signed Divide
DIVU	Unsigned Divide
EOR	Exclusive Or
EXG	Exchange Registers
EXT	Sign Extend
JMP	Jump
JSR	Jump to Subroutine
LEA	Load Effective Address
LINK	Link Stack
LSL	Logical Shift Left
LSR	Logical Shift Right
MOVE	Move
MOVEM	Move Multiple Registers
MOVEP	Move Peripheral Data
MULS	Signed Multiply
MULU	Unsigned Multiply
NBCD	Negate Decimal with Extend
NEG	Negate
NOP	No Operation
NO	Ones Complement
OR	Logical Or
PEA	Push Effective Address
RESET	Reset External Devices
ROL	Rotate Left without Extend
ROR	Rotate Right without Extend
ROXL	Rotate Left with Extend
ROXR	Rotate Right with Extend
RTE	Return from Exception
RTR	Return and Restore
RTS	Return from Subroutine
SBCD	Subtract Decimal with Extend
Scc	Set Conditional
STOP	Stop
SUB	Subtract
SWAP	Swap Data Register Halves
TAS	Test and Set Operand
TRAP	Trap
TRAPV	Trap on Overflow
TST	Test
UNLK	Unlink

Figure 3-15 Instruction set summary (Motorola, Inc.).

Instruction Type	Variation	Description
ADD	ADD	Add
	ADDA	Add Address
	ADDQ	Add Quick
	ADDI	Add Immediate
	ADDX	Add with Extend
AND	AND	Logical AND
	ANDI	AND Immediate
	ANDI to CCR	AND Immediate to Condition Code
	ANDI to SR	AND Immediate to Status Register
CMP	CMP	Compare
	CMPA	Compare Address
	CMPM	Compare Memory
	CMPI	Compare Immediate
EOR	EOR	Exclusive OR
	EORI	Exclusive OR Immediate
	EORI to CCR	Exclusive Immediate to Condition Codes
	EORI to SR	Exclusive OR Immediate to Status Register
MOVE	MOVE	Move
	MOVEA	Move Address
	MOVEQ	Move Quick
	MOVE to CCR	Move to Condition Codes
	MOVE to SR	Move to Status Register
	MOVE from SR	Move from Status Register
	MOVE to USP	Move to User Stack Pointer
NEG	NEG	Negate
	NEGX	Negate with Extend
OR	OR	Logical OR
	ORI	OR Immediate
	ORI to CCR	OR Immediate to Condition Codes
	ORI to SR	OR Immediate to Status Register
SUB	SUB	Subtract
	SUBA	Subtract Address
	SUBI	Subtract Immediate
	SUBQ	Subtract Quick
	SUBX	Subtract with Extend

Figure 3-16 Variations of instruction types (Motorola, Inc.).

are shown in Fig. 3.17. Notice that it includes the following instructions: *move* (MOVE), *move multiple* (MOVEM), *load effective address* (LEA), *exchange* (EXG), *swap* (SWAP), and *clear* (CLR).

Move Instruction—MOVE

The first of the basic data transfer instructions in Fig. 3.17 is the MOVE instruction. This instruction has the ability to perform all three of the earlier mentioned data transfer operations. That is, data transfers from register to register, between register and memory, or memory to memory. Looking at Fig. 3.17, we see that there are eight different forms of this instruction. Notice that they differ in both the size of operands they process and the types of operands that they can access.

The first form of the MOVE instruction is

MOVE   EAs,EAd

It permits movement of a source operand location identified by effective address EAs into a destination location identified by effective address EAd. The source and

Mnemonic	Meaning	Type	Operand Size	Operations
MOVE	Move	MOVE EAs,EAd	8, 16, 32	(EAs) → EAd
		MOVE EA,CCR	16	(EA) → CCR
		MOVE EA,SR	16	(EA) → SR
		MOVE SR,EA	16	SR → EA
		MOVE USP,An	32	USP → An
		MOVE An,USP	32	An → USP
		MOVEA EA,An	16, 32	(EA) → An
		MOVEQ #XXX,Dn	8	#XXX → Dn
MOVEM	Move multiple	MOVEM Reg_list,EA	16, 32	Reg_list → EA
		MOVEM EA,Reg_list	16, 32	(EA) → Reg_list
LEA	Load effective address	LEA EA,An	32	EA → An
EXG	Exchange	EXG Rx,Ry	32	Rx ↔ Ry
SWAP	Swap	SWAP Dn	16	Dn 31:16 ↔ Dn 15:0
CLR	Clear	CLR EA	8, 16, 32	0 → EA

Figure 3-17 Data transfer instructions.

destination operands can be located in data registers, address registers, or storage locations in memory. Moreover, this instruction can be used to process byte, word, or long-word operands.

Whenever this instruction is processing word or long-word data, the source operand can be specified using any addressing mode. However, for operation on byte data, address register direct addressing mode cannot be used. This is because the address registers can be accessed only as word or long-word operands.

For the destination operand, only the alterable addressing modes are allowed. The addressing modes in this group were identified in Fig. 3.14. In other words, program counter relative and the immediate data addressing modes cannot be used to specify the location of the destination operand. Moreover, when processing byte operands, address register direct addressing cannot be used.

Another thing that may be important to note is how the condition code bits in the user byte of the 68000's status register are affected by execution of the MOVE instruction. The condition codes affected are the negative (N) bit, the zero (Z) bit, the overflow (V) bit, and the carry (C) bit. N and Z are set or cleared based on the result of the instruction: that is, the value copied into the destination location. If the result is negative, N is set; otherwise, it is cleared. Similarly, if the result is zero, Z is set, and if it is nonzero, it is cleared. The V and C bits are always cleared.

Here is an example of the move instruction that performs a word-copy operation.

$$\text{MOVE.W   D0,D1}$$

The source operand in D_0 is specified using data register direct addressing mode. Let us assume that the contents of register D_0 are 12345678_{16}. The destination operand in D_1 is also specified using data register direct addressing mode. Execution of the instruction causes the least significant word in D_0, which equals 5678_{16}, to be copied into the lower 16 bits of D_1. Since the result in D_1 is positive and nonzero, the condition codes are affected as follows: N = 0, Z = 0, V = 0, C = 0, and X is not affected.

The next two forms shown in Fig. 3.17 for the MOVE instruction are provided for initialization of the status register. The instruction

$$\text{MOVE   EA,CCR}$$

allows only the condition code part of the status register to be specified as the destination operand. This operand is identified by CCR. On the other hand, any of the data addressing modes can be used for the source operand. This instruction can be used to load the user byte of SR from memory or an internal register. Even though the source operand size is specified as a word, just its eight least significant bits are used to modify the condition code bits in SR.

The second instruction

$$\text{MOVE   EA,SR}$$

is used to load all 16 bits of the status register. Therefore, its execution loads both the system byte and user byte. Since this instruction updates the most significant byte in SR, it can be executed only when the 68000 is in the supervisor state (privileged instruction).

Example 3.1

What will be the result of executing the following sequence of instructions?

$$\text{MOVE.W   \#12,D0}$$

$$\text{MOVE   D0, SR}$$

Assume that the 68000 is in the supervisor state.

Solution.   Execution of the first instruction loads the lower word of D_0 with immediate source operand 12_{10}.

$$12_{10} = 000C_{16} = 0000000000001100_2$$

After execution of this instruction, the condition code bits of SR are as follows:

$$X = \text{unchanged}$$

$$N = 0$$

$$Z = 0$$

$$V = 0$$

$$C = 0$$

Check Fig. 2.7 for the meaning of each of these bits. The result of executing the second instruction depends on the state of the 68000. We have assumed that it is operating in the supervisor state; therefore, SR is loaded with the lower word of D_0, which is 0000000000001100_2.

$$D0 = XXXXXXXXXXXXXXXX0000000000001100_2$$

$$SR = 0000000000001100_2$$

This gives the condition codes that follow:

$$X = 0$$
$$N = 1$$
$$Z = 1$$
$$V = 0$$
$$C = 0$$

The next form of the MOVE instruction shown in Fig. 3.17 is

MOVE SR,EA

Notice that its source operand is always the contents of SR and that the destination operand is represented by the effective address EA. Therefore, this instruction permits the programmer to save the contents of the status register in an address register, data register, or a storage location in data memory. In specifying the destination operand, only those addressing modes identified in Fig. 3.14 as alterable can be used.

For example, executing the instruction

MOVE SR,D7

causes the contents of SR to be copied into data register D_7. No condition codes are affected due to the execution of this instruction. Since this instruction reads but does not modify the contents of SR, it can be executed when the 68000 is in either the user state or the supervisor state.

The move user stack pointer instructions are shown in Fig. 3.17 to be

MOVE   USP,An

and

MOVE   An,USP

Notice that the data transfer that takes place is always between the user stack pointer (USP) register and one of the address registers. For this reason, these instructions are used to read and to modify the user stack pointer, respectively. Since USP is a 32-bit register, both the source and destination operands are always long word in size. Both of the instructions are privileged and must only be executed when the 68000 is in the supervisor state.

An efficient way of loading an address register from another address register, data register, or storage location in memory is with the *move address instruction*. In Fig. 3.17, this form of the MOVE instruction is given as

MOVEA EA,An

This instruction allows the operand to be either 16 bits or 32 bits in length. If the source operand is specified as a word, the address word is sign-extended to give a long word before it is moved into the address register.

The source operand can be specified using any of the 68000's addressing modes. For instance, the instruction

(Bufend) Buffer

MOVEA.L   (A0),A6

employs address register indirect addressing. Execution of this instruction causes the long-word contents of the memory location pointed to by the address in A_0 to be loaded into address register A_6. Condition codes are not affected by execution of this instruction.

The last form of the MOVE instruction we find in Fig. 3.17 is

MOVEQ   #XXX,Dn   *upto 255 only for a byte*

This instruction, *move quick,* is used to load a data register efficiently with a byte-wide immediate operand. An example is the instruction

MOVEQ   #4,D1

The immediate operand, which is decimal number 4, is encoded directly into the instruction operation word. When this instruction is executed, the immediate data are loaded into data register D_1. However, before the value is loaded, it is sign extended to 32 bits. Therefore, the value loaded into D_1 is 00000004_{16}.

Move Multiple Registers Instruction—MOVEM

The move multiple registers (MOVEM) instruction provides an efficient mechanism for saving the contents of the internal registers into memory or to restore their contents from memory. One use of this instruction is to initialize a group of registers from a table in memory. This operation can be done with a series of MOVE instructions or with just one MOVEM instruction.

Another operation for which it can be useful is when working with subroutines. For instance, if a subroutine is to be initiated, typically the contents of the registers that are used during its execution must be saved in memory. Moreover, after its execution is complete, their contents must be restored. In this way, when program control is returned to the main program, the registers reflect the same information that they contained prior to entry into the subroutine. Either the save or restore operation can be performed with a single MOVEM instruction.

The two forms of MOVEM are shown in Fig. 3.17. The first form,

MOVEM   Reg-list,EA

is employed to save the contents of the registers specified in *register list* (Reg-list) in memory. They are saved at consecutive addresses in memory starting at the address specified by the destination operand. Any of the control addressing modes and address register indirect with predecrement can be used in conjunction with the destination operand.

The register list can include any combination of data and address registers. A list of the registers to be saved is coded into a second word of the instruction. This word is called the _register list mask_. As shown in Fig. 3.18(a), each bit of this mask corresponds to one of the 68000's internal registers. Setting a bit to 1 indicates that the corresponding register is included in the list and 0 indicates that it is not included. Notice that data registers D_0 through D_7 correspond to bits 0 through 7 of the mask, respectively, and address registers A_0 through A_7 correspond to bits 8 through 15, respectively. When address register indirect with predecrement addressing is used, the meaning of the bits of the mask word are changed as shown in Fig. 3.18(b). The register corresponding to the first set bit is saved first, followed by the register corresponding to the next set bit and so on. The last saved register corresponds to the last set bit.

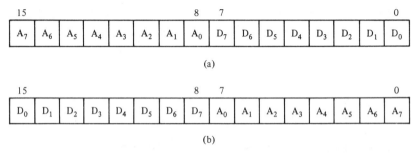

Figure 3-18 (a) Register list mask word format for control mode and postincrement addressing; (b) format for address register indirect with predecrement addressing.

This instruction can be written to perform word or long-word data transfers. In a word operation, only the least significant word parts of the specified registers are saved in memory. In this case, it requires one word of memory storage for each register. However, if long-word transfers are specified, each register needs two words of memory.

The second form of the MOVEM instruction shown in Fig. 3.17 permits the internal registers of the 68000 to be initialized or restored from memory. It is written as

MOVEM   EA,Reg-list

Execution of this instruction causes the word or long-word contents of the registers in Reg-list to be loaded one after the other from memory. When specifying the source operand, the starting address of the table of values to be loaded can only use the control or postincrement addressing modes.

Example 3.2

Write an instruction that will do the reverse of the instruction

MOVEM.W   D0/D1/A5,$AF00

Solution. This instruction will save the lower words of registers D_0, D_1, and A_5 in memory at word addresses $AF00_{16}$, $AF02_{16}$, and $AF04_{16}$, respectively. To restore the registers, the instruction is written as

MOVEM.W $AF00,D0/D1/A5

Figure 3.19 illustrates what happens due to the execution of these two instructions.

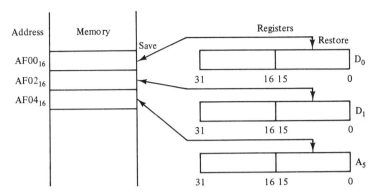

Figure 3-19 Save and restore of processor register contents as implemented with the MOVEM instructions.

Load Effective Address Instruction—LEA

A way of directly loading an address register with an address is with the load effective address (LEA) instruction. The form of this instruction is given in Fig. 3.17 as

$$\text{LEA} \quad \text{EA,An}$$

Execution of this instruction does not load the destination operand with the contents of the specified source operand. Instead, it computes an effective address based on the addressing mode used for the source operand and loads this value into the address register specified as the destination. Only the control addressing modes listed in Fig. 3.14 can be used to describe the source operand.

Example 3.3

Describe what happens when the instruction

$$\text{LEA} \quad \text{6(A1,D0),A2}$$

is executed. Assume that $A_1 = 00004000_{16}$ and $D_0 = 000012AB_{16}$.
Solution. This instruction uses address register indirect with index addressing for the source operand. Its destination is simply address register A_2. Execution of the instruction causes A_2 to be loaded with the effective address

$$A2 = A1 + D0 + 6_{10}$$

Using the values given for the contents of A_1 and D_0, we find that the effective address loaded into A_2 equals

$$A2 = 00004000_{16} + 000012AB_{16} + 6_{16}$$

$$= 000052B1_{16}$$

Exchange Instruction—EXG

Earlier we showed how the MOVE instruction could be used to move the contents of one of the internal registers of the 68000 to another internal register. Another type of requirement for some applications is to exchange efficiently the contents of two registers. It is for this reason that the exchange (EXG) instruction is included in the instruction set of the 68000.

This instruction is shown in Fig. 3.17 to have the form

EXG   Rx,Ry

Here Rx and Ry stand for arbitrarily selected data or address registers. An example is the instruction

EXG   D0,A3

It will load data register D_0 with the contents of address register A_3 and A_3 with the contents of D_0. For example, if D_0 contains $FFFFFFFF_{16}$ and A_3 contains 00000000_{16}, the result after executing the instruction is that D_0 now contains 00000000_{16} and A_3 contains $FFFFFFFF_{16}$. The data transfers that take place are always 32 bits long and no condition code bits are affected.

Swap Instruction—SWAP

The swap (SWAP) instruction is similar to the exchange instruction in that it has the ability to exchange two values. However, it is used to exchange the upper and lower words in a data register. The general form of SWAP is given in Fig. 3.17 as

SWAP Dn

An example is

SWAP   D0

When this instruction is executed, the contents of the lower 16 bits of D_0 are swapped with its upper 16 bits. If the original contents of D_0 are $FFFF0000_{16}$, execution of the instruction results in the value $0000FFFF_{16}$ in D_0. The 32-bit value that results in D_0 after the swap operation is used to set or reset the condition code flags.

Clear Instruction—CLR

The CLR instruction can be used to initialize the contents of an internal register or storage location in data memory to zero. Figure 3.17 shows that the instruction is written in general as

CLR   EA

and that it can perform its operation on byte, word, or long-word operands. All alterable addressing modes except address register direct can be used to access the operand.

For instance, to clear the least significant 8 bits of D_0, the following instruction is executed:

CLR.B   D0

Whenever this instruction is executed, the Z bit of SR is set and the N, V, and C bits are cleared. Moreover, the X bit is not affected.

3.7 INTEGER ARITHMETIC INSTRUCTIONS

The instruction set of the 68000 provides instructions to perform binary arithmetic operations, such as add, subtract, multiply, and divide. These instructions can process both signed and unsigned numbers. Moreover, the data being processed can be organized as bytes, words, or long words. The instructions in this group are shown in Fig. 3.20.

Mnemonic	Meaning	Type	Operand Size	Operation
ADD	Add|	ADD EA, Dn	8, 16, 32	(EA) + Dn → Dn
		ADD Dn, EA	8, 16, 32	Dn + (EA) → EA
		ADDI #XXX, EA	8, 16, 32	#XXX + (EA) → EA
		ADDQ #XXX, EA	8, 16, 32	#XXX + (EA) → EA
		ADDX Dy, Dx	8, 16, 32	Dy + Dx + X → Dx
		ADDX ⁻(Ay), ⁻(Ax)	8, 16, 32	⁻(Ay) + ⁻(Ax) + X → (Ax)
		ADDA EA, An	16, 32	(EA) + An → An
SUB	Subtract|	SUB EA, Dn	8, 16, 32	Dn − (EA) → Dn
		SUB Dn, EA	8, 16, 32	(EA) − Dn → EA
		SUBI #XXX, EA	8, 16, 32	(EA) − #XXX → EA
		SUBQ #XXX, EA	8, 16, 32	(EA) − #XXX → EA
		SUBX Dy, Dx	8, 16, 32	Dx − Dy → Dx
		SUBX ⁻(Ay), ⁻(Ax)	8, 16, 32	⁻(Ax) − ⁻(Ay) → (Ax)
		SUBA EA, An	16, 32	An − (EA) → An
NEG	Negate	NEG EA, Dn	8, 16, 32	0 − (EA) → EA
		NEGX EA, Dn	8, 16, 32	0 − (EA) − X → EA
MUL	Multiply	MULS EA, Dn	16	(EA) · Dn → Dn
		MULU EA, Dn	16	(EA) · Dn → Dn
DIV	Divide	DIVS EA, Dn	32 ÷ 16	Dn ÷ (EA) → Dn
		DIVU EA, Dn	32 ÷ 16	Dn ÷ (EA) → Dn
EXT	Extend sign	EXT.W Dn	8 → 16	Dn byte → Dn word
		EXT.L Dn	16 → 32	Dn word → Dn long word

Figure 3-20 Integer arithmetic instructions.

The condition code bits in the SR register are set or reset as per the result of arithmetic instructions. For ADD, SUB, and NEG instructions the five condition code bits are affected as follows:

N is set if the result is negative, cleared otherwise

Z is set if the result is zero, cleared otherwise

V is set if an overflow occurs, cleared otherwise

X and C are set if carry is generated or borrow is taken, cleared otherwise

For MUL, DIV, and EXT instructions, V and C are always cleared, X is not affected, and N and Z are set or cleared like that in other arithmetic instructions: ADD, SUB, and NEG.

Addition Instructions—ADD, ADDI, ADDQ, ADDX, and ADDA

For implementing the binary addition operation, the 68000 provides five types of add instructions. All five forms together with their permitted operand sizes are shown in Fig. 3.20. The different types of instructions are provided for dealing with different kinds of addition requirements. For instance, when addresses are manipulated, we want to operate on data in the address registers and do not want to affect the condition codes in SR. Thus for this situation a special address addition (ADDA) instruction is provided.

The first four forms of the add instruction in Fig. 3.20 are generally used to process data and the last form is for modifying addresses. Two forms of the basic *add* (ADD) instruction are shown. The first form

$$ADD \quad EA,Dn$$

adds the contents of the location specified by the effective address EA to the contents of data register D_n; that is,

$$(EA) + Dn \rightarrow Dn$$

The source operand can be located in an internal register or a storage location in memory. Moreover, its effective address can be specified with any of the addressing modes of the 68000. The only exception is that the size of the operand cannot be specified as a byte when address register direct addressing mode is used.

For instance, the instruction

$$ADD.L \quad D0,D1$$

causes the contents of D_0 to be added to the contents of D_1. If the original contents of D_0 are \$00013344 and that of D_1 are \$00000FFF, the sum that is produced equals \$00014343 and it is saved in D_1.

The second form is similar except that it represents the addition of the contents of a source data register to the contents of a destination operand that is identified by the effective address EA.

$$ADD \quad Dn,EA$$

$$Dn + (EA) \rightarrow EA$$

In this case only the alterable memory addressing modes are applicable to the destination operand.

Example 3.4

Write an instruction sequence that can be used to add two long words whose locations in memory are specified by the contents of address registers A_1 and A_2, respectively. The sum is to replace the contents of the storage location pointed to by the address in A_2.

Solution. We will use D_0 as an intermediate storage location for implementing the memory-to-memory add. The instruction sequence is

```
CLR.L     D0
ADD.L     (A1),D0
ADD.L     D0,(A2)
```

The instruction *add immediate* (ADDI) operates similarly to the ADD instruction we just introduced. The important difference is that now the value of the source operand is always located in program memory as an immediate operand. That is, it is encoded as the second word of the instruction for byte and word operands or as a second and third word for long-word operands. The general instruction format as shown in Fig. 3.20 is

ADDI   #XXX,EA

Here #XXX stands for the immediate source operand and EA is the effective address of the destination operand. For example, the instruction

ADD.L #$0FFFF,D0

causes the value $FFFF_{16}$ to be added to the long-word contents of D_0.

The *add quick* (ADDQ) instruction of Fig. 3.20 is a special variation of the add-immediate instruction. It limits the size of the source operand to the range 1 through 8.

An example is the instruction

ADDQ #3,D1

It stands for add the number 3 to the contents of D_1. These immediate data are encoded directly into the instruction word. For this reason, ADDQ encodes in fewer bytes and executes faster than ADDI. Therefore, it is preferred when memory requirement and execution times are to be minimized. Of course, the addition that is performed cannot involve a number larger than 8 as the source operand.

The next type of addition instruction in Fig. 3.20 is the *add extend* (ADDX) instruction. It differs from the earlier instructions in that the addition it performs involves the two operands along with the extend (X) bit of SR. One form of the instruction is

ADDX   Dy,Dx

and the arithmetic operation it performs is

$$Dy + Dx + X \rightarrow Dx$$

That is, the contents of data register Dy are added to the contents of data register Dx and extend bit X. The sum that results is placed in Dx. Notice that both operands must always be in data registers.

The other form of the ADDX instruction, as shown in Fig. 3.20, specifies its operands with predecrement address register indirect addressing. It permits access to data stored in memory.

The last form of the addition instruction in Fig. 3.20 is the *add address* (ADDA) instruction. Its form is

$$\text{ADDA EA,An}$$

and its execution results in

$$(EA) + An \rightarrow An$$

The source operand can employ any of the addressing modes of the 68000. For this reason the source operand can reside in an internal register or storage location in memory. On the other hand, the destination is always an address register. Since the destination operand is always an address register, only word or long-word operations are permitted.

Example 3.5

If the values in D_3 and A_3 are 76543210_{16} and $0000ABCD_{16}$, respectively, what is the result produced by executing the instruction

$$\text{ADDA.W D3,A3}$$

Solution. Execution of this instruction causes the word value in D_3 to be added to the contents of A_3. This gives

$$A_3 = XXXX3210_{16} + 0000ABCD_{16}$$
$$= 0000DDDD_{16}$$

Subtraction Instructions—SUB, SUBI, SUBQ, SUBX, and SUBA

Having covered the addition instructions of the 68000, let us look at the instructions provided to perform binary subtraction. As shown in Fig. 3.20, the subtraction instruction also has five basic forms. Notice that these forms are identical to those already described for the addition operation. For this reason we will present the subtraction instructions in less detail.

The general *subtraction* (SUB) instruction of the 68000 can be written in general using either the form

$$\text{SUB EA,Dn}$$

or

$$\text{SUB Dn,EA}$$

The first form permits the contents of an internal register or storage location in memory to be subtracted from the contents of a data register. The difference that is obtained is stored in the selected destination data register. This operation can be expressed as

$$Dn - (EA) \rightarrow Dn$$

For instance, the instruction

$$\text{SUB D0,D1}$$

performs a register-to-register subtraction. The difference $D_1 - D_0$ is saved in D_1.

The second SUB instruction in Fig. 3.20 performs the opposite subtraction operation. Its source operand is a data register within the 68000 and the location of the destination is specified by an effective address. Therefore, it can be a data register, address register, or storage location in data memory.

The next two subtraction instructions in Fig. 3.20, *subtract immediate* (SUBI) and *subtract quick* (SUBQ), permit an immediate operand in program memory to be subtracted from the destination operand identified by EA. The destination operand can be a data register or a storage location in data memory. These instructions operate the same as their addition counterparts except that they calculate the difference between their source and destination operands instead of their sum.

For instance,

$$\text{SUBI.W } \#\$1234,\text{D0}$$

causes the value 1234_{16} to be subtracted from the contents of D_0. Assuming that D_0 initially contains $0000FFFF_{16}$, the difference produced in D_0 is

$$FFFF_{16} - 1234_{16} = EDCB_{16}$$

Extend subtract (SUBX), just like ADDX, includes the extend (X) bit of SR in the subtraction. Moreover, the same source and destination operand variations are permitted as for the ADDX instruction. For example, the first form in Fig. 3.20 is

$$\text{SUBX Dy,Dx}$$

and it performs the subtraction

$$\text{Dx} - \text{Dy} - \text{X} \rightarrow \text{Dx}$$

For example, if D_1 and D_2 contain the values 76543210_{16} and $0000ABCD_{16}$, respectively, and the extend bit is 1_2, the result produced by executing the instruction

$$\text{SUBX.W   D1,D2}$$

is

$$D_2 = 0000ABCD_{16} - XXXX3210_{16} - 1_{16}$$
$$= 79BC_{16}$$

Finally, *subtract address* (SUBA) of Fig. 3.20 is used to modify addresses in A_0 through A_6 by subtraction. For example, it can be used to subtract the contents of data register D_7 from the address in A_5 with the instruction

$$\text{SUBA   D7,A5}$$

Negate Instructions—NEG and NEGX

Another type of arithmetic instruction is the negate instruction. Two forms of this instruction are shown in Fig. 3.20. The negate instructions are similar to the subtract instructions in that the specified operand is subtracted from another operand.

However, in this case, the other operand is always assumed to be zero. Subtracting any number from zero gives its negative.

The basic *negate* (NEG) instruction is used to form the negative of the specified operand. It is given in general by

NEG   EA

and an example is the instruction

NEG.W   D0

If the original contents of D_0 are $00FF_{16}$, execution of the instruction produces the result $FF01_{16}$.

Negate with extend (NEGX) differs from NEG in that it subtracts both the contents of the specified operand and the extend (X) flag from 0. That is, it performs the operation

$$0 - (EA) - X \rightarrow EA$$

Both instructions can be written to process bytes, words, or long words of data. Moreover, the addressing modes permitted for the operand are the alterable addressing modes that were shown in Fig. 3.14.

Multiplication Instructions—MULS and MULU

The 68000 provides instructions that perform the multiplication arithmetic operation on unsigned or signed numbers. Separate instructions are provided to process these two types of numbers. As shown in Fig. 3.20, they are signed multiply,

MULS EA,Dn

and unsigned multiply,

MULU EA,Dn

Both MULS and MULU have two 16-bit operands that are labeled EA and Dn. The source operand EA can be specified with any of the data addressing modes and the destination operand always uses data register direct addressing. Both the source and destination operands are treated as signed numbers when executing MULS and as unsigned numbers when executing MULU. The result, which is a 32-bit number, is placed in the destination data register.

Here is an example of the instruction needed to multiply the unsigned word number in data register D_1 by the unsigned word number in D_0.

MULU   D0,D1

At completion of execution of the instruction, the long-word product that results is in D_1.

As in most arithmetic instructions, the condition code bits of SR are updated based on the product that results. Two of the condition code bits, zero (Z) and negative (N), are affected based on the results. On the other hand, carry (C) and overflow (V) are always cleared.

Division Instructions—DIVS and DIVU

Similar to the multiplication instructions of the 68000, there is a *signed divide* (DIVS) instruction and an *unsigned divide* (DIVU) instruction. They are expressed in general as

DIVS   EA,Dn

and

DIVU   EA,Dn

The destination operand, which is the dividend, must be the contents of one of the data registers. The source operand, which is the divisor, can be accessed using any of the data addressing modes of the 68000.

Execution of either of these instructions causes the 32-bit dividend identified by the destination operand to be divided by the 16-bit divisor specified by the effective address. The 16-bit quotient that results is produced in the lower word of the destination data register and the remainder is placed in the upper word of the same register. The sign of the remainder produced by a signed division is always the same as that of the dividend.

The condition codes that are affected by the division instruction are zero (Z) and negative (N). They are set or reset based on the quotient value and its sign. Furthermore, the carry flag is always cleared. If the result turns out to be over 16 bits, the overflow condition code bit is set and the destination operand is not changed. Thus one should check the V flag for an overflow after executing a division instruction. An attempt to divide by zero is also automatically detected by the 68000.

Sign Extend Instruction—EXT

The 68000 provides the *sign extend* (EXT) instruction for *sign extension* of byte or word operands. As shown in Fig. 3.20, the general form of this instruction is given by

EXT   Dn

Notice that its operand must be located in a data register. When EXT is executed, the sign bit of the operand is copied into the most significant bits of the register.

For instance, when the word value in D_1 must be extended to a long word, the instruction

EXT.L   D1

can be executed. It causes the value in bit 15 (the sign bit) to be copied into bits 16 through 31 of D_1.

Sign extension is required before data of unequal lengths can be involved in signed arithmetic operations. For instance, if one of the operands for an addition instruction that is written to process word data is expressed as a signed byte, it must first be extended to a signed word.

Example 3.6

Assume that data registers D_0, D_1, and D_2 contain a signed byte, a signed word, and a signed long word in 2's-complement form, respectively. Write a sequence of instructions that will produce the signed result of the operation that follows:

$$D_0 + D_1 - D_2 \rightarrow D_0$$

Solution. Before any addition or subtraction can be performed, we must extend each value of data to a signed long word. To convert the byte in D_0 to its equivalent long word, we must first convert it to a word and then to a long word. This is done with the following instructions:

> EXT.W   D0
>
> EXT.L   D0

Similarly, to convert the word in D_1 to a long word, we execute the instruction

> EXT.L   D1

Since the contents of D_2 are already a signed long word, no sign extension is necessary.

To do the required arithmetic operations, we just use the appropriate arithmetic instructions. For instance, to add the contents of D_0 and D_1, we use ADD, and to subtract the contents of D_2 from this sum, we use SUB. This leads us to the following sequence of instructions.

> ADD.L   D1,D0
>
> SUB.L   D2,D0

The complete program is listed in Fig. 3.21.

```
EXT.W    D0
EXT.L    D0
EXT.L    D1
ADD.L    D1, D0
SUB.L    D2, D0
```

Figure 3-21 Addition and subtraction of signed numbers.

3.8 DECIMAL ARITHMETIC INSTRUCTIONS

The arithmetic instructions we considered in the preceding section process data that is expressed as binary numbers. However, data are frequently provided that are coded as BCD numbers instead of as binary numbers. Traditionally, BCD-to-binary and binary-to-BCD conversion routines are used to process BCD data. However, the 68000 microprocessor has the ability to perform the add, subtract, and negate arithmetic operations directly on packed BCD numbers. Three BCD arithmetic instructions, ABCD, SBCD, and NBCD, are provided for this purpose. They provide an efficient and easy-to-use method for implementing BCD arithmetic. As per the result of these instructions, the condition code bits, Z, C, and X, are affected, whereas N and V are undefined.

Add Decimal with Extend Instruction—ABCD

Let us begin with the *add binary-coded decimal* (ABCD) instruction. In Fig. 3.22 we see its permitted operand variations, operand size, and the operation it performs. Notice that only two addressing modes can be used to specify its operands. The first form,

$$\text{ABCD} \quad \text{Dy,Dx}$$

uses data register direct addressing for both source and destination operands. Therefore, both operands must reside in internal data registers of the 68000.

The other form,

$$\text{ABCD} \quad -(\text{Ay}), -(\text{Ax})$$

employs predecrement address register indirect addressing to specify both operands. Use of this addressing mode permits access of data stored in memory.

Execution of either of the ABCD instructions adds the contents of the source and destination operands together with the extend (X) bit of SR. The sum that results is saved in the destination operand location.

Mnemonic	Meaning	Type	Operand Size	Operation
ABCD	Add BCD numbers	ABCD Dy, Dx ABCD $^-$(Ay), $^-$(Ax)	8 8	Dy + Dx + X → Dx $^-$(Ay) + $^-$(Ax) + X → (Ax)
SBCD	Subtract BCD numbers	SBCD Dy, Dx SBCD $^-$(Ay), $^-$(Ax)	8 8	Dx − Dy − X → Dx $^-$(Ax) − $^-$(Ay) − X → (Ax)
NBCD	Negate BCD numbers	NBCD EA	8	0 − (EA) − X → EA

Figure 3-22 Binary-coded decimal arithmetic instructions.

These instructions perform decimal addition operations; therefore, we must start with decimal operands instead of binary operands. These decimal operands are expressed in packed BCD. The sum that is produced is also a decimal number coded in packed BCD. However, the operand size is always byte wide; therefore, two BCD digits can be processed at a time.

An example is the instruction

$$\text{ABCD} \quad \text{D0,D1}$$

If D_0 initially contains the value $12_{10} = 00010010_2$, D_1 contains $37_{10} = 00110111_2$, and X is clear, execution of the instruction produces the sum

$$D0 + D1 + X = 12_{10} + 37_{10} + 0_{10}$$
$$= 49_{10}$$

At completion of the instruction, D_0 still contains 12_{10} but the contents of D_1 are changed to 49_{10}. X remains cleared because no carry results.

Condition code bits Z, X, and C are affected based on the result produced by the addition. Bits C and X are always set to the same logic level. The other two condition code bits, V and N, are undefined after execution of the instruction and do not provide any usable information.

Subtract Decimal with Extend Instruction—SBCD

The *subtract binary-coded decimal* (SBCD) instruction works similar to the ABCD instruction just discussed. Of course, in this case, the subtraction arithmetic operation is performed and not the addition operation.

As shown in Fig. 3.22, the two forms of the instruction are

$$SBCD \quad Dy,Dx$$

and

$$SBCD \quad -(Ay),-(Ax)$$

Notice that the permitted addressing modes are identical to those employed by the ABCD instruction.

An example is the instruction

$$SBCD \quad -(A0),-(A1)$$

When this instruction is executed, the byte-wide (two BCD digits) contents of the source operand and X bit of SR are subtracted from the destination operand. The difference that is produced is saved at the destination location.

In our example, we are using address register indirect with predecrement addressing. Therefore, the contents of address registers A_0 and A_1 are first decremented by 1. For instance, if their original contents were $0000110F_{16}$ and $0000120F_{16}$, respectively, decrementing by 1 gives $A_0 = 0000110E_{16}$ and $A_1 = 0000120E_{16}$. These are the addresses that are used to access the operands in memory. Then the BCD data at memory location $00110E_{16}$ and X are subtracted from the BCD value at $00120E_{16}$. We will assume that the value stored at $00120E_{16}$ is 37_{10}, the value at $00110E_{16}$ is 12_{10}, and X is 1. Then the difference calculated by the instruction is

$$(00120E_{16}) - (00110E_{16}) - X = 37_{10} - 12_{10} - 1_{10}$$
$$= 24_{10}$$

This value is saved at destination address $00120E_{16}$ and the condition code bits Z, X, and C are cleared.

Negate Decimal Instruction—NBCD

The last of the decimal arithmetic instructions in Fig. 3.22 is *negate binary-coded decimal* (NBCD). It is expressed in general as

$$NBCD \quad EA$$

NBCD is effectively an SBCD instruction in which the subtrahend always equals zero. For this reason, it implements the operation

$$0 - (EA) \rightarrow EA$$

The operand identified as EA can be specified using the alterable addressing modes. One exception is address register direct addressing, which cannot be used.

Here is an example with the operand accessed through address register indirect addressing mode with postincrement:

$$NBCD \quad (A5)+$$

The condition code bits affected by the NBCD instruction are the same as those affected by the SBCD instruction.

Example 3.7

Write a program segment that will add two four-digit packed BCD numbers that are held in registers D_0 and D_1 and place their sum in D_0. The organization of the original BCD data in the data registers is shown in Fig. 3.23(a).

Solution.   Remember that only the contents of the 8 least significant bits of a data register can be processed with the BCD instructions. Moreover, up to this point in the chapter we have not shown any direct way of exchanging the most significant byte of a word in a data register with its least significant byte. One solution to this problem is to move the contents of D_0 and D_1 to memory. This reorganizes the BCD digits at separate byte addresses, as shown in Fig. 3.23(b). To move D_0 and D_1 to memory, say D_0 to address MEM_0 and D_1 to address MEM_1, the following instructions can be used:

$$MOVE.W \qquad D0,MEM0$$

$$MOVE.W \qquad D1,MEM1$$

Now we can use the predecrement address register indirect form of the BCD addition instruction to perform the decimal arithmetic operations. Therefore, address registers must be loaded with pointers to the data in memory. Let us use A_0 and A_1 for this purpose. Since the predecrement mode of addressing must be used, A_0 should be loaded with $MEM_0 + 2$ and A_1 with $MEM_1 + 2$. This is done with the instructions

$$LEA \quad MEM0 + 2, A0$$

$$LEA \quad MEM1 + 2, A1$$

Moreover, in order to use the BCD instructions, we must start with X = 0. To do this, we execute the instruction

$$MOVE \quad \#0,CCR$$

Now that the address pointers and the extend bit of SR are initialized, we are ready to perform the addition operation. Executing the instructions

$$ABCD \quad -(A1), -(A0)$$

and

$$ABCD \quad -(A1), -(A0)$$

gives the sum in MEM_0.

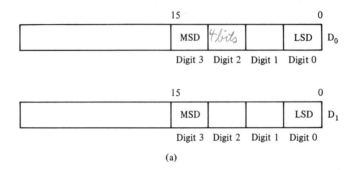

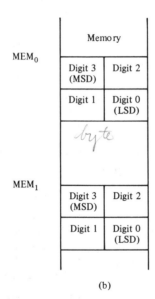

(b)

```
MOVE.W      D0, MEM0
MOVE.W      D1, MEM1
LEA         MEM0 + 2, A0
LEA         MEM1 + 2, A1
MOVE        #0, CCR
ABCD        -(A1), -(A0)
ABCD        -(A1), -(A0)
MOVE.W      MEM0, D0
```

(c)

Figure 3-23 (a) Four-digit BCD numbers in data registers D_0 and D_1; (b) storage of the BCD numbers in memory; (c) program for adding two four-digit BCD numbers.

To put the sum into D_0, the instruction is

MOVE.W   MEM0,D0

The complete program is repeated in Fig. 3.23(c).

3.9 LOGIC INSTRUCTIONS

To implement logic functions, such as AND, OR, exclusive-OR, and NOT, the instruction set of the 68000 provides a group of logic instructions. The instructions in this group are shown in Fig. 3.24 together with their different forms, operand sizes, and operations. The execution of a logic instruction sets the condition code bits N and Z as per the result, clears V and C, and does not affect the X bit.

AND Instructions—AND and ANDI

As shown in Fig. 3.24, there are four forms of the AND instruction. The general form, which uses the mnemonic AND, permits the contents of a data register and an operand specified by the effective address EA to be ANDed together. Let us look at the first form of the instruction

AND   EA,Dn

The source operand can use the data addressing modes to generate EA. Therefore, the source operand can use any addressing mode except address register direct addressing. On the other hand, the destination operand can be specified only with data register direct addressing and will always be one of the eight data registers inside the 68000.

Mnemonic	Meaning	Type	Operand Size	Operation
AND	Logical AND	AND EA,Dn	8, 16, 32	$(EA) \cdot Dn \rightarrow Dn$
		AND Dn,EA	8, 16, 32	$Dn \cdot (EA) \rightarrow EA$
		ANDI #XXX,EA	8, 16, 32	$\#XXX \cdot (EA) \rightarrow EA$
		ANDI #XXX,CCR	8	$\#XXX \cdot CCR \rightarrow CCR$
		ANDI #XXX,SR	16	$\#XXX \cdot SR \rightarrow SR$
OR	Logical OR	OR EA,Dn	8, 16, 32	$(EA) + Dn \rightarrow Dn$
		OR Dn,EA	8, 16, 32	$Dn + (EA) \rightarrow EA$
		ORI #XXX,EA	8, 16, 32	$\#XXX + (EA) \rightarrow EA$
		ORI #XXX,CCR	8	$\#XXX + CCR \rightarrow CCR$
		ORI #XXX,SR	16	$\#XXX + SR \rightarrow SR$
EOR	Logical exclusive-OR	EOR Dn,EA	8, 16, 32	$Dn \oplus (EA) \rightarrow EA$
		EORI #XXX,EA	8, 16, 32	$\#XXX \oplus (EA) \rightarrow EA$
		EORI #XXX,CCR	8	$\#XXX \oplus CCR \rightarrow CCR$
		EORI #XXX,SR	16	$\#XXX \oplus SR \rightarrow SR$
NOT	Logical NOT	NOT EA	8, 16, 32	$(\overline{EA}) \rightarrow EA$

Figure 3-24 Logic instructions.

An example of the instruction, which uses register direct addressing for both the source and destination operands, is

$$\text{AND.B} \quad \text{D0,D1}$$

Execution of this instruction causes a bit for bit AND operation to be performed on the byte contents of D_0 and D_1. The result is saved in destination register D_1.

For instance, if D_1 contains $0000ABCD_{16}$ and D_0 contains $00000F0F_{16}$, the AND operation between the least significant bytes gives

$$CD_{16} \cdot 0F_{16} = 11001101_2 \cdot 00001111_2$$
$$= 00001101_2$$
$$= 0D_{16}$$

Therefore, the new contents of D_1 are $0000AB0D_{16}$. Notice that the four most significant bits of the least significant byte of D_1 have been masked off. The affected condition code bits in SR are Z, N, C, and V. The C and V bits are always cleared, but Z and N are set or reset based on the result produced in the destination register.

The second form,

$$\text{AND} \quad \text{Dn,EA}$$

permits the contents of a source operand held in a data register to be ANDed with a destination operand identified by EA. This time the location of the destination operand can be specified using any of the alterable memory addressing modes. These addressing modes are identified in Fig. 3.14.

The next three types of the AND group are *AND immediate* (ANDI) instructions. These instructions AND an immediate source operand identified as #XXX with the contents of a specified destination operand. The immediate operand is stored as part of the instruction in program memory.

The first form,

$$\text{ANDI} \quad \text{\#XXX,EA}$$

permits ANDing of an immediate source operand with the contents of a destination operand whose location is specified by effective address EA. This destination operand can be in a data register, address register, or storage location in data memory.

An example is the instruction

$$\text{ANDI.B} \quad \text{\#7,D1}$$

Execution of this instruction causes the binary form of decimal number 7 to be ANDed with the contents of D_1. Let us assume that D_1 originally contained $FFFFFFFF_{16}$; then, executing the instruction gives

$$D_1 = FFFFFFFF_{16} \cdot 7_{16}$$
$$= FFFFFFF7_{16}$$

The next two forms,

$$\text{ANDI} \quad \text{\#XXX,SR}$$

and

ANDI   #XXX,CCR

are used to AND the contents of the complete status register and the condition code byte part of SR with immediate data, respectively. The first of these two operations is privileged and can only be executed when the 68000 is in the supervisor state.

OR Instructions—OR and ORI

The OR instruction has the same five forms that we just introduced for the AND instruction. Figure 3.24 shows that they include two forms of the *general OR* instruction and three forms of the *OR immediate* (ORI) instruction.

The general OR instruction permits the OR logic operation to be performed between the contents of a data register specified using one operand and the contents of another data register, an address register, or a location in memory specified by the data addressing mode of the other operand. For example, the instruction

OR.B   (A0),D0

ORs the contents of the byte location whose effective address is the contents of A_0 with the byte contents of D_0. The result is saved in D_0. That is, it performs the logic operation

(EA) + D0 → D0

Assuming that the contents of the storage location pointed to by the address in A_0 is $AAAAAAAA_{16}$ and the data held in D_0 is 55555555_{16}, the results obtained by executing the instruction are

$$D0 = AAAAAAAA_{16} + 55555555_{16}$$
$$= FFFFFFFF_{16}$$

The OR immediate forms of the instruction allow an immediate operand to be ORed with the contents of a storage location in data memory, a data register, or the status register. An example is the instruction

ORI   #FF00,SR

Execution of this instruction causes all of the bits in the upper byte of SR to be set to 1 without changing the bits in the lower byte. Since the status register's upper byte is changed, the operation can only be performed when in the supervisor state.

Exclusive-OR Instructions—EOR and EORI

Looking at Fig. 3.24, we see that the same basic instruction forms are also provided for the *exclusive-OR* (EOR) instruction. The difference here is that they perform the exclusive-OR logic function on the contents of the source and destination operands.

Let us now look at some examples. A first example of the instruction is

EOR.L   A0,D0

When it is executed, the operation performed is

$$A0 \oplus D0 \rightarrow D0$$

Another example is

$$EOR \quad \#\$0F,CCR$$

Execution of this instruction performs the operation

$$\$0F \oplus CCR \rightarrow CCR$$

NOT Instruction—NOT

The *NOT* instruction differs from the AND, OR, and EOR instructions we just described in that only one operand is specified. Its general form, as shown in Fig. 3.24, is

$$NOT \quad EA$$

When this instruction is executed, the contents of the specified operand are replaced by its 1's complement. To address the operand, only the alterable addressing modes can be used. However, one exception exists: it is that address register direct addressing is not permitted.

Example 3.8

Write a sequence of logic instructions that will clear the bits in register D_1 that correspond to the bits that are set in D_0.

Solution. To clear a bit that is set, it should be ANDed with logic 0. Moreover, to obtain a logic 0 from logic 1, it should be inverted. Thus if the contents of D_0 are inverted and then ANDed with D_1, the required result will be generated in D_1. The instructions that do this are

$$NOT.L \quad D0$$
$$AND.L \quad D0,D1$$

3.10 SHIFT AND ROTATE INSTRUCTIONS

The shift and rotate instructions of the 68000 are used to change bit positions of the data bits in an operand. These types of operations are useful to multiply or divide a given number by a power of 2, check the status of individual bits in an operand, or simply shift the position of data bits in a register or memory location.

Shift Instructions—LSL, LSR, ASL, and ASR

There are two kinds of shift operations: the *logical shift* and the *arithmetic shift*. Moreover, each of these two shifts can be performed in the *left direction* or *right direction*. As shown in Fig. 3.25, these variations lead to four basic shift instructions.

The two logical shift instructions are *logical shift left* (LSL) and *logical shift right* (LSR). The operation of these instructions is illustrated with diagrams in Fig.

Mnemonic	Meaning	Type	Operand Size	Operation
LSL	Logical shift left	LSL #XXX,Dy LSL Dx,Dy LSL EA	8, 16, 32 8, 16, 32 8, 16, 32	X/C ◄── ◄── ◄──0
LSR	Logical shift right	LSR #XXX,Dy LSR Dx,Dy LSR EA	8, 16, 32 8, 16, 32 8, 16, 32	0──► ──► ──► X/C
ASL	Arithmetic shift left	ASL #XXX,Dy ASL Dx,Dy ASL EA	8, 16, 32 8, 16, 32 8, 16, 32	X/C ◄── ◄── ◄──0
ASR	Arithmetic shift right	ASR #XXX,Dy ASR Dx,Dy ASR EA	8, 16, 32 8, 16, 32 8, 16, 32	──► ──► X/C MSB

Figure 3-25 Shift instructions.

3.25. Looking at the illustration for LSL, we see that its execution causes the bits of the operand to be shifted to the left by a specific number of bit positions. At the same time, the vacated bit positions on the least significant bit end of the operand are filled with zeros and bits are shifted out from the most significant bit end. The last bit shifted out on the left is copied into both the extend (X) and carry (C) bits of SR.

Notice in Fig. 3.25 that there are three forms of the LSL instruction. The first two forms differ in the way the shift count is specified. In the first form,

$$LSL \quad \#XXX,Dy$$

the count is specified by the immediate operand #XXX. The value of this operand can be from 0 through 7. A value of zero stands for "shift left eight bit positions." In this way, we see that this form of the instruction limits the shift left to the range of from 1 to 8 bits. For instance,

$$LSL.W \quad \#5,D4$$

initiates a shift left by five bit positions for the word contents of data register D_4.

The second form

$$LSL \quad Dx,Dy$$

specifies the count as residing in data register Dx. Only the six least significant bits of this register are used for the shift count. Therefore, the shift count is extended to a range of from 1 to 63 bit positions.

An example is the instruction

$$LSL \quad D0,D1$$

Assuming that D_0 contains 4_{16} and D_1 contains $0000FFFF_{16}$, execution of the instruction results in

$$D_1 = 000FFFF0_{16}$$

and

$$C = 0$$

Both of the forms of the LSL instruction that we have considered up to this point only have the ability to shift the bits of an operand that is held in one of the internal data registers of the 68000. The third form,

LSL   EA

permits a shift left operation to be performed on the contents of a storage location in memory. Actually, any of the data-alterable addressing modes that relate to external memory can be used to specify EA. One restriction is that the size specified for the operand must always be a word. Moreover, since no shift count is specified, execution of the instruction causes a shift left of just one bit position.

Looking at Fig. 3.25, we see that the logical shift right (LSR) instruction can be written using the same basic forms as the LSL instruction. Moreover, the operations that they perform are the exact opposite of that just described for their corresponding LSL instruction. Now data are shifted to the right instead of to the left; zeros are loaded into vacated bits from the MSB end instead of the LSB end; and the last bit shifted out from the LSB is copied into both X and C.

There are also two basic arithmetic shift instructions: *arithmetic shift left* (ASL) and *arithmetic shift right* (ASR). Their forms and operations are also shown in Fig. 3.25. Here we see that the operation performed by ASL is essentially the same as that performed by the LSL instruction. However, there is a difference in the way in which the overflow flag is handled by the two instructions. It is always 0 for the LSL instruction, but for ASL it is set to 1 if the MSB changes logic level.

On the other hand, ASR is not the same as LSR. Notice that it does not only shift the bits of its operand but also preserves its sign. The illustration of operation of ASR in Fig. 3.25 shows that vacated more significant bit positions are filled with the original value for the MSB—that is, the sign bit.

Rotate Instructions—ROL, ROR, ROXL, and ROXR

The rotate instructions of the 68000 are similar to its shift instructions in that they can be used to shift the bits of data in an operand to the left or right. However, the shift operation they perform differs in that the bits of data that are shifted out at one end are shifted back in at the other end. Hence, the bits of data appear to have been rotated.

Based on the path in which bits are rotated, two kinds of rotate operations are defined. As shown in Fig. 3.26, the basic rotate operation performed by the *rotate left* (ROL) instruction or *rotate right* (ROR) instruction use a path in which bits are shifted out from one end of the operand into the carry (C) bit of SR, and at the same time they are reloaded at the other end. Notice that the path for the other two instructions, ROXL and ROXR, differs in that both C and X are loaded with the bits as they are shifted out. Moreover, bits that are reloaded at the other end pass through X.

Mnemonic	Meaning	Type	Operand Size	Operation
ROL	Rotate left	ROL #XXX,Dy ROL Dx,Dy ROL EA	8, 16, 32 8, 16, 32 8, 16, 32	
ROR	Rotate right	ROR #XXX,Dy ROR Dx,Dy ROR EA	8, 16, 32 8, 16, 32 8, 16, 32	
ROXL	Rotate left through extend	ROXL #XXX,Dy ROXL Dx,Dy ROXL EA	8, 16, 32 8, 16, 32 8, 16, 32	
ROXR	Rotate right through extend	ROXR #XXX,Dy ROXR Dx,Dy ROXR EA	8, 16, 32 8, 16, 32 8, 16, 32	

Figure 3-26 Rotate instructions.

Let us begin with the ROL instruction. Looking at the diagram of its operation in Fig. 3.26, we see that it causes the bits of the specified operand to be rotated to the left. Bits shifted out from the most significant bit position are both loaded into C and the least significant bit position. The number of bit positions through which the data are to be rotated are specified as part of the instruction.

Notice that the allowed operand variations for ROL are identical to those shown in Fig. 3.25 for the shift instructions. The first form,

$$\text{ROL} \quad \#XXX,Dy$$

permits an immediate operand in the range 0 to 7, to specify the count. This limits the amount of rotation to 1 to 8 bit positions. A value of 0 for XXX is actually a special case. It causes an 8-bit rotate to the left. The next form,

$$\text{ROL} \quad Dx,Dy$$

uses the contents of the six least significant bits of data register Dx to specify the count. This extends the rotate range to from 1 to 63 bit positions. When either of these instructions are used, the operand that is to be processed by the rotate operation must reside in one of the data registers.

An example is the instruction

$$\text{ROL.L} \quad D0,D1$$

If D_0 contains 00000004_{16}, execution of the instruction causes the long-word contents of D_1 to be rotated four bit positions to the left. For instance, if the original contents of D_1 were $0000FFFF_{16}$, after the rotate operation is complete, the new contents of D_1 are $000FFFF0_{16}$ and C equals 0.

The last form of the rotate left instruction

$$\text{ROL} \quad EA$$

permits the operand to reside in a storage location in memory. This instruction may only be used to perform a 1-bit rotate left on a word operand.

In Fig. 3.26 we see that the rotate right (ROR) instruction is capable of performing the same operations as ROL. However, in this case, the data are rotated in the opposite direction.

As we indicated earlier, the *rotate left with extend* (ROXL) and *rotate right with extend* (ROXR) instructions essentially perform the same rotate operations as ROL and ROR, respectively. However, this time the last bit rotated out is loaded into both X and C, not just C, and bits that are reloaded at the other end pass through X. Therefore, execution of the instruction

$$\text{ROXL.L} \quad \text{D0,D1}$$

when $D_0 = 4_{16}$, $D_1 = 000FFFF0_{16}$, $C = 1$, and $X = 1$, results in $D_1 = 00FFFF08_{16}$ with $C = 0$ and $X = 0$.

Example 3.9

Implement the operation described in Example 3.7 using the rotate and decimal arithmetic instructions to add two four-digit packed BCD numbers that are held in D_0 and D_1, respectively. Place the result in D_0.

Solution. We first start with $X = 0$ and add the two least significant digits. The instructions required to do this are

$$\text{MOVE} \quad \text{\#0,CCR}$$

$$\text{ABCD} \quad \text{D1,D0}$$

Let us save this result in D_2 by executing the instruction

$$\text{MOVE.B} \quad \text{D0,D2}$$

To add the most significant digits, we can rotate the words in D_1 and D_0 8 bits to the right. The instructions for this are

$$\text{ROR.W} \quad \text{\#0,D0}$$

$$\text{ROR.W} \quad \text{\#0,D1}$$

This does not change the X bit, which must be used in the addition. Now the least significant bytes in D_0 and D_1 can be added as BCD numbers by the instruction

$$\text{ABCD} \quad \text{D1,D0}$$

The result of D_0 can now be rotated to the left and the least significant result saved in D_2 can be placed back in D_0. The instructions to do this are

$$\text{ROL.W} \quad \text{\#0,D0}$$

$$\text{MOVE.B} \quad \text{D2,D0}$$

This completes the BCD addition. The entire program is shown in Fig. 3.27.

MOVE	#0,CCR
ABCD	D1,D0
MOVE.B	D0,D2
ROR.W	#0,D0
ROR.W	#0,D1
ABCD	D1,D0
ROL.W	#0,D0
MOVE.B	D2,D0

Figure 3-27 BCD addition program.

ASSIGNMENT

Section 3.2

1. Can the 68000 directly store a word of data starting at an odd address?
2. Compare a data register and an address register from a software point of view.
3. List the basic data types on which the 68000 can operate directly.

Section 3.3

4. Identify the three parts of an assembly language instruction in each of the following statements:

AGAIN   ADD D0,D1   ADD THE REGISTERS

MOVE D1,D5   SAVE THE RESULT

5. Identify the source and destination operands for each of the statements in problem 4.

Section 3.4

6. Make a list of the addressing modes available on the 68000.
7. Identify the addressing modes for both the source and destination operands in the instructions that follow.

   (a) MOVE.W   D3,D2
   (b) MOVE.B   D3,A2
   (c) MOVE.L   D3,$ABCD
   (d) MOVE.L   XYZ,D2
   (e) MOVE.W   XYZ(D0.L),D2
   (f) MOVE.B   D3,(A2)
   (g) MOVE.L   A1,(A2)+
   (h) MOVE.L   −(A2),D3
   (i) MOVE.W   10(A2),D3
   (j) MOVE.B   10(A2,A3.L),$A123
   (k) MOVE.W   #$ABCD,$1122

8. Compute the memory address for the source operand and/or destination operand in each of the instructions in problem 5.

9. Specify the conditions that make the following instructions equivalent.

$$
\begin{array}{ll}
\text{MOVE.L} & \text{D0,\$ABCD} \\
\text{MOVE.L} & \text{D0,\$10(A1)} \\
\text{MOVE.L} & \text{D0,\$100(A2,D1.L)} \\
\text{MOVE.L} & \text{D0,(A3)}
\end{array}
$$

Section 3.6

10. Given that $D_0 = \$12345678$, $D_1 = \$ABCDEF01$, and $A_0 = \$87654321$, specify the memory contents of address $A000 to address $A002 after executing the instruction

$$\text{MOVEM.B} \quad \text{D0/D1/A0,\$A000}$$

11. Write an instruction that places the long-word contents of memory locations $B000, $B004, and $B008 into registers D_5, D_6, and D_7, respectively.

12. What will be the contents of D_0 and D_1 after executing the following sequence of instructions?

$$
\begin{array}{ll}
\text{MOVE.L} & \text{\$13579BDF,D0} \\
\text{MOVE.L} & \text{\$02468ACE,D1} \\
\text{SWAP} & \text{D0} \\
\text{EXG.W} & \text{D0,D1}
\end{array}
$$

Section 3.7

13. Two word-wide unsigned integers are stored at the memory addresses $A000 and $B000, respectively. Write an instruction sequence that computes and stores their sum, difference, product, and quotient. Store these results at consecutive memory locations starting at address $C000 in memory. To obtain the difference, subtract the integer at $B000 from the integer at $A000. For the division, divide the integer at $A000 by the integer at $B000. Use register indirect relative addressing mode through register A_1 to store the various results.

Section 3.8

14. Two long-word BCD integers are stored at the symbolic addresses NUM1 and NUM2, respectively. Write an instruction sequence to generate their difference and store it at NUM3. The difference is to be formed by subtracting the value at NUM1 from that at NUM2. Use the predecrement indirect mode of addressing.

Section 3.9

15. Write an instruction sequence that generates a byte-size integer in the memory location identified by label RESULT. The value of the byte integer is to be calculated using logic operations as follows:

$$(\text{RESULT}) = \text{D0} \cdot \text{NUM1} + \text{NUM2} \cdot \text{D0} + \text{D1}$$

Assume that all parameters are byte size.

Section 3.10

16. Implement the following operation using shift and arithmetic instructions.

$$7 \cdot D1 - 5 \cdot D2 - \frac{1}{8} D2 \to D0$$

Assume that the parameters are all long word in size.

17. Write a program that stores the long-word contents of D_0 into memory starting at address location $B001.

4

68000 MICROPROCESSOR PROGRAMMING 2

4.1 INTRODUCTION

In Chapter 3, we introduced the addressing modes and many of the instructions in the instruction set of the 68000 microprocessor. Using these instructions, we also covered some preliminary programming techniques. Here we will cover the rest of the instructions and introduce some more complex programming methods. Specifically, the following topics are presented in this chapter:

1. Compare and test instructions
2. Jump and branch instructions
3. Programs employing loops
4. Subroutines and subroutine handling instructions
5. Bit manipulation instructions

4.2 COMPARE AND TEST INSTRUCTIONS

The instruction set of the 68000 includes instructions to compare two operands or an operand with zero. The comparison is done by subtracting the source operand from the destination operand. The result of the subtraction does not modify either of the operands; instead, it is used to set or reset condition code bits (flags) in the status register. The flags affected are: negative (N), zero (Z), overflow (V), and carry (C). These flags can then be examined by other instructions to make the decision as to whether to execute one part of the program or another.

The instructions that have the ability to compare operands are shown in Fig. 4.1. Basically, two types of instructions are available: the *compare* (CMP) instruction and *test* (TST) instruction. Notice that the CMP instruction always compares two operands. On the other hand, the TST instruction compares the specified operand with zero.

Mnemonic	Meaning	Type	Operand Size	Status Bits Affected
CMP	Compare	CMP EA,Dn	8, 16, 32	N, Z, V, C
		CMPA EA,An	16, 32	N, Z, V, C
		CMPI #XXX,EA	8, 16, 32	N, Z, V, C
		CMPM $(Ay)^+,(Ay)^+$	8, 16, 32	N, Z, V, C
TST	Test	TST EA	8, 16, 32	N, Z, V, C

Figure 4-1 Compare and test instructions.

Let us begin by looking in detail at the compare instruction of the 68000. Looking at Fig. 4.1, we see that there are four forms of this instruction. These forms are: *compare* (CMP), *compare address* (CMPA), *compare immediate* (CMPI), and *compare memory* (CMPM). They differ in the manner their operands are obtained for comparison.

The CMP instruction is used to compare a source operand with the contents of a data register. To specify the location of the source operand, any of the 68000's addressing modes can be used. On the other hand, the destination operand must always be one of the internal data registers. As indicated in Fig. 4.1, the specified operand size may be a byte, a word, or a long word. However, when an address register contains the source operand, byte-size comparisons cannot be made.

The result of the comparison is reflected by changes in four of the 68000's status flags. Notice in Fig. 4.1 that it affects the sign, zero, overflow, and carry flags. The logic state of these flags can be referenced by instructions in order to make a decision whether or not to alter the sequence in which the program executes.

The process of comparison performed by the CMP instruction is basically a subtraction operation. The source operand is subtracted from the destination operand. However, the result of this subtraction is not saved in the destination. Instead, based on the result the appropriate flags are set or reset.

The subtraction is done using 2's complement arithmetic. For example, let us assume that the destination operand equals $10011001_2 = -103_{10}$ and that the source operand equals $00011011_2 = +27_{10}$. Subtracting the source from the destination, we get

$$10011001_2 = -103_{10}$$
$$-00011011_2 = -(+27_{10})$$

Replacing the destination operand with its 2's complement and adding yields

$$10011001_2 = -103_{10}$$
$$-11100101_2 = -27_{10}$$
$$\overline{01111110_2 = +126_{10}}$$

In the process of obtaining this result, we set the status flags as follows:

1. Bit 7 of the difference is zero and therefore sign flag N is at logic 0.
2. The difference that is produced is nonzero, which makes zero flag Z logic 0.
3. Even though a carry out is generated from bit 7, there is no carry from bit 6 to bit 7. This represents an overflow condition and therefore the V flag is logic 1.
4. There is a carry out from bit 7. Thus, carry flag C is logic 1.

Notice that the result produced by subtracting the two 8-bit numbers is not correct. This condition is indicated by the fact that the overflow flag is set.

An example of the instruction is

CMP.W   D1,D0

When this instruction is executed, the word contents of D_1 are subtracted from that of D_0 and the flags are affected according to the result produced by the subtraction. For instance, if the value in D_1 is the same as that in D_0, the Z bit in SR is set and N, V, and C are all reset. Even though a subtraction is performed to determine this status, the values in D_1 and D_0 are not changed.

For instance, if the word contents of D_1 and D_0 are 1000_{16} and 4000_{16}, respectively, execution of the instruction CMP.W D1,D0 subtracts 1000_{16} from 4000_{16} and sets or resets the status flags based on the difference that results. Since this result is positive and nonzero, both N and Z are reset. Moreover, no carry is generated by the subtraction; therefore, C is also reset. Finally, in the process of performing the subtraction, an overflow condition does not occur and V is also reset. In this way, we find that at completion of execution of the instruction the statuses are N = 0, Z = 0, V = 0, and C = 0.

Compare address (CMPA) is the same as CMP except that the destination operand must reside in an address register instead of a data register. For this reason only word and long-word operands can be specified. A word source operand is sign extended to a long word before making the comparison. Here is an instruction that does a long-word comparison of the value of a long word in memory to the contents of A_0.

CMPA.L   (A1),A0

Notice that the address in A_1 is used to point to the long word in memory.

The next instruction, compare immediate (CMPI), is used to compare a byte, word, or long-word immediate operand to a destination operand that resides in a data register, address register, or storage location in memory. The location of the destination operand can be specified using any of the data-alterable addressing modes of the 68000. An example is the instruction

CMPI.B   #$FF,D0

The last type of compare instruction in Fig. 4.1 is compare memory (CMPM). Here both operands are located in memory and must be specified using the automatic postincrement indirect address register addressing modes. Since this instruction updates the address pointers each time it is executed, we are always ready to compare the next two pieces of data in memory. For this reason, it is very useful for performing string comparisons.

Example 4.1

Determine how the condition codes will change as the following instructions are executed.

CLR.L	D0
MOVE.B	#$5A,D0
CMP.B	D0,D0
CMPI.B	#$60,D0

Solution. What happens to the condition codes as these instructions are executed is summarized in Fig. 4.2. Here we see that the first instruction clears data register D_0. This is written as a long-word instruction; therefore, all 32 bits of D_0 are cleared. That is, it is loaded with 00000000_{16}. Due to the execution of the first instruction, the Z condition code bit is set while N, V, and C are cleared.

Instruction	Function	Condition Codes				
		X	N	Z	V	C
CLR.L D0	Clear D_0	X	0	1	0	0
MOVE.B #$5A,D0	Load $5A_{16}$ into D_0	X	0	0	0	0
CMP.B D0,D0	Compare D_0 with D_0	X	0	1	0	0
CMPI.B #$60,D0	Compare 60_{16} with D_0	X	1	0	0	1

Figure 4-2 Example program employing compare instructions.

The next instruction loads the lower byte of D_0 with the number $5A_{16}$. Since this number is positive and greater than zero, the N and Z bits of SR are cleared. Moreover, it always clears the V and C bits.

The third instruction compares the contents of D_0 with itself. Thus the Z bit is set and N, V, and C are cleared.

The last instruction compares 60_{16} with the contents of D_0. Therefore, it subtracts 60_{16} from $5A_{16}$. This subtraction yields a negative result; therefore, the N bit is set. Furthermore, to subtract a larger number from a smaller one, a borrow is required. Thus the C bit is also set. The result of subtracting the two numbers can be correctly represented as a byte. That is, no overflow has occurred. Therefore, V is reset. Moreover, the result is not zero; therefore, Z is also reset.

Test Instruction—TST

The last instruction in Fig. 4.1 is the test (TST) instruction. This instruction performs an operation that is similar to the compare instruction except that its destination operand is always assumed to be zero. The specified source operand is subtracted from zero and based on the result, the condition code bits in SR are set or reset. Any of the data-alterable addressing modes can be used to specify the source operand and it can be a byte, word, or long word.

The same four condition code bits are affected by the TST instruction. But in this case only N and Z are set or reset based on the result of the comparison. The other two bits, V and C, are always cleared.

An example is the instruction

$$\text{TST.B} \quad \text{D0}$$

Let us assume that D_0 contains 10_{16}. Executing the instruction causes 10_{16} to be subtracted from 0 and then the flags are set or reset based on the difference that results. For this value of data, the difference that is produced is negative and nonzero; therefore, N is set to 1 and Z is cleared to 0.

Set According to Condition Instruction—Scc

Earlier we pointed out that the condition code bits set or reset by the compare and test instructions are examined through software to decide whether or not branching should take place in the program. One way of using these bits is to test them directly with the branch instructions. Another approach is to test them for a specific condition and then save a flag value representing whether the tested condition is true or false. This flag value can then be used for program branching decisions. An instruction that performs this operation is *set according to condition* (Scc).

The form of the Scc instruction is shown in Fig. 4.3(a). The "cc" part of the mnemonic stands for a general condition code relationship and must be replaced with a specific relationship when writing the instruction. Figure 4.3(b) is a list of the mnemonics and condition code relationships that can be used to replace cc. For instance, replacing cc by LE gives the instruction mnemonic SLE. This stands for *set if less than or equal to* and tests status to determine if the logical value of

$$Z + N \cdot \overline{V} + \overline{N} \cdot V$$

is equal to 0 or 1.

Looking at Fig. 4.3(a), we see that a byte-wide destination operand is also specified in the instruction. Its location can be identified using any of the data-alterable addressing modes. For example, an instruction could be written as

$$\text{SGT} \quad \text{D0}$$

When this instruction is executed, it causes the condition code bits to be checked to determine if the relationship

$$N \cdot V \cdot \overline{Z} + \overline{N} \cdot \overline{V} \cdot \overline{Z} = 1$$

Mnemonic	Meaning	Format	Operand Size	Operation
Scc	Set according to condition code	Scc EA	8	11111111 → EA if cc is true 00000000 → EA if cc is false

(a)

Mnemonic	Meaning	Condition Code Relationship
SCC	Set if carry clear	$C = 0$
SCS	Set if carry set	$C = 1$
SEQ	Set if equal	$Z = 1$
SNE	Set if not equal	$Z = 0$
SMI	Set if minus	$N = 1$
SPL	Set if plus	$N = 0$
SVC	Set if overflow clear (signed)	$V = 0$
SVS	Set if overflow set (signed)	$V = 1$
SHI	Set if higher (unsigned)	$\overline{C} \cdot \overline{Z} = 1$
SLS	Set if lower or same (unsigned)	$C + Z = 1$
SGT	Set if greater than (signed)	$NV\overline{Z} + \overline{N}\,\overline{V}\overline{Z} = 1$
SGE	Set if greater or equal (signed)	$NV + \overline{N}\,\overline{V} = 1$
SLT	Set if less than	$N\overline{V} + \overline{N}V = 1$
SLE	Set if less or equal (signed)	$Z + N\overline{V} + \overline{N}V = 1$

(b)

Figure 4-3 (a) Set according to condition code instruction; (b) conditional tests of the Scc instruction.

is satisfied. If this relationship is true, the bits of the byte part of destination register D_0 are all set. On the other hand, if the relationship is false, they are all reset. For example, if $N = V = 0$, and $Z = 1$, the condition code relationship evaluates as

$$N \cdot V \cdot \overline{Z} + \overline{N} \cdot \overline{V} \cdot \overline{Z} = 0 \cdot 0 \cdot 0 + 1 \cdot 1 \cdot 0 = 0$$

Therefore, the relationship is false and the byte part of D_0 becomes 00_{16}.

4.3 JUMP AND BRANCH INSTRUCTIONS

For all the programs we have studied up to this point, the sequence in which the instructions were written was also the sequence in which they were executed. In other words, after execution of an instruction the program counter always points to the next sequential instruction.

For most applications, one must be able to alter the sequence in which instructions of the program execute. The changes in sequence may have to be unconditionally done or may be subject to satisfying a conditional relationship. To support these types of operations, the 68000 is equipped with jump and branch instructions.

The Unconditional and Conditional Branch

The 68000 microprocessor allows two different types of branch operations. They are the *unconditional branch,* and the *conditional branch.* In an unconditional branch, no status requirements are imposed for the branch to occur. That is, as the instruction is executed, the branch always takes place to change the execution sequence.

This concept is illustrated in Fig. 4.4(a). Notice that when the instruction BRA AA in part I is executed, program control is passed to a point in part III identified by the label AA. Execution resumes with the instruction corresponding to AA. In this way, the instructions in part II of the program have been bypassed. That is, they have been jumped over.

On the other hand, for a conditional branch instruction, status conditions that exist at the moment the branch instruction is executed decide whether or not the branch will occur. If this condition or conditions are met, the branch takes place; otherwise,

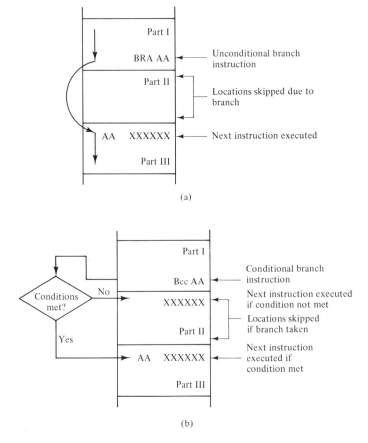

(a)

(b)

Figure 4-4 (a) Unconditional branch program sequence; (b) conditional branch program sequence.

execution continues with the next sequential instruction of the program. The conditions that can be referenced by a conditional branch instruction are status flags such as carry (C), zero (Z), negative (N), and overflow (V).

Looking at Fig. 4.4(b), we see that execution of the conditional branch instruction in part I causes a test to be initiated. If the conditions of the test are not met, the NO path is taken and execution continues with the next sequential instruction. This corresponds to the first instruction in part II. However, if the result of the conditional test is YES, a branch is initiated to the segment of the program identified as part III and the instructions in part II are bypassed.

Unconditional Jump and Branch Instructions—JMP and BRA

Unconditional changes in the execution sequence of a program are supported by both the jump and branch instructions. The first instruction in Fig. 4.5 is the *jump* (JMP) instruction. The effect of executing this instruction is to load the program counter with the contents of the effective address specified by the operand in the instruction. Therefore, program execution resumes at the location specified by the effective address.

An example of the instruction is

$$\text{JMP} \quad (\text{A0})$$

In this case, program execution is directed to the instruction at the address specified by the contents of address register A_0. Only the control addressing modes can be used to specify the operand.

A second way of initiating unconditional changes in the program execution sequence is by means of the *branch always* (BRA) instruction. The format of this instruction is also shown in Fig. 4.5. Notice that BRA differs from JMP in the manner by which the address of the next instruction to be executed is encoded. In JMP, this address is specified directly by an EA operand. This permits it to reside in a data register or a storage location in memory. On the other hand, in BRA the difference between the address of the new instruction and that of the BRA instruction (displacement) is encoded following the opcode. Thus, for the BRA instruction the microprocessor computes the next address by adding the displacement to the current value in PC.

The branch instruction allows the displacement d to be encoded either as an 8-bit (*short-form*) integer or 16-bit (*long-form*) integer. With an 8-bit displacement, the instruction is encoded as one word, but the branch to location must reside within

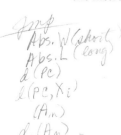

Mnemonic	Meaning	Format	Operand Size	Operation
JMP	Jump	JMP EA	— —	EA → PC
BRA	Branch always	BRA Label	8, 16	PC + d → PC

Figure 4-5 Jump and branch always instructions.

byte

+ 129 or − 126 bytes of the current value in PC. On the other hand, the 16-bit displacement is encoded as a second instruction word, thereby making it a two-word instruction. This long displacement extends the range of the branch operation to + 32769 to − 32766 bytes relative to the current PC.

The programmer does not normally specify the displacement in the branch instruction. Instead, a label is written in the program to identify the branch to location. For example, the instruction

BRA   START

causes a transfer of program control to the instruction in the program with the label START. It is the duty of the assembler program to compute the actual displacement and encode it into the instruction. In this example, the displacement will be encoded as a 16-bit word. If displacement must be encoded as a byte, the instruction should be written as

BRA.S   START

JMP and BRA are called *unconditional branch* instructions. This is because the change in instruction sequence that they initiate takes place independent of any conditions in the processor status.

Conditional Branch Instruction—Bcc

The 68000 provides a *conditional branch* instruction called *branch conditionally* (Bcc). As shown in Fig. 4.6(a), its general form is

Bcc   LABEL

Here "cc" is used to specify one of many conditional relationships. Figure 4.6(b) is a list of all the valid relationships and their mnemonics. For instance, selecting EQ we get the *branch on equal* (BEQ) instruction.

The conditional branch instruction passes control to the specified label only if the conditional relationship is true. In the example BEQ, the Z bit of SR is tested. If it is set, the branch takes place to the location specified by LABEL. If it is not set, the next sequential instruction is executed. The amount of displacement allowed with the conditional branch instruction is the same as for the branch always instruction.

Let us now consider an example. The instruction

BVS   START

means branch to the instruction identified by START if the overflow (V) bit is set. If V is not set, the instruction that follows the BVS instruction is executed. The displacement between the address of BVS plus two and the instruction with label START is computed by the assembler and encoded into the instruction as a 16-bit integer. For encoding the displacement as a byte, the instruction should be written as

BVS.S   START

Mnemonic	Meaning	Format	Operand Size	Operation
Bcc	Branch conditionally	Bcc Label	8, 16	$(PC) + d \rightarrow PC$ if cc is true; otherwise, next sequential instruction executes

(a)

Mnemonic	Meaning	Conditional Code Relationship
BCC	Branch if carry clear	$C = 0$
BCS	Branch if carry set	$C = 1$
BEQ	Branch if equal	$Z = 1$
BNE	Branch if not equal	$Z = 0$
BMI	Branch if minus	$N = 1$
BPL	Branch if plus	$N = 0$
BVC	Branch if overflow clear (signed)	$V = 0$
BVS	Branch if overflow set (signed)	$V = 1$
BHI	Branch if high (unsigned)	$\overline{C} \cdot \overline{Z} = 1$
BLS	Branch if less or same (unsigned)	$C + Z = 1$
BGT	Branch if greater than (signed)	$NV\overline{Z} + \overline{N}\,\overline{V}\overline{Z} = 1$
BGE	Branch if greater or equal (signed)	$NV + \overline{N}\,\overline{V} = 1$
BLT	Branch if less than	$N\overline{V} + \overline{N}V = 1$
BLE	Branch if less or equal (signed)	$Z + N\overline{V} + \overline{N}V = 1$

(b)

Figure 4-6 (a) Branch conditionally instruction; (b) conditional tests of the Bcc instruction.

Example 4.2

It is required to move a set of N, 16-bit data points that are stored in a block of memory that starts at location BLK1 to a new block that starts at location BLK2. Write a program to implement this operation.

Solution.   The flowchart in Fig. 4.7(a) shows a plan for implementing the block move function. Initially, we set up two pointers, one for the beginning of BLK1 and the other for the beginning of BLK2. Address registers A_1 and A_2, respectively, can be used as these pointers. The count for the number of points to be moved is placed in D_0. This can be accomplished by the instruction sequence

```
LEA        BLK1,A1

LEA        BLK2,A2

MOVE.L     N,D0
```

To move a word from BLK1 to BLK2, we can use a move word instruction with address register indirect addressing with postincrement mode for both its source and destination operands. Moreover, each time a data point is moved, the count in D_0 must be decreased by 1. The move instruction must be repeated if the count has not reached zero. The instructions that follow will perform these operations.

NXTPT	MOVE.W	(A1) + ,(A2) +
	SUBQ.L	#1,D0
	BNZ	NXTPT

The entire program is shown in Fig. 4.7(b).

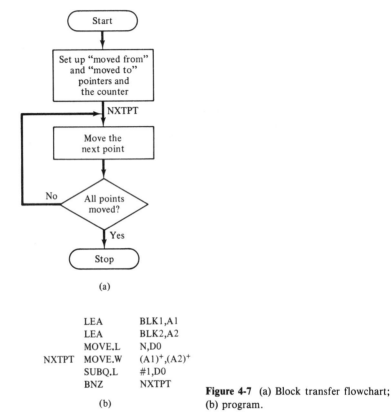

(a)

	LEA	BLK1,A1
	LEA	BLK2,A2
	MOVE.L	N,D0
NXTPT	MOVE.W	$(A1)^+,(A2)^+$
	SUBQ.L	#1,D0
	BNZ	NXTPT

(b)

Figure 4-7 (a) Block transfer flowchart; (b) program.

4.4 THE TEST CONDITION, DECREMENT, AND BRANCH INSTRUCTION AND PROGRAMS INVOLVING LOOPS

The program we considered in the preceding section was an example of a *software loop*. In the earlier example we found that when a software loop is executed, a group of instructions are executed repeatedly. The repetition may be unconditional or conditional. To design a loop, one can use the previously introduced compare, jump, and branch instructions. This was the approach employed in Example 4.2. However, the 68000 provides another instruction that is especially useful for handling loops. This instruction is called *test condition, decrement, and branch* (DBcc) and has the general form

DBcc   Dn,Label

Here "cc" represents the same conditions that were available for the Bcc instruction. They are listed in the table of Fig. 4.6(b). In fact, two more conditions, always true (T) and always false (F), are also available for the DBcc instruction. Dn is the data register that contains the count of how many times the loop is to be repeated, and Label identifies the location to which control is to be returned by the branch operation.

When the DBcc instruction is executed, first the condition identified by cc is tested. If it is true, no branch takes place; instead, the loop is terminated and the next sequential instruction is executed. On the other hand, if the condition is not true, the contents of the specified data register are decremented by 1. Then another test is performed. This one is on the count in Dn. If it is equal to -1, the branch does not take place because the loop operation has run to completion. In this case, execution continues with the next sequential instruction. However, if the count is not -1, program control branches to the location corresponding to Label.

An example of the instruction is as follows:

DBLE   D0,NXTPT

During the execution of this instruction, first the condition code bits of SR are tested to determine if the relationship

$$Z + N \cdot \overline{V} + \overline{N} \cdot V = 1$$

is satisfied. If true, the instruction following the DBLE instruction is executed. If false, D_0 is decremented. Next, D_0 is tested to determine if it has become -1. If it has, the next sequential instruction is executed. But if D_0 is any number other than -1, execution continues at the label NXTPT.

For example, if $Z = 0$, $N = 1$, $V = 1$, and the contents of D_0 are 03_{16}, the condition code relationship evaluates as

$$Z + N \cdot \overline{V} + \overline{N} \cdot V = 0 + 1 \cdot 0 + 0 \cdot 1$$
$$= 0$$

Since the result is 0, the relationship is false. Thus, the value in D_0 is decremented by 1, which gives 02_{16}, and tested for -1. Since D_0 does not contain -1, control is passed to the instruction corresponding to label NXTPT.

Example 4.3

Given N data points that are signed 16-bit numbers stored in consecutive memory locations starting at address DATA, write a program that finds their average value. The average value that results is to be stored at location AVERAGE in memory. Assume that N is in the range $0 < N < 32K$.

Solution.   A flowchart that solves this problem is shown in Fig. 4.8(a). It implements an algorithm that finds the average of N data points by adding their values and then dividing the sum by N.

Initially we set the sum, which will reside in D_7, to 0, the address pointer in A_1 to DATA so that it points to the first data point, and the counter in D_0 equal to $N - 1$. Notice that the value of the count is 1 less than the number of data points to be processed.

The reason for this is that we intend to use the DBcc instruction which branches out of the loop when the count in a data register becomes equal to -1 and not 0. This initialization is performed by executing the following instructions

CLR.L	D7
LEA	DATA,A1
MOVE.L	#(N – 1),D0

To add a new data point to sum, we first move it into D_1. Since the data point is of word length, it must be sign extended to a long word before it can be added to the previous sum. Then the sign-extended data point in D_1 is added to the sum in D_7. Next the count in D_0 is decremented by 1 and checked to determine if it has become equal to -1. A value of -1 means that all points have been added. If it is not -1, there are still data points to be added and we must repeat the set of instructions that add a new data point. On the other hand, if the count shows that all points have been added, we are ready to divide the sum in D_7 by N to obtain the average. This value can then be moved from D_7 to the storage location AVERAGE in memory. All this can be done by the following sequence of instructions.

NXTPT	MOVE.W	(A1)+,D1
	EXT.L	D1
	ADD.L	D1,D7
	DBF	D0,NXTPT
	DIVS	#N,D7
	MOVE.W	D7,AVERAGE

The complete program is listed in Fig. 4.8(b).

Example 4.4

Given a four-digit BCD number located in memory location BCDNUM, write a program to convert it to its equivalent binary number and place the result in memory location BINNUM.

Solution. Let us begin by defining an algorithm that can be used to convert a BCD number to its equivalent binary number. For the general BCD number

$$N_{BCD} = D_3 D_2 D_1 D_0$$

its equivalent decimal number is given by the expression

$$N_{10} = 1000(D_3) + 100(D_2) + 10(D_1) + D_0$$

This expression can be reorganized to give

$$N_{10} = D_0 + 10(D_1 + 10(D_2 + 10(D_3)))$$

D_0, D_1, D_2, and D_3 in this expression stand for BCD digits and not for data registers within the 68000. This expression suggests an algorithm that can be implemented using a software loop. Notice that if we start with the MSD D_3, multiply it by 10, and then add the next MSD D_2, we will get our first temporary result. This same sequence can

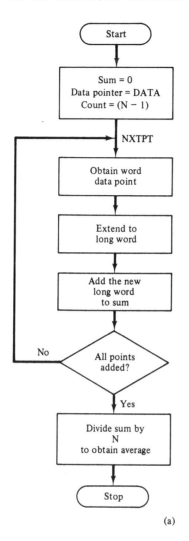

D_0 = counter
D_7 = sum
A_1 = pointer to data points
D_1 = temporary register for holding data point

(a)

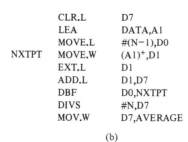

```
         CLR.L      D7
         LEA        DATA,A1
         MOVE.L     #(N−1),D0
NXTPT    MOVE.W     (A1)+,D1
         EXT.L      D1
         ADD.L      D1,D7
         DBF        D0,NXTPT
         DIVS       #N,D7
         MOV.W      D7,AVERAGE
```

(b)

Figure 4-8 (a) Flowchart of a program for finding the average of N signed numbers; (b) program.

be performed twice more on the temporary result, first adding D_1 to the product and then adding D_0 to the product, to produce the final result.

The flowchart in Fig. 4.9(a) shows how this algorithm can be implemented on the 68000. Initialization involves setting the result, which is in D_7, to zero, setting the digit counter in D_0 to 3, and the shift counter in D_1 to 12. The BCD number at memory location BCDNUM is copied into D_2. Notice that the value of the digit counter is actually one less than the number of digits to be processed. This is due to the fact that we intend to use the DBcc instruction, which branches on the contents of a data register being equal to -1. The shift counter will be used to extract the appropriate digit from the number. This initialization can be performed with the instruction sequence that follows.

```
CLR.L       D7

MOVE.L      #3,D0

MOVE.L      #12,D1

MOVE.W      BCDNUM,D2
```

To program the conversion equation, we begin with the most significant digit of BCDNUM. To extract the MSD, the BCD number in register D_2 is first copied into register D_3 and then the contents of D_3 are shifted right logically by 12 bit positions. This places the MSD in the 4 least significant bits of register D_3. Now this digit value is added to the result in D_7. To prepare for the extraction of the next MSD, we shift the contents of register D_2 left by four bit positions. This places the next MSD in the most significant digit position so that this digit can now be treated exactly like the preceding one. The counter in register D_0 is decremented and tested; if it is not equal to -1, we repeat the process with the next digit. If we repeat, we must multiply the result by 10 before adding the value of the next digit. All this can be done by the following sequence of instructions:

```
NXTDGT      MULU        #10,D7

            MOVE.W      D2,D3

            LSR.W       D1,D3

            ADD.W       D3,D7

            LSL.W       #4,D2

            DBF         D0,NXTDGT

            MOVE.W      D7,BINNUM
```

The entire program is shown in Fig. 4.9(b).

Example 4.5

It is required to sort an array of 16-bit signed binary numbers such that they are arranged in ascending order. For instance, if the original array is

$$5, 1, 29, 15, 38, 3, -8, -32$$

after sorting, the array that results would be

$$-32, -8, 1, 3, 5, 15, 29, 38$$

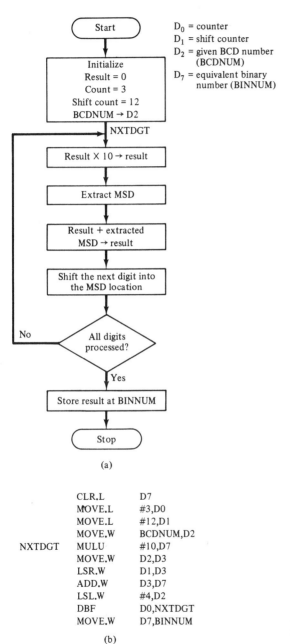

D_0 = counter
D_1 = shift counter
D_2 = given BCD number (BCDNUM)
D_7 = equivalent binary number (BINNUM)

(a)

```
          CLR.L      D7
          MOVE.L     #3,D0
          MOVE.L     #12,D1
          MOVE.W     BCDNUM,D2
NXTDGT    MULU       #10,D7
          MOVE.W     D2,D3
          LSR.W      D1,D3
          ADD.W      D3,D7
          LSL.W      #4,D2
          DBF        D0,NXTDGT
          MOVE.W     D7,BINNUM
```

(b)

Figure 4-9 (a) Flowchart for BCD-to-binary conversion routine; (b) program.

Assume that the array of numbers is stored at consecutive memory locations from addresses $F400_{16}$ through $F4FE_{16}$ in memory. Write a sort program.

Solution.   First we will develop an algorithm that can be used to sort an array of elements A(0), A(1), A(2), through A(N) into ascending order. One way of doing this is to take the first number in the array, which is A(0), and compare it to the second number A(1). If A(0) is greater than A(1), the two numbers are swapped; otherwise, they are left alone. Next A(0) is compared to A(2) and based on the result of this comparison they are either swapped or left alone. This sequence is repeated until A(0) has been compared with all numbers up through A(N). When this is complete, the smallest number will be in the A(0) position.

Now A(1) must be compared to A(2) through A(N) in the same way. After this is done, the second smallest number is in the A(1) position. Up to this point, just two of the N numbers have been put in ascending order. Therefore, the procedure must be continued for A(2) through A(N − 1) to complete the sort.

Figure 4.10(a) illustrates the use of this algorithm for an array with just four numbers. The numbers are A(0) = 5, A(1) = 1, A(2) = 29, and A(3) = −8. During the sort sequence, A(0) = 5 is first compared to A(1) = 1. Since 5 is greater than 1, A(0) and A(1) are swapped. Now A(0) = 1 is compared to A(2) = 29. This time 1 is less than 29; therefore, the numbers are not swapped and A(0) remains equal to 1. Next, A(0) = 1 is compared with A(3) = −8. A(0) is greater than A(3). Thus A(0) and A(3) are swapped and A(0) becomes equal to −8. Notice in Fig. 4.10(a) that the lowest of the four numbers now resides in A(0).

The sort sequence in Fig. 4.10(a) continues with A(1) = 5 being compared first to A(2) = 29 and then to A(3) = 1. In the first comparison, A(1) is less than A(2). For this reason, their values are not swapped. But in the second comparison, A(1) is greater than A(3); therefore, the two values are swapped. In this way, the second lowest number, which is 1, is sorted into A(1).

It just remains to sort A(2) and A(3). Comparing these two values, we see that 29 is greater than 5. This causes the two values to be swapped such that A(2) = 5 and A(3) = 29. As shown in Fig. 4.10(a), the sorting of the array is now complete.

I	0	1	2	3	Status
A(I)	5	1	29	−8	Original array
A(I)	1	5	29	−8	Array after comparing A(0) and A(1)
A(I)	1	5	29	−8	Array after comparing A(0) and A(2)
A(I)	−8	5	29	1	Array after comparing A(0) and A(3)
A(I)	−8	5	29	1	Array after comparing A(1) and A(2)
A(I)	−8	1	29	5	Array after comparing A(1) and A(3)
A(I)	−8	1	5	29	Array after comparing A(2) and A(3)

(a)

Figure 4-10   (a) Sort example.

A_1 = $PNTR_1$ = pointer to first element
A_2 = $PNTR_2$ = pointer to next element
A_3 = $PNTR_3$ = pointer to last element

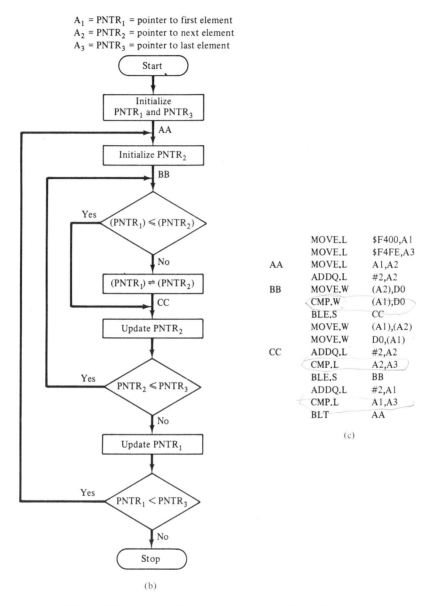

Figure 4-10 *(cont.)*   (b) Flowchart for sort algorithm; (c) program.

We will implement this algorithm for the 68000 microprocessor. The flowchart for the sort algorithm is shown in Fig. 4.10(b).

The first block represents initialization of pointers PNTR1 and PNTR3. They contain addresses that point to the storage locations of the first and last elements of the array, respectively. Since registers A_1 and A_3 are used as these pointers and the addresses of the first and last elements are $F400 and $F4FE, respectively, the instructions used to perform the initialization are

$$\text{MOVE.L} \qquad \text{\$F400,A1}$$

$$\text{MOVE.L} \qquad \text{\$F4FE,A3}$$

Address register A_2 contains another pointer. It is called PNTR2 and points to the next element to be processed in the array. To initialize PNTR2, we can load register A_2 with the contents of A_1, which is PNTR1, and then increment this value by 2. In this way, the next word address is established for PNTR2. This is done with the instructions

$$\text{AA} \qquad \text{MOVE.L} \qquad \text{A1,A2}$$

$$\text{ADDQ.L} \qquad \text{\#2,A2}$$

As shown in the flowchart, the label AA is used to implement a branch point.

Next, starting with label BB, we first compare the two numbers. To implement the comparison, the number pointed to by PNTR2 can be copied into register D_0; next, the value pointed to by PNTR1 can be compared to it; and then a conditional branch can be made if status shows that

$$\text{PNTR1} \leq \text{PNTR2}$$

The branch passes control to the point in the program identified by label CC. If the value pointed to by PNTR1 is greater than the value pointed to by PNTR2, the two values must be swapped. These operations are performed with the instructions

$$\text{BB} \qquad \text{MOVE.W} \qquad \text{(A2),D0}$$

$$\text{CMP.W} \qquad \text{(A1),D0}$$

$$\text{BLE.S} \qquad \text{CC}$$

To implement swapping of the two numbers, the number pointed to by PNTR1 is copied into the memory location pointed to by PNTR2. Next, the contents of D_0 are copied to the storage location pointed to by PNTR1. This completes the swap. The corresponding instructions are

$$\text{MOVE.W} \qquad \text{(A1),(A2)}$$

$$\text{MOVE.W} \qquad \text{D0,(A1)}$$

Now pointer PNTR2 is updated by incrementing it by 2 and then it is compared to PNTR3 to find out if the last element has been compared. If the result of this comparision shows that

$$\text{PNTR2} \leq \text{PNTR3}$$

control is returned to the point in the program identified by BB. Otherwise, program execution continues on to the next block in the flowchart. These operations are done with the instructions

$$\text{CC} \qquad \text{ADDQ.L} \qquad \text{\#2,A2}$$

$$\text{CMP.L} \qquad \text{A2,A3}$$

$$\text{BLE.S} \qquad \text{BB}$$

When the answer to the comparison is that

$$PNTR2 > PNTR3$$

we must update PNTR1 by adding 2 and then compare it to PNTR3. If it turns out that

$$PNTR1 < PNTR3$$

we must start all over again from AA. Otherwise, the program is complete. The instructions for this part of the program are

ADDQ.L	#2,A1
CMP.L	A1,A3
BLT	AA

The entire program is shown in Fig. 4.10(c).

4.5 SUBROUTINES AND SUBROUTINE-HANDLING INSTRUCTIONS

A *subroutine* is a special segment of program that can be called for execution from any point in a program. Figure 4.11 illustrates the concept of a subroutine. Here we see a program structure where one part of the program is called the *main program*. In addition to this, we find a smaller segment attached to the main program, known as a subroutine. The subroutine is written to provide a function that must be performed at various points in the main program. Instead of including this piece of code in the main program each time the function is needed, it is put into the program just once as a subroutine.

Wherever the function must be performed, a single instruction is inserted into the main body of the program to "call" the subroutine. Remember that the contents of PC always identifies the next instruction to be executed. Thus, to branch to a subroutine that starts elsewhere in memory, the value in PC must be modified. After executing the subroutine, we want to return control to the instruction that follows

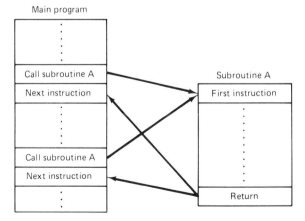

Figure 4-11 Subroutine concept.

the one that called the subroutine. In this way, program execution resumes in the main program at the point where it left off due to the subroutine call. A return instruction must be included at the end of the subroutine to initiate the *return sequence* to the main program environment.

The instructions provided to transfer control from the main program to a subroutine and return control back to the main program are called *subroutine handling instructions*. Let us now examine the instructions provided for this purpose.

Subroutine Control Instructions—JSR, BSR, RTS, and RTR

The four subroutine handling instructions of the 68000 microprocessor are shown in Fig. 4.12. These instructions include *jump to subroutine* (JSR), *branch to subroutine* (BSR), *return from subroutine* (RTS), and *return and restore condition codes* (RTR). These instructions provide for efficient subroutine handling and nesting.

The instructions jump to subroutine (JSR) and branch to subroutine (BSR) serve essentially the same purpose. This is to pass control to the starting point of a subroutine. As shown in Fig. 4.12, they both save the current contents of PC by pushing it to the active stack. This preserves a return address for use at completion of the subroutine. Then they pass control to the starting point of the subroutine.

These two instructions differ in how they specify the starting address of the subroutine. For the JSR instruction this address is specified as an effective address and only the control addressing modes are allowed. Therefore, the starting address can reside in a data register, address register, or in either program or data storage memory. For instance, using address register indirect addressing through register A_1, we get

JSR   (A1)

On the other hand, in the BSR instruction, the *displacement* between the current instruction and the first instruction of the subroutine is determined and encoded into the instruction. That is, it is stored in program storage memory. An example is

BSR   STARTSUB

Mnemonic	Meaning	Format	Operand Size	Operation
JSR	Jump to subroutine	JSR EA	32	$PC \rightarrow {}^- (SP)$ $EA \rightarrow PC$
BSR	Branch to subroutine	BSR Label	8, 16	$PC \rightarrow {}^- (SP)$ $PC + d \rightarrow PC$
RTS	Return from subroutine	RTS	—	$(SP)^+ \rightarrow PC$
RTR	Return and restore	RTR	—	$(SP)^+ \rightarrow CCR$ $(SP)^+ \rightarrow PC$

Figure 4-12 Subroutine control instructions.

Thus JSR provides the ability to jump to a subroutine that resides anywhere in the 16M-byte address space of the 68000. But BSR only permits branching to a subroutine that is located within the maximum allowable displacement value. The displacement can be either 8 bits for the short form of the BSR instruction or 16 bits for the long form.

The other two instructions return from subroutine (RTS) and return and restore (RTR) provide the means for returning from a subroutine back to the calling program. In Fig. 4.12, we see that executing RTS simply restores the program counter by popping the value that was saved on the active stack when the subroutine was called. The second instruction RTR restores both the condition code part of SR and PC from the stack. One of these instructions is always the last instruction of a subroutine.

Example 4.6

In a Fibonacci series, the first number is 0, the second is 1, and each subsequent number is obtained by adding the previous two numbers. For example, the first 10 numbers of the series are

$$0, 1, 1, 2, 3, 5, 8, 13, 21, 34$$

Write a program to generate the first 20 elements of a Fibonacci series. The numbers of the series are to be stored at consecutive locations in memory starting at address FIBSER. Use a subroutine to implement the part of the procedure by which the next number of the series is obtained from the previous two numbers.

Solution. A flowchart for this program together with the assignments of various registers is shown in Fig. 4.13(a). The first part of the program initializes the registers and stores the first two numbers. The instructions used for this purpose are

MOVE.L	#$11,D0	SET THE COUNTER TO 17
LEA	FIBSER,A1	SET THE POINTER TO FIBSER
CLR.W	D1	D1 = 0
MOVEQ.W	#1,D2	D2 = 1
MOVE.W	D1,(A1)+	STORE THE FIRST NUMBER
MOVE.W	D2,(A1)+	STORE THE SECOND NUMBER

The next-to-last instruction causes 0 to be loaded into address FIBSER and increments the pointer in A_1 by 2 such that it points to the storage location of the next number in the series. Then a similar instruction is executed to load FIBSER + 2 with 1 and A_1 is again incremented.

We are now ready to call the subroutine that does the addition to form the next number in the series. Since the subroutine will be called repeatedly, the BRS instruction is identified by a label to which the program can loop back. This instruction is

$$\text{NXTNM} \quad \text{BRS.S} \quad \text{SBRTF}$$

The subroutine starts at the instruction with label SBRTF. The purpose of the subroutine is to add the contents of D_1 and D_2 so that the next number in the series is generated,

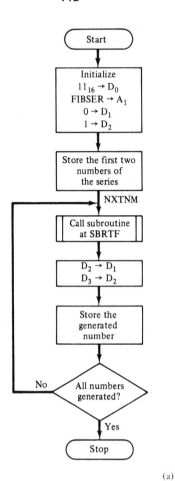

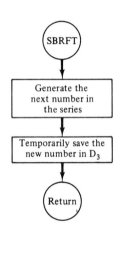

D_0 = counter for the numbers to be generated

A_1 = pointer to the address at which the number is to be stored

D_1 = first number used in the generation

D_2 = second number used in the generation

D_3 = generated number

(a)

```
                MOVE.L      #$11,D0
                LEA         FIBSER,A1
                CLR.W       D1
                MOVEQ.W     #1,D2
                MOVE.W      D1,(A1)+
                MOVE.W      D2,(A1)+
NXTNM           BSR.S       SBRTF
                MOVE.W      D2,D1
                MOVE.W      D3,D2
                MOVE.W      D3,(A1)+
                DBF         D0,NXTNM
DONE            BRA         DONE
SBRTF           ADD.W       D2,D1
                MOVE.W      D1,D3
                RTS
```

(b)

Figure 4-13 (a) Flowchart for the Fibonacci series program; (b) program.

temporarily save this number in D_3, and then return back to the main program. This can be done by the instruction sequence

SBRTF	ADD.W	D2,D1
	MOVE.W	D1,D3
	RTS	

At this point in the main program, we get ready for generating the next number. This is done by saving the contents of D_2 in D_1 and that of D_3 in D_2. Next we save the new number that was generated in D_3 by moving it to memory. To do this, the instructions are

	MOVE.W	D2,D1
	MOVE.W	D3,D2
	MOVE.W	D3,(A1)+

Now the count in D_0 is decremented and tested for -1. If it is not equal to -1, we loop back to the label NXTNM. However, if it is -1, we are done. The instruction for this is

	DBF	D0,NXTNM
DONE	BRA	DONE

The entire program is repeated in Fig. 4.13(b).

Link and Unlink Instructions—LINK and UNLK

Before the main program calls a subroutine, quite often it is necessary for the calling program to pass the values of some *variables* (*parameters*) to the subroutine. It is a common practice to push these variables onto the stack before calling the routine. Then during the execution of the subroutine, they are accessed by reading them from the stack and used in computations. Two instructions are provided to allocate and deallocate a data area called a *frame* in the stack part of memory. This data area is used for local storage of parameters or other data. The two instructions, as shown in Fig. 4.14, are *link and allocate* (LINK) and *unlink* (UNLK). They make the process of passing and retrieving parameters much easier.

The LINK instruction is used at the beginning of a subroutine to create a data frame. Looking at the format of the instruction in Fig. 4.14, we see that it has two

Mnemonic	Meaning	Format	Operation
LINK	Link and allocate	LINK An, d	$An \rightarrow {}^-(SP)$ $SP \rightarrow An$ $SP - d \rightarrow SP$
UNLK	Unlink	UNLK An	$An \rightarrow SP$ $(SP)^+ \rightarrow An$

Figure 4-14 Link and unlink instructions.

operands. The one denoted A_n is always an address register. The address held in A_n is known as the *frame pointer* and it points to the lowest storage location in the data frame. The other operand is an immediate operand that specifies the value of a displacement. This displacement specifies the size of the data space. Since it can be as long as 16 bits, a *frame data space* can be as large as 32K words.

An example of this instruction is

LINK   A1, – #$A

Execution of this instruction causes the current contents of A_1 to be pushed onto the active stack; then the updated contents of the active SP register are loaded into A_1; finally, A_{16} is subtracted from the new value in SP.

Figure 4.15 shows what happens by executing this instruction. First we see that pushing the contents of A_1 to the stack saves the frame pointer for the prior data frame. This is identified as "Prior frame pointer" and is stored at A_{1new}. Loading A_1 with the contents of SP establishes a frame pointer to the new data frame. Subtracting the displacement from (SP) modifies the stack pointer so that the active stack is located in memory just below the data frame. Since the displacement is A_{16}, the data frame is 10 bytes in length.

The frame pointer A_1 provides a fixed reference into the data frame and old stack. Parameters that were loaded into the stack prior to calling the subroutine can be accessed using address register indirect with displacement addressing for the operand. For example, the instruction

MOVE.W   4(A1),D0

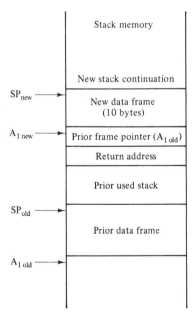

Figure 4-15 Creation of a data frame with the link instruction.

causes the word parameter stored four bytes from frame pointer A_1 to be copied into D_0. This parameter is in the old stack.

After performing the operation defined by the subroutine and just before returning to the calling program, the prior data frame must be restored. The UNLK instruction is used for this purpose. Notice in Fig. 4.14 that it causes address register A_n, which is used for the frame pointer, to be loaded into the active stack pointer register. Then the address held at the top of the stack is popped into A_n.

For our example, the unlink instruction would be

$$\text{UNLK} \quad \text{A1}$$

Earlier we pointed out that execution of the LINK instruction saved the old frame pointer on the stack and then created a new data frame. Executing UNLK A1 causes SP to be loaded from A_1. Looking at Fig. 4.15, we find that the stack pointer now points to the location of the prior frame pointer. Then A_1 is loaded from the stack. Therefore, the prior frame pointer is put back in A_1 and the prior stack and data frame environment is restored.

To understand this concept better, let us consider the example illustrated in Fig. 4.16. As we begin to execute the first instruction of the program segment shown in Fig. 4.16(a), we will assume that the active SP points to the top of the data frame identified in Fig. 4.16(b) as local storage area for the calling routine. Execution of the first two instructions

$$\text{MOVE.W} \quad \text{D0}, -(\text{SP})$$

$$\text{MOVE.W} \quad \text{D1}, -(\text{SP})$$

passes the contents of D_0 and D_1 as parameters onto the stack. Looking at Fig. 4.16(b), we see that at the completion of these two instructions SP points to the location where parameter 2 is stored.

```
          MOVE.W    D0, ¯ (SP)      ; parameter 1 passed to stack
          MOVE.W    D1, ¯ (SP)      ; parameter 2 passed to stack
   AA     JSR       SBRT            ; call subroutine SBRT
          .          .
          .          .
          .          .
          .          .
          .          .
          .          .

  SBRT    LINK      A0, −#$8        ; FP and local storage established for called routine
          .          .
          .          .
          MOVE.W    10(A0), D5      ; parameter 1 accessed
          .          .
          .          .
          UNLK      A0              ; FP for the calling routine established
          RTS                       ; return to main program
```

(a)

Figure 4-16   (a) Program example with LINK and UNLK instructions.

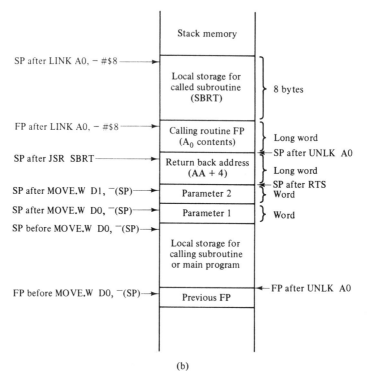

Figure 4-16 *(cont.)*   (b) Stack for the example program.

The next instruction,

$$\text{JSR} \quad \text{SBRT}$$

which has the label AA, calls the subroutine starting at label SBRT. It causes the address of the instruction that follows it to be pushed onto the stack. This return address is AA + 4 since the JSR instruction takes up four bytes of program memory. Secondly PC is loaded with the address of SBRT such that program control picks up execution from the first instruction of the subroutine.

The subroutine starts with the instruction

$$\text{LINK} \quad \text{A0}, - \#\$8$$

It causes the contents of A_0 to be saved on the stack and then loads A_0 from the active stack pointer register. This sets up a new frame pointer FP (A_0 register). Then 8 is subtracted from the value in SP. Therefore, it points to the top of the data area identified in Fig. 4.16(b) as *local storage* for the called subroutine.

As subroutine SBRT is being executed, we may need to access parameter 1. The frame pointer serves as a reference into the called routines data frame. Parameter 1 is at a displacement of 10 bytes from the frame pointer; therefore, the instruction

$$\text{MOVE.W} \quad 10(\text{A0}),\text{D5}$$

can be used to access it. Execution of this instruction copies parameter 1 into D_5.
    The next instruction we see is

UNLK   A0

It loads SP with the contents of A_0 and then pops the contents at the top of the stack into A_0. Now A_0 once again contains the frame pointer for the calling routine and SP points to the location where the return address $AA + 4$ is stored.
    The last instruction

RTS

loads the return address into the program counter so that execution resumes in the calling routine.

4.6 BIT-MANIPULATION INSTRUCTIONS

The bit manipulation instructions of the 68000 enable a programmer to test the logic level of a bit in either a data register or storage location in memory. The tested bit can also be set, reset, or changed during the execution of the instruction. The four bit manipulation instructions in the 68000's instruction set are shown in Fig. 4.17. They are: *test a bit* (BTST), *test a bit and set* (BSET), *test a bit and clear* (BCLR), and *test a bit and change* (BCHG).

Test a Bit Instruction—BTST

The test a bit (BTST) instruction has the ability to test any one bit in a 32-bit data register or any one bit of a byte storage location in memory. The logic state of the tested bit is inverted and copied into the Z bit of SR. That is, when the bit is tested as 1, Z is set to 0 or when the bit is tested as 0, Z is set to 1. The two valid forms of the BTST instruction are shown in Fig. 4.17. In both forms, the destination operand, which contains the bit to be tested, is specified by an effective address.
    These two forms differ in the way the number of the bit to be tested is specified. In the first form, the number of the bit is supplied as an immediate source operand

Mnemonic	Meaning	Format	Operand Size	Operation
BTST	Test a bit	BTST #XXX,EA BTST Dn,EA	8, 32 8, 32	$\overline{\text{EA bit}} \rightarrow Z$
BSET	Test a bit and set	BSET #XXX,EA BSET Dn,EA	8, 32 8, 32	$\overline{\text{EA bit}} \rightarrow Z$ $1 \rightarrow \text{EA bit}$
BCLR	Test a bit and clear	BCLR #XXX,EA BCLR Dn,EA	8, 32 8, 32	$\overline{\text{EA bit}} \rightarrow Z$ $0 \rightarrow \text{EA bit}$
BCHG	Test a bit and change	BCHG #XXX,EA BCHG Dn,EA	8, 32 8, 32	$\overline{\text{EA bit}} \rightarrow Z$ $\overline{\text{EA bit}} \rightarrow \text{EA bit}$

Figure 4-17 Bit-manipulation instructions.

that gets coded as part of the instruction in program memory. An example is the instruction

$$\text{BTST} \quad \#5,\text{D7}$$

Execution of this instruction tests bit 5 in data register D_7. The complement of the value found in this bit position is copied into Z. For example, if D_7 contains 25_{16}, that is

$$D_7 = 00000000000000000000000001001101_2$$

bit 5 is logic 1. Thus, the complement of 1, which is 0, is copied into the Z flag.

The second form uses the contents of one of the data registers to specify the bit position. For instance, if D_0 contains number 5, then executing the instruction

$$\text{BTST} \quad \text{D0,D7}$$

produces the same result as the instruction that employed an immediate operand.

Other Test Bit Instructions—BSET, BCLR, and BCHG

The other instructions in Fig. 4.17, BSET, BCLR, and BCHG, operate similarly to BTST. However, they not only copy the complement of the tested bit into Z, but also set, clear, or invert the bit in the destination operand, respectively.

An example is the instruction

$$\text{BSET} \quad \#7,(\text{A1})$$

When this instruction is executed, bit 7 of the memory location pointed to by (A1) is tested. The complement of its logic level is copied into Z and then bit 7 is set to 1. For instance, if the byte memory location pointed to by the address in A_1 contains $7F_{16}$, which is 01111111_2 in binary form, bit 7 is logic 0. Therefore, execution of the instruction causes Z to be set to 1 and the contents of the memory location to be changed to FF_{16}.

When a memory bit is addressed, BTST allows use of the data addressing modes to specify the effective address of the destination operand. The instructions BSET, BCLR, and BCHG allow the use of data-alterable addressing modes for EA.

Test and Set Operand Instruction—TAS

Another instruction that is similar to the test bit instruction is *test and set operand* (TAS). As shown in Fig. 4.18, TAS differs from BTST in that it tests a byte operand in a data register or storage location in memory. The test is performed by comparing the operand with zero and setting or resetting condition code bits N and Z based on the result. N is set to the logic level of the most significant bit of the operand and Z is set if the operand is zero. Second, independent of the result of the test, the most significant bit of the accessed byte is set to 1. An example is the instruction

$$\text{TAS} \quad \text{D0}$$

Mnemonic	Meaning	Format	Operand Size	Operation
TAS	Test and set an operand	TAS EA	8	If destination is zero, $1 \rightarrow Z$; otherwise, $0 \rightarrow Z$ If destination is negative, $1 \rightarrow N$; otherwise, $0 \rightarrow N$ $0 \rightarrow V$ $0 \rightarrow C$ $1 \rightarrow$ most significant bit of byte addressed by EA

Figure 4-18 TAS instruction.

The TAS instruction is specifically designed to support *multiprocessing* and *multitasking system environments*. For instance, in a multiprocessing system, a bit called a semaphore in a byte in memory is set for resolving which processor can access a memory section reserved for a specific resource. If a processor needs to access this resource, it will first test and set the memory byte. If the resource is already in use, the test will indicate that condition and the processor can wait until it is available. Once it is done using the resource, it resets the *semaphore* bit, thus allowing access by other processors. This is illustrated in Fig. 4.19.

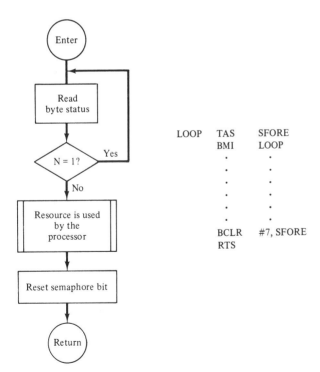

LOOP	TAS	SFORE
	BMI	LOOP
	.	.
	.	.
	.	.
	.	.
	.	.
	.	.
	BCLR	#7, SFORE
	RTS	

Figure 4-19 Use of TAS for multiprocessing.

ASSIGNMENT

Section 4.2

1. Assuming that condition codes N, Z, V, and C are initially zero, specify their status as each of the instructions that follow is executed.

SUB.L	A0,A0
CMPI.W	#$A000,A0
TST	A0

2. Use move, shift, and logic instructions to compute the results of the logic equation

$$F = Z + N \cdot \overline{V} + \overline{N} \cdot V$$

where N, V, and Z are the condition code bits of the 68000. Store the result F at a location in memory identified as RESULT as a byte of all 1s or all 0s, depending on whether F is 1 or 0.

Section 4.3

3. Describe the difference between a JMP instruction and a BRA instruction.
4. Consider the delay loop program that follows:

	MOVE.B	#$10,D7
DLY	SUBQ.B	#1,D7
	BGT	DLY
NXT	---	---

   (a) How many times does the instruction BGT DLY get executed?
   (b) Change the program so that BGT DLY is executed just 17 times.
   (c) Change the program so that BGT DLY is executed 2^{32} times.

Section 4.4

5. Given a number N in the range $0 < N \leqslant 5$, write a program that computes its factorial and saves the result in the memory location corresponding to FACT.
6. Write a program that compares the elements of two arrays, A(I) and B(I). Each array contains one hundred 16-bit integer numbers. The comparison is to be done by comparing the corresponding elements of the two arrays until either two elements are found to be unequal or all elements of the arrays have been compared and found to be equal. Assume that the arrays start at addresses $A000 and $B000, respectively. If the two arrays are found to be unequal, save the address of the first unequal element of A(I) at memory location FOUND. On the other hand, if all elements are equal, write a byte of 0s into FOUND.
7. Given an array A(I) with one hundred 16-bit signed numbers, write a program to generate two new arrays, P(J) and N(K). P(J) is to contain all the positive numbers from A(I) and N(K) is to contain all of its negative numbers. A(I) starts at address $A000 in memory and the two new arrays, P(J) and N(K), are to start at addresses $B000 and $C000, respectively.

8. Given an array A(I) of one hundred 16-bit signed integers, write a program to generate a new array, B(I), according to the following directions.

$$B(I) = A(I) \quad \text{for } I = 1, 2, 99, \text{ and } 100$$

and

$$B(I) = \text{median of } A(I-2), A(I-1), A(I), A(I+1), \text{ and } A(I+2) \quad \text{for all}$$

other Is

Section 4.5

9. Write a subroutine that converts a given 32-bit binary number to its equivalent BCD number. The binary number is to be passed to the subroutine as a parameter in D_7 and the subroutine also returns the result in D_7.

10. Given an array A(I) of 100 signed 16-bit integer numbers, generate another array B(I) given by

$$B(I) = A(I) \quad \text{for } I = 1 \text{ and } 100$$

and

$$B(I) = \frac{1}{4}(A(I-1) + 2A(I) + A(I+1)) \quad \text{for all other Is}$$

Use a subroutine to generate the terms of B(I). Parameters A(I−1), A(I), and A(I+1) are to be passed to the subroutine on the stack and the subroutine returns the result B(I) on the stack.

Section 4.6

11. Write the segment of main program and show its subroutine structure to perform the following operations. The program is to check repeatedly the 3 least significant bits of D_0 and depending on their settings, executes one of three subroutines: SUBA, SUBB, or SUBC. The subroutines are selected according to the priority that follows:

3 LSB of D_0	Execute
XX1	SUBA
X10	SUBB
100	SUBC

If a subroutine is executed, before returning to the main program, the corresponding bit or bits in register D_0 are to be cleared. After returning from the subroutine, the main program continues.

5 USING THE MC68000 EDUCATIONAL MICROCOMPUTER FOR PROGRAM DEVELOPMENT

5.1 INTRODUCTION

In the previous two chapters, we studied the instruction set of the 68000 microprocessor and how to write simple assembly language programs. In this chapter, we shall describe how to use the *MC68000 educational microcomputer* to verify whether or not a program correctly performs the application for which it was written. This microcomputer is manufactured by Motorola, Inc., as an educational tool that can be used to teach 68000 microcomputer system architecture and assembly language programming. Here we will learn the commands of the microcomputer's monitor program and use them to assemble, execute, and debug programs. The following topics are covered:

1. The 68000 microcomputer development system
2. The monitor program
3. Monitor commands
4. Register display/modify commands
5. Memory display/modify/search commands
6. Commands for control of I/O resources
7. Assembly and disassembly of instructions and programs
8. Program execution control commands
9. Executing a program
10. Debugging a program

5.2 THE 68000 MICROCOMPUTER DEVELOPMENT SYSTEM

A *development system* is an instrument that is used to develop programs and hardware for a microprocessor-based system. Typically, the development system is designed to permit development work to be done for only specific microprocessors—for instance, devices produced by a specific manufacturer. It can be a sophisticated system that gives the microcomputer designer important capabilities, such as the ability to develop programs in either assembly language or a variety of high-level languages, powerful tools for efficient debugging of programs, facilities for connection to external hardware for debugging of circuit operation, and the ability to integrate the user's software and hardware together for testing and debugging. Use of this type of development system is essential for major microcomputer development projects. Its use results in much saved time and higher-quality hardware and software.

The MC68000 educational microcomputer is a simplified development system that is intended to be used by students and designers to learn how to develop hardware and assembly language programs for 68000-based microcomputers. Figure 5.1 shows the microcomputer board of the MC68000 educational microcomputer. Since this system is intended to serve educational needs and not a complete microcomputer-based system design project, it provides only limited development support. However, the microcomputer board includes all the hardware of a complete microcomputer: 32K bytes of RAM for data and user program storage, 16K bytes of PROM for storage of the monitor program, and interfaces for a variety of input/output (I/O) devices, such as a CRT terminal, a printer, and a cassette player/recorder. The board also has a prototyping area that allows the user to build custom interfaces easily into the microcomputer.

The MC68000 educational microcomputer system can be configured in a number of different ways. The complete system configuration, as shown in Fig. 5.2, includes the microcomputer module (MEX68KECB), a power supply, an RS-232C compatible terminal, an audio cassette recorder, a printer, and even a communications link to a host computer. This complete system configuration provides greater ease and flexibility for program development. However, a more limited system configuration can be used if necessary. For example, the host computer interface is frequently not employed. The minimum hardware configuration is enclosed by dashed lines in Fig. 5.2. Here we see that the only items required in a minimum system are the microcomputer module, the power supply, and the terminal.

In a minimum system configuration, the terminal acts as both the input and output device. Programs and data entered at the keyboard of the terminal are stored in the microcomputer's RAM. They also are echoed back to the screen of the terminal so that their entry can be verified by the user. Commands, such as those used to execute or debug a program, also are issued to the microcomputer from the keyboard. These commands are interpreted and executed by the monitor program that is stored in PROM.

The terminal communicates with the microcomputer through an *RS-232C port*. An RS-232C compatible port is an industry standard interface that defines the voltage

Figure 5-1 The MC68000 educational microcomputer board (Motorola, Inc.).

levels, data format, and control lines for an asynchronous communications interface. Data are passed through the interface in serial form—that is, one bit after the other over a single communication line. The rate at which data is transferred over this line is identified as the baud rate. In this case, baud rate means the number of bits of data per second. The data transmission rate is jumper selectable on the microcomputer board and can be set at a variety of speeds from 110 to 9,600 baud.

The use of an audio cassette recorder in the MC68000 educational microcomputer allows the user to save information, such as programs, on audio cassette tape. In this way, the programmer can reload the program from tape at a later time instead of having to retype it at the keyboard. The audio cassette recorder

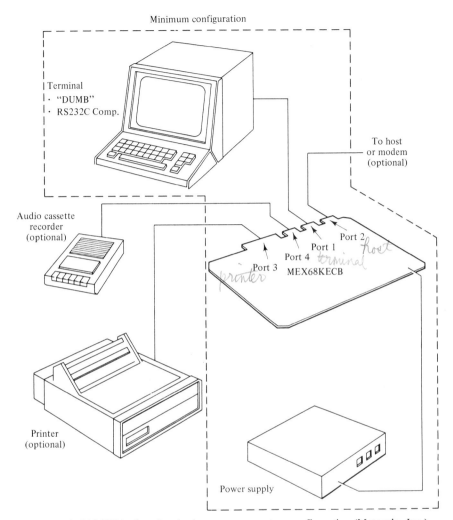

Minimum configuration

Terminal
· "DUMB"
· RS232C Comp.

To host
or modem
(optional)

Audio cassette
recorder
(optional)

Port 2
Port 1   *host*
Port 4   *terminal*
Port 3   MEX68KECB
printer

Printer
(optional)

Power supply

Figure 5-2 MC68000 educational microcomputer system configuration (Motorola, Inc.).

interface is implemented as part of the parallel I/O interface on the microcomputer board. Data transmissions between the microcomputer and cassette recorder are also in serial form. However, in this case the data rate is between 1,000 and 2,000 baud, depending on the bits being transferred through the interface.

The printer can be used to produce hard copies of programs, results produced by executing programs, and debug sequences. The printer interface used in the MC68000 educational microcomputer is what is called a *parallel printer interface (Centronics interface),* and it is also implemented using parallel I/O ports on the microcomputer board.

5.3 THE MONITOR PROGRAM

In Chapter 4, we wrote a number of programs in the 68000's assembly language. For instance, we wrote a block transfer program that could be used to move a block of data from one location in memory called the *source location* to another location called the *destination*. Once a program such as this has been written, we are ready to verify its operation by running it on a microcomputer such as the MC68000 educational microcomputer. To do this we must assemble the program into the microcomputer's memory and then execute it. After execution is complete, the correct operation of the program can be verified by examining the results that it produces, and if necessary any errors that are found can be analyzed by performing what are known as *debug* operations. The *Tutor monitor program* that is provided with the MC68000 educational microcomputer is what permits us to assemble, execute, and debug programs. We pointed out earlier that the monitor is stored in PROM on the microcomputer board.

Tutor is the software interface through which the user can talk to the MC68000 educational microcomputer. It is a simple monitor program that provides a set of commands for use in the entry, execution, and debugging of assembly language programs. The monitor program itself consists of a number of subroutines that are written to perform the various operations that are needed to support assembly language program development. When the microcomputer is being used by a programmer, the monitor program receives a command that is keyed in by the programmer at the keyboard, analyzes it to determine what operation is to be performed, initiates a subroutine to perform the operation specified by the command, and displays the information produced during the execution of the command on the screen of the terminal.

The general operation of the monitor program is overviewed by the flowchart in Fig. 5.3. Here we find that after power is turned on and the microcomputer's reset button is depressed, the monitor program begins to run. It first initializes the memory and I/O resources of the microcomputer system. For instance, all of the storage locations in data memory are initially cleared. After initialization is complete, the command prompt

TUTOR 1.3 >

is displayed on the screen. Here, 1.3 stands for the revision level of the monitor program software. The monitor is now waiting for a command to be entered from the keyboard.

When a command is entered, the Tutor program first verifies that it is a valid command. If the command is invalid, the error message "SYNTAX ERROR" is displayed and software control is returned so that the command prompt is redisplayed. The monitor is again waiting for entry of a command.

On the other hand, if the command is valid, Tutor next determines whether it specifies a monitor operation or execution of the user's program. Let us assume for the moment that the command that was entered asked for the data in a certain

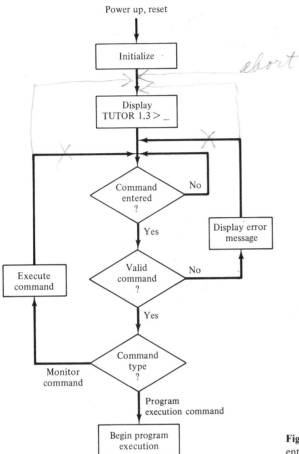

Figure 5-3 Monitor program command entry/execution sequence.

part of the microcomputer's memory to be displayed. This represents the "execute command" path in the flowchart. In this case, control is passed to the subroutine for this monitor function; the command is performed by the microcomputer; and then control is returned to the point in the monitor that calls for entry of another command. If the command asked for execution of the user program instead of a monitor operation, the other path in the flowchart is taken. This time, software control is passed to the starting point of the user's program and its execution is begun. Depending on how the program was specified to execute, control may or may not be returned to the monitor. However, control can always be returned to the monitor if necessary by depressing the ABORT switch.

5.4 THE MONITOR COMMANDS

In Section 5.3, we introduced the Tutor monitor, how it prompts for command entry, and how it processes commands after they are entered. Here we will discuss the commands that are provided in the monitor program. Figure 5.4 is a list of the *command set* of the Tutor monitor. This list includes the mnemonic and a functional description for each of the monitor's thirty-three commands. These commands give the programmer the ability to initiate operations such as to examine or modify the contents of memory or the registers within the 68000, control the execution of a

Command mnemonic	Description
√MD	Memory Display
√MM, M	Memory Modify
MS	Memory Set
.A0 to .A7	Display/Set Address Register
.D0 to .D7	Display/Set Data Register
.PC	Display/Set Program Counter
.SR	Display/Set Status Register
.SS	Display/Set Supervisor Stack Pointer
.US	Display/Set User Stack Pointer
DF	Display Formatted Registers
OF	Display Offsets
.R0 to .R6	Display/Set Relative Offset Register
BF	Block of Memory Fill
BM	Block of Memory Move
BT	Block of Memory Test
BS	Block of Memory Search
DC	Data Conversion
BR	Breakpoint Set
NOBR	Breakpoint Remove
GO, G	Go
GT	Go Until Breakpoint
GD	Go Direct
TR, T	Trace
TT	Temporary Breakpoint Trace
PA	Printer Attach
NOPA	Reset Printer Attach
PF	Port Format
TM	Transparent Mode
*	Send Message to Port 2 — *host computer*
HE	Help
DU	Dump Memory
LO	Load
VE	Verify

Figure 5-4 Tutor's command set (Motorola, Inc.).

program, trace the state of the microprocessor as a program is executed, and control the operation of I/O resources.

Also included as part of Tutor is a line-by-line assembler/disassembler. The assembler capability lets the programmer enter programs in assembly language form and have them automatically translated into machine code and stored into memory. The disassembler function allows the programmer to verify that a program has been loaded into memory correctly by translating its machine code into assembly-language-like instructions and displaying them on the screen of the terminal.

Syntax of a Monitor Command

When commands are keyed in from the keyboard of the terminal, they must always be entered using a special form that is understood by the monitor program. This is known as the command's *syntax,* and if it is not correctly followed, the command entry will result in the display of a syntax error message. The general format for a command entry is

$$[NO] \; <command> \; [<parameters>] \; [;<options>]$$

Notice that there are four fields within the format: the *negative form (NO) field,* the *command field,* the *parameters field,* and the *options field.* When entered, each of these fields must be separated by a space.

In the general format, any field that is enclosed within square brackets is optional. Therefore, the minimum command entry response to the Tutor prompt is just

$$<command>$$

A field enclosed with an angle bracket is to be replaced by a syntactical variable. For instance, the command field can be replaced with a mnemonic from the list in Fig. 5.4. An example of a command that only requires entry of a command field is the *display formatted registers* command. It is issued by entering

$$TUTOR \; 1.3 \; > \; DF \qquad (cr)$$

Execution of this command causes the contents of the 68000's internal registers to be displayed on the screen.

Most monitor commands also require one or more entries in the parameter field. Examples of information that is entered as parameters are: starting and ending addresses, data, counts, and port numbers. For instance, entry of the GO command

$$TUTOR \; 1.3 \; > \; GO \; 100 \qquad (cr)$$

means begin execution of the program that starts at address 000100_{16}. Notice that numeric information that is entered as parameters is assumed to have been expressed in hexadecimal form. However, the interpretation of a number by the monitor can be converted to decimal form by preceding the number with the & symbol. For instance, the GO command that we just introduced can be written using a decimal starting address as

$$TUTOR \; 1.3 \; > \; GO \; \&256 \qquad (cr)$$

The parameter also may be written as an expression. In the expression, numeric information can be combined with the + and − operators. For example, data that are to be loaded into a memory location could be specified with the expression

$$100 + \&25$$

This expression is interpreted by the monitor as a parameter having the hexadecimal value

$$119_{16}$$

Parameters that represent address information can be expressed using a variety of special address formats. The allowed address formats are shown in Fig. 5.5. Here, we find that the monitor program references all address parameters that are specified as a numeric value or expression to the contents of what is called an *offset register*. The monitor defines eight offset registers that are identified as R_0 through R_7. They are software registers that exist in the microcomputer's memory, not hardware registers such as those within the 68000.

When executing a command, the monitor program combines the contents of the specified offset register with the value specified as the address parameter to generate a physical address. For instance, in Fig. 5.5, we see that if an address parameter is specified simply as

140

Format	Example	Description
expression	140	Absolute address (*Note:* offset zero is added)
expression + offset	130 + R5	Absolute address plus offset five (not an assembler-accepted syntax)
expression + offset	150 + R7	Absolute address (*Note:* offset seven is always zero) (not an assembler-accepted syntax)
(A@)	(A5)	Address register indirect
(A@,D@) (A@,A@)	(A6,D4)	Address register indirect with index
expression (A@)	120(A3)	Address register indirect with displacement
expression (A@,D@) expression (A@,A@)	110(A2,D1)	Address register indirect with index plus displacement
[expression]	[100]	Memory indirect (not an assembler-accepted syntax)

Figure 5-5 Parameter field address formats (Motorola, Inc.).

the address parameter is automatically referenced to register R_0. Therefore, the value used as the physical address is actually

$$140_{16} + R0$$

An example of a command like this is

TUTOR 1.3 > GO 140

and when executed it initiates program execution at the physical address obtained by adding 140_{16} and the offset value held in register R_0. If an offset register other than R_0 is to be referenced in the generation of a physical address, its register name is simply added to the expression that specifies the value of the address in the command. For example, the command

TUTOR 1.3 > GO 140+R5

references R_5 instead of R_0 in the generation of the address.

At power up and whenever the reset switch is depressed, all of the offset registers are initialized to zero. The values held in registers R_0 through R_6 can be modified with the *display/set relative offset register* command. However, the value in R_7 is fixed at zero.

The last five address formats in Fig. 5.5 show how the 68000's internal address and data registers can be used to specify the physical address in a monitor command. In general, address registers A_0 through A_6 can be used to hold either the indirect address or an index that is to be added to the indirect address. However, data registers D_0 through D_7 can be used only to hold an index. For instance, the command

TUTOR 1.3 > GO (A5)

specifies that the address at which program execution is to begin is that held in address register A_5. This is an example of what is called *address register indirect addressing*. Notice that indirect addressing is specified by enclosing the register name with parentheses.

Another example is the command

TUTOR 1.3 > GO (A6,D4)

In this command, the indirect address is held in A_6 and the value in D_4 is used as an index. The index is added to the value in A_6 to obtain the starting address for the GO command.

The last address format in Fig. 5.5 shows how a storage location in memory can be referenced for an indirect address. Notice that the expression that specifies the memory address is simply enclosed with a set of square brackets. For example, the command

TUTOR 1.3 > GO [100]

indicates that execution is to resume at the address held in memory location 000100_{16}.

For the purpose of our discussion, we will divide the commands of Tutor's command set into four groups. These groups are the register display/modify commands, the memory display/modify/search commands, the program execution control commands, and the I/O control commands. In the sections that follow, we will study the commands in each of these categories.

5.5 REGISTER DISPLAY/MODIFY COMMANDS

The first group of Tutor commands that we will examine in detail are those in the *register display/modify* group. The commands that are in this group are shown in Fig. 5.6. These commands give the programmer the ability to display and modify the contents of the internal registers of the 68000 as well as the software offset registers of the Tutor monitor.

The ability to examine the contents of the 68000's internal registers is essential for debugging the execution of programs. For instance, the contents of a register can be examined prior to and just after the execution of an instruction. In this way, we can verify that the instruction performed its intended function. Moreover, we need to use the modify capability of these commands to initialize the contents of internal registers before executing an instruction or the complete program.

One way of displaying the contents of the internal registers of the 68000 is by using the *display formatted registers* (DF) command. In Fig. 5.6, we find that this command is issued to the monitor by responding to the command prompt by first entering DF and then depressing the carriage return (cr) key. That is,

Command	Meaning	Format	Explanation
DF	Display formatted registers	DF	Displays the contents of the 68000's internal registers
.A0 to .A7 .D0 to .D7 .PC	Display/set registers	.\<Register>	Display the contents of the specified registers
.SR .SS .US		.\<Register>\<Data>	Loads the specified register with the specified data
OF	Display offset registers	OF	Display the contents of the offset registers
.R0 to .R6	Display/set offset register	.RX	Display the specified offset register contents
		.RX\<Data>	Loads the specified offset register with the specified data
		.RX\<Data> + RX	Loads the specified offset register with the specified data via RX

Figure 5-6 Register display/modify commands.

TUTOR 1.3 > DF   (cr)

Execution of the DF command causes the contents of all of the registers within the 68000 to be displayed in the format shown in Fig. 5.7. Looking at this information, we find that the current value in the program counter (PC) is $00009C72_{16}$; the current value in D_0 is $0000FF0D_{16}$; and the current value in A_0 is 00010040_{16}. Notice that the last line displayed is the address, machine code, and assembly language version of the instruction pointed to by the current value in PC.

```
TUTOR  1.3 > DF
PC=00009C72 SR=2700=.S7..... US=FFFFFFFF SS=00000756
D0=0000FF0D D1=00000000 D2=12100010 D3=00000000
D4=00000231 D5=00000FFF D6=00000004 D7=00000000
A0=00010040 A1=FFFFFFFF A2=00000414 A3=00000554
A4=00009FAC A5=00000540 A6=00000540 A7=00000756
--------------------------009C72    41F900010040          LEA.L     $00010040,A0

TUTOR  1.3 >
```

Figure 5-7 Register data display format for the DF command.

Example 5.1

In Fig. 5.7 what is the value displayed for the current value held in the user's stack pointer register?

Solution. Looking at the first line of register information in Fig. 5.7, we find that the value of the user's stack pointer is that preceded with the mnemonic US and that it's current value is

$$US = FFFFFFFF_{16}$$

The DF command does not let us examine the contents of just a specific register or modify the value held in a register. To do these types of operations, we must use another command, the *display/set registers* command. This is the second command in the chart of Fig. 5.6. As shown in the format column of this chart, the display/set register command can be initiated by entering a "." followed by the name of the register whose contents are to be displayed and then depressing carriage return (cr). This form of the command is used to examine the contents of a register. For instance, to examine the contents of data register D_5, the keyboard entry is

TUTOR 1.3 > .D5   (cr)

The monitor responds to this command by displaying the value held in D_5 in the form

.D5 = 00000FFF

Example 5.2

What is the effect of issuing the command

TUTOR 1.3 > .SS   (cr)

Solution. This command causes the monitor to display the value held in the user's stack pointer register in the form

.SS = 00000756

To modify the value in a register, such as D_5, the second command format in Fig. 5.6 is used. Here we see that the command is initiated in the same way as we just did to examine the register contents, but this time the new value of data is entered prior to depressing (cr). For example, to load the value AAA_{16} into D_5, the command is

TUTOR 1.3 > .D5 AAA   (cr)

When this command is executed by the monitor, D_5 is loaded with the value $00000AAA_{16}$. This can be verified by displaying the new value in D_5 as follows

TUTOR 1.3 > .D5   (cr)

.D5 = 00000AAA

Example 5.3

Show the command sequence needed to initialize PC with the value 2000_{16} and A_3 with the value 2500_{16}. Verify this initialization with a DF command.

Solution.   The new values are loaded into PC and A_3 with the commands

TUTOR 1.3 > .PC 2000   (cr)

TUTOR 1.3 > .A3 2500   (cr)

and initialization is verified with the command

TUTOR 1.3 > DF   (cr)

The information displayed as a result of executing these commands is shown in Fig. 5.8.

```
TUTOR   1.3 > .PC 2000

TUTOR   1.3 > .A3 2500

TUTOR   1.3 > DF
PC=00002000 SR=2700=.S7..... US=FFFFFFFF SS=00000756
D0=0000FF0D D1=00000000 D2=12100010 D3=00000000
D4=00000231 D5=00000FFF D6=00000004 D7=00000000
A0=00010040 A1=FFFFFFFF A2=00000414 A3=00002500
A4=00009FAC A5=00000540 A6=00000540 A7=00000756
--------------------------002000      FF5B              DC.W    $FF5B

TUTOR   1.3 >
```

Figure 5-8 Display sequence for example 5.3.

The last two commands in Fig. 5.6, *display offset registers* and *display/set offset registers,* operate similar to the commands we just introduced; however, these commands are used to examine or modify the contents of the monitor's software offset registers instead of the 68000's internal registers. For instance, the values in all of the offset registers are displayed by entering the command

TUTOR 1.3 > OF   (cr)

To examine the value held in a specific offset register, we use the display/set offset register command. For example, the command

TUTOR 1.3 > .R0   (cr)

displays the contents of offset register R_0. This same command can be used to modify the value in offset registers R_0 through R_6. As an example, let us change the value held in R_0 to $F000_{16}$. This is done by issuing the command

TUTOR 1.3 > .R0 F000   (cr)

It is important to note that when modifying the contents of an offset register other than R_0 the value held in R_0 is always added to the data entered as part of the command before it is loaded into the specified register. That is, the command

TUTOR 1.3 > .R1 FF   (cr)

is really equivalent to the command

TUTOR 1.3 > .R1 FF + R0   (cr)

Assuming that R_0 already contains $F000_{16}$, the value loaded into R_1 when this command is executed is

$$R_1 = FF_{16} + R_0$$
$$= FF_{16} + F000_{16} = F0FF_{16}$$

Remember that the value in R_7 is always 00000000_{16}. Therefore, it can be used as the reference register if we want to load an offset register with a value and not have the current value in R_0 added. For instance, issuing the command

TUTOR 1.3 > .R1 FF + R7   (cr)

causes just the value FF_{16} to be loaded into R_1.

5.6 MEMORY DISPLAY/MODIFY/SEARCH COMMANDS

In the last section, we learned how to use Tutor commands to examine or modify the contents of the internal registers of the 68000 microprocessor. The second group of commands we will examine, the *memory display/modify/search* commands, are the ones that allow the programmer to display or change the contents of storage locations in memory or search through a block of memory locations looking for specific data. These capabilities are essential for both debugging of programs and for initializing memory before executing an instruction or program. The commands in this group are summarized in Fig. 5.9. Let us next look at each of these commands in detail.

Examining Memory—MD

To examine the contents of memory, Tutor provides the *memory display* (MD) command. In Fig. 5.9, we see that the general format for this command is

MD [<port number>] <address> [<count>] [;<options>]

The port number field determines the output device to which the memory data that is to be examined is output. Remember that the MC68000 educational microcomputer

Command	Meaning	Format	Explanation
MD	Memory display	MD [<port number>] <address> [<count>] [;<options>]	Displays the contents of the specified number (count) of bytes of memory starting from the given address, by outputting them to the specified port as hexadecimal data
MM	Memory modify	MM <address> [;<options>]	The byte contents of the specified address are displayed or modified
M		M <address> [;<options>]	
MS	Memory set	MS <address> <data>	Loads the list of data starting at the specified address
BF	Block fill	BF <starting address> <ending address> <data>	Fills the block of memory locations beginning at starting address and continuing through ending address with the word specified as data
BM	Block move	BM <starting address> <ending address> <destination address>	Moves the contents of the block of memory locations beginning at starting address and continuing through ending address to another block of memory locations starting at destination address
BS	Block search	BS <starting address> <ending address> 'literal string'	Scans the block of memory locations from starting address through ending address for the literal string or data
		BS <starting address> <ending address> <data> [<mask>] [;<options>]	

Figure 5-9 Memory display/modify/search commands.

has three ports that can be used as outputs: port 1, which is the port where the terminal is connected; port 2, which is the host computer interface; and port 3, which is for the printer. Any of these three port numbers can be specified in the port number field. If no port number is entered, the default port, which is port 1, is used by Tutor and the information is displayed on the screen of the terminal.

The next field is for the address of the storage location at which we will begin to examine memory. In the MC68000 educational microcomputer, data storage memory is located in the address range from 000900_{16} through $007FFF_{16}$. However, the address entry made as part of an MD command does not need to be restricted to this range. Information from the program storage memory part of the address space also can be displayed. The count field tells the monitor how many of the bytes of data that follow the specified starting address are to be displayed. This field is also optional, and if no entry is made a default value of 16 is used. Finally, the option field is related to use of the disassembler, which we will discuss in a later section.

Notice that the only field other than the command field that is not optional is the address field. Let us assume that the default port is to be used and that no count or options are to be specified. Then the command format simplifies to

$$\text{MD} < \text{address} >$$

and if we want to display the contents of the first 16 bytes of data memory the command is

$$\text{TUTOR 1.3} > \text{MD 900} \quad \text{(cr)}$$

Execution of this command causes Tutor to display the data shown in Fig. 5.10. Here we see that the starting address 000900_{16} is displayed at the left margin and the 16 bytes of data in the range 000900_{16} through $00090F_{16}$ are listed one after the other to the right.

```
TUTOR  1.3 > MD 900
000900      EE 7B FF FF FF FF FF FF   FF FF FF FF FF FF FF FF   n{..............

TUTOR  1.3 >
000910      FF FF FF FF FF FF FF FF   FF FF FF FF FF FF FF FF   ................
000920      FF FF FF FF FF FF FF FF   FF FF FF FF FF FF FF FF   ................
000930      FF FF FF FF FF FF FF FF   FF FF FF FF FF FF FF FF   ................
000940      FF FF FF FF FF FF FF FF   FF FF FF FF FF FF FF FF   ................
000950      FF FF FF FF FF FF FF FF   FF FF FF FF FF FF FF FF   ................
000960      FF FF FF FF FF FF FF FF   FF FF FF FF FF FF FF FF   ................
000970      FF FF FF FF FF FF FF FF   FF FF FF FF FF FF FF FF   ................
000980      00 00 00 00 00 00 00 00   00 00 00 00 00 00 00 00   ................
000990      00 00 00 00 00 00 00 00   00 00 00 00 00 00 00 00   ................
0009A0      00 00 00 00 00 00 00 00   00 00 00 00 00 00 00 00   ................
0009B0      00 00 00 00 00 00 00 00   00 00 00 00 00 00 00 00   ................
0009C0      00 00 00 00 00 00 00 00   00 00 00 00 00 00 00 00   ................
0009D0      00 00 00 00 00 00 00 00   00 00 00 00 00 00 00 00   ................
0009E0      00 00 00 00 00 00 00 00   00 00 00 00 00 00 00 00   ................
0009F0      00 00 00 00 00 00 00 00   00 00 00 00 00 00 00 00   ................
000A00      FF FF FF FF FF FF FF FF   FF FF FF FF FF FF FF FF   ................

TUTOR  1.3 >
```

Figure 5-10 Examining the contents of memory with the MD command.

Once a memory display command operation has been initiated, the next 256 consecutive bytes in memory can be displayed by simply responding to the Tutor prompt by depressing the return key. For instance, if the next command is

TUTOR 1.3 >   (cr)

the data for storage locations 000910_{16} through $000A0F_{16}$ are displayed, as shown in Fig. 5.10.

Another example is the command

TUTOR 1.3 > MD 1000 15   (cr)

Since the count is expressed in hexadecimal form, we would expect the command to cause values in the 21 storage locations from address 1000_{16} through 1015_{16} to be displayed. However, this is not exactly what happens. The way the MD command works is that it always displays groups of 16 storage locations. Therefore, for this command, the contents of the 32 storage locations from 1000_{16} through $101F_{16}$ are actually displayed.

Example 5.4

How many bytes of data are displayed when the command

TUTOR 1.3 > MD 1200 40   (cr)

is executed? What is the range of the addresses that are examined with the command? Rewrite the command with the count specified in decimal form.

Solution. The count in the command is 40_{16}. In decimal form, this is the number 64. Therefore, 64 bytes of data are displayed with the command. The starting address of the range of memory that is examined is 1200_{16} and the ending address is $123F_{16}$.

To use the decimal value of the count in the command, we must precede it with the & symbol. This gives

TUTOR 1.3 > MD 1200 &64   (cr)

Modifying Memory—MM, MS, BF, and BM

The MD command lets us examine data that are stored in memory, but it does not let us change the value of these data. For use in modifying the contents of memory, Tutor is provided with four commands: *memory modify* (MM), *memory set* (MS), *block fill* (BF), and *block move* (BM). In general, these commands give the programmer the ability to change individually the contents of storage locations in memory, initialize a block of storage locations with specific data, and copy the contents from one block of memory locations to another block of locations in memory.

The format of the memory modify (MM) command is shown in Fig. 5.9. Here we see that it is initiated by entering MM followed by the address of the memory location whose value is to be changed. If no option is included as part of the command, its execution causes the byte of data stored at <address> to be displayed on the screen. For instance, the command

TUTOR 1.3 > MM 900   (cr)

causes the following information to be displayed

000900 00 ?___

We have assumed that the original data held at address 900_{16} is 00_{16}. Notice that the cursor is displayed following the question mark. This is because the command is not yet complete and the monitor is waiting for another entry. If the data that is displayed is already the value that is needed at address 900_{16}, the response is simply to depress the return key. This entry causes the contents of the next consecutive byte of data to be displayed in the form

000901 00 ?___

Let us assume that the value at address 901_{16} is to be FF_{16}. To make this change, we simply enter the new value and then depress return. Therefore, the displayed information on the screen now looks like

000901 00 ?FF

000902 00 ?___

Assume that these two memory locations are the only ones that need to have their contents initialized. Since this has already been done, the MM command can now be terminated. To do this, type in the period (.) symbol and then depress the return key. This entry results in display of the lines of information that follow

000902 00 ? .   (cr)

TUTOR 1.3 >___

The monitor is now waiting for a new command to be entered. The series of information displayed for this command is shown in Fig. 5.11.

```
TUTOR   1.3 > MM 900
000900      00 ?
000901      00 ?FF
000902      00 ?.
TUTOR   1.3 >
```

Figure 5.11 Examining and modifying the contents of memory with the MM command.

By including an option as part of the command, we can control the way in which data are displayed and modified. In the example we just used to illustrate the operation of the MM command, memory was displayed and modified one byte at a time. This is the default mode of operation. However, by adding the option ;W after the address, we can display and modify memory data as words. For instance, our earlier example also could have been performed as

TUTOR 1.3 > MM 900;W   (cr)

000900 0000 ?00FF   (cr)

000902 0000 ? .   (cr)

TUTOR 1.3 >___

Notice that inclusion of the ;W option caused the word contents of address 900_{16} to be displayed as 0000_{16} and then we changed the complete word by entering $00FF_{16}$.

Another option allows us to display memory contents as long words. This is the ;L option, and an example using it is the command

TUTOR 1.3 > MM 1004;L   (cr)

Execution of this command displays the data held at memory addresses 1004_{16} through 1007_{16} as a long word.

001004 00000000 ?___

With what we have learned up to this point, there are just three responses we can issue after the ? symbol. They are: depress (cr) to display the contents of the next long word address; key in a new value of data for the current long word address and depress (cr); or terminate the command by entering the . symbol followed by (cr). However, the MM command does allow other entries. Let us now look at them briefly. One choice is to enter the symbol ˆand then depress (cr). For instance, the command entry can be

001004 00000000 ? ˆ   (cr)

This causes the address to be decremented instead of incremented to display the contents of the new address. Therefore, the data at long word address 001000_{16} is displayed

001000 00FF0000 ? ___

The last way of completing an MM entry is to enter a new value followed by the = symbol and a (cr). This entry updates the value at the current address and then redisplays it to verify that the change has taken place. For instance, if we load long word address 001000_{16} with the value $FFFFFFFF_{16}$ the displayed response is

001000 00000000 ? FFFFFFFF = (cr)

001000 FFFFFFFF ?___

There are two other options that can be used in the MM command. They are ;O, which stands for display odd bytes only, and ;V, which stands for display even bytes only. These commands are useful in conjunction with examining and modifying the contents of internal registers of LSI I/O devices. This is because their registers typically reside at consecutive odd or even addresses.

Example 5.5

Explain what is being done with the command sequence that follows

TUTOR 1.3 > MM 1200;L   (cr)

001200 00000000 ?FFFFFFFF   (cr)

001204 00000000 ?FFFFFFFF   (cr)

TUTOR 1.3 >___

Solution.   This series of long word memory modify commands initialize the eight bytes of memory from address 1200_{16} through 1207_{16} with the value FF_{16}.

Another command that can be used to initialize memory is *memory set* (MS). Looking at the general format of the memory set command in Fig. 5.9, we see that it differs from the memory modify command in that the data to be entered is included in the command right after the address. This data can be a string of up to eight hexadecimal numbers or ASCII characters. In fact, multiple strings of data with up to eight numbers or characters can be entered in the data field. When doing this, the strings must be separated by a space.

An example of an MS command that is used to load hexadecimal numbers is

TUTOR 1.3 > MS 2000 ABCD   (cr)

Execution of this command causes AB_{16} and CD_{16} to be loaded into memory at addresses 2000_{16} and 2001_{16}, respectively. Another example is

TUTOR 1.3 > MS 2000 'ABCD'   (cr)

Here the single quote marks around the data field indicate that the data are ASCII data and not numeric data. Therefore, execution of this command loads the four bytes of memory starting at address 2000_{16} with the codes for characters A, B, C, and D. That is, the values 41, 42, 43, and 44 are stored starting at address 2000_{16}.

Example 5.6

Write an MS command that performs the same function as the MM commands given in Example 5.5.

Solution.   The MM commands in Example 5.5 load the eight bytes of memory starting at address 1200_{16} each with the value FF_{16}. This operation can be done with the single MS command

TUTOR 1.3 > MS 1200 FFFFFFFF FFFFFFFF   (cr)

In Examples 5.5 and 5.6, we showed how a block of consecutive memory locations can be filled with the same value. This type of operation is better performed with the *block fill* (BF) command. As shown in Fig. 5.9, the first field of the command is the starting address of the block of memory locations. It is followed by the ending address of the block and the word of data that is to be stored into these locations. Notice that the data is always entered as a word; therefore, both the starting and ending addresses must be word addresses. That is, they both must be even. To perform the same operation as done in our earlier examples, the BF command is written as

TUTOR 1.3 > BF 2000 2006 FFFF   (cr)

and its execution loads word addresses 2000_{16} through 2006_{16} with the value $FFFF_{16}$.

The block fill command is the most efficient command to use when initializing large blocks of memory. For instance, the command

TUTOR 1.3 > BF 900 9FE 0000   (cr)

could be used to clear the first 256 words of data memory.

The last command that can be used to modify the contents of memory is the *block move* (BM) command. It can be used to copy a block of data that already exists in one location in memory, called the *source block,* to another location, called the *destination block.* Looking at Fig. 5.9, we see that the command requires three addresses. The first two addresses identify the starting and ending points of the source block, while the third address identifies the starting location of the destination block. For instance, the command

TUTOR 1.3 > BM 1000 10FE 1200   (cr)

copies the contents of the 128 word addresses in the range 1000_{16} through $10FE_{16}$ to the block of storage locations from 1200_{16} through $12FE_{16}$. During the execution of the command, the data in the source block is not affected in any way.

Block Search Command—BS

The last of the commands given in Fig. 5.9 is the *block search* (BS) command. This command can be used to scan through a specified block of memory locations looking for the occurrence of a special data pattern or string of characters. The general format of the command is given in Fig. 5.9. Here we see that the first two fields are the starting and ending addresses of the block of storage locations. The third field is for entry of the data pattern or character string. For example, to search for the ASCII character string ABCD in the memory range from 1000_{16} to 1500_{16}, the command is

TUTOR 1.3 > BS 1000 1500 'ABCD'   (cr)

Every time a match to the character string is found, the starting address of the string and the character string are displayed. For instance, if the pattern ABCD was found starting at address 1034_{16}, the information displayed is

001034 'ABCD'

Looking at Fig. 5.9, we find that the block search command for a numeric data pattern also can include an optional mask and option. For now, let us assume that there is no mask and look at what options are available. The three allowed options are ;B, ;W, and ;L, and they stand for byte, word, and long word, respectively. If no option is entered, the default option, which is byte, is used. An example that uses the default option is the command

TUTOR 1.3 > BS 1000 1500 AB   (cr)

When this command is executed, a search is made of all byte-wide storage locations in the block of memory looking for the data pattern AB_{16}, and the address and data pattern are displayed for each match condition that is found. If this command is modified with the ;W option, we get

TUTOR 1.3 > BS 1000 1500 ABAB ;W   (cr)

The search performed by this command differs from that performed for the previous command in that a match condition requires a word-wide occurrence of the pattern. That is, the search is for the pattern $ABAB_{16}$.

The mask field makes the block search command more versatile. The specification of a mask allows us to ignore some of the bits of the data pattern. In this case, the mask and data pattern are ANDed together and the bits that are masked off are not used in the comparison with the data being searched. Therefore, all bits that are logic 0 in the mask are set to 0 in the data pattern and are ignored. For instance, in the command

TUTOR 1.3 > BS 1000 1500 AB F0   (cr)

ANDing the data pattern AB_{16} with the mask $F0_{16}$ masks off the four LSBs and they are don't-care bits. For this reason, during the search the match condition is based on the data pattern of AX_{16}. Here the X stands for a don't-care byte; therefore, all bytes that have A_{16} in their most significant byte location represent a match condition. The original contents of the storage location are displayed along with the address.

5.7 COMMANDS FOR CONTROL OF I/O RESOURCES

The MC68000 educational microcomputer has four I/O ports that are provided for reception of data from or transmission of data to peripheral devices such as a terminal and printer. These ports are shown in Fig. 5.2. Here we find that the terminal, which provides the keyboard input and display output of the microcomputer, connects to port 1; port 2 is for a modem through which the microcomputer can be connected to a host computer; port 3 is the port that is used to attach a printer to the microcomputer; and port 4 is provided for connection of a cassette player/recorder. Tutor's command set includes four commands that are for control of these I/O resources. These commands are listed in Fig. 5.12.

Let us start by looking at the function of the commands that control the printer's interface (port 3). The first two commands in Fig. 5.12, *printer attach* (PA) and *no printer attach* (NOPA), allow the programmer to select or deselect the printer. The PA command is issued as

TUTOR 1.3 > PA   (cr)

and when executed it directs information that is normally output on the display at port 1 to the printer at port 3 as well. That is, now the information is both displayed and printed. If we no longer want the information to be printed, the NOPA command must be issued as

TUTOR 1.3 > NOPA   (cr)

After executing this command, data are no longer directed to the printer. They are again only displayed at the terminal.

The two serial communication ports of the microcomputer can be configured with a variety of operating characteristics. The operation of each port is defined by four port parameters. They are its *format, character nulls, carriage return nulls,* and *options.* The *port format* (PF) command can be used either to display the current port parameters of both port 1 and port 2 or to change the parameters to give a port new operating characteristics.

Command	Meaning	Format	Explanation
PA	Printer attach	PA	Attaches the printer so that information sent to the terminal is also printed
NOPA	No printer attach	NOPA	Disconnects the printer from the microcomputer so that information output to the terminal is not printed
PF	Port format	PF [<port number>]	Displays or modifies the characteristics of the serial ports: format, character nulls, CR nulls, and options
TM	Transparent mode	TM [<exit character>] [<trailing character>]	Enters the transparent mode and specifies the exit and trailing characters
DU4	Dump onto cassette tape	DU4 <starting address> <ending address>	Dumps the contents of the specified address range to port 4 where it is saved on cassette tape
VE4	Verify cassette tape	VE4	Verifies that the data saved on tape matches the contents of memory
LO4	Load from cassette tape	LO4	Loads memory with the data held on a cassette tape

Figure 5-12 Commands for control of the I/O resources.

The format parameter specifies the number of stop bits used during the transmission and reception of character data. Either one or two stop bits can be assigned. One stop bit is selected by making the format parameter equal to 15 and two stop bits are selected by making it 11.

Nulls are needed when communicating with slow-reacting devices such as a printer. For instance, when a carriage return is sent to the printer, a short interval of time is required to move the printhead back to the beginning of the next line. In such a case, nulls may be sent out to the printer before any more character information is output. These are what are called *carriage return nulls*. Moreover, if the baud rate is very high, nulls may need to be sent out after each character as well. These nulls are called character nulls. The number of carriage return and character nulls that are output can both be set with the PF command.

The last characteristic of the two serial ports that can be changed with the PF command is their options. The options specify a RAM address where 6 bytes of information are stored. This information is used during what is called *transparent mode* of operation. When in this mode, the terminal port gets directly connected to the host computer port.

The syntax of the port format command is shown in Fig. 5.12. An example where PF is used to display the characteristics of both ports is

TUTOR 1.3 > PF   (cr)

FORMAT = 15 15

CHAR NULL = 00 00

C/R NULL = 00 00

OPTIONS = @XXXXX

Here we see that both ports are set for one stop bit, no character nulls, and no carriage return nulls.

To change the characteristics of a port—for instance, port 2—we begin by issuing the command

TUTOR 1.3 > PF2   (cr)

Tutor responds by displaying the current format setting and prompts with a ? for entry of a new value. That is,

FORMAT = 15?

At this point, (cr) can be depressed if the value of format is not to be changed. However, let us assume that it is to be changed for two stop bits. Then the entry is

FORMAT = 15? 11 (cr)

After this entry is made, the character null parameter is displayed as

CHAR NULL = 00?

Assuming that this parameter is not to be changed, the entry is simply

CHAR NULL = 00?   (cr)

and then the carriage return null parameter is displayed

C/R NULL = 00?

We will change this parameter to 4; therefore, the entry is

C/R NULL = 00? 4   (cr)

The next command in Fig. 5.12 is the *transparent mode* (TM) command. Transparent mode operation can be initiated by issuing the command

TUTOR 1.3 > TM   (cr)

Execution of this command connects the terminal port and the modem port together. In this way, the terminal port is connected directly to a host computer; therefore, commands can now be issued to Tutor from the host computer. When transparent mode is initiated in this way, default values, which are CTRL A and CRTL X, are used for what are called the *exit character* and *trailing character* parameters.

When operating in the transparent mode, the microcomputer accepts inputs from the host computer just as though it was the terminal. However, it also watches the input from the host computer for the occurrence of an exit character (CTRL A). If the exit character is received, transparent mode is exited and Tutor once again accepts inputs from the terminal at port 1.

5.8 ASSEMBLING INSTRUCTIONS AND PROGRAMS

The assembly language instructions of a source program are not in a form that can be executed by a 68000-based microcomputer. They first must be converted to their equivalent machine language instructions. We pointed out earlier that the program used to convert assembly language instructions to machine language is called an assembler. Let us now look at how the Tutor monitor can be used to assemble and disassemble instructions of a program.

The Line-by-Line Assembler

The assembler provided in the Tutor monitor of the MC68000 educational microcomputer is what is called a *line-by-line assembler*. It is an assembler that translates each line of source code into its equivalent machine code as it is entered from the keyboard of the terminal and then stores the machine code in memory.

Use of a line-by-line assembler imposes a few restrictions on the writing of source programs. For instance, it does not allow the programmer to use labels or symbols; instead, the specific memory address or numeric data must be entered into the instruction.

Assembly Language Statement Syntax

When entering assembly language statements into the microcomputer with the line-by-line assembler, certain syntax must be used. *Syntax* is the rules that govern how assembly language source statements are to be written. Source programs written for the MC68000 educational microcomputer can consist of two types of statements. The first type, called an *instruction statement,* specifies an instruction of the program. The other type, which is called a *directive,* defines a constant that is to be used by the program. We will begin by looking at the syntax of instruction statements.

The notations and syntax that we used for writing instructions in Chapters 3 and 4 are those required by the line-by-line assembler of the MC68000 educational microcomputer. Therefore, we will briefly review this format here. All instruction statements in a source program must have the following format

$$\_\_ \ <\text{operation field}> \ \_\_ \ [<\text{operand field}>]$$

Here, the first __ means that a space must be entered at the beginning of every source statement and the second __ means that a space must be used to separate the operation field from the operand field. Moreover, notice that the operand field is enclosed in square brackets ([ ]). This means that the field is optional in some instructions.

The operation field part of the instruction statement format specifies the operation that is to be performed. That is, the mnemonic for the instruction. For instance, when writing an addition instruction for long-word data, this field is filled with ADD.L. The operand field specifies the operand or operands that are to be processed during the execution of the instruction. For example, the source operand could reside in data register D_1 and the destination operand could reside in data register D_2. Therefore, the add instruction statement would be written as

ADD.L   D1,D2

Now that we have reviewed instruction statement format, let us continue with the directive. Only one directive is accepted by the line-by-line assembler. It is called *define constant* (DC.W) and is used to define a constant in a word storage location in memory. The define constant directive uses the same format as we just showed for the instruction statement. An example is

DC.W $A000

Entry of this directive assigns the value $A000_{16}$ to the current memory location.

Tutor allows the programmer to specify the operands in instructions or directives with decimal numbers (no prefix), hexadecimal numbers ($ sign prefix), or ASCII strings (enclosed in apostrophes). For instance, if the earlier directive was written as

DC.W   7000

the binary equivalent of decimal number 7000 is loaded into the storage location. Moreover, if the directive is written as

DC.W   'AA'

the ASCII form of character A is loaded into both the most significant byte and least significant byte of the current memory location.

Assembly and Disassembly of Instructions

The line-by-line assembler function is one of the optional modes of operation for the memory modify (MM) command. Actually the operation provided by this command is a combined disassembler/assembler function. It is invoked by specifying *disassemble instruction* (DI) as the option. Therefore, the general syntax for the command is

TUTOR 1.3 > MM   < address >;DI

The value of address specified in the command is the starting address of the machine code instruction when it is assembled into memory.

For instance, to assemble the instruction

MOVE.B   D5,D0

into memory starting at address 002000_{16}, we bring up the assembler with the command

TUTOR 1.3 > MM   2000;DI   (cr)

Tutor responds to this command by displaying

002000   2248   MOVE.L   A0,A1 ?

This demonstrates the disassembler mode of operation. Notice that the current contents held at address 002000_{16} are displayed as 2248_{16} and that this is the machine code for the instruction

MOVE.L   A0,A1

To replace this instruction with the new instruction, we must assemble the instruction into memory. This is done by simply typing it following the ? prompt and then depressing the carriage return key. That is,

002000   2248   MOVE.L   A0,A1 ? MOVE.B D5,D0   (cr)

Remember that for correct syntax a space must be entered before MOVE.B and another before D_5. Tutor responds to this entry by displaying the information that follows:

002000   1005   MOVE.B   D5,D0

002002   4EF81012   JMP.S $00000012 ?

Here we find that the first line of displayed information consists of the starting address of the instruction, which is 002000_{16}, followed by the machine code form of the instruction, 1005_{16}, and the assembly language instruction statement

MOVE.B   D5,D0

This completes the assembly operation. However, notice that the next sequential instruction has been disassembled and displayed as a second line of information. It is again followed by the ? prompt. We can now either enter another instruction or terminate instruction disassembly/assembly by entering period (.) followed by carriage return (cr). Let us assume that instruction assembly is to be terminated, then the entry is

002002   4EF81012   JMP.S $00000012 ? .   (cr)

and Tutor responds by prompting for a new command

TUTOR 1.3 >

The assembly of this instruction is shown in Fig. 5.13.

```
TUTOR  1.3 > MM 2000;DI
002000      1005                  MOVE.B   D5,D0
002002      4EF81012              JMP.S    $00000012 ?.


TUTOR   1.3 >
```

Figure 5-13 Assembly of an instruction.

When a source statement is entered, the line-by-line assembler first checks it for correct syntax. If invalid syntax is encountered, the assembler responds by displaying an error message and then prompts for reentry of the statement. The error conditions may be due to an attempt to access a location at which no memory exists, use of improper characters or symbols, use of too large a number, use of an invalid opcode, or even a missing space where one is required. In most cases, the error condition can be rectified simply by reentering the instruction. The error messages and the conditions which generate them are discussed in the MC68000 educational microcomputer's user's manual.

Let us assume that we want to assemble the instruction

$$\text{OR.B   D5,(A6)}$$

at address 006000_{16}. Using the memory modify command, we enter

TUTOR 1.3 > MM 6000;DI   (cr)

06000 FFFF   DC.W $FFFF   ?OR.B D5, (A6)   (cr)

Notice that we forgot to leave a space after the prompt before beginning to type in the instruction's mnemonic. This is a syntax error. Therefore, Tutor responds with

X?

which means that a syntax error has been identified. To correct the syntax error, we just reenter the complete instruction after the ? this time preceding OR with a space. That is,

X?   OR.B   D5, (A6)   (cr)

After this entry is made, Tutor responds with

006000   8B16   OR.B   D5, (A6)

006002   00000000   OR.B   #0, D0 ?

Here 006000_{16} is the address at which the instruction is entered into memory and $8B16_{16}$ is the machine code for the OR instruction. This operation of the assembler is shown in Fig. 5.14.

TUTOR 1.3 > MM 6000;DI
006000   1005   MOVE.B D5,D0 ?OR.B D5,(A6)
(a)

006000   X? OR.B D5,(A6)
(b)
006000   8B16   OR.B D5,(A6)
006002   00000000   OR.B #0,D0?
(c)

Figure 5-14 (a) Syntax error in the entry of an instruction; (b) Tutor's response to a syntax error; (c) corrected instruction entry.

The disassembly capability of the MM command also can be used to view instructions stored in memory without modifying them. To do this, we initiate the disassemble/assembly mode of operation and then respond to the prompt for a new instruction by simply depressing (cr). In this way, the machine code and assembly language statement is displayed for one instruction after the other. Figure 5.15 shows the disassembly of three instructions.

```
TUTOR   1.3 > MM 6000;DI
006000      8B16              OR.B      D5,(A6)  ?
006002      00000000          OR.B      #0,D0  ?
006006      00000000          OR.B      #0,D0  ?.

TUTOR   1.3 >
```

Figure 5-15 Disassembly of an instruction.

Assembly/Disassembly of a Complete Program

Now that we have shown how to assemble an instruction into the memory of the MC68000 educational microcomputer and also disassemble it to verify its loading, let us look at how a complete program is loaded with the line-by-line assembler. The assemble option of the MM command allows for easy entry of a series of instructions. The starting address of the program is first set up as part of calling up the line-by-line assembler. Then one instruction after the other is typed in and after each instruction the carriage return key is depressed. When the last instruction of the program has been entered, the assembly process is terminated by entering . and then (cr).

Here we will show how to enter the program in Fig. 5.16 into the memory of the microcomputer. Let us begin by briefly describing the operation of this program. The program in Fig. 5.16 implements what is known as a *block-move* data transfer operation. Its function is to move a block of data called the source block from one location in memory to another location called the destination block. The source block of data starts at memory address 001000_{16} and is 16 words in length. It is to be moved to a destination block, which starts at address 002000_{16}. That is, execution of the program causes the contents of each address in the source block to be copied into the corresponding address in the destination block. For instance, if before the program was executed all storage locations in the source block contained $FFFF_{16}$ and all storage locations in the destination block contained 0000_{16}, at completion of executing the program all storage locations in both blocks would contain $FFFF_{16}$.

Let us assume that the program in Fig. 5.16 is to be entered into memory starting at address 003000_{16}. To do this, a memory modify (MM) command with the DI option specified is first used to bring up the assembler. This is done by issuing the command

TUTOR 1.3 > MM 3000;DI

Tutor responds with

003000   1005   MOVE.B   D5,D0   ?

```
         LEA        $1000,A1      SOURCE BLOCK STARTS AT $1000
         LEA        $2000,A2      DESTINATION BLOCK STARTS AT $2000
         MOVE.L     #16,D0        BLOCK LENGTH EQUALS 16 WORDS
NXTPT    MOVE.W     (A1)+,(A2)+   MOVE WORD AND POINT TO NEXT WORD
         SUBQ.L     #1,D0         UPDATE COUNT
         BNE        NXTPT         REPEAT FOR NEXT WORD
HERE     BRA        HERE
```

Figure 5-16 Block transfer program.

Here we have assumed that the memory location 003000_{16} originally contains 1005_{16}, which when disassembled is the instruction

$$\text{MOVE.B D5,D0}$$

The ? displayed at the end of the disassembled instruction is a prompt for us to enter the new instruction. Now we enter the first instruction of the program preceded by a space. The display appears

003000   1005   MOVE.B   D5,D0 ?   LEA $1000,A1   (cr)

Execution of this command replaces the current contents of address 003000_{16} and prompts for entry of the next instruction. The response displayed on the screen of the terminal is

003000   43F81000   LEA $1000,A1

003004   DC.W $FFFF ?

The next instruction is now entered followed by (cr):

003004 DC.W $FFFF ? LEA $2000,A2   (cr)

In the same way, the rest of the instructions of the program are entered as follows:

003008   DC.W $FFFF   ?   MOVE.L   #16,DO   (cr)

```
    .            .            .       .        .           .        .
    .            .            .       .        .           .        .
    .            .            .       .        .           .        .
```

003014   DC.W $FFFF   ?   BRA *   .   (cr)

Notice that the last instruction is followed by a period and a carriage return. This entry is required to exit the line-by-line assembler. The results produced by assembling this program are shown in Fig. 5.17.

Since the program is entered using a line-by-line assembler, symbols and labels cannot be used. For instance, the label NXTPT in the BNE instruction is replaced by the starting address of the instruction MOVE.W (A1)+,(A2)+, which is 300_{16}. When a forward label reference is encountered, the corresponding addresses may not be available as yet. In this case, the label can be entered as a '*' as a first step. When the rest of the program has been entered, the addresses will be known and the instructions that contain asterisks can be reentered with the correct values of addresses.

```
TUTOR   1.3  >  MM  3000;DI
003000      43F81000            LEA       $1000,A1
003004      45F82000            LEA       $2000,A2
003008      203C00000010        MOVE.L    #16,DO
00300E      34D9                MOVE.W    (A1)+,(A2)+
003010      5380                SUBQ.L    #1,DO
003012      66FA                BNE       $300E
003014      60FE                BRA       *
003016      FFFF                DC.W      $FFFF  ?.


TUTOR   1.3  >
```

Figure 5-17 Assembling the block transfer program into memory.

We can disassemble a series of instructions that are stored at sequential memory addresses by initiating the disassemble process by using the memory display (MD) command. Assuming that the information is to be displayed on the terminal, the general format of the disassemble command is

MD   <address> [<count>];DI

In this command statement, <address> is the starting address of the first instruction in the group of instructions that are to be disassembled; the optional count specifies the number of consecutive bytes that are to be disassembled; and DI selects disassemble mode of operation. For instance, to disassemble the instructions of the program we just loaded into the memory range from address 003000_{16} to 003014_{16}, the command is issued as

TUTOR 1.3 > MD   3000   16;DI

The information that is displayed for this command is shown in Fig. 5.18.

```
TUTOR   1.3  >  MD  3000  16;DI
003000      43F81000            LEA.L     $00001000,A1
003004      45F82000            LEA.L     $00002000,A2
003008      203C00000010        MOVE.L    #16,DO
00300E      34D9                MOVE.W    (A1)+,(A2)+
003010      5380                SUBQ.L    #1,DO
003012      66FA                BNE.S     $00300E
003014      60FE                BRA.S     $003014

TUTOR   1.3  >
```

Figure 5-18 Disassembly of the block–move data transfer program.

Saving and Loading Programs with the Cassette Recorder/Player

The block-move program that we just entered into memory would be lost if we turned off the microcomputer's power. The cassette recorder/player interface is provided as part of the MC68000 educational microcomputer so that a permanent record can be made of a program by recording it on a magnetic tape. In this way, the programmer can simply reload the program from tape the next time it is to be run, instead of having to reenter it from the keyboard.

Three commands are provided for saving, verifying, and loading machine code programs with the cassette recorder/player. These commands are *dump memory* (DU), *verify* (VE), and *load* (LO). Let us now look at how these commands can be used to save the block-move program on cassette and then reload it into the microcomputer's memory.

Earlier, we found that the block-move program was assembled into word addresses in the range 003000_{16} through 003014_{16}. To save this program, we type in the command

TUTOR 1.3 > DU 3000   3014

but do not yet depress the carriage return key. Notice that the command mnemonic is followed by the starting address and ending address of the program. Next the cassette recorder/player must be set up for recording and then started. After the motor of the tape player is up to speed, the carriage return key is depressed. Tutor now reads the program out of memory, formats it for recording, and outputs it to the tape. When the dump memory command is complete, Tutor signals that fact by prompting for another command.

It is a good practice to verify that the program has been correctly recorded on tape. This is one of the intended uses of the verify command. Before issuing a verify command, the tape should be rewound to a point somewhat before the place where the program was recorded. Then the verify command is typed in as

TUTOR 1.3 > VE4

Again, the carriage return key is not yet depressed; instead, the tape is rewound and then the cassette recorder/player is set up to play instead of record and started. When the motor is up to speed, the carriage return key is depressed. Now the microcomputer reads the machine code of the program from tape and compares it to what is held in memory. If no differences are found, the Tutor prompt is simply displayed when the verify operation is complete. However, if any differences are identified, the errors are displayed below the verify command statement. Assuming that the verify operation is performed without detecting any error, a permanent record of the block-move program now exists on tape.

Now that we know how to save machine code programs on cassette tape, let us look into how they can be reloaded from tape into the microcomputer. First, the tape with the program is inserted into the cassette recorder/player and the tape is rewound to a point just prior to the spot where the program was recorded. Next, the load command is typed in as

TUTOR   1.3 > LO4

Now the tape player is set to play mode, and as the motor comes up to full speed the carriage return key is depressed. The microcomputer proceeds to read the program from tape and load it into the appropriate location in memory. The loading of the program can be verified by rewinding the tape and issuing the command

TUTOR 1.3 > VE4   (cr)

Assuming that it verifies correctly, we now can disassemble the program with the command

> TUTOR 1.3 > MD   3000   16;DI   (cr)

This command causes the assembly language source statements to be displayed on the screen of the terminal.

5.9 PROGRAM EXECUTION CONTROL COMMANDS

Once a program has been loaded into the memory of the MC68000 educational microcomputer, it is ready to be executed. By executing the program and then examining the results that it produces, we can verify that it operates correctly. Tutor contains three groups of commands that are specifically provided for controlling the execution of programs: the *trace commands*, the *go commands*, and the *breakpoint commands*. These commands are shown in Fig. 5.19. Let us now look at the operation of the commands in each of these groups and how they can be used to control execution of programs.

Command	Meaning	Format	Explanation
TR	Trace	TR [<count>]	Execute and trace the operation of the specified number of instructions starting with the instruction
T		T [<count>]	pointed to by the current value in PC.
TT	Trace to temporary breakpoint	TT <breakpoint address>	Executes and traces the operation of instructions starting from the current value in PC and continues until either the specified breakpoint address or a prior set breakpoint address is encountered.
GO	Go execute	GO [<address>]	Initiates execution of the program from the specified address or if no address is
G		G [<address>]	included from the current value in PC. Trace information related to instruction execution is displayed and execution is terminated if a set breakpoint address is encountered.

Figure 5-19 Commands for program execution control.

GD	Go execute direct	GD [<address>]	Initiates execution of the program directly from the specified address or if no address is included from the current value in PC. No trace information related to instruction execution is displayed and execution is not terminated if a set breakpoint address is encountered.
GT	Go until breakpoint	GT <breakpoint address>	Initiates execution of the program from the current value in PC. Trace information related to instruction execution is displayed and execution is terminated when either the specified breakpoint address or a prior set breakpoint address is encountered.
BR	Breakpoint set	BR [<address> [;<count>]]. . .	Sets one or more breakpoints by putting the specified addresses into the breakpoint address table.
NOBR	Breakpoint remove	NOBR [<address> <address>. . .]	Removes the breakpoints for the specified addresses.

Figure 5-19 *(Cont.)*

Trace Commands—TR (T) and TT

During the early stages of program development, an operation known as *single-stepping* the program is very useful. By single stepping, we mean that one instruction of the program is executed at a time. The state of the microprocessor's internal registers and data in memory that are affected by the instruction can be examined just before and just after it is executed. In this way, the operation of the program can be verified instruction by instruction. The trace commands are the commands provided in Tutor for single-stepping through a program.

Tutor has two trace commands called *trace* (TR or T) and *trace to temporary breakpoint* (TT). We will begin with the TR command. This command can be used to execute either one or several instructions. To execute one instruction, the command is issued as either

TUTOR 1.3 > TR   (cr)

or just

TUTOR 1.3 > T   (cr)

In response to this command, the microcomputer executes the instruction pointed to by the current value in PC and then it displays the contents of the 68000's internal registers.

In Fig. 5.20, we have initialized PC to the address 003000_{16} and then executed the instruction

LEA.L $1000,A1

with a TR command. The format in which the trace information is displayed for the TR command is shown in Fig. 5.20. Notice that the original value in PC is 00003000_{16}. After executing the TR command, we find that the new value in PC is 00003004_{16} and that A_1 has been loaded with 00001000_{16}. Moreover, the disassembled form of the instruction that starts at this address, which is

LEA.L $2000,A2

is displayed in the last line of information. This type of information allows the programmer to verify easily that the instruction performed the correct operation.

Once a TR command has been issued, Tutor enters what is called the *trace mode*. When in this mode, the prompt is issued as

TUTOR 1.3 :>

Here we see that it now includes a : before the > symbol. This colon tells the programmer that the monitor is in the trace mode. While in trace mode, the next instruction is executed by simply depressing the return key. That is, by making the entry

TUTOR 1.3 : >   (cr)

the instruction at address 00003004_{16} is executed and the new contents of the registers and next instruction are again displayed. To get out of trace mode, just enter any

```
TUTOR   1.3  > .PC 3000

TUTOR   1.3  > DF
PC=00003000  SR=2700=.S7..... US=FFFFFFFF SS=00000756
D0=0000FF0D D1=00000000 D2=12100010 D3=00000000
D4=00000231 D5=00000FFF D6=00000004 D7=00000000
A0=00010040 A1=00001000 A2=00000414 A3=00002500
A4=00009FAC A5=00000540 A6=00000540 A7=00000756
-------------------003000      43F81000           LEA.L    $00001000,A1

TUTOR   1.3  > TR
PHYSICAL ADDRESS=00003000
PC=00003004  SR=2700=.S7..... US=FFFFFFFF SS=00000756
D0=0000FF0D D1=00000000 D2=12100010 D3=00000000
D4=00000231 D5=00000FFF D6=00000004 D7=00000000
A0=00010040 A1=00001000 A2=00000414 A3=00002500
A4=00009FAC A5=00000540 A6=00000540 A7=00000756
-------------------003004      45F82000           LEA.L    $00002000,A2

TUTOR   1.3  :> .PC
.PC=00003004

TUTOR   1.3  >
```

Figure 5-20 Executing an instruction with the trace command.

command after :> and then depress the return key. This entry causes the specified command to be performed and the prompt to be redisplayed as

TUTOR 1.3 >

Notice in the TR command format in Fig. 5.19 that an optional count field can be specified as part of the command. This count is what lets the TR command execute more than one instruction. For instance, the command

TUTOR 1.3 > TR 5   (cr)

executes five instructions. After execution of each instruction, the internal state of the 68000 is displayed.

The second trace command, trace to temporary breakpoint (TT), is used to execute and trace the operation of instructions until what is called a *breakpoint* is reached. A breakpoint is an address that identifies a point in the program where execution is to be stopped. Looking at the format of the TT command in Fig. 5.19, we see that the breakpoint address is specified in the field that follows the command's mnemonic. An example is the command

TUTOR 1.3 > TT   1000   (cr)

This causes all instructions starting from the current value in PC and up to breakpoint address 1000_{16} to be executed. The name of the command implies that the breakpoint is temporary. By this we mean that the breakpoint that is set up by the address specified in the command is automatically cleared after the address is reached and execution stopped.

Go Commands—GD, GO, and GT

The go commands allow us to execute either a whole program or a program as several segments of instructions. For this reason, they are typically used to execute programs that are completely functional or to aid in the later stages of the debugging process. For example, if the early part of a program is already operating correctly, a go command can be used to execute through this group of instructions and stop execution at the point in the program where additional debugging is to begin. The point at which execution is to stop and debugging is to continue is identified by a breakpoint address.

Let us begin with the *go direct* (GD) command. The general format of the GD command is shown in Fig. 5.19. Here we see that the command can be used to begin program execution directly from the current value of PC or from an optional address that is specified in the command. To initiate program execution from the current value in PC, the command is issued as

TUTOR 1.3 > GD   (cr)

After entering this command, the program begins execution and runs to completion or until either the ABORT or RESET switch is depressed. No trace information is displayed as the program runs.

Alternately, the command can be issued with an address in the starting address field. For instance, to start program execution at address 002000_{16}, the command is issued as

$$\text{TUTOR } 1.3 > \text{GD } 2000 \quad \text{(cr)}$$

Looking at Fig. 5.19, we see that the format of the *go* (GO or G) command is identical to that of the GD command. However, its operation differs in two ways from that of the GD command. First, trace information is displayed after execution of the first instruction, and second execution automatically stops if a breakpoint is encountered. Two examples of the GO command are

$$\text{TUTOR } 1.3 > \text{GO} \quad \text{(cr)}$$

and

$$\text{TUTOR } 1.3 > \text{G } 2000 \quad \text{(cr)}$$

The address, 2000_{16}, which is specified in the second go command, is not a breakpoint address. It specifies the point at which program execution is to start. We pointed out earlier that execution initiated with the go command will stop when a breakpoint is reached. This breakpoint must have been set up already by a special breakpoint command.

The last go command, *go until* (GT), has the ability to set a temporary breakpoint and then initiate program execution with the instruction pointed to by the current value in PC. Program execution continues until the temporary breakpoint address is reached, another breakpoint is encountered, or the ABORT or RESET switch is depressed. When execution stops, the temporary breakpoint is cleared.

For example, if we have already set up breakpoints at addresses $00100A_{16}$, 001010_{16}, and 001020_{16}, execution of the command

$$\text{TUTOR } 1.3 > \text{GT } 1006 \quad \text{(cr)}$$

when PC equals 001000_{16} initiates program execution and it continues until address 001006_{16} is reached. At this point in the program, instruction execution stops. By next issuing the command

$$\text{TUTOR } 1.3 > \text{GT } 100C \quad \text{(cr)}$$

program execution resumes down through breakpoint address $00100A_{16}$. In this case, a breakpoint was encountered before reaching the temporary breakpoint. Even though the temporary breakpoint did not cause the break in program execution, it is cleared.

Breakpoint Commands—BR and NOBR

In our description of the trace and go commands, we found that the operation of certain commands in both groups were affected by breakpoints. Remember that a breakpoint is the address of the end of a program segment; that is, the addresss of the first byte of the instruction at which execution is to stop. We found that a temporary breakpoint must be specified directly in both the TT and GT commands. Moreover, if any additional breakpoints already existed, they also would affect the operation of these two commands. On the other hand, we found that the GO command did not specify a temporary breakpoint; instead, it was only affected by breakpoints that were already defined when the command was issued. Commands are provided in Tutor for setting and clearing of breakpoints. Let us next look at the operation of these commands.

The command that is used to set up breakpoints is called *breakpoint set* (BR). The format for this command is shown in Fig. 5.19. Here we find that the address of the breakpoint is simply included after the command's mnemonic. In fact, up to eight breakpoint addresses can be specified and, if desired, they all could be defined with one BR command. An example is the command

$$\text{TUTOR } 1.3 > \text{BR} \quad 100\text{A} \quad 1010 \quad 1020 \quad \text{(cr)}$$

Execution of this command causes addresses $00100A_{16}$, 001010_{16}, and 001020_{16} to be placed into a table called the *breakpoint address table*.

Another way of using the breakpoint command is to enter it as

$$\text{TUTOR } 1.3 > \text{BR} \quad \text{(cr)}$$

In this form, the command causes the locations of all of the currently defined breakpoints to be displayed.

In programs that involve loops, we may want to stop execution at a breakpoint address only after that address has been encountered a specific number of times. For instance, the last time that the loop is repeated. In Fig. 5.19, we find that an optional count can be specified with each breakpoint address in a BR command. This count gives the programmer the ability to execute a program in this way. For instance, the command

$$\text{TUTOR } 1.3 > \text{BR } 1200;5 \quad \text{(cr)}$$

sets up a breakpoint at address 001200_{16} and configures the breakpoint such that it will stop program execution the fifth time the address is encountered.

Unlike the temporary breakpoints defined in a TT or GT command, breakpoint addresses set up with the BR command are not cleared when encountered during the execution of a program with the TT, GO, or GT command. The only way that they may be cleared is if the programmer uses a *remove breakpoint* (NOBR) command. For instance, to remove all breakpoint addresses from the breakpoint table, the command is issued as

$$\text{TUTOR } 1.3 > \text{NOBR} \quad \text{(cr)}$$

However, the NOBR command also can be used to remove specific breakpoints that are no longer needed. For example, to remove just the breakpoints at addresses 001010_{16} and 001020_{16}, the command

$$\text{TUTOR } 1.3 > \text{NOBR } 1010 \quad 1020 \quad \text{(cr)}$$

is used.

5.10 EXECUTING A PROGRAM

By executing a program and examining the results that it produces, we can tell whether or not it performs the operation for which it was written. As discussed earlier, Tutor provides GO and TRACE commands for use in executing programs. Let us now demonstrate how programs can be run on the microcomputer by using the block-move program we assembled into memory in Section 5.8.

Before going any further, let us disassemble the program to verify that it still resides in memory. In Fig. 5.18, we find that the program resides in the address range 3000_{16} through 3014_{16}. Therefore, the program is disassembled with the command

TUTOR 1.3 > MD 3000 16;DI

We will assume that the sequence of assembly language instructions displayed by execution of this command is the same as that shown in Fig. 5.18. Therefore, the complete block-move program is still held in memory.

We still are not ready to run the program on the microcomputer. The internal registers and storage locations in memory that are used by the program must first be initialized. For instance, the status register, the selected stack pointer register, the program counter, and the blocks of data in memory must all be assigned initial values. Let us first display the current contents of all registers with the command

TUTOR 1.3 > DF   (cr)

The information displayed with this command is shown in Fig. 5.21.

Next, we choose to execute the program in the user state. To accomplish this, bit 13 of the status register must be reset. This is done with the command

TUTOR 1.3 > .SR 0704   (cr)

Next, the user stack must be located in memory just below address 004000_{16}. The command needed to do this is

TUTOR 1.3 > .US 4000   (cr)

Remember that the program starts at address 003000_{16}. Therefore, PC is initialized as

TUTOR 1.3 > .PC 3000   (cr)

To verify that the register initialization has been done correctly, we again use the DF command to display the current contents of all of the 68000's registers.

TUTOR 1.3 > DF   (cr)

From the displayed information in Fig. 5.21, we see that the values in SR, US, and PC have been loaded correctly.

We are not yet finished initializing the microcomputer—the blocks of storage locations in memory must still be loaded. The sixteen words in the source block are to be filled with the value $FFFF_{16}$. This is done with the command

TUTOR 1.3 > BF 1000 101E FFFF   (cr)

```
TUTOR  1.3 > DF
PC=00003004 SR=2700=.S7..... US=FFFFFFFF SS=00000756
D0=0000FF0D D1=00000000 D2=12100010 D3=00000000
D4=00000231 D5=00000FFF D6=00000004 D7=00000000
A0=00010040 A1=00001000 A2=00000414 A3=00002500
A4=00009FAC A5=00000540 A6=00000540 A7=00000756
--------------------003004    45F82000           LEA.L    $00002000,A2


TUTOR  1.3 > .SR 0704

TUTOR  1.3 > .US 4000

TUTOR  1.3 > .PC 3000

TUTOR  1.3 > DF
PC=00003000 SR=0704=..7..Z.. US=00004000 SS=00000756
D0=0000FF0D D1=00000000 D2=12100010 D3=00000000
D4=00000231 D5=00000FFF D6=00000004 D7=00000000
A0=00010040 A1=00001000 A2=00000414 A3=00002500
A4=00009FAC A5=00000540 A6=00000540 A7=00004000
--------------------003000    43F81000           LEA.L    $00001000,A1


TUTOR  1.3 > BF 1000 101E FFFF
PHYSICAL ADDRESS=00001000 0000101E


TUTOR  1.3 > BF 2000 201E 0000
PHYSICAL ADDRESS=00002000 0000201E


TUTOR  1.3 > MD 1000 1E
001000    FF FF FF FF FF FF FF FF  FF FF FF FF FF FF FF FF   ................
001010    FF FF FF FF FF FF FF FF  FF FF FF FF FF FF FF FF   ................

TUTOR  1.3 > MD 2000 1E
002000    00 00 00 00 00 00 00 00  00 00 00 00 00 00 00 00   ................
002010    00 00 00 00 00 00 00 00  00 00 00 00 00 00 00 00   ................

TUTOR  1.3 > BR 3014

BREAKPOINTS
003014    003014

TUTOR  1.3 > GO
PHYSICAL ADDRESS=00003000

AT BREAKPOINT
PC=00003014 SR=0704=..7..Z.. US=00004000 SS=00000756
D0=00000000 D1=00000000 D2=12100010 D3=00000000
D4=00000231 D5=00000FFF D6=00000004 D7=00000000
A0=00010040 A1=00001020 A2=00002020 A3=00002500
A4=00009FAC A5=00000540 A6=00000540 A7=00004000
--------------------003014    60FE             BRA.S    $003014

TUTOR  1.3 > MD 1000 1E
001000    FF FF FF FF FF FF FF FF  FF FF FF FF FF FF FF FF   ................
001010    FF FF FF FF FF FF FF FF  FF FF FF FF FF FF FF FF   ................

TUTOR  1.3 > MD 2000 1E
002000    FF FF FF FF FF FF FF FF  FF FF FF FF FF FF FF FF   ................
002010    FF FF FF FF FF FF FF FF  FF FF FF FF FF FF FF FF   ................

TUTOR  1.3 >
```

Figure 5-21 Executing the block–move data transfer program.

On the other hand, the storage locations in the destination block are all to be cleared to zero. To do this, we issue the command

TUTOR 1.3 > BF 2000 201E 0000   (cr)

Finally, the initialization of the blocks of data can be verified by executing the commands

TUTOR 1.3 > MD 1000 1E   (cr)

TUTOR 1.3 > MD 2000 1E   (cr)

By again looking at the displayed information in Fig. 5.21, we find that memory initialization also was correctly done.

Now we are ready to execute the program. Since PC has already been loaded with 003000_{16}, the go command that we use to initiate program execution will not need to specify the starting address of the program. However, to return to the monitor at the end of the program, we must specify the address of the last instruction of the program as a breakpoint address. From the disassembled version of the program in Fig. 5.18, we find that the last instruction is at address 003014_{16}. A breakpoint is set up at this address with the command

TUTOR 1.3 > BR 3014   (cr)

Now the program is executed by issuing the command

TUTOR 1.3 > GO   (cr)

and it runs to completion.

The operation of the program can be verified by looking at the blocks of data in memory. This is done by entering the commands.

TUTOR 1.3 > MD 1000 1E   (cr)

TUTOR 1.3 > MD 2000 1E   (cr)

Looking at the displayed information in Fig. 5.21, we find that all storage locations in both blocks now contain $FFFF_{16}$. Therefore, the contents of the source block have been copied into the destination block.

5.11 DEBUGGING A PROGRAM

In Sections 5.8 and 5.10, we showed how to load a program into the memory of the MC68000 educational microcomputer and how to execute it. Moreover, we verified that when executed the program did perform the block-move data transfer operation for which it was written. However, in practice it is common to have errors in programs, and even a single error can render the program useless. For instance, if the address to which a branch instruction passes control is wrong, the program may get hung up. Errors in a program are also referred to as *bugs*. The process of removing them is called *debugging*.

The two types of errors that can be made by a programmer are *syntax errors* and *execution errors*. A syntax error is an error caused by not following the rules for coding or entering an instruction. These types of errors are typically identified by the microcomputer's assembler or monitor and signaled to the user with error messages. For this reason, they are usually easy to find and correct.

For example, if an instruction is entered as

BEQU.S $3012

an error condition exists. This is because the mnemonic BEQU.S is invalid. The correct instruction is written as

BEQ.S $3012

This incorrect entry is signaled by the Tutor monitor with an error message during assembly.

An execution error is an error in the logic behind the development of the program. That is, the program is correctly coded and entered, but it does not perform the operation for which it was planned. This type of error can be identified by entering the program into the microcomputer and executing it. Even when an execution error problem has been identified, it can be difficult to find the exact cause of the problem.

Our ability to debug execution errors in a program is aided by the commands of the Tutor monitor. For instance, the TR command allows us to step through the program by executing just one instruction at a time. In this way, we can use the register and memory display commands to determine the state of the microcomputer prior to execution of an instruction and again just after its execution. This information will tell us whether the instruction has performed the operation planned for it. If an error is found, the cause can be determined and corrected.

To illustrate the process of debugging a program, let us once again consider the program in Fig. 5.16. Its assembled version is given in Fig. 5.18 and we showed how to enter the program into the microcomputer in Sec. 5.8. Remember that this program implements a block-move data transfer operation. The block of data that is to be moved starts at memory address 001000_{16} and is sixteen words in length. It is to be moved to another block location starting at address 002000_{16}. We will assume that the program already resides in memory starting at address 003000_{16}.

Before executing the program, let us issue commands to initialize the block of memory locations from address 001000_{16} through $00101E_{16}$ with the value $FFFF_{16}$ and those from 002000_{16} through $00201E_{16}$ with zero. As shown in Fig. 5.22, this is done with the command sequence

TUTOR   1.3   >   BF   1000   101E   FFFF   (cr)

TUTOR   1.3   >   BF   2000   201E   0   (cr)

Furthermore, we must initialize the status register, user stack pointer, and the program counter to the values 0704_{16}, 4000_{16}, and 3000_{16}, respectively. To do this, the commands *block fill*   *bytes*

{fills all mem location inclusively with FFFF

```
TUTOR  1.3 > BF 1000 101E FFFF
PHYSICAL ADDRESS=00001000 0000101E

TUTOR  1.3 > BF 2000 201E 0
PHYSICAL ADDRESS=00002000 0000201E
```

{load registers, leading zeros

```
TUTOR  1.3 > .SR 0704
```

user stack or SP

```
TUTOR  1.3 > .US 4000

TUTOR  1.3 > .PC 3000
```

mem display

```
TUTOR  1.3 > MD 1000 1E
001000    FF FF FF FF FF FF FF FF  FF FF FF FF FF FF FF FF   ...............
001010    FF FF FF FF FF FF FF FF  FF FF FF FF FF FF FF FF   ...............

TUTOR  1.3 > MD 2000 1E
002000    00 00 00 00 00 00 00 00  00 00 00 00 00 00 00 00   ...............
002010    00 00 00 00 00 00 00 00  00 00 00 00 00 00 00 00   ...............
```

displays registers

```
TUTOR  1.3 > DF
PC=00003000 SR=0704=..7..Z.. US=00004000 SS=00000786
D0=0000FF00 D1=00000002 D2=10BC5380 D3=00000000
D4=00005330 D5=FFFFFF2C D6=00000002 D7=00000000
A0=00010040 A1=000000C0 A2=00000414 A3=00000554
A4=00009F86 A5=00000540 A6=00000540 A7=00004000
--------------------003000    43F81000           LEA.L   $00001000,A1

TUTOR  1.3 > BR 300E

BREAKPOINTS
00300E     00300E
```

1st   last   *{execution begins at PC value*

```
TUTOR  1.3 > GO
PHYSICAL ADDRESS=00003000
```

{run til brkpt

stops before executing 300E

```
AT BREAKPOINT
PC=0000300E SR=0700=..7..... US=00004000 SS=00000786
```

earlier load?

```
D0=00000010 D1=00000002 D2=10BC5380 D3=00000000
D4=00005330 D5=FFFFFF2C D6=00000002 D7=00000000
A0=00010040 A1=00001000 A2=00002000 A3=00000554
A4=00009F86 A5=00000540 A6=00000540 A7=00004000
--------------------00300E    34D9               MOVE.W  (A1)+,(A2)+

TUTOR  1.3 > T
PHYSICAL ADDRESS=0000300E
```

current addr

```
PC=00003010 SR=0708=..7.N... US=00004000 SS=00000786
D0=00000010 D1=00000002 D2=10BC5380 D3=00000000
D4=00005330 D5=FFFFFF2C D6=00000002 D7=00000000
A0=00010040 A1=00001002 A2=00002002 A3=00000554
A4=00009F86 A5=00000540 A6=00000540 A7=00004000
--------------------003010    5380               SUBQ.L  #1,D0
```

execute til next instruc

```
TUTOR  1.3 :> T
PHYSICAL ADDRESS=00003010
PC=00003012 SR=0700=..7..... US=00004000 SS=00000786
D0=0000000F D1=00000002 D2=10BC5380 D3=00000000
D4=00005330 D5=FFFFFF2C D6=00000002 D7=00000000
A0=00010040 A1=00001002 A2=00002002 A3=00000554
A4=00009F86 A5=00000540 A6=00000540 A7=00004000
--------------------003012    66FA               BNE.S   $00300E
```

Figure 5-22 Demonstration of program debugging.

```
TUTOR  1.3 :> T
PHYSICAL ADDRESS=00003012

AT BREAKPOINT
PC=0000300E SR=0700=..7..... US=00004000 SS=00000786
D0=0000000F D1=00000002 D2=10BC5380 D3=00000000
D4=00005330 D5=FFFFFF2C D6=00000002 D7=00000000
A0=00010040 A1=00001002 A2=00002002 A3=00000554
A4=00009F86 A5=00000540 A6=00000540 A7=00004000
--------------------00300E    34D9          MOVE.W  (A1)+,(A2)+
                    check mem
TUTOR  1.3 :> MD 2000 1E
002000    FF FF 00 00 00 00 00 00   00 00 00 00 00 00 00 00  ................
002010    00 00 00 00 00 00 00 00   00 00 00 00 00 00 00 00  ................

TUTOR  1.3 > GO        {til brkpt
PHYSICAL ADDRESS=0000300E

AT BREAKPOINT
PC=0000300E SR=0700=..7..... US=00004000 SS=00000786
D0=0000000E D1=00000002 D2=10BC5380 D3=00000000
D4=00005330 D5=FFFFFF2C D6=00000002 D7=00000000
A0=00010040 A1=00001004 A2=00002004 A3=00000554
A4=00009F86 A5=00000540 A6=00000540 A7=00004000
--------------------00300E    34D9          MOVE.W  (A1)+,(A2)+

TUTOR  1.3 > MD 2000
002000    FF FF FF FF 00 00 00 00   00 00 00 00 00 00 00 00  ...............

TUTOR  1.3 > NOBR

BREAKPOINTS

TUTOR  1.3 > BR 3014
                    {new brkpt
BREAKPOINTS
003014    003014

TUTOR  1.3 > GO
PHYSICAL ADDRESS=0000300E

AT BREAKPOINT
PC=00003014 SR=0704=..7..Z.. US=00004000 SS=00000786
D0=00000000 D1=00000002 D2=10BC5380 D3=00000000
D4=00005330 D5=FFFFFF2C D6=00000002 D7=00000000
A0=00010040 A1=00001020 A2=00002020 A3=00000554
A4=00009F86 A5=00000540 A6=00000540 A7=00004000
--------------------003014    60FE          BRA.S   $003014

TUTOR  1.3 > MD 2000 1E
002000    FF FF FF FF FF FF FF FF   FF FF FF FF FF FF FF FF  ................
002010    FF FF FF FF FF FF FF FF   FF FF FF FF FF FF FF FF  ................
```

Figure 5-22 *(Cont.)*

TUTOR	1.3	>	.SR	0704	(cr)
TUTOR	1.3	>	.US	4000	(cr)
TUTOR	1.3	>	.PC	3000	(cr)

are issued. The initialization of the microcomputer can be verified using the following memory display and register display commands.

TUTOR	1.3	>	MD	1000	1E	(cr)
TUTOR	1.3	>	MD	2000	1E	(cr)
TUTOR	1.3	>	DF			(cr)

The displayed information in Fig. 5.22 shows that the initialization is correct.

Let us now execute the first three instructions of the program. To do this, we first set a breakpoint at the address of the fourth instruction. In Fig. 5.18, we find that this instruction starts at address $300E_{16}$. The breakpoint is set by issuing the command

TUTOR   1.3 > BR   300E   (cr)

The Tutor response shown in Fig. 5.22 verifies that the breakpoint address has been set. Now the three instructions are executed by issuing the GO command

TUTOR   1.3 > GO   (cr)

At this point, we can verify that registers A_1, A_2, and D_0 have been loaded with 00001000_{16}, 00002000_{16}, and 00000010_{16}, respectively.

The following trace commands are used to execute the next three instructions.

TUTOR	1.3	>	T	(cr)
TUTOR	1.3	>	T	(cr)
TUTOR	1.3	>	T	(cr)

From Fig. 5.22, we find that the first T command executes the instruction

MOVE.W (A1)+, (A2)+

and then displays the contents of the 68000's internal registers. Notice that A_1 now contains 00001002_{16} and A_2 contains 00002002_{16}. Therefore, they point to the second word in the source block and destination block, respectively. The displayed information for the second trace command shows that the contents of D_0 have been decremented by one and that for the third command shows that PC has been reloaded with the address of the instruction

MOVE.W   (A1)+, (A2)+

This completes one iteration of the block transfer loop.

To verify that the source word at 001000_{16} has moved to the destination location at 002000_{16}, we use the memory display command

TUTOR   1.3 > MD   2000   1E   (cr)

The displayed information in Fig. 5.22 shows that word address 2000_{16} now contains $FFFF_{16}$. This confirms that the data transfer has taken place.

At this point the rest of the iterations of the loop can be executed by issuing GO commands. Figure 5.22 shows that first a GO command was issued followed by an MD command. This command sequence did not run the program to completion; instead, the displayed information shows that just the second word of data has been moved into the destination block.

To run the program to completion, we must first remove the breakpoint that exists at address $300E_{16}$ and then set a new one at the address of the last instruction in the program, which is 3014_{16}. This is done with the commands

$$\text{TUTOR} \quad 1.3 \quad > \quad \text{NOBR} \quad \text{(cr)}$$

$$\text{TUTOR} \quad 1.3 \quad > \quad \text{BR} \quad 3014 \text{ (cr)}$$

Now the rest of the program is executed by issuing the command

$$\text{TUTOR} \quad 1.3 > \text{GO} \quad \text{(cr)}$$

To verify that all of the contents of the source block have been moved to the destination block, we use the command

$$\text{TUTOR} \quad 1.3 \quad \text{MD} \quad 2000 \quad 1E \quad \text{(cr)}$$

As shown in Fig. 5.22, all word locations in the destination block contain $FFFF_{16}$ thereby verifying that the program functions correctly.

ASSIGNMENT

Section 5.2

1. What purpose is served by a development system?
2. How much RAM is provided on the MC68000 educational microcomputer for storage of user programs?
3. How many ports are provided on the MC68000 educational microcomputer board for connection of I/O devices?
4. Which I/O port implements the Centronics parallel printer interface? Which port implements a serial communications interface for connection of the terminal?

Section 5.3

5. What is a monitor program? Where is it stored?
6. List the main functions of the Tutor monitor.
7. What size is the MC68000 educational microcomputer's monitor program?

Section 5.4

8. What is meant by a line-by-line assembler/disassembler?
9. Which field of the monitor's command syntax is always required in a command?
10. Describe the difference between an offset register of the monitor and an internal register of the 68000.
11. If $A_0 = 100_{16}$, $D_0 = 200_{16}$, $R_0 = 1000_{16}$, and $R_3 = 2000_{16}$, specify the memory addresses at which execution starts when the commands that follow are issued.

    (a) TUTOR   1.3   >   GO   1000
    (b) TUTOR   1.3   >   GO   100 + R3

(c) TUTOR   1.3   >   GO   (A0)
(d) TUTOR   1.3   >   GO   (A0,D0)

Section 5.5

12. Write a series of commands that will load PC, A_0, D_3, and D_7, with decimal numbers 100, 200, 500, and 800, respectively.

13. If R_0 contains 1000_{16}, what is loaded into R_5 as a result of executing the following commands.
(a) TUTOR   1.3   >   .R0   1000
(b) TUTOR   1.3   >   .R5   1000 + R7

Section 5.6

14. What happens when we issue the following series of commands?
TUTOR   1.3   >   MD   1000   (cr)
TUTOR   1.3   >   (cr)

15. Write a command sequence that will fill the block of memory locations from 1000_{16} through $10FE_{16}$ with the ASCII string ABCD and the block of locations from 2000_{16} through $20FE_{16}$ with data 5555_{16}. Verify the initialization of these two blocks and then move the contents of the block of locations from 1000_{16} through $100F_{16}$ to the block of locations starting at 3000_{16}.

Section 5.7

16. Write a command sequence to set port 2 for one stop bit, two character nulls, and ten carriage return nulls.

17. Wite a command that when issued will set up the MC68000 educational microcomputer so that a host computer can be used to send commands to it.

Section 5.8

18. List two limitations experienced when working with a line-by-line assembler.

19. Show how directives can be used to initialize consecutive memory locations starting at address 1000_{16} with word data $ABCD_{16}$ and 1234_{16}.

20. Which command is used to assemble/disassemble instructions into the memory of the MC68000 educational microcomputer?

Section 5.9

21. Which command is best used to:
(a) Execute one instruction of a program?
(b) Execute an entire program?
(c) Execute a group of instructions in a program?

22. What is the use of a breakpoint during program execution? How can a breakpoint be set?

23. Write a command that will set up a breakpoint at address 1150_{16} so that execution will stop on the tenth occurrence of this address.

Section 5.10

24. Why must some registers be initialized before executing a program?

25. Write a command sequence that when executed initializes PC to point to the beginning of a program which starts at address 2000_{16} and executes the program until the address 2014_{16} is encountered three times. Before beginning execution, the appropriate breakpoint should be set up.

Section 5.11

26. What is the difference between a syntax error and an execution error?

27. How does Tutor provide debugging support?

28. Repeat the debug demonstration presented in Section 5.11, but this time use the TT and GD commands to execute the program.

6

MEMORY AND INPUT/OUTPUT INTERFACES OF THE 68000 MICROPROCESSOR

6.1 INTRODUCTION

The preceding four chapters were devoted to the architecture of the 68000, its instruction set, and assembly language programming. In this chapter we study the *memory and input/output interfaces* of this microprocessor together with the instructions that are provided to implement stack and I/O operations. In particular, the following topics are the subject of this chapter:

1. The asynchronous memory and I/O interface
2. Address space
3. Data organization
4. Dedicated and general use of memory
5. Program and data storage memory
6. Memory function codes
7. Memory and I/O read and write cycles
8. User and supervisor stacks
9. 64K-byte software refreshed dynamic RAM subsystem
10. I/O instruction—MOVEP
11. 6821 peripheral interface adapter
12. Asynchronous bus interface I/O circuitry
13. Synchronous memory and I/O interface
14. Synchronous bus I/O interface circuitry

15. Serial communication interface

16. The 6850 asynchronous communications interface adapter

17. Special purpose interface controllers

6.2 ASYNCHRONOUS MEMORY AND I/O INTERFACE

The *asynchronous memory and input/output interface* of the 68000 is shown in Fig. 6.1. It consists of the address bus, data bus, function code bus, and control bus. The address and data buses of the 68000 are *demultiplexed*. That is, they do not share pins on the package of the IC. The advantage of this is that the interface circuitry between microprocessor and memory is simplified.

Moreover, in the 68000 microcomputer I/O devices are always *memory-mapped*. By this, we mean that memory and I/O do not have separate address spaces. Instead, the designer allocates a part of the memory address space to the I/O devices. Therefore, both memory and I/O are accessed in the same way through the asynchronous bus interface.

We have indicated several times that the bus between the 68000 and memory or I/O is *asynchronous*. By "asynchronous" we mean that once a bus cycle is initiated to read (input) or write (output) instructions or data, it is not completed until a response is provided by the memory or I/O subsystem. This response is an acknowledge signal that tells the 68000 that it should complete its current bus cycle. For this reason, the timing of the bus cycle in a 68000 microcomputer system can be easily matched to slow memories or I/O devices. This results in efficient use of the system bus.

6.3 ADDRESS SPACE AND DATA ORGANIZATION

Notice in Fig. 6.1 that the address bus of the 68000 consists of 23 independent address lines, which are labeled A_1 through A_{23}. The address information output on these lines selects the storage location in memory or the I/O device that is to be accessed. With this large 23-bit address, the 68000 is capable of generating 8M unique addresses. As shown in Fig. 6.2, they represent a *word address space* in the address range 000000_{16} through $FFFFFE_{16}$. Here we see that word information such as instructions, word operands, or long-word operands must always be aligned at even address boundaries.

Coupling the upper data strobe ($\overline{UDS}$) and lower data strobe ($\overline{LDS}$) control signals with this address bus gives the 68000 the ability to access bytes of data. Figure 6.3 illustrates how these two signals can be used to enable *byte-wide upper* and *lower data banks* in memory. Address lines A_1 through A_{23} are applied in parallel to both memory banks.

From an address point of view, memory can now be considered to be organized as bytes, and as shown in Fig. 6.4, bytes of data can be stored at odd or even addresses.

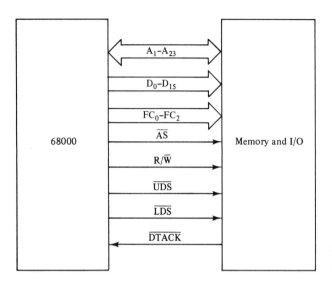

Figure 6-1 Asynchronous memory and I/O interface.

Word Addresses   Memory Contents

Word Addresses	Memory Contents
000000_{16}	Word 0
000002_{16}	Word 1
000004_{16}	Word 2
$FFFFFC_{16}$	Word 8,388,606
$FFFFFE_{16}$	Word 8,388,607

24-bit address

Figure 6-2 Word address space.

When expressed in this way, the size of the *physical address space* is said to be 16M bytes.

The address strobe ($\overline{AS}$) control signal is output by the 68000 along with the address on A_1 through A_{23}. It is used to signal memory and I/O devices that valid address information is available on the bus.

In Fig. 6.1 we find a second bus between the 68000 and the memory or I/O device. It is the data bus and consists of the 16 bidirectional data lines D_0 through D_{15}. Data are input to the microprocessor over these lines during read (input) operations and are output by the processor over these lines during write (output) operations.

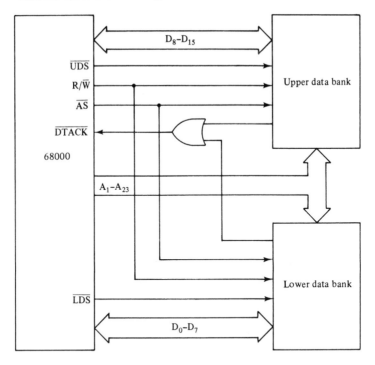

Figure 6-3 Memory organized as upper and lower data banks.

Even Byte Addresses	Memory Contents		Odd Byte Addresses
hi lo 000000_{16}	Byte 0	Byte 1	000001_{16}
000002_{16}	Byte 2	Byte 3	000003_{16}
000004_{16}	Byte 4	Byte 5	000005_{16}
.	.	.	.
$FFFFFE_{16}$	Byte 16,777,214	Byte 16,777,215	$FFFFFF_{16}$

Figure 6-4 Byte address space.

The control signals that coordinate the data transfers that take place between the 68000 and memory or I/O devices are also shown in Fig. 6.1. They are the read/write ($R/\overline{W}$) output and the data transfer acknowledge ($\overline{DTACK}$) input. The 68000 sets $R/\overline{W}$ to the appropriate logic level to tell external circuitry whether data are being input or output by the microprocessor during the current bus cycle.

On the other hand, $\overline{\text{DTACK}}$ acknowledges that the transfer between microprocessor and memory or I/O subsystem has taken place. When the 68000 executes a read operation, it always waits until the $\overline{\text{DTACK}}$ input goes active before completing the bus cycle. $\overline{\text{DTACK}}$ is asserted by the memory or I/O device when the data it has put on the bus are valid. In response to $\overline{\text{DTACK}}$ equal to 0, the 68000 latches in the data from the bus and completes the read cycle. During a write operation, $\overline{\text{DTACK}}$ indicates to the 68000 that data have been written; therefore, it terminates the bus cycle.

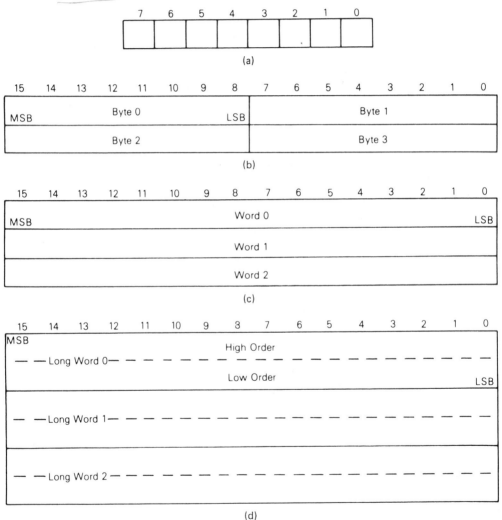

Figure 6-5 Data organization in memory (Motorola, Inc.).

Remember that most of the instructions in the instruction set of the 68000 have the ability to process operands expressed in *byte, word*, or *long-word formats*. Let us now look at how data expressed in these forms are stored in memory. From Fig. 6.5(a), we see that within a byte of data bit 0 represents the least significant bit and bit 7 represents the most significant bit. Next, Fig. 6.5(b) shows that two bytes of data can be stored at each word address. Notice that even-addressed bytes such as byte 0 and byte 2 are stored in most significant byte locations and odd-addressed bytes such as byte 1 and byte 3 are stored in least significant byte locations. Figure 6.5(c) and (d) show that a word is simply stored at each word address and that a long word is stored at two consecutive word addresses.

Looking at the memory subsystem hardware configuration in Fig. 6.3, we see that for an addressed word storage location the upper 8 bits of the word are in the upper data bank. This is the even byte and it is transferred between memory and microprocessor over data bus lines D_8 through D_{15}. The lower 8 bits of the word, the odd byte, are in the lower data bank. They are transferred between microprocessor and memory over D_0 through D_7.

For a word transfer to take place over the bus, both $\overline{UDS}$ and $\overline{LDS}$ must be active at the same time. Therefore, they are both switched to the 0 logic level. Moreover, the direction in which data are transferred is identified by the logic level of $R/\overline{W}$. For instance, if the word of data is to be written into memory, $R/\overline{W}$ is set to logic 0. $\overline{UDS}$ and $\overline{LDS}$ can also be set to access just the upper byte or lower byte of data. In this case, either $\overline{UDS}$ or $\overline{LDS}$ remains at its inactive 1 logic level.

Figure 6.6 summarizes the types of data transfers that can take place over the data bus and the corresponding control signal logic levels. For example, when an even byte is read from the high memory bank $\overline{UDS} = 0$, $\overline{LDS} = 1$, $R/\overline{W} = 1$ and data are transferred from memory to the 68000 over data lines D_8 through D_{15}.

$\overline{UDS}$	$\overline{LDS}$	$R/\overline{W}$	D8-D15	D0-D7
High	High	—	No valid data	No valid data
Low	Low	High	Valid data bits 8-15	Valid data bits 0-7
High	Low	High	No valid data	Valid data bits 0-7
Low	High	High	Valid data bits 8-15	No valid data
Low	Low	Low	Valid data bits 8-15	Valid data bits 0-7
High	Low	Low	Valid data bits 0-7	Valid data bits 0-7
Low	High	Low	Valid data bits 8-15	Valid data bits 8-15

Figure 6-6 Relationship between bus control signals and data bus transfers (Motorola, Inc.).

6.4 DEDICATED AND GENERAL USE MEMORY

Now that we have introduced the memory interface of the 68000, its address space, and data organization, let us continue by looking at which parts of the address space have dedicated uses and which parts are for general use. In Fig. 6.7 we see that the lower end of the address space has a *dedicated function*. That is, the word storage locations over the address range from 000000_{16} to $0003FE_{16}$ are allocated for storage of an address vector table. As shown, it contains the 68000's exception vector table. Each vector address is 24 bits long and takes up two words of memory. An example of 68000 exceptions are its hardware interrupts. The exception processing capability of the 68000 is the subject of Chapter 7.

From the *memory map* in Fig. 6.7 we see that the rest of the address space is for *general use*. Therefore, it can be used to store instructions of the program, data operands, or address information.

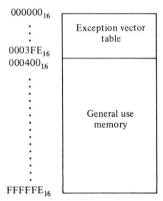

000000_{16}

$0003FE_{16}$
000400_{16}

Exception vector table

General use memory

$FFFFFE_{16}$

Figure 6-7 Memory map.

6.5 PROGRAM AND DATA STORAGE MEMORY AND THE FUNCTION CODES

In the preceding section, we showed how the memory address space of the 68000 is partitioned into a dedicated use area and a general use area. Another way of partitioning the memory subsystem in a 68000 microcomputer system is in terms of *program and data storage memory*. In general, the program segment of memory contains the opcodes of the instructions in the program, direct addresses of operands, and data of immediate source operands. It can be implemented with ROM or RAM.

On the other hand, the data segment is generally implemented with RAM. This is because it contains data operands that are to be processed by the instructions. Therefore, it must be able to be read from or written into.

During all bus cycles to memory, the 68000 outputs bus status codes to indicate whether it is accessing program or data memory. The bus status code is known as the *function code* and is output on function code bus lines FC_0 through FC_2. The

Function code output			Reference class
FC_2	FC_1	FC_0	
0	0	0	(Unassigned)
0	0	1	User data
0	1	0	User program
0	1	1	(Unassigned)
1	0	0	(Unassigned)
1	0	1	Supervisor data
1	1	0	Supervisor program
1	1	1	Interrupt acknowledge

Figure 6-8 Memory function codes (Motorola, Inc.).

table in Fig. 6.8 lists all function codes output by the 68000 and the corresponding type of bus cycle. Notice that program and data memory accesses are further categorized based on whether they occur when the 68000 is in the user state or supervisor state. For instance, an instruction acquisition bus cycle performed when the 68000 is in the user state is accompanied by the function code $FC_2FC_1FC_0 = 010$, but the same type of access when in the supervisor state is accompanied by $FC_2FC_1FC_0 = 110$.

One use of the function codes is to partition the memory subsystem hardware. This can be done by decoding the function codes in external logic to produce enable signals for the *user program segment, user data segment, supervisor program segment*, and *supervisor data segment*.

One approach is illustrated in Fig. 6.9. Here the memory subsystem has been partitioned into a user memory segment and a supervisor memory segment. Looking

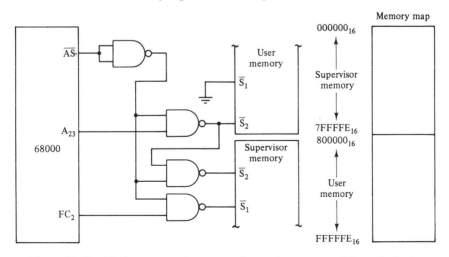

Figure 6-9 Partitioning memory into user and supervisor segments (Motorola, Inc.).

at Fig. 6.8, we see that the logic level of function code line FC_2 indicates whether the 68000 is in the user or supervisor state. Notice that in this circuit FC_2 is gated with address strobe $\overline{AS}$ to produce select input $\overline{S}_1$ for the supervisor memory bank. In this way, the 68000 can access either the user or supervisor memory banks when it is in the supervisor state, but when it is in the user state the supervisor memory bank is locked out.

Another approach would be to partition the memory subsystem such that it has an independent 16M-byte program memory segment and a 16M-byte data memory segment. This expands the address space of the 68000 to 32M bytes in a segmented fashion.

6.6 MEMORY AND I/O READ CYCLE TIMING

To read a word or byte from an input device or memory, the signal lines that are used are address lines A_1 through A_{23}, data lines D_0 through D_{15}, and asynchronous control lines: address strobe ($\overline{AS}$), upper and lower data strobes ($\overline{UDS}$ and $\overline{LDS}$), read/write ($R/\overline{W}$), and data transfer acknowledge ($\overline{DTACK}$). Figure 6.10(a) is a flowchart that shows the sequence of events that take place in order to read a byte of data from the memory subsystem in Fig. 6.3. A timing diagram for an upper bank *read bus cycle* is shown in Fig. 6.10(b).

From the timing diagram, we see that a read cycle can be completed in as few as four clock cycles. Each clock cycle consists of a high and low state for a total of eight states. They are labeled S_0 through S_7 in the timing diagram. With the 100-ns clock cycle of the 10-MHz 68000, this gives a minimum read bus cycle time of 400 ns.

In Fig. 6.10(a) we see that the read bus cycle begins with $R/\overline{W}$ being switched to logic 1. As shown in Fig. 6.10(b), this happens at the leading edge of state S_0. During S_0, a function code $FC_2FC_1FC_0$ is output and address lines A_1 through A_{23} are put in the high-Z state. Next the address is output during the S_1 state followed by address strobe $\overline{AS}$ and the appropriate data strobes during S_2. In our example, we are to read only the upper byte; therefore, $\overline{UDS}$ is switched to its active 0 logic level. The address phase of the bus cycle is now complete.

Next the memory or I/O subsystem must decode the address and put the selected data on bus lines D_8 through D_{15}. This must happen during S_3. Then in S_4 it must assert $\overline{DTACK}$ by switching it to logic 0. This signals the 68000 that valid data are on the bus and that the bus cycle should be continued through to completion.

$\overline{DTACK}$ is tested by the 68000 during S_5. If it is active (logic 0), data are read off the bus at the end of S_6. During S_7, the 68000 returns $\overline{AS}$ and $\overline{UDS}$ to their inactive logic levels and the address bus and data lines to the high-Z state. Moreover, the memory or I/O subsystem must return $\overline{DTACK}$ to the 1 level before another bus cycle can be initiated.

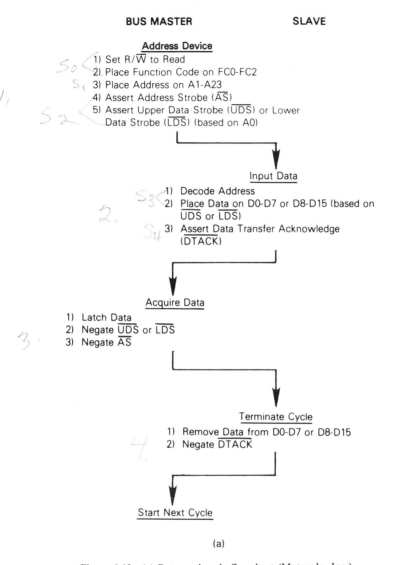

BUS MASTER   **SLAVE**

Address Device
1) Set R/$\overline{\text{W}}$ to Read
2) Place Function Code on FC0-FC2
3) Place Address on A1-A23
4) Assert Address Strobe ($\overline{\text{AS}}$)
5) Assert Upper Data Strobe ($\overline{\text{UDS}}$) or Lower
   Data Strobe ($\overline{\text{LDS}}$) (based on A0)

Input Data
1) Decode Address
2) Place Data on D0-D7 or D8-D15 (based on
   $\overline{\text{UDS}}$ or $\overline{\text{LDS}}$)
3) Assert Data Transfer Acknowledge
   (DTACK)

Acquire Data
1) Latch Data
2) Negate $\overline{\text{UDS}}$ or $\overline{\text{LDS}}$
3) Negate $\overline{\text{AS}}$

Terminate Cycle
1) Remove Data from D0-D7 or D8-D15
2) Negate $\overline{\text{DTACK}}$

Start Next Cycle

(a)

Figure 6-10   (a) Byte read cycle flowchart (Motorola, Inc.).

If the 68000 finds $\overline{\text{DTACK}}$ not asserted during S_5, it inserts wait clock cycles until $\overline{\text{DTACK}}$ goes low to indicate that valid data are on the data bus.

Accesses of byte or word data require execution of one bus cycle by the 68000. On the other hand, long-word accesses require two words of data to be transferred over the bus. Therefore, they take two bus cycles.

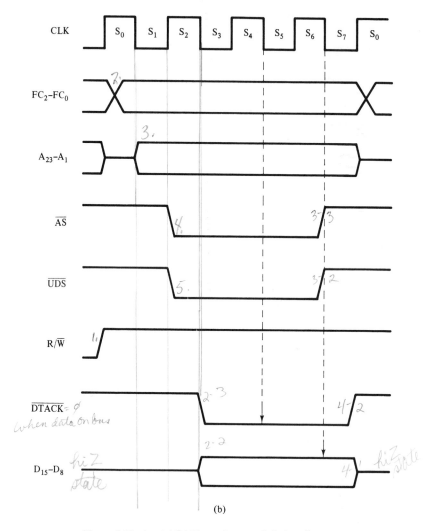

Figure 6-10 *(cont.)* (b) Upper byte read timing diagram.

6.7 MEMORY AND I/O WRITE CYCLE TIMING

To write a word or a byte of data to memory or an I/O device, the same basic interface signals we identified for the read operation are used. The flowchart and timing diagram for a bus cycle that writes a word of data are shown in Fig. 6.11(a) and (b), respectively. Here we see that a minimum of five clock cycles, which equals 10 states S_0 through S_9, are required to perform a *write bus cycle*. At 10 MHz this takes 500 ns.

Looking at Fig. 6.11(a), we see that the bus cycle begins with a function code being output on the FC bus during S_0. The address lines that are floating during S_0 are asserted with a valid address during S_1 and $\overline{AS}$ and R/$\overline{W}$ go active during S_2.

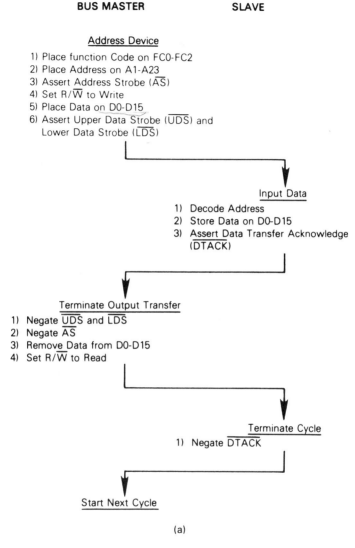

Figure 6-11   (a) Word write cycle flowchart (Motorola, Inc.).

This time, R/$\overline{\text{W}}$ is set to 0 to indicate that a write operation is to take place and data are output on the complete bus D_0 through D_{15} during S_3.

Selection of byte or word data is made by the 68000 asserting the data strobe signals. For a word access, both $\overline{\text{UDS}}$ and $\overline{\text{LDS}}$ are switched to their active 0 logic level. This is done during the S_4 state.

Up to this point, the 68000 has output the address of the storage location and put the data on the bus. External circuitry must now decode the address to select the memory location or I/O device. Then the data, which were put on the bus during

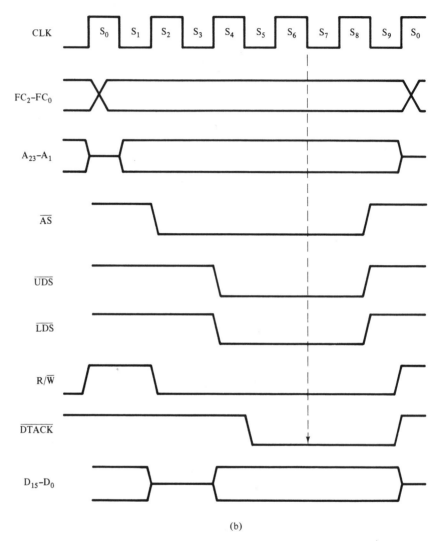

(b)

Figure 6-11 *(cont.)* (b) Timing diagram for word write

S_3, are written into the enabled device during S_4. After the write of data has been completed, the memory or I/O device must inform the 68000 of this condition by pulling $\overline{DTACK}$ to its active 0 logic level. DTACK is tested by the 68000 at the beginning of S_7 and if it is not asserted, wait clock cycles are inserted between the S_6 and S_7 states. This extends the duration of the write cycle. However, if $\overline{DTACK}$ is found to be at its active 0 level, $\overline{UDS}$, $\overline{LDS}$, and $\overline{AS}$ are returned to their inactive 1 logic levels at the beginning of the S_9 state. Furthermore, at the end of S_9, the address and data lines are returned to the high-Z state and $R/\overline{W}$ is switched to 1.

Before the S_0 state of the next bus cycle, $\overline{\text{DTACK}}$ must be returned to logic 1. However, this is done by the memory or I/O subsystem, not the 68000.

6.8 THE USER AND SUPERVISOR STACKS

The 68000 employs a stack-oriented architecture. In Chapter 2 we indicated that the 68000 has two internal stack pointer registers and that these stack pointers are called the user stack pointer (USP) and supervisor stack pointer (SSP). As shown in Fig. 6.12, the addresses held in these registers point to the top storage locations in their respective stacks: that is, their tops of stacks. The storage locations identified as bottom of stack represent the locations pointed to by the initial values loaded into the stack pointers. When the stacks are empty, the stack pointers point to these locations. The *user stack* is active whenever the 68000 is in the user state and the *supervisor stack* is active whenever it is in the supervisor state. Both stacks can be located in memory anywhere in the address space of the 68000, and they are not limited in size.

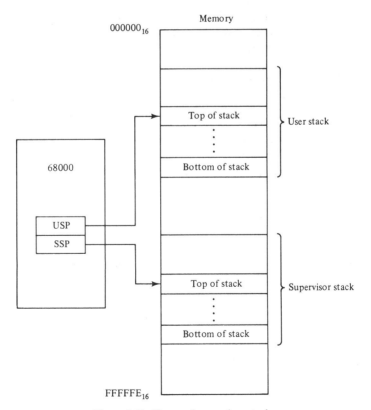

Figure 6-12 User and supervisor stacks.

During exception processing or subroutine calls, the contents of certain internal registers of the 68000 are saved on the stack. For instance, when exception processing is initiated for a hardware interrupt, the current contents of the program counter (PC) and status register (SR) are automatically pushed to the stack. In this way, they are temporarily saved.

Additional stack operations are usually performed as part of the exception processing service routine or subroutine. These are push operations that save the contents of registers that are to be used within the service routine on the stack. For instance, instructions in a hardware interrupt service routine can cause the contents of data registers D_0, D_1, and D_2 to be pushed to the user stack. One way of doing this is with the instruction sequence

$$\text{MOVE.W}\quad \text{D2}, -(\text{USP})$$

$$\text{MOVE.W}\quad \text{D1}, -(\text{USP})$$

$$\text{MOVE.W}\quad \text{D0}, -(\text{USP})$$

These examples all push word data to the user stack. Byte data also can be pushed to the stack. However, each byte also consumes one word of stack. The byte of data is stored in the most significant byte location of the word storage location and the least significant byte is not affected.

At the completion of processing of the exception routine, the saved contents of internal registers can be restored by popping them from the stack. When pushing or popping a number of registers, the move multiple (MOVEM) instruction can be used to perform the operation efficiently. For example, the instruction

$$\text{MOVEM}\quad (\text{USP})+, \text{D0/D1/D2}$$

would restore the contents of D_0, D_1, and D_2 from the user stack.

Moreover, the return instructions for exception processing and subroutines cause automatic reloading of some internal registers. An example is the *return from exception* (RTE) instruction. It causes the contents of both PC and SR to be restored from the top of the stack.

6.9 64K-BYTE SOFTWARE-REFRESHED DYNAMIC RAM SUBSYSTEM

The circuit diagram in Fig. 6.13 shows one way of implementing a dynamic RAM subsystem for a 68000 microcomputer system. This circuit is designed to provide 64K bytes of memory which are mapped into the address range 008000_{16} through $017FFF_{16}$ of the 68000's address space.

Due to the large memory support capability of the 68000, it is essential to buffer all of the memory interface signals. This is done by the leftmost group of circuits in Fig. 6.13. For example, two 74245 devices are used to buffer bidirectional data bus lines D_0 through D_{15} and two 74LS244 devices are used to buffer address lines A_1 through A_{16}. These buffers increase the drive capability of the address and data buses over that supplied directly by the lines of the 68000.

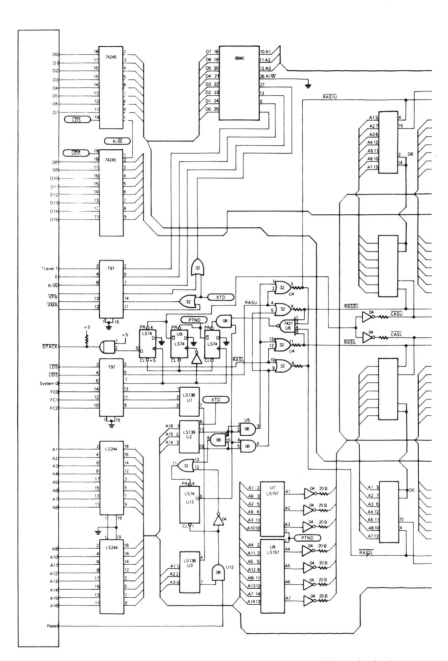

Figure 6-13 Software-refreshed dynamic RAM subsystem (Motorola, Inc.).

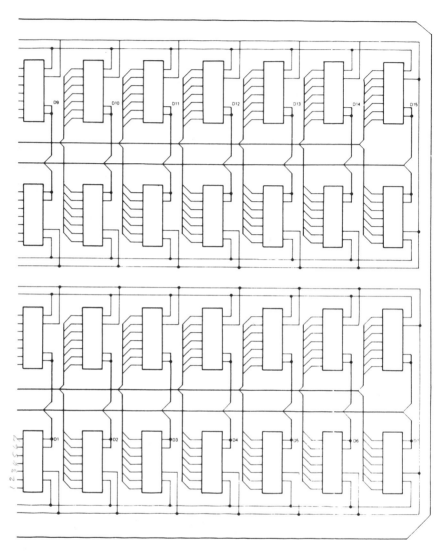

Figure 6-13 *(cont.)*

Let us next look at the storage array of the memory subsystem. It is located at the right of the circuit diagram and employs thirty-two 16K by 1 dynamic RAMs. The type of memory device used is the MCM4116. The circuit is set up to implement a structure similar to that shown in Fig. 6.3. The upper 16 devices form a 32K-byte upper data bank. This bank is used to store even-addressed bytes of data and they are transferred between microprocessor and memory over data bus lines D_8 through D_{15}. The lower 16 devices form a 32K-byte lower data bank. It stores odd bytes of data which are carried between the 68000 and memory over data lines D_0 through D_7.

Since dynamic RAMs are in use instead of static RAMs, the address output by the 68000 on A_1 through A_{14} must be multiplexed into separate row and column addresses before it can be applied to the memory devices. In Fig. 6.13 we see that these address lines are input to two 74LS157 multiplexers which produce 7-bit row and column addresses at their outputs, A_1 through A_7. The timing of the address output on these lines is determined by the PTND output of a 74LS74 flip-flop in IC U_9.

Both bank and byte/word selection is performed through the generation of $\overline{\text{RAS}}$ signals. Notice that the control logic implemented with ICs U_2, U_4, U_5, and U_9 produces four RAS signals. They are denoted as $\overline{\text{RAS}}_{1U}$, $\overline{\text{RAS}}_{2U}$, $\overline{\text{RAS}}_{1L}$, and $\overline{\text{RAS}}_{2L}$. Also, two CAS signals, $\overline{\text{CAS}}_U$ and $\overline{\text{CAS}}_L$, are produced by this section of circuitry. The inputs from which the row select and column select signals are derived are address bits A_{14} through A_{16}, upper and lower data select $\overline{\text{UDS}}$ and $\overline{\text{LDS}}$, and the system clock SYSTEM 0.

For example, to perform a word access from the group 1 RAMs, both $\overline{\text{LDS}}$ and $\overline{\text{UDS}}$ are logic 0. This makes both the $\overline{\text{RAS}}_L$ and $\overline{\text{RAS}}_U$ signals active. At the same time, the address code $A_{16}A_{15}A_{14}$ is decoded by ICs U_2 and U_5 to enable both $\overline{\text{RAS}}_{1U}$ and $\overline{\text{RAS}}_{1L}$ to the memory array. These signals are synchronized to the output of the row address from the multiplexer. A short time later, the $\overline{\text{CAS}}_U$ and $\overline{\text{CAS}}_L$ signals are produced. They are synchronized to the output of the column address from the multiplexer.

Notice that the data acknowledge ($\overline{\text{DTACK}}$) signal is also produced by this section of control logic. It is buffered and then sent to the 68000.

This memory subsystem employs *software refresh* and not *hardware refresh*. The 6840 device is provided for this purpose. It contains a timer that is set up to initiate an interrupt to the 68000 every 1.9 ms. This interrupt has a priority level of 7 and execution of its service routine performs the software-refresh function. The advantage of software refresh is that the interface hardware is simplified. However, it also has a disadvantage—the software and time overhead required to perform the refresh operation.

6.10 AN I/O INSTRUCTION—MOVEP

The 68000 microprocessor has one instruction that is specifically designed for communicating with LSI peripherals that interface over an 8-bit data bus. It is the *move peripheral data* (MOVEP) instruction. An example of an LSI peripheral that can be used in the 68000 microcomputer system is the *6821 peripheral interface adapter* (PIA). Internal to this device is a group of byte-wide control registers. When the device is built into the microcomputer system, these registers will all reside at either odd addresses or even addresses. This poses a problem if we attempt to make multibyte transfers by specifying word or long-word data operands. For instance, a MOVE instruction for word data would cause the two bytes to be transferred to consecutive byte addresses, one of which is even and the other is odd. This problem is overcome by using the MOVEP instruction.

The general formats of the instruction are

$$\text{MOVEP} \quad \text{Dn,d(An)}$$

and

$$\text{MOVEP} \quad \text{d(An),Dn}$$

The first form of the instruction is for output of data. It copies the contents of a source operand that is in data register D_n to the location at the effective address specified by the destination operand. Notice that the destination operand must always be specified using address register indirect with displacement addressing.

As an example, let us write an instruction that will transfer a word of data that is in D_0 to two consecutive output ports. Assume that the contents of A_0 are 16000_{16} and it is a pointer to the first of a group of eight byte-wide registers in an LSI peripheral. These registers are at consecutive even addresses. That is, register 0 is at address 16000_{16}, register 1 at 16002_{16}, and so on. We want to transfer data to the last two of these registers, registers 6 and 7. The displacement of register 6 from the address in A_0 is C_{16}; therefore, the instruction is

$$\text{MOVEP.W} \quad \text{D0,12(A0)}$$

Execution of this instruction causes the bytes of the word contents of D_0 to be output to two consecutive even-byte addresses. The most significant byte is output to the effective destination address, which is $1600C_{16}$. This is register 6. Then the address is incremented by 2 to give $1600E_{16}$ and the least significant byte is output to register 7. The pointer address in A_0 remains unchanged.

A MOVEP instruction that employs long-word operands operates in a similar way except that it would output four bytes to consecutive odd or even addresses. As an example, let us assume that four byte-wide input ports are located at odd-byte addresses 16001_{16}, 16003_{16}, 16005_{16}, and 16007_{16}. The data at these 32 input lines can be read into a data register by executing a single MOVEP instruction. If A_1 contains a pointer to the first input port, the long word of data can be input to D_1 with the instruction

$$\text{MOVEP.L} \quad \text{0(A1),D1}$$

6.11 THE 6821 PERIPHERAL INTERFACE ADAPTER

In the 68000 microcomputer system, parallel input/output ports can be implemented by using the 6821 peripheral interface adapter (PIA). The 6821 is one of the simpler LSI peripherals that is designed for implementing parallel input/output. It has two byte-wide I/O ports called A and B. Each line at both of these ports can be independently configured as an input or output.

Figure 6.14 is a block diagram that shows the internal architecture of the 6821 device. Here we find six programmable registers. They include an *output register* (OR), *data direction register* (DDR), and *control register* (CR) for each of the I/O ports. Let us overview the function of each of these registers before going on.

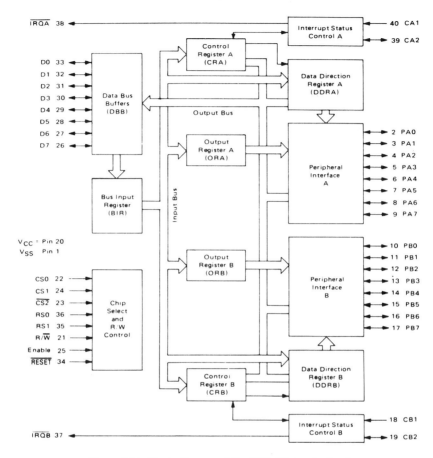

Figure 6-14 Block diagram of the 6821 (Motorola, Inc.).

All input/output data transfers between the microprocessor and PIA take place through the output data registers. These registers are 8 bits wide and their bits correspond to the I/O port lines. For example, to set the logic level of an output line at port A to logic 1, we simply write logic 1 into the corresponding bit in port A's output register.

Each I/O line of the 6821 also has a bit corresponding to it in the A or B data direction register. The logic level of this bit decides whether the corresponding line works as an input or an output. Logic 0 in a bit position selects input mode of operation for the corresponding I/O line and logic 1 selects output operation. For instance, port A can be configured as a byte-wide output port by initializing its data direction register with the value FF_{16}.

The control register (CR) serves three main functions. First, it is used to configure the operation of *control inputs* CA_1, CA_2, CB_1, and CB_2. A second function is that it can be read by the 68000 to identify control status. However, its third function is what we are interested in right now. This is how it is used to select between the

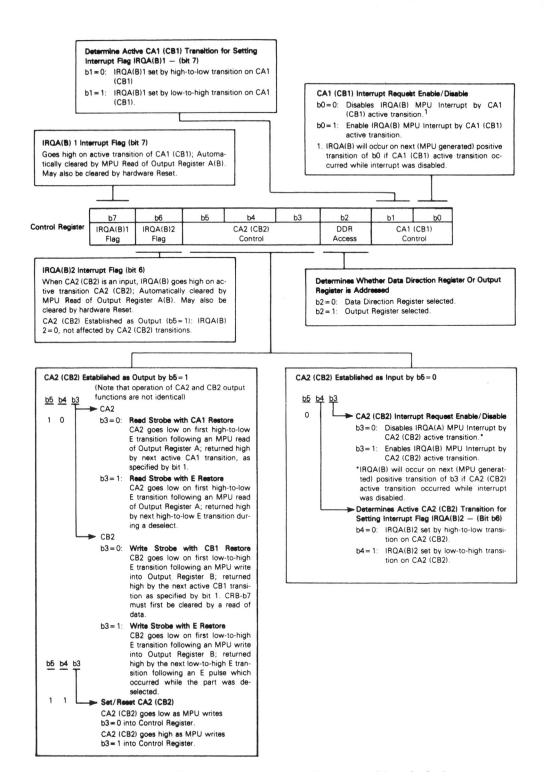

Figure 6-15 Control register bit functions (Motorola, Inc.).

DDR and OR registers when they are loaded or read by the 68000. In Fig. 6.15 we see that the logic level of bit b_2 in CR selects DDR when it is zero and OR when it is 1.

Looking at Fig. 6.14, we find that the microprocessor interface of the 6821 is shown on the left. The key signals here are the eight *data bus lines* D_0 through D_7. It is over these lines that the 68000 can initialize the registers of the 6821, write commands to the control registers, read status from the control registers, and read from or write into the peripheral data registers. The direction in which data are to be transferred is signaled to the 6821 by the logic level of R/$\overline{W}$. For example, logic 0 on R/$\overline{W}$ indicates that data are to be written into one of its registers.

Even though the 6821 has six addressable registers, only two *register select lines* have been provided. They are labeled RS_0 and RS_1. The table in Fig. 6.16 shows how they are used together with bit b_2 of the control registers to select the internal registers. Notice that if both RS_1 and RS_0 are logic 0, the data direction register and output register for port A are selected. As we pointed out earlier, the setting of b_2 in the A control register selects between the two registers. For instance, if this bit is logic 0, the data transfer takes place between the microprocessor and the DDR for port A. In this way we see that bit 2 in control register A must be set to select the appropriate register before initiating the data transfer.

| RS1 | RS0 | Control Register Bit | | Location Selected |
		CRA-2	CRB-2	
0	0	1	X	Peripheral Register A
0	0	0	X	Data Direction Register A
0	1	X	X	Control Register A
1	0	X	1	Peripheral Register B
1	0	X	0	Data Direction Register B
1	1	X	X	Control Register B

X - Don't Care

Figure 6-16 User-accessible register selection (Motorola, Inc.).

As part of the microprocessor interface, there are also three *chip select inputs*. They are labeled CS_0, CS_1, and $\overline{CS_2}$ and must be 1, 1, and 0, respectively, to enable the microprocessor interface.

At the right side of the 6821 block diagram in Fig. 6.14, we find the A and B byte-wide I/O ports. The individual I/O lines at these ports are labeled PA_0 through PA_7 and PB_0 through PB_7, respectively.

Two more lines are associated with each I/O port. They are control lines. For instance, looking at the A port, we find control lines CA_1 and CA_2. Notice that CA_1 is a dedicated output, but CA_2 is bidirectional and can be configured to operate as either an input or an output. The mode of operation of these control lines are determined by the settings of the bits in port A's control register.

These control lines permit the user of the 6821 to implement a variety of different *I/O handshake mechanisms*. For example, port A could be configured for a *strobed mode* of operation. If this is the case, a pulse is output at CA_2 whenever new data are available at PA_0 through PA_7. Moreover, the 6821 can be configured such that the pulse at CA_2 is automatically produced by the 6821 or is generated under software control from the 68000. In the *automatic mode*, the pulse that is output is of a fixed duration. But if the pulse is initiated by the 68000, it can be set to any duration.

6.12 DUAL 16-BIT PORTS FOR THE 68000 MICROCOMPUTER USING 6821s

The circuit in Fig. 6.17 shows how 6821 PIAs can be used to implement a parallel I/O interface for a 68000 microcomputer system. At the left of the circuit diagram, we find the asynchronous interface bus signals. Included are address lines A_1 through A_{16}, data lines D_0 through D_{15}, and control signals $\overline{AS}$, $R/\overline{W}$, and $\overline{DTACK}$.

In order to construct two 16-bit ports, we use two 6821 ICs, U_{14} and U_{15}. The A ports on the two 6821 ICs are cascaded to make a word-wide output port. On the other hand, the B ports on the two devices are cascaded to make a word-wide input port.

This circuit has been designed such that the registers of the PIAs reside in the address range 18000_{16} through 18007_{16}. The chart in Fig. 6.18(a) shows the address for each register. Notice that the data direction registers corresponding to the bytes of the 16-bit output port are at addresses 18000_{16} and 18001_{16}. Those of the 16-bit input port are at 18004_{16} and 18005_{16}.

The address decoding for selecting between the two chips and their internal registers is shown in Fig. 6.18(b). Notice that bits A_1 and A_2 of the address are applied to register select inputs RS_0 and RS_1, respectively. Moreover, A_3 and A_4 are applied to the CS_1 and CS_0 chip select inputs of both 6821 devices. The rest of the address lines, A_5 to A_{16}, and $\overline{AS}$ are decoded by gates U_{9A}, U_{9B}, U_{10E}, U_{11A}, and U_{11B}. Their output is synchronized with a 2-MHz externally generated clock signal by flip-flops U_{13A} and U_{13B}. The output of this circuit is the third chip select signal, $\overline{CS_2}$, for the PIAs.

The data bus lines are simply buffered and then applied to both PIAs in parallel. Notice that the upper PIA device is coupled to the 68000 over the lower eight data bus lines and the lower PIA by the upper eight data lines. Therefore, as shown in Fig. 6.18(a), the registers of the upper device reside at odd byte addresses and those of the lower device are at even byte addresses.

To use the B ports on the two 6821 devices as inputs, their B port DDRs must be initialized with all zeros. These two registers are located at addresses 18004_{16} and 18005_{16}, respectively. However, to select these DDRs, bit 2 in the corresponding control registers must be loaded with logic 0. These control registers are located at addresses 18006_{16} and 18007_{16}. Thus, to configure the B ports as inputs, we can execute the following instruction sequence:

```
MOVE.W   #$0,$18006      SELECT DATA-DIRECTION REGISTERS B
MOVE.W   #$0,$18004      PORT B IS INPUT-PORT
```

Execution of these instructions loads the word-wide memory locations at addresses 18006_{16} and 18004_{16} with 0000_{16}.

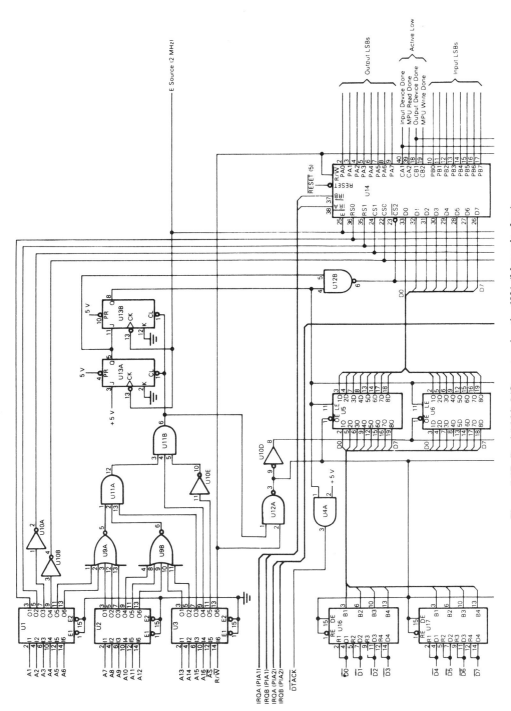

Figure 6-17 Dual 16-bit I/O ports using the 6821 (Motorola, Inc.).

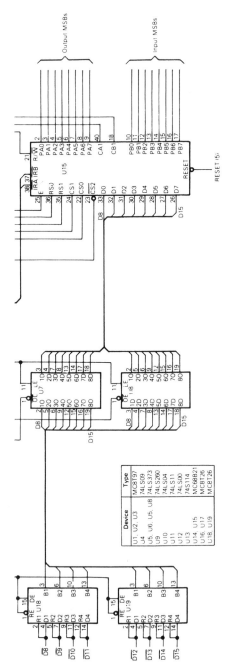

Figure 6-17 *(cont.)*

18000	Peripheral Data/DDRA	(U15)
18001	Peripheral Data/DDRA	(U14)
18002	CRA	(U15)
18003	CRA	(U14)
18004	Peripheral Data/DDRB	(U15)
18005	Peripheral Data/DDRB	(U14)
18006	CRB	(U15)
18007	CRB	(U14)

(a)

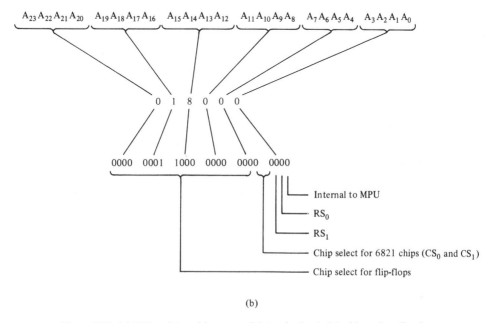

(b)

Figure 6-18   (a) 6821 register address map (Motorola, Inc.); (b) address decoding for port selection.

To configure the A ports on the two chips, we first select the DDRs for port A by clearing bit 2 in their control registers. These CRs are located at addresses 18002_{16} and 18003_{16}. The DDRs are located at 18000_{16} and 18001_{16}. To configure the A ports as outputs, we must load their DDRs with all 1s. This gives the following instruction sequence:

MOVE.W   #$0,$18002   SELECT DATA-DIRECTION REGISTERS A

MOVE.W   #$FFFF,$18000   PORT A IS OUTPUT-PORT

Now to use the ports for inputting or outputting of data, we must select the peripheral data (output) registers. To select the two output registers for port A, we must load their control registers so that bit 2 is logic 1. A similar configuration is needed for port B. To do this, the following instructions can be executed:

  MOVE.W #$0404,$18002 SELECT DATA REGISTERS A

  MOVE.W #$0404,$18006 SELECT DATA REGISTERS B

Now the two ports are ready to perform I/O operations.

  As an example of how data are input and output, let us show how to read a 16-bit word from the input port, increment it by 1, and output the new value to the output port. This can be accomplished by the following instructions:

    MOVE.W $18004,D1

    ADDQ.W #1,D1

    MOVE.W D1,$18000

The first instruction moves the contents of the input port to D_1. Then we increment the value in D_1 by 1. Finally, the third instruction outputs the value in D_1 to the output port.

6.13 SYNCHRONOUS MEMORY AND I/O INTERFACE

Up to this point in the chapter, we have been considering the asynchronous bus interface of the 68000 microprocessor. However, the 68000 also provides a *synchronous bus interface*. This capability is provided primarily for interface with slower 8-bit LSI peripherals such as those in the 6800 family. The synchronous interface is shown in Fig. 6.19. This interface looks quite similar to the asynchronous

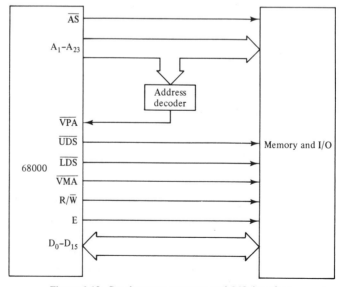

Figure 6-19 Synchronous memory and I/O interface.

interface of Fig. 6.1. It includes the complete address bus A_1 through A_{23}, the 16-bit data bus D_0 through D_{15}, and control signals $\overline{UDS}$, $\overline{LDS}$, $\overline{AS}$, and $R/\overline{W}$. Notice that $\overline{DTACK}$ is not part of this interface. Instead, it is replaced by three synchronous bus control signals. They are valid peripheral address ($\overline{VPA}$), valid memory address ($\overline{VMA}$), and enable (E).

Let us look briefly at the function of each of these control signals. $\overline{VPA}$ is an input to the 68000. It must be switched to the 0 logic level to tell the 68000 to perform a synchronous bus cycle. As shown in Fig. 6.19, external decoder circuitry is supplied in the interface to detect that the address on the bus is in the address space of the synchronous peripherals. On the other hand, $\overline{VMA}$ is an output produced by the 68000 only during synchronous bus cycles. It signals that a valid address is on the bus.

E is an enable clock that is produced within the 68000. It is at a rate equal to 1/10 that of the system clock. For instance, in a 10-Mz 68000 microcomputer system, E is at 1 MHz. The duty cycle of this signal is such that the pulse is at the 1 logic level for four clock states and at the 0 logic level for six clock states. This signal is applied to the E clock input of 6800 LSI peripherals.

Synchronous Bus Cycle

A flowchart of the 68000's *synchronous bus cycle* is shown in Fig. 6.20(a). Moreover, a general timing diagram for the key interface signals involved in a synchronous read/write operation is shown in Fig. 6.20(b). Notice that the waveforms of the FC, $R/\overline{W}$, $\overline{UDS}$, and $\overline{LDS}$ signals are not shown. They have the same function and timing as in the asynchronous bus cycle.

The synchronous bus cycle starts out just like an asynchronous bus cycle with a function code being output on the FC bus during state S_0. It is followed by the address on A_1 through A_{23} during S_1. When the address is stable in S_2, $\overline{AS}$ is switched to the 0 logic level. At this time $R/\overline{W}$ is set to 0 if a write cycle is in progress; otherwise, it stays at the 1 logic level. Moreover, if a write operation is in progress, the data are output on D_0 through D_{15} and it is maintained valid during the rest of the bus cycle.

By the end of S_4, external circuitry must have decoded the address on the bus. At this time, it asserts $\overline{VPA}$ by switching it to the 0 logic level. In response to this, the 68000 begins to assert wait states to extend the bus cycle. At the end of the next clock state, the $\overline{VMA}$ output is switched to the 0 level. This signals external circuitry that an address is on the bus. The peripheral transfers the data after E is active. For a read cycle, the MPU reads the data when E goes low. The data transfer cycle is terminated by the processor by negating control signals $\overline{VMA}$, $\overline{AS}$, $\overline{UDS}$, and $\overline{LDS}$.

Interfacing the 6821 PIA to the Synchronous Interface Bus

The circuit diagram of Fig. 6.17 illustrates how 6821 PIAs are interfaced to the 68000's asynchronous bus. This circuit can be easily modified so that the LSI peripherals

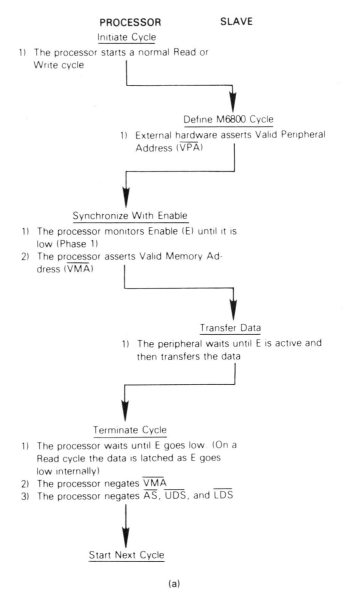

PROCESSOR   SLAVE

Initiate Cycle
1) The processor starts a normal Read or
   Write cycle

Define M6800 Cycle
1) External hardware asserts Valid Peripheral
   Address ($\overline{VPA}$)

Synchronize With Enable
1) The processor monitors Enable (E) until it is
   low (Phase 1)
2) The processor asserts Valid Memory Address ($\overline{VMA}$)

Transfer Data
1) The peripheral waits until E is active and
   then transfers the data

Terminate Cycle
1) The processor waits until E goes low. (On a
   Read cycle the data is latched as E goes
   low internally)
2) The processor negates $\overline{VMA}$
3) The processor negates $\overline{AS}$, $\overline{UDS}$, and $\overline{LDS}$

Start Next Cycle

(a)

Figure 6-20 (a) Synchronous bus cycle flowchart (Motorola, Inc.).

work off a synchronous bus cycle instead of an asynchronous bus cycle. Figure 6.21 shows a simple circuit that makes this modification. First, the ICs U_{11A}, U_{12B}, U_{13A}, and U_{13B} are removed from the circuit of Fig. 6.17. This is because $\overline{DTACK}$ is not required to support the synchronous bus. Moreover, the E output of the 68000 now gets directly connected to the E input of both 6821 devices in parallel.

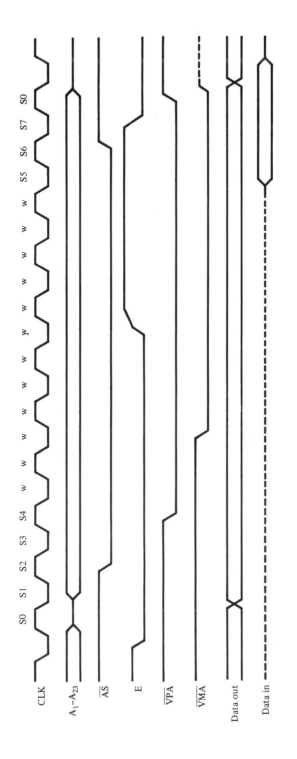

Figure 6-20 *(cont.)* (b) Timing diagram (Motorola, Inc.).

199

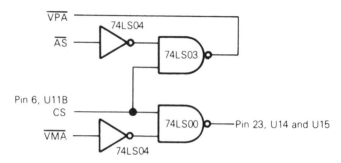

Figure 6-21   Conversion circuit for implementing synchronous bus cycle (Motorola, Inc.).

Looking at Fig. 6.21, we see that the chip select (CS) output at pin 6 of U_{11B} gets connected to one input of the 74LS00 NAND gate. The other input of this gate is supplied by the $\overline{VMA}$ output of the 68000 after it is inverted. The output of the NAND gate goes to the $\overline{CS_2}$ input of both 6821 devices in parallel. In this way, we see that the 6821s get chip-selected only when one of their addresses is on the bus and the 68000 has signaled that a valid address is on the bus during a synchronous bus cycle.

The upper NAND gate in this circuit also has CS as one of its inputs and $\overline{AS}$ as the other. Therefore, it detects when an address corresponding to one of the LSI peripherals is on the bus. When this condition occurs, it switches $\overline{VPA}$ to logic 0, thereby signaling to the processor that a synchronous bus cycle should be performed.

6.14 SERIAL COMMUNICATIONS INTERFACE

Another type of I/O interface that is widely used in microcomputer systems is known as a *serial communications port*. This is the type of interface that is used to connect peripheral units, such as CRT terminals and printers, to a microcomputer. It permits data to be transferred between the various units of the system. For instance, data input at the keyboard of a terminal are passed to the MPU part of the microcomputer through this type of interface. Let us now look into the different types of serial interfaces that are implemented in microcomputer systems.

Synchronous and Asynchronous Data Communications

Two types of *serial data communications* are widely used in microcomputer systems. They are called *asynchronous communications* and *synchronous communications*. By synchronous, we mean that the receiver and transmitter sections of the two pieces of equipment that are communicating with each other must run synchronously. For this reason, as shown in Fig. 6.22(a), the interface includes a Clock line as well as Transmit Data, Receive Data, and Signal Common lines. It is the clock signal that synchronizes both the transmission and reception of data.

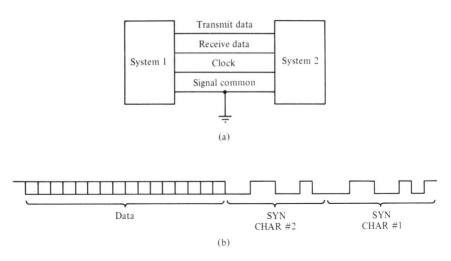

(a)

(b)

Figure 6-22 (a) Synchronous communications interface; (b) synchronous data transmission format.

The format used for synchronous communication of data is shown in Fig. 6.22(b). To initiate synchronous transmission, the transmitter first sends out synchronization characters to the receiver. The receiver reads the synchronization bit pattern and compares it to a known sync pattern. Once they are identified as being the same, the receiver begins to read character data off the communications line. Transfer of data continues until the complete block of data is received or synchronization is lost between the receiver and transmitter. If large blocks of data are being sent, the synchronization characters may be periodically resent to assure that synchronization is maintained. The synchronous type of communications is typically used in applications where high-speed data transfer is required.

The asynchronous method of communications eliminates the need for the Clock signal. As shown in Fig. 6.23(a), the simplest form of an asynchronous communication interface could consist of a Receive Data, Transmit Data, and Signal Common communication lines. In this case, the data to be transmitted are sent out one character at a time and at the receiver end of the communication line synchronization is performed by examining synchronization bits that are included at the beginning and end of each character.

The format of a typical asynchronous character is shown in Fig. 6.23(b). Here we see that the synchronization bit at the beginning of the character is called the *start bit* and that at the end of the character the *stop bit*. Depending on the communications scheme and device used, 1, $1\frac{1}{2}$, or 2 STOP bits can be used. The bits of the character are embedded between the start and stop bits. Notice that the start bit is always input or output first. It is followed in the serial bit stream by the LSB of the character, the other 6 bits of the character, a parity bit, and the stop bits. For instance, 7-bit ASCII can be used and parity added as an eighth bit for higher reliability in transmission. The duration of each bit in the format is called a *bit time*.

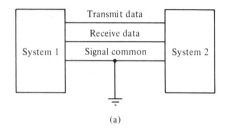

(a)

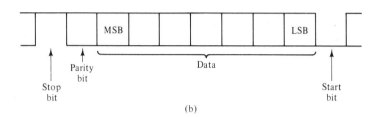

(b)

Figure 6-23 (a) Asychronous communications interface; (b) asynchronous data transmission format.

The fact that an 0 or 1 logic level is being transferred over the communication line is identified by whether the voltage level on the line corresponds to that of a *mark* or a *space*. The start bit is always to the mark level. It synchronizes the receiver to the transmitter and signals that the unit receiving data should start assembling the character. Stop bits are to the space level. This assures that the receiving unit sees a transition of logic level at the start bit of the next character.

The USART and UART

Since serial communication interfaces are so widely used in modern electronic equipment, special LSI peripheral devices have been developed to permit easy implementation of these types of interfaces. Some of the names that these devices go by are *UART* (*universal asynchronous receiver/transmitter*) and *USART* (*universal synchronous/asynchronous receiver/transmitter*).

Both UARTs and USARTs have the ability to perform the parellel-to-serial conversions needed in the transmission of data and the serial-to-parallel conversions needed in the reception of data. For data that are transmitted asynchronously, they also have the ability to frame the character automatically with a start bit, parity bit, and the appropriate stop bits.

Moreover, for reception of data, UARTs and USARTs typically have the ability to check characters automatically as they are received for correct parity, and for two other errors, known as *framing error* and *overrun error*. A framing error means that after the detection of the beginning of a character with a start bit the appropriate number of stop bits were not detected. This means that the character that was transmitted was not received correctly and should be resent. An overrun error means that the prior character that was received was not read out of the UARTs receive data register by the microprocessor before another character was received. Therefore, the first character was lost and should be retransmitted.

A block diagram of a typical UART is shown in Fig. 6.24. Here we see that it has four key signal interfaces: the microprocessor interface, the transmitter interface, the receiver interface, and the handshake control interface. Let us now look at each of these interfaces in more detail.

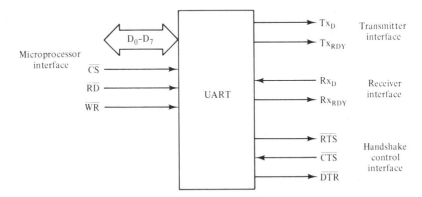

Figure 6-24 Block diagram of a UART.

LSI USARTs and UARTs cannot stand alone in a communication system. Their operation must be controlled by a general-purpose processor such as a microprocessor. The *microprocessor interface* is the interface that is used to connect the UART to an MPU. Looking at Figure 6.24, we see that this interface consists of an 8-bit bidirectional data bus ($D_0 - D_7$) and a minimum of three control lines, $\overline{CS}$, $\overline{RD}$, and $\overline{WR}$.

All data transfers between the UART and MPU take place over the 8-bit data bus. Two uses of this bus are for the input of character data from the receiver of the UART and for the output of character data to its transmitter. Other types of information are also passed between the MPU and UART. Examples are mode control information, operation commands, and status.

LSI UARTs, just like the 6821 LSI peripheral we discussed earlier in the chapter, can be configured for various modes of operation through software. Mode control instructions are what must be issued to a UART to initialize its control registers for the desired mode of operation. For example, the format of the data frame used for transmitted or received data can be configured through software. Typical options are character length equal to from 5 to 8 bits; even, odd, or no parity; and 1, $1\frac{1}{2}$, or 2 stop bits.

We pointed out earlier that a UART cannot perform the communication function on its own. Instead, the sequence of events that is needed to initiate transmission and reception is controlled by commands issued to the UART by the MPU. For instance, the MPU can initiate a request for transmission of data to another unit by writing a command to the UART that forces its $\overline{RTS}$ control output to its active 0 logic level. The logic 0 at $\overline{RTS}$ signals the system at the other end of the communication line to prepare to receive data. At the receiver end of the communication line, the MPU can acknowledge that it is ready to receive data by sending a command to its UART that forces the $\overline{DTR}$ control output to logic 0.

Most UARTs have a *status register* that contains information related to its current state. For example, it may contain flag bits that represent the current logic state of signal lines such as $\overline{CTS}$. This permits the MPU to examine the logic state of the line through software.

Besides information about the logic level of control lines, the status register typically contains flag bits for error conditions such as parity error, overrun error, and framing error. After reception of a character, the MPU can first read these bits to assure that a valid character has been received, and if the bits are at their inactive levels, the character should be read from the receive data register within the UART.

At the other side of the block in Fig. 6.24, we find the *transmitter* and *receiver interfaces*. The transmitter interface has two signal lines: transmit data (Tx_D) and transmitter ready (Tx_{RDY}). Tx_D is the line over which the transmitter section of the UART outputs serial character data. As shown in Fig. 6.25, this output line is connected to the receive data (Rx_D) input of the receiver section in the system at the other end of the communication line.

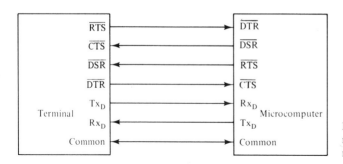

Figure 6-25 Simple asynchronous communications interface between a microcomputer and terminal.

Usually, the transmitter section of an LSI UART can hold only one character at a time. This character datum is held in the *transmit data register* within the UART. Since only one character can be held within the UART, it must signal the MPU when it has completed transmission of this character. The Tx_{RDY} line is provided for this purpose. As soon as transmission of the character is complete, the transmitter switches Tx_{RDY} to its active logic level. This signal should be returned to an interrupt input of the MPU. In this way, its occurrence can cause program control to be passed quickly to a service routine that will output another character to the transmitter data register and then reinitiate transmission. In some UARTs, the transmitter empty condition is identified by a status bit instead of an external signal. In this case the status bit can be polled through software.

The receiver section is similar to the transmitter we just described. However, here the receive data (Rx_D) line is the input that accepts bit-serial character data that are transmitted from the other system's transmitter. Moreover, the receiver ready (Rx_{RDY}) output is again used as an interrupt to the MPU. But this time it signals the MPU that a character has been received. The service routine that is initiated must first determine whether or not the character is valid, and if it is, it must read the character out of the UART's *receive data register*. Here again a status bit instead of a signal bit can be used to signal the receiver full condition.

Using the handshake control signals $\overline{RTS}$, $\overline{DSR}$, $\overline{DTR}$, and $\overline{CTS}$, different types of *asynchronous communication protocols* can be implemented through the serial I/O interface. By protocol we mean a handshake sequence by which two systems signal each other that they are ready to communicate.

A simple asynchronous communication interface that uses these control lines is shown in Fig. 6.25. In this example, a protocol can be set up such that when the terminal wants to send data to the microcomputer it will issue a request at its request to sent ($\overline{RTS}$) output. To do this, the MPU of the terminal must issue a command to the UART that causes it to set the $\overline{RTS}$ line to its active 0 logic level. $\overline{RTS}$ of the terminal is applied to the data terminal ready ($\overline{DTR}$) input of the microcomputer. In this way, it tells the microcomputer that the terminal wants to transmit data to it.

When the microcomputer is ready to receive data, it acknowledges this fact to the terminal by activating the data set ready ($\overline{DSR}$) output of its UART. The MPU in the microcomputer does this by issuing a command to the UART that switches $\overline{DSR}$ to its active 0 logic level. This signal is returned to the clear to send ($\overline{CTS}$) input of the terminal's UART and tells the UART in the terminal to start outputting data on Tx_D. At the same time, the receiver section in the UART within the microcomputer begins to read data from its Rx_D input.

If a UART does not have true $\overline{DSR}$, $\overline{DTR}$, or $\overline{CTS}$ signal lines, external logic circuitry can be used to generate these signal functions from the provided signals.

Baud Rate and the Baud Rate Generator

The rate at which data transfers take place over the receive and transmit lines is known as the *baud rate*. By baud rate we mean the number of bits of data that are transferred per second of time. For instance, some of the common data transfer rates are 300 baud, 1200 baud, and 9600 baud. They correspond to 300 bits/second (bps), 1200 bps, and 9600 bps, respectively.

The baud rate at which data are transferred determines the *bit time*. That is, the amount of time each bit of data is on the communication line. At 300 baud, the bit time is found to be

$$t_{BT} = 1/300 \text{ bps} = 3.33 \text{ ms}$$

Baud rate is set by a part of the serial communication interface called the *baud rate generator*. This part of the interface generates the clock signal that is used to drive the receiver and transmitter parts of the UART. Some LSI UARTs have a built-in baud rate generator; others need an external circuit to provide this function.

The RS-232C Interface

The *RS-232C interface* is a standard hardware interface for implementing asynchronous serial data communication ports on devices such as printers, CRT terminals, keyboards, and modems. The pin definitions and electrical characteristics of this interface are defined by the Electronic Industries Association (EIA). The aim behind publishing standards such as the RS-232C is to assure compatibility between equipment made by different manufacturers.

Peripherals that connect to a microcomputer can be located anywhere from several feet to many feet from the system. For instance, in large systems it is common to have the microcomputer part of the system in a separate room from the terminals and printers. This leads us to the main advantage of using a serial interface to connect peripherals to a microcomputer, which is that as few as three signal lines can be used to connect the peripheral to the MPU: a Receive Data line, a Transmit Data line, and a Common Ground. This results in a large savings in wiring costs and the small number of lines that need to be put in place also leads to higher reliability.

The RS-232C standard defines a 25-pin interface. Figure 6.26 lists each pin and its function. Note that the three signals that we mentioned earlier, Transmit Data, Receive Data, and Signal Common, are located at pins 2, 3, and 7, respectively. Pins are also provided for additional control functions. For instance, pins 4 and 5 are the Request To Send and Clear To Send control signals. These two signals are also frequently used when implementing an asynchronous communication interface.

The RS-232C interface is specified to operate correctly over a maximum distance of 100 feet. To satisfy this distance specification, a bus driver is used to buffer the transmit line to provide the appropriate drive current and a bus receiver is used at the receive line. RS-232C drivers and receivers are available as standard ICs. These buffers do both the voltage-level translation needed to convert the TTL-compatible outputs of the UART to the mark and space voltage levels defined for the RS-232C interface. The voltage levels that are normally transmitted for a mark and a space are $+ 12$ V dc and $- 12$ V dc, respectively. For the RS-232C interface, all voltages below $- 3$ V dc are equal to a mark and all voltages above $+ 3$ V dc are considered a space.

The RS-232C interface is specified to support baud rates of up to 20,000 bps. In general, the receive and transmit baud rates do not have to be the same; however, in most simpler systems they are set to the same value. For instance, a baud rate that is widely used in communication between an MPU and a printer is 1200 bps. This corresponds to a bit time equal to .833 ms.

Simplex, Half-Duplex, and Full-Duplex Communication Links

Applications require different types of asynchronous links to be implemented. For instance, the *communication link* needed to connect a printer to a microcomputer just needs to support communications in one direction. That is, the printer is an

Pin	Signal
1	Protective Ground
2	Transmitted Data
3	Received Data
4	Request to Send
5	Clear to Send
6	Data Set Ready
7	Signal Ground (Common Return)
8	Received Line Signal Detector
9	Reserved for Data Set Testing
10	Reserved for Data Set Testing
11	Unassigned
12	Secondary Received Line Signal Detector
13	Secondary Clear to Send
14	Secondary Transmitted Data
15	Transmission Signal Element Timing
16	Secondary Received Data
17	Receiver Signal Element Timing
18	Unassigned
19	Secondary Request to Send
20	Data Terminal Ready
21	Signal Quality Detector
22	Ring Indicator
23	Data Signal Rate Selector
24	Transmit Signal Element Timing
25	Unassigned

Figure 6-26 RS-232C interface pins and functions.

output-only device; therefore, the MPU only needs to transmit data to the printer. Data are not transmitted back. In this case, as shown in Fig. 6.27(a), a single unidirectional communication line can be used to connect the printer and microcomputer together. This type of connection is known as a *simplex communication link*.

Other devices, such as the CRT terminal with keyboard shown in Fig. 6.27(b), need to both transmit data to and receive data from the MPU. That is, they must both input and output data. This requirement can also be satisfied with a single communication line by setting up a *half-duplex communication link*. In a half-duplex link, data are transmitted and received over the same line; therefore, a system cannot transmit and receive data at the same time.

If higher-performance communication is required, separate transmit and receive lines can be used to connect the peripheral and microcomputer. When this is done, data can be transferred in both directions at the same time. This type of link is illustrated in Fig. 6.27(c). It is called a *full-duplex communication link*.

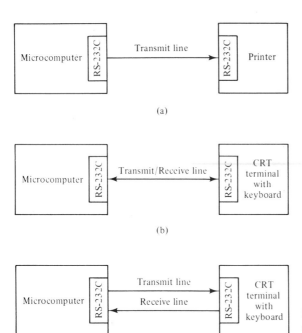

(a)

(b)

(c)

Figure 6-27 (a) Simplex communications link; (b) half-duplex communications link; (c) full-duplex communications link.

6.15 THE 6850 ASYNCHRONOUS COMMUNICATIONS INTERFACE ADAPTER

The 6850 *asynchronous communications interface adapter* is another important LSI peripheral that is frequently used in 68000 microcomputer systems. It permits simple implementation of a serial data communications interface. As its name implies, the 6850 is capable of implementing an asynchronous communication interface. For instance, the 6850 can be used to implement an RS-232C port. This is the type of interface that is used to connect a CRT terminal or printer to a microcomputer. To support connection of these two peripheral devices, the microcomputer would need two independent RS-232C I/O ports.

The programmability of the 6850 provides for implementation of a very flexible asynchronous communication interface. It contains a full-duplex receiver and transmitter that can be configured through software for communication of data using formats with character lengths of 7 or 8 bits, with either even or odd parity and 1 or 2 stop bits. Moreover, the 6850 has the ability to detect automatically the occurrence of parity, framing, and overrun errors during data reception.

A block diagram showing the internal architecture of the 6850 is shown in Fig. 6.28. From this diagram, we find that it includes four key sections: the bus interface section, which consists of the data bus buffers block and the chip select and read/write control block; the transmit section, which consists of the transmit data register,

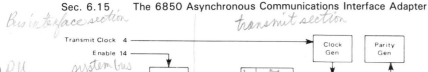

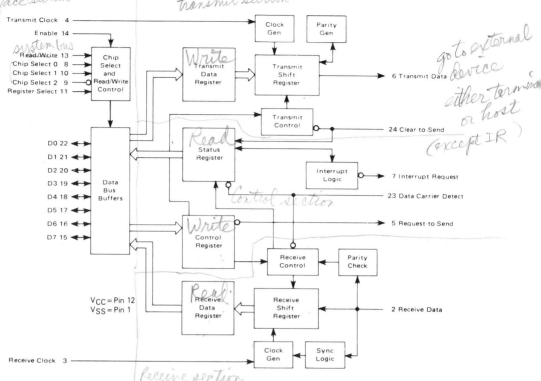

Bus interface section

CPU system

system bus

transmit section

Write

Read

Write

Read

Control section

Receive section

go to external device either terminal or host (except IR)

Figure 6-28 Block diagram of the 6850 ACIA device (Motorola, Inc.).

transmit shift register, and transmit control blocks; the receive section, which consists of the receive data register, receive shift register, and receive control blocks; and the control section, which consists of the control register, status register, and interrupt logic blocks. Let us now look at each of these sections in more detail.

The bus interface section is used to connect the 6850 to a microprocessor such as the 68000. Notice that the interface includes an 8-bit bidirectional data bus D_0 through D_7 that is driven by the data bus buffers. It is over these lines that the microprocessor transfers configuration information to the 6850's control register, reads its status register, and inputs or outputs character data.

Data transfers take place over the bus under control of the signals read/write ($R/\overline{W}$), register select (RS), enable (E), and chip selects CS_0, CS_1, and $\overline{CS_2}$. All of these signals are inputs to the chip select and read/write control block. Typically, the 6850 is located at a specific address in the microcomputer's memory address space. When the microprocessor is to access registers within the 6850, it puts this address on the address bus. The address is decoded by external circuitry and must produce logic 1 at the CS_0 and CS_1 inputs and logic 0 at the $\overline{CS_2}$ input. These three inputs must be at these logic levels for a read or write bus cycle to take place to the 6850.

The other two control signals, $R/\overline{W}$ and RS, tell the 6850 what type of data transfer is to take place over the bus. Figure 6.29 shows the various types of read/write

Data Bus Line Number	RS • $\overline{R/W}$ Transmit Data Register (Write Only)	RS • R/W Receive Data Register (Read Only)	Buffer Address RS • $\overline{R/W}$ Control Register (Write Only)	$\overline{RS}$ • R/W Status Register (Read Only)
0	Data Bit 0*	Data Bit 0	Counter Divide Select 1 (CR0)	Receive Data Register Full (RDRF)
1	Data Bit 1	Data Bit 1	Counter Divide Select 2 (CR1)	Transmit Data Register Empty (TDRE)
2	Data Bit 2	Data Bit 2	Word Select 1 (CR2)	Data Carrier Detect ($\overline{DCD}$)
3	Data Bit 3	Data Bit 3	Word Select 2 (CR3)	Clear to Send ($\overline{CTS}$)
4	Data Bit 4	Data Bit 4	Word Select 3 (CR4)	Framing Error (FE)
5	Data Bit 5	Data Bit 5	Transmit Control 1 (CR5)	Receiver Overrun (OVRN)
6	Data Bit 6	Data Bit 6	Transmit Control 2 (CR6)	Parity Error (PE)
7	Data Bit 7***	Data Bit 7**	Receive Interrupt Enable (CR7)	Interrupt Request ($\overline{IRQ}$)

   * Leading bit = LSB = Bit 0
   ** Data bit will be zero in 7 bit plus parity modes.
   *** Data bit is "don't care" in 7 bit plus parity modes.

Figure 6-29   Control signals and corresponding bus data transfers (Motorola, Inc.).

operations that can occur. For example, the first state in the table, RS · $\overline{R/W}$, corresponds to a write of character data from the microprocessor to the transmit data register within the 6850. Notice that in general $R/\overline{W} = 0$ signals that the microprocessor is writing data to the 6850, $R/\overline{W} = 1$ indicates that data are being read from the 6850, and the logic level of RS indicates whether character data, control information, or status information is on the data bus.

Example 6.1

   What type of data transfer is taking place over the bus if the control signals are RS = 0 and $R/\overline{W}$ = 1?

   Solution.   Looking at the table in Fig. 6.29, we see that RS = 0 and $R/\overline{W}$ = 1 correspond to the condition $\overline{RS}$ · $R/\overline{W}$; therefore, status information is being read from within the 6850.

   The receiver section of the 6850 is responsible for reading the serial bit-stream of data at the receive data (Rx_{DATA}) input and converting it to parallel form. When a mark voltage level is detected on this line, the receiver enables a counter. As the counter increments to a value equal to 1/2 a bit time, the logic level at the Rx_{DATA} line is sampled again. If it is still at the mark level, a valid start pulse has been detected. Then Rx_{DATA} is examined every time the counter increments through another bit time. This continues until a complete character is assembled in the receive shift register and the stop bit is read. After this, the complete character is transferred in parallel into the receive data register.

During reception of a character, the receiver automatically checks the character data for parity, framing, or overrun errors. If one of these error conditions occurs, it is flagged by setting a corresponding bit in the status register. Then the receive data register full (RDRF) status bit is set to 1 and, assuming that the receive interrupt enable bit in the control register is set to 1, the interrupt request ($\overline{\text{IRQ}}$) output switches to logic 0. This signal can be sent to the microprocessor to tell it that a character is available and should be read from the receive data register. RDRF is automatically reset to logic 0 when the MPU reads the contents of the receive data register.

The 6850 does not have a built in baud rate generator. For this reason, the clock signal that is used to set the baud rate must be externally generated and applied to the receive clock (Rx_{CLK}) input of the receiver. Through software the 6850 can be set up to internally divide the clock signal input at Rx_{CLK} by 1, 16, or 64.

The 6850's transmitter section does the opposite of the receiver section. The MPU loads its transmit data register with parallel character data by writing data to it over the data bus. The character is automatically framed with the start bit, the appropriate parity bit, and the correct number of stop bits, and then is put into the transmit data register. It is then shifted through the transmit shift register to produce a bit-serial output on the transmit (Tx_{DATA}) line. When the transmit data register becomes empty, the transmit data register empty (TDRE) bit of the status register is set to logic 1 and, assuming that the interrupt on transmitter data register empty function is enabled with its control bit, the $\overline{\text{IRQ}}$ output is switched to logic 0. This signal can be returned to the MPU to tell it that another character should be output to the transmitter section. When the MPU writes another character out to the transmit data register, the TDRE status bit is reset automatically.

Data are output on the transmit data (Tx_{DATA}) line at a baud rate set by the external transmit clock signal that is input at Tx_{CLK}. In most applications, the transmitter and receiver operate at the same baud rate. Therefore, both Rx_{CLK} and Tx_{CLK} are supplied by the same baud rate generator. The diagram in Fig. 6.30 shows this type of system configuration.

The operation of the 6850 is controlled through the setting of bits in two internal registers: the control register and the status register. For instance, the way in which the 6850's receiver and transmitter operate is determined by the contents of the control register. The control register has eight bits, which are labeled CR_0 through CR_7. Figure 6.31(a) through (d) shows the function of each of the control register's bits.

The two least significant bits, CR_0 and CR_1, are the counter divide select bits. Notice in Fig. 6.31(a) that these two bits determine how the signals applied to the external baud rate inputs, Rx_{CLK} and Tx_{CLK}, are divided within the 6850. For example, if these two bits are $CR_1CR_0 = 10$, it is set for divide-by-64 operation. The three bits that follow, CR_2 through CR_4, are called the word select bits. In Fig. 6.31(b), we find that they select the length of the character, the type of parity, and the number of stop bits. For instance, when information is to be transmitted and received as 7-bit ASCII characters, with odd parity, and one stop bit, these bits must be loaded with $CR_4CR_3CR_2 = 011$.

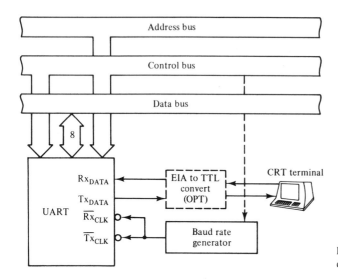

Figure 6-30 Receiver and transmitter driven at the same baud rate.

The next two bits, CR_5 and CR_6, are the transmitter control bits and are used to set the active logic level of $\overline{RTS}$, enable or disable the $\overline{IRQ}$ output for transmitter operation, and select the transmission of a break logic level (SPACE) at the Tx_{DATA} output. Looking at Fig. 6.31(c), we see that selecting $CR_6 CR_5 = 01$ sets the active level of $\overline{RTS}$ to logic 0, enables the automatic assertion of the $\overline{IRQ}$ output when the transmit data register is empty, and does not cause transmission of a break level at the Tx_{DATA} output.

The last bit, CR_7, is the receiver control bit. By making it logic 1, we enable the automatic assertion of the $\overline{IRQ}$ output whenever the receive data register becomes full, an overrun error occurs, or on the low-to-high transition of the data carrier detect ($\overline{DCD}$) signal.

Example 6.2

What value must be written into the control register in order to configure the 6850 such that it works with the baud clock internally divided by 16, character size equal to eight bits for EBCDIC, even parity, one stop bit, $\overline{RTS}$ active high, and the transmitter and receiver interrupts are to be disabled?

Solution.   From Fig. 6.31(a), we find that CR_1CR_0 must be set to 01 in order to select divide by 16 for the external baud rate inputs.

$$CR_1CR_0 = 01$$

To select a character length of eight bits, even parity, and one stop bit, the next three bits in the control register must be made 110. This gives

$$CR_4CR_3CR_2 = 110$$

To set up the 6850 for $\overline{RTS}$ active high with the transmitter interrupt disabled, we make the next two CR bits

$$CR_6CR_5 = 10$$

CR$_1$	CR$_0$	Function
0	0	$\div 1$
0	1	$\div 16$
1	0	$\div 64$
1	1	Master reset

(a)

CR$_4$	CR$_3$	CR$_2$	Function
0	0	0	7 bits + even parity + 2 stop bits
0	0	1	7 bits + odd parity + 2 stop bits
0	1	0	7 bits + even parity + 1 stop bit
0	1	1	7 bits + odd parity + 1 stop bit
1	0	0	8 bits + 2 stop bits
1	0	1	8 bits + 1 stop bit
1	1	0	8 bits + even parity + 1 stop bit
1	1	1	8 bits + odd parity + 1 stop bit

(b)

CR$_6$	CR$_5$	Function $Request\ to\ Send$
0	0	$\overline{RTS}$ = low, transmitting interrupt disabled
0	1	$\overline{RTS}$ = low, transmitting interrupt enabled
1	0	$\overline{RTS}$ = high, transmitting interrupt disabled
1	1	$\overline{RTS}$ = low, transmits a break level on the transmit data output. Transmitting interrupt disabled.

(c)

CR$_7$	Function
0	Receiving interrupt disabled
1	Receiving interrupt ~~disabled~~ enabled

(d)

Figure 6-31 Control register bit functions (Motorola, Inc.).

Finally, the receiver interrupt is disabled by making

$$CR_7 = 0$$

Therefore, the complete control word is

$$CR_7 CR_6 \ldots\ldots CR_0 = 01011001_2$$
$$= 59_{16}$$

Before the 6850 can be used to receive or transmit characters, its control register must be initialized. As the microcomputer powers up, it should issue a software reset to the 6850. This is done by writing a byte to the control register with bits CR_0 and CR_1 both one. Looking at Fig. 6.31(a), we see that this represents a master reset

interr enable sets IRQ to 1

command. This command causes the status register to be cleared and initializes both the receiver and transmitter sections. After this, another write operation is performed to load the configuration byte into the control register. Assuming that the 6850 is at address $00F000_{16}$ of the 68000's address space, the command byte formed in Example 6.2 can be written to the command register with the instruction sequence

$$\text{MOVE.B} \quad \#\$C9,D0$$
$$\text{MOVE.L} \quad \#\$0F000,A0$$
$$\text{MOVE.B} \quad D0,(A0)$$

Now that the configuration for asynchronous communications has been set up in the control register, the 6850 is ready for operation.

The status register of the 6850 is shown in Fig. 6.32. We already looked briefly at the function of bits 0 and 1 of the status register. The first bit RDRF (receive data register full) is set to 1 to indicate that a character has been received in the receiver section. That is, the receive data register is full. If the interrupt request ($\overline{\text{IRQ}}$) line is disabled, the microprocessor must poll (read) this bit through software to determine if character data has been received through the communication interface. When it

Keyint

is 1, the character held in the receive data register must be read by the microprocessor. On the other hand, the second bit, TDRE (transmit data register empty), is set to 1 when the transmit data register is empty. This means that another character can be written to the transmit data register.

B$_7$	B$_6$	B$_5$	B$_4$	B$_3$	B$_2$	B$_1$	B$_0$
$\overline{\text{IRQ}}$	PE	OVRN	FE	$\overline{\text{CTS}}$	$\overline{\text{DCD}}$	TDRE	RDRF

Figure 6-32 Status register bit functions.

Notice in Fig. 6.32 that bits FE, OVRN, and PE are the error flags for the receiver. If the incoming character is found to have a parity error, the PE (parity error) bit gets set. On the other hand, if an overrun or framing error condition occurs, the OVRN (overrun error) or FE (framing error) flag is set, respectively. The MPU should always examine these error bits before reading a character from the receive data register. If an error is found to have occurred, a software routine can be initiated to cause the character to be retransmitted.

The other three bits in the status register, bit 2, bit 3, and bit 7, represent the logic level of input signals $\overline{\text{DCD}}$, $\overline{\text{CTS}}$, and $\overline{\text{IRQ}}$, respectively. The fact that these three signals are represented by bits in the status register permits the MPU to examine their current logic levels through software.

Skip

6.16 SPECIAL-PURPOSE INTERFACE CONTROLLERS

Up to this point in the chapter, we have introduced LSI controllers for two of the most widely used I/O interfaces. They are the 6821, which is used to implement parallel input/output ports, and the 6850, which is used to implement asynchronous communication ports. A large number of other LSI devices are available to simplify the implementation of complex I/O interfaces. Some examples are CRT controllers, floppy disk controllers, Winchester disk controllers, and IEEE-488 bus controllers. Here we will introduce just one of these types of devices, the 68230 parallel interface/timer controller.

The 68230 Parallel Interface/Timer PI/T

Earlier in this chapter, we examined the 6821 parallel interface adapter IC. Here we will examine a more general-purpose LSI device, the 68230, which has I/O ports that provide for implementation of parallel I/O interfaces and a timer that can be used as an interval timer or event counter. We will concentrate on its use in implementing parallel I/O ports.

The block diagram in Fig. 6.33 shows the internal architecture of the 68230 device. From this diagram, we find that there are four key sections of circuitry. They are the microprocessor interface, which consists of the data bus interface and interrupt vector registers; I/O interfaces for port A, port B, port C, and the handshake interface logic; the timer; and control logic sections for the port interrupt, DMA, handshake lines, and mode of operation.

Microprocessor Interface of the 68230

Let us now look at how the 68230 is interfaced to an MPU. Figure 6.34 shows a 68230 connected to a 68000 microprocessor. The 68000 communicates with the 68230 by reading or writing to its internal control registers bytes of data, control information, and status information. Data transfers between the 68000 and the internal registers of the 68230 take place over bidirectional data bus lines D_0 through D_7. The 68000 tells the 68230 whether data are to be written into or read from its registers with the $R/\overline{W}$ signal. Logic 0 at $R/\overline{W}$ means that the 68000 is writing information to the 68230, and logic 1 means that information is being read from the 68230.

The 68230 does not receive data during all bus cycles performed by the MPU. Instead, its microprocessor interface is active only when the chip select ($\overline{CS}$) input is at the 0 logic level. Notice in Fig. 6.34 that the address decoder circuit decodes part of the address output by the MPU along with $\overline{LDS}$ and function code FC_0 through FC_2 to produce $\overline{CS}$ whenever an address corresponding to a register within the 68230 is on the address bus. The register select inputs, RS_1 through RS_5, of the 68230 are supplied by another part of the address. The 5-bit code applied to these inputs determines which one of the 68230's registers is to be accessed during the current bus cycle. Figure 6.35 shows that the 68230 has 23 internal registers. Each of these registers is assigned to a unique register select code. For instance, if the code applied to the RS inputs is

$$RS_5RS_4RS_3RS_2RS_1 = 00010_2$$

register R_2, which is also known as the port A data direction register, is accessed. Notice that each of the registers also can be identified with its mnemonic name. For

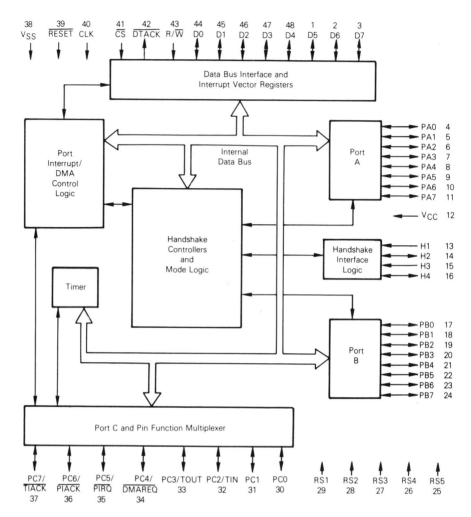

Figure 6-33 Block diagram of the 68230 PI/T device (Motorola, Inc.).

example, the port A data direction register that we just introduced is denoted by the mnemonic PADDR.

The type of access that the 68000 has to the 68230's internal registers is shown in Fig. 6.35. Looking at the column labeled "accessible," we see that all registers can be read from but not all can be written into. For instance, the PADDR register that we have been using as an example can be accessed either through a read or write operation. On the other hand, R_{10} (PAAR) and R_{11} (PBAR) are read-only registers.

Example 6.3

What code must be applied to the RS inputs of the 68230 during a bus cycle in which the contents of the port status register are read by the MPU? What is the mnemonic

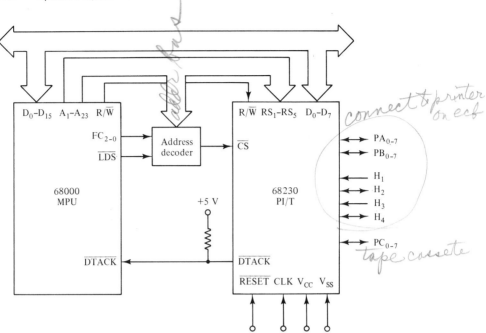

Figure 6-34 Connecting the 68230 PI/T to the 68000 MPU (Motorola, Inc.).

used to identify the port status register? Could this register also be accessed with a write bus cycle?

Solution.   Looking at Fig. 6.35, we find that to select the port status register the register select code

$$RS_5RS_4RS_3RS_2RS_1 = 01101_2$$

must be applied to the 68230. Moreover, in the table of Fig. 6.35 we see that the port status register is identified by the mnemonic PSR and that it also can be written into.

Remember that the 68000 performs asynchronous bus cycles. That is, once started a bus cycle is not completed until the data acknowledge ($\overline{DTACK}$) input is switched to logic 0. Since the 68230 is a 68000 family LSI peripheral, it is designed to produce the $\overline{DTACK}$ signal automatically. For this reason, as shown in Fig. 6.34, the $\overline{DTACK}$ output of the 68230 is simply returned directly to the $\overline{DTACK}$ input of the 68000.

I/O Port Configurations

From Fig. 6.34, we see that ports A, B, and C of the 68230 are bidirectional and are all byte wide. Together, they give 24 input/output lines, which are labeled PA_0 through PA_7, PB_0 through PB_7, and PC_0 through PC_7. There are also four handshake lines, H_1 through H_4, that can be used to implement input and output

Register	Register name	Register select code					Accessible
		5	4	3	2	1	
R_0	Port General Control Register (PGCR)	0	0	0	0	0	R W
R_1	Port Service Request Register (PSRR)	0	0	0	0	1	R W
R_2	Port A Data Direction Register (PADDR)	0	0	0	1	0	R W
R_3	Port B Data Direction Register (PBDDR)	0	0	0	1	1	R W
R_4	Port C Data Direction Register (PCDDR)	0	0	1	0	0	R W
R_5	Port Interrupt Vector Register (PIVR)	0	0	1	0	1	R W
R_6	Port A Control Register (PACR)	0	0	1	1	0	R W
R_7	Port B Control Register (PBCR)	0	0	1	1	1	R W
R_8	Port A Data Register (PADR)	0	1	0	0	0	R W
R_9	Port B Data Register (PBDR)	0	1	0	0	1	R W
R_{10}	Port A Alternate Register (PAAR)	0	1	0	1	0	R
R_{11}	Port B Alternate Register (PBAR)	0	1	0	1	1	R
R_{12}	Port C Data Register (PCDR)	0	1	1	0	0	R W
R_{13}	Port Status Register (PSR)	0	1	1	0	1	R W*
R_{14}	Timer Control Register (TCR)	1	0	0	0	0	R W
R_{15}	Timer Interrupt Vector Register (TIVR)	1	0	0	0	1	R W
R_{16}	Counter Preload Register High (CPRH)	1	0	0	1	1	R W
R_{17}	Counter Preload Register Middle (CPRM)	1	0	1	0	0	R W
R_{18}	Counter Preload Register Low (CPRL)	1	0	1	0	1	R W
R_{19}	Count Register High (CNTRH)	1	0	1	1	1	R
R_{20}	Count Register Middle (CNTRM)	1	1	0	0	0	R
R_{21}	Count Register Low (CNTRL)	1	1	0	0	1	R
R_{22}	Timer Status Register (TSR)	1	1	0	1	0	R W*

*A write to this register may perform a special status resetting operation.   R = Read
W = Write

Figure 6-35 Registers and their select codes (Motorola, Inc.).

handshake protocols. An example of a simple handshake protocol for input of data is to have the external I/O device that is supplying data to the input port signal the 68230 that new data is available at the port by setting H_1 to its active logic level. Then after the 68000 reads data from the port, the H_2 output of the 68230 can be set to its active logic level to signal the I/O device that the data has been read and that it may now apply another byte of data to the port.

Notice in Fig. 6.33 that six of the lines at port C can be configured under software control to serve special functions. For instance, the PC_2 line also can be set up to work as a timer input (T_{IN}). When the 68230's timer is being used as an event counter, pulses applied to this input by external circuitry are used to decrement the value in the counter. That is, T_{IN} is the clock input of the timer. T_{IN} also can be configured to operate as a run/halt input for the timer. When operated in this way, logic 1 at T_{IN} enables the internal timer clock of the 68230 to the input of the timer circuit.

That is, the timer is running when T_{IN} equals 1. On the other hand, logic 0 at T_{IN} turns off the clock and halts the timer. Another example is PC_6. This line has a second label $\overline{PIRQ}$, which stands for parallel interrupt request. This signal is an output that is used when the 68230 implements an interrupt-driven parallel I/O configuration. In this way, we see that lines PC_2 through PC_7 at port C may or may not be available for use as general-purpose inputs or outputs.

Example 6.4

What is the special function performed by the PC_6 line at port C of the 68230?

Solution. In Fig. 6.33, we see that PC_6 is also labeled $\overline{PIACK}$. This mnemonic stands for parallel interrupt acknowledge and is an input with which the 68000 can tell the 68230 that it has been granted service in response to a parallel I/O interrupt request initiated with the $\overline{PIRQ}$ output.

Internal Registers of the 68230

We pointed out earlier that the 68230 PI/T has 23 internal registers, R_0 through R_{22}. The register model in Fig. 6.36 identifies each of these registers along with the function of each of their bits. In general, these registers are used to configure the mode of operation of the I/O ports and timer, input and output data, and input status information about the I/O ports and timer.

The I/O ports of the 68230 are very versatile and can be programmed for a wide variety of different modes of operation. Let us begin our study of these registers and how they control the operation of the 68230 by just briefly looking at some of the ways in which ports A and B can be configured.

Ports A and B of the 68230 can be configured to work in one of four general ways called *modes*. The first two of these modes correspond to the use of ports A and B separately as byte-wide unidirectional or bidirectional ports. In the other two modes, ports A and B are used together to form a single word-wide unidirectional or bidirectional port. Ports that are set up for unidirectional operation must be further configured with what is called a *submode* of operation. The submode defines whether the lines of the port all work as inputs, all work as outputs, or act as bit addressable inputs or outputs. In addition to the modes and submodes of operation, the ports can also be set up for latched input operation, interrupt driven operation, direct memory accessed operation, and with a number of input/output handshake protocols. The operation of the ports is defined and controlled by the contents of registers R_0 through R_{13} of the 68230's register set. For this reason, we will now look at the function of the bits in each of these control registers in more detail.

Register R_0 is called the port general control register and is identified by the mnemonic PGCR for short. Figure 6.37(a) shows the control functions of its bits. Notice that the two most significant bits are used together as a 2-bit port mode control code. The binary combination in these bits select one of four modes of operation for both port A and port B. These modes of operation are called mode 0, mode 1, mode 2, and mode 3. For instance, in Fig. 6.37(b), we find that if B_7B_6 equals 00

meaning of bits

name of register

out or in 68230

Register	7	6	5	4	3	2	1	0	
R_0	Port Mode Control		H34 Enable	H12 Enable	H4 Sense	H3 Sense	H2 Sense	H1 Sense	Port General Control Register
R_1	*	SVCRQ Select		Interrupt PFS		Port Interrupt Priority Control			Port Service Request Register
R_2	Bit 7	Bit 6	Bit 5	Bit 4	Bit 3	Bit 2	Bit 1	Bit 0	Port A Data Direction Register
R_3	Bit 7	Bit 6	Bit 5	Bit 4	Bit 3	Bit 2	Bit 1	Bit 0	Port B Data Direction Register
R_4	Bit 7	Bit 6	Bit 5	Bit 4	Bit 3	Bit 2	Bit 1	Bit 0	Port C Data Direction Register
R_5	Interrupt Vector Number						*	*	Port Interrupt Vector Register
R_6	Port A Submode		H2 Control			H2 Int Enable	H1 SVCRQ Enable	H1 Stat Ctrl	Port A Control Register
R_7	Port B Submode		H4 Control			H4 Int Enable	H3 SVCRQ Enable	H3 Stat Ctrl	Port B Control Register
R_8	Bit 7	Bit 6	Bit 5	Bit 4	Bit 3	Bit 2	Bit 1	Bit 0	Port A Data Register
R_9	Bit 7	Bit 6	Bit 5	Bit 4	Bit 3	Bit 2	Bit 1	Bit 0	Port B Data Register
R_{10}	Bit 7	Bit 6	Bit 5	Bit 4	Bit 3	Bit 2	Bit 1	Bit 0	Port A Alternate Register
R_{11}	Bit 7	Bit 6	Bit 5	Bit 4	Bit 3	Bit 2	Bit 1	Bit 0	Port B Alternate Register
R_{12}	Bit 7	Bit 6	Bit 5	Bit 4	Bit 3	Bit 2	Bit 1	Bit 0	Port C Data Register
R_{13}	H4 Level	H3 Level	H2 Level	H1 Level	H4S	H3S	H2S	H1S	Port Status Register
	*	*	*	*	*	*	*	*	(null)
	*	*	*	*	*	*	*	*	(null)
R_{14}	TOUT/TIACK Control		Z D Ctrl		*	Clock Control		Timer Enable	Timer Control Register
R_{15}	Bit 7	Bit 6	Bit 5	Bit 4	Bit 3	Bit 2	Bit 1	Bit 0	Timer Interrupt Vector Register
	*	*	*	*	*	*	*	*	(null)
R_{16}	Bit 23	Bit 22	Bit 21	Bit 20	Bit 19	Bit 18	Bit 17	Bit 16	Counter Preload Register (High)
R_{17}	Bit 15	Bit 14	Bit 13	Bit 12	Bit 11	Bit 10	Bit 9	Bit 8	(Mid)
R_{18}	Bit 7	Bit 6	Bit 5	Bit 4	Bit 3	Bit 2	Bit 1	Bit 0	(Low)
	*	*	*	*	*	*	*	*	(null)
R_{19}	Bit 23	Bit 22	Bit 21	Bit 20	Bit 19	Bit 18	Bit 17	Bit 16	Count Register (High)
R_{20}	Bit 15	Bit 14	Bit 13	Bit 12	Bit 11	Bit 10	Bit 9	Bit 8	(Mid)
R_{21}	Bit 7	Bit 6	Bit 5	Bit 4	Bit 3	Bit 2	Bit 1	Bit 0	(Low)
R_{22}	*	*	*	*	*	*	*	ZDS	Timer Status Register
	*	*	*	*	*	*	*	*	(null)
	*	*	*	*	*	*	*	*	(null)
	*	*	*	*	*	*	*	*	(null)
	*	*	*	*	*	*	*	*	(null)
	*	*	*	*	*	*	*	*	(null)

Figure 6-36 Register Model of the 68230 (Motorola, Inc.).

7	6	5	4	3	2	1	0
Port Mode Control		H34 Enable	H12 Enable	H4 Sense	H3 Sense	H2 Sense	H1 Sense

(a)

PGCR

7	6	Port Mode Control
0	0	Mode 0 (Unidirectional 8-Bit Mode)
0	1	Mode 1 (Unidirectional 16-Bit Mode)
1	0	Mode 2 (Bidirectional 8-Bit Mode)
1	1	Mode 3 (Bidirectional 16-Bit Mode)

PGCR

5	H34 Enable
0	Disabled
1	Enabled

PGCR

4	H12 Enable
0	Disabled
1	Enabled

PGCR

3-0	Handshake Pin Sense
0	The associated pin is at the high-voltage level when negated and at the low-voltage level when asserted.
1	The associated pin is at the low-voltage level when negated and at the high-voltage level when asserted.

(b)

written to affect operation of chip

actively

Figure 6-37 (a) Port general control register (PGCR) format; (b) control bit functions (Motorola, Inc.).

the A and B ports are configured for mode 0 (unidirectional 8-bit mode) operation. That is, they are set up to work as either byte-wide input or byte-wide output ports. The fact that the port lines are inputs or outputs is determined by what is called a submode. The submodes of operation are selected by bits in another control register.

The rest of the bits in PGCR are used to enable and set the active logic levels of handshake lines H_1 through H_4. For example, bit B_4 is the H_{12} enable bit. As shown in Fig. 6.37(b), it must be set to logic 1 to enable the H_1 and H_2 lines for operation. The sense (active logic level) of the handshake lines is also programmable. This is done with bits B_0 through B_3 of PGCR. Notice that the value in bits B_0 and B_1 sets the active logic level of H_1 and H_2, respectively. For instance, making B_0 logic 1 sets the high-voltage level as the active state for handshake line H_1. On the other hand, if B_1 is set to logic 0, the low-voltage level is set as the active state for H_2.

Example 6.5

What value will need to be written into PGCR if mode 1 operation is to be selected for ports A and B; H_{12} is to be disabled and H_{34} is to be enabled; and all of the handshake lines are to be set up with the low-voltage level as their active logic level?

Solution. In Fig. 6.37(b), we find that mode 1 operation is selected by making the mode select code equal to 01.

$$B_7 B_6 = 01$$

Next, H_{34} is enabled by setting bit 5 to logic 1 and H_{12} is disabled by making bit 4 logic 0.

$$B_5 = 1$$
$$B_4 = 0$$

Finally, to set the active logic levels of the H lines for the low-voltage level, sense bits 0 through 3 are all set to logic 0.

$$B_3 \ B_2 \ B_1 \ B_0 \ = 0000$$

Therefore, the control byte that is to be loaded into PGCR as

$$B_7 \ B_6 \ B_5 \ B_4 \ B_3 \ B_2 \ B_1 \ B_0 = 01100000_2$$
$$= 60_{16}$$

It must be noted that this control byte cannot be directly loaded into PGCR. This is because the mode control bits should only be altered when bits H_{12} and H_{34} are both logic 0. For this reason, PGCR should be loaded in two steps. For instance, first the byte

$$B_7 \ B_6 \ B_5 \ B_4 \ B_3 \ B_2 \ B_1 \ B_0 = 01000000_2$$
$$= 40_{16}$$

can be loaded to initialize the mode and disable the handshake lines. Then the register's state is finalized by writing the byte

$$B_7 \ B_6 \ B_5 \ B_4 \ B_3 \ B_2 \ B_1 \ B_0 = 01100000_2$$
$$= 60_{16}$$

Now that we have described the control functions performed by the bits of R_0, let us continue with another register that controls general operations of the A and B ports: register R_1, the port service request register (PSRR). Earlier in this section we indicated that the parallel I/O ports of the 68230 can be operated in a way that involves the interrupt interface of the 68000. When using interrupt-driven mode of operation for I/O, control bits in PSRR are used to configure signal lines of port C as interrupt request and interrupt acknowledge lines instead of as I/O lines and to assign a priority scheme to the handshake lines. Ports A and B of the 68230 also can be operated in a direct memory access (DMA) mode. This mode of operation is configured with control bits in R_1.

Figure 6.38(a) shows the format of the control bits in PSRR. The * in bit position 7 means that it is not in use. It is followed in bit positions 5 and 6 with a two-bit service request (SVCRQ) select code. This code determines whether the $PC_4/\overline{DMAREQ}$ pin at port C is configured as an I/O pin (PC_4) or as the DMA request output ($\overline{DMAREQ}$). Notice in Fig. 6.38(b) that making bit 6 logic 0 selects I/O mode of operation and making it 1 selects the DMA mode. Moreover, we find that bit 5 determines whether DMA operations are associated with the port

7	6	5	4	3	2	1	0
*	SVCRQ Select		Interrupt PFS		Port Interrupt Priority Control		

(a)

PSRR

6 5   **SVCRQ Select**

0 X The PC4/$\overline{\text{DMAREQ}}$ pin carries the PC4 function; DMA
      is not used.

1 0 The PC4/$\overline{\text{DMAREQ}}$ pin carries the $\overline{\text{DMAREQ}}$ function
      and is associated with double-buffered transfers con-
      trolled by H1. H1 is removed from the PI/T's interrupt
      structure, and thus, does not cause interrupt requests
      to be generated. To obtain $\overline{\text{DMAREQ}}$ pulses, Port A
      Control Register bit 1 (H1 SVCRQ Enable) must be a 1.

1 1 The PC4/$\overline{\text{DMAREQ}}$ pin carries the $\overline{\text{DMAREQ}}$ function
      and is associated with double-buffered transfers con-
      trolled by H3. H3 is removed from the PI/T's interrupt
      structure, and thus, does not cause interrupt requests
      to be generated. To obtain $\overline{\text{DMAREQ}}$ pulses, Port B
      Control Register bit 1 (H3 SVCRQ Enable) must be 1.

PSRR

4 3   **Interrupt Pin Function Select**

0 0 The PC5/$\overline{\text{PIRQ}}$ pin carries the PC5 function.
      The PC6/$\overline{\text{PIACK}}$ pin carries the PC6 function.

0 1 The PC5/$\overline{\text{PIRQ}}$ pin carries the $\overline{\text{PIRQ}}$ function.
      The PC6/$\overline{\text{PIACK}}$ pin carries the PC6 function.

1 0 The PC5/$\overline{\text{PIRQ}}$ pin carries the PC5 function.
      The PC6/$\overline{\text{PIACK}}$ pin carries the $\overline{\text{PIACK}}$ function.

1 1 The PC5/$\overline{\text{PIRQ}}$ pin carries the $\overline{\text{PIRQ}}$ function.
      The PC6/$\overline{\text{PIACK}}$ pin carries the $\overline{\text{PIACK}}$ function.

PSRR			Port Interrupt Priority Control			
2	1	0	Highest	....		Lowest
0	0	0	H1S	H2S	H3S	H4S
0	0	1	H2S	H1S	H3S	H4S
0	1	0	H1S	H2S	H4S	H3S
0	1	1	H2S	H1S	H4S	H3S
1	0	0	H3S	H4S	H1S	H2S
1	0	1	H3S	H4S	H2S	H1S
1	1	0	H4S	H3S	H1S	H2S
1	1	1	H4S	H3S	H2S	H1S

(b)

Figure 6-38 (a) Port service request register (PSRR) format; (b) control bit functions (Motorola, Inc.).

corresponding to the H_1 or H_3 handshake line. For instance, the code

$$B_6B_5 = 10$$

selects DMA operation associated with H_1 and port A.

The next two bits in PSRR, bits 3 and 4, define the operation of the $PC_5/\overline{PIRQ}$ and $PC_6/\overline{PIACK}$ pins of the 68230. In Fig. 6.38(b), we see that making them both logic 0

$$B_4B_3 = 00$$

sets up both PC_5 and PC_6 to operate as I/O lines. On the other hand, setting these control bits to

$$B_4 B_3 = 01$$

selects the interrupt request output ($\overline{PIRQ}$) mode of operation for the $PC_5/\overline{PIRQ}$ pin and leaves PC_6 as an I/O line.

The three least significant bits in PSRR, B_0, B_1, and B_2, assign interrupt priorities to handshake lines H_1 through H_4. The table in Fig. 6.38(b) shows all of the allowed priority schemes. Notice that making

$$B_2 B_1 B_0 = 000$$

assigns priorities in what is called ascending order. That is, H_1 has the lowest priority, it is followed by H_2 with the next higher priority, H_3 follows H_2 with still higher priority, and finally H_4 has the highest priority. In Fig. 6.38(b), we find that changing the port interrupt priority control code to

$$B_2 B_1 B_0 = 111$$

assigns priorities in the reverse order; that is, descending order.

Example 6.6

With what value should PSRR be initialized in order to configure the 68230 such that $PC_4/\overline{DMAREQ}$ acts as an I/O line, $PC_5/\overline{PIRQ}$ acts as an interrupt request output, $PC_6/\overline{PIACK}$ acts as an interrupt acknowledge input, and handshake lines H_1 through H_4 are configured in descending priority order (H_1 has the highest priority and H_4 has the lowest priority).

Solution. From the information in Fig. 6.38(b), we see that making bits 5 and 6 both logic 0 configures $PC_4/\overline{DMAREQ}$ to act as an I/O line

$$B_6 B_5 = 00$$

Then by making bits 3 and 4 both logic 1, $PC_5/\overline{PIRQ}$ acts as an interrupt request output and $PC_6/\overline{PIACK}$ acts as an interrupt acknowledge input.

$$B_4 B_3 = 11$$

Finally, the handshake lines are assigned priorities in descending order by making bits 2 through 0 all logic 0.

$$B_2 B_1 B_0 = 000$$

Assuming that bit 7 is set to logic 0, the complete control byte is

$$B_7 B_6 B_5 B_4 B_3 B_2 B_1 B_0 = 00011000_2$$
$$= 18_{16}$$

The next three registers in Fig. 6.36, R_2 through R_4, are the port A data direction register (PADDR), port B data direction register (PBDDR), and port C data direction register (PCDDR). The logic level of the bits in these registers control the direction of the I/O lines at the respective I/O port when the ports are configured for unidirectional mode of operation. The format of the bits in PADDR is shown in Fig. 6.39. Each of the eight bits in PADDR corresponds to one of the I/O lines at

7	6	5	4	3	2	1	0
Bit 7	Bit 6	Bit 5	Bit 4	Bit 3	Bit 2	Bit 1	Bit 0

Figure 6-39 Port A data direction register (PADDR).

port A. That is, the logic level of bit 0 in PADDR sets the direction of I/O line PA_0; the logic level of bit 1 sets the direction of PA_1; and so on. If an I/O line in port A is to be used as an input, its corresponding bit in PADDR is initialized to logic 0. On the other hand, if it is to operate as an output, the bit is set to 1 instead of 0. Therefore, to configure all of the I/O lines at port B as outputs, PBDDR must be loaded with FF_{16}.

Example 6.7

What value must be loaded into PCDDR to configure all lines of port C as inputs?

Solution. The lines of an I/O port are configured as inputs by setting the bits in the corresponding port data direction register to logic 0. Therefore, all lines of port C are configured as inputs by making all bits of the PCDDR register logic 0.

Register R_5 in Fig. 6.36 is used in conjunction with interrupt-driven mode of operation for the parallel I/O ports. It is the port interrupt vector register (PIVR). Looking at the format diagram in Fig. 6.40, we see that just six of its bits are implemented and that they are loaded under software control with the upper six bits of an interrupt vector number. The two least significant bits of the vector are supplied by the prioritization logic within the 68230 and represent the priority of the active handshake line.

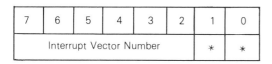

Figure 6-40 Port interrupt vector register (PIVR) format (Motorola, Inc.).

Before introducing the port A and B control registers, let us look at the two groups of registers that follow them in Fig. 6.36. The first group, R_8 and R_9, are the port A and B data registers, PADR and PBDR. Each bit in these registers corresponds to one of the lines at the corresponding I/O port. The format of the port A data register (PADR) is shown in Fig. 6.41. Here bit 0 corresponds to signal line PA_0 at port A and bit 7 corresponds to signal line PA_7.

These are the registers through which the 68000 inputs or outputs data to the I/O ports of the PI/T. If port A is configured as an input port, the logic levels applied to the PA inputs can be latched into the PADR register and then read out of the register by the 68000 MPU. In the case of port A configured as an output port, data are output by the MPU to PADR instead of directly to the output ports.

As shown in Fig. 6.36, the next group, R_{10} and R_{11}, are the alternate data registers: the port A alternate data register (PAADR) and port B alternate data register

7	6	5	4	3	2	1	0
Bit 7	Bit 6	Bit 5	Bit 4	Bit 3	Bit 2	Bit 1	Bit 0

Figure 6-41 Port A data register (PADR) format.

(PABDR). These registers are similar to the data register we just described in that they contain a bit for each bit of the corresponding I/O port. However, these registers can only be read and when read the data received by the MPU represents the instantaneous logic levels at the I/O pins of the port.

Now we will continue with the port A and B control registers (PACR and PBCR) that we skipped earlier. In Fig. 6.36, they are identified as registers R_6 and R_7. Figure 6.42(a) shows the formats of PACR and PBCR. Notice that corresponding bits in the two registers serve the same basic function; however, for their respective ports.

Earlier in this section we found that two of the bits in the port general control register (R_0) are used to select between mode 0, mode 1, mode 2, or mode 3 operation for the A and B ports and that submodes of operation exist within each of the general modes. It is the function of control bits within PACR and PBCR to select the submodes of operation. In the format of PACR and PBCR in Fig. 6.42(a), we see that the two most significant bits of each register define the submode of operation for the corresponding port. For example, if the mode select bits in PGCR configure port A for mode 0 operation and the submode bits in PACR are set to 00 for submode 00, the I/O configuration is as shown in Fig. 6.42(b). Notice that port lines PA_0 through PA_7 act as a byte-wide latched double-buffered input port. By latched, we mean that data applied to the PA input pins are latched into flip-flops within the 68230 synchronously with the transition of the logic level of the H_1 input. Remember that the active level of the H_1 handshake input can be set to logic 1 or logic 0 by the sense bit in PGCR. For this reason, data can be latched into the port A data register on a positive-going transition or negative-going transition at the H_1 input.

Let us now look just briefly at what is meant by double buffered. This means that the I/O ports of the 68230 have dual latches. Use of this double buffering permits an overlapping mode of operation in which the current data in the port A data register can be read by the MPU and at the same time external circuitry can strobe new data into the register. This capability of the 68230 results in a higher maximum input/output data rate.

Example 6.8

How would port B operate if the mode control bits in PGCR are 00 and the submode bits in PBCR are 01?

Solution. 00 in the mode control bits of PGCR selects mode 0 operation for both port A and port B, and 01 in the submode bits of PBCR selects submode 01 operation for port B. Looking at Fig. 6.42(b), we see that this selects the I/O configuration labeled mode 0 submode 01. Notice that in this case the B port is configured as a double-buffered byte-wide output port with H_3 and H_4 as its handshake lines. H_3 is an input by which the external device that is reading data from the PB output lines can signal the 68230

Port A Control Register (PACR) —

7	6	5	4	3	2	1	0
Port A Submode		H2 Control			H2 Int. Enable	H1 SVCRQ Enable	H1 Stat. Ctrl.

Port B Control Register (PBCR) —

7	6	5	4	3	2	1	0
Port B Submode		H4 Control			H4 Int. Enable	H3 SVCRQ Enable	H3 Stat. Ctrl.

(a)

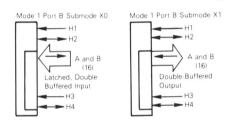

(b)

Mode 0 (Unidirectional 8-Bit Mode)
Port A
    Submode 00 — Double-Buffered Input
        H1 — Latches input data
        H2 — Status/interrupt generating input, general-purpose output, or operation with H1 in the interlocked or pulsed input handshake protocols
    Submode 01 — Double-Buffered Output
        H1 — Indicates data received by peripheral
        H2 — Status/interrupt generating input, general-purpose output, or operation with H1 in the interlocked or pulsed output handshake protocols
    Submode 1X — Bit I/O
        H1 — Status/interrupt generating input
        H2 — Status/interrupt generating input or general-purpose output
Port B, H3 and H4 — Identical to Port A, H1 and H2

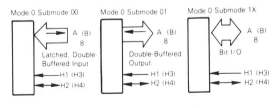

(c)

Mode 1 (Unidirectional 16-Bit Mode)
    Port A — Double-Buffered Data (Most significant)
        Submode XX (not used)
            H1 — Status/interrupt generating input
            H2 — Status/interrupt generating input or general-purpose output
    Port B — Double-Buffered Data (Least significant)
        Submode X0 — Unidirectional 16-Bit Input
            H3 — Latches input data
            H4 — Status/interrupt generating input, general-purpose output, or operation with H3 in the interlocked or pulsed input handshake protocols
        Submode X1 — Unidirectional 16-Bit Output
            H3 — Indicates data received by peripheral
            H4 — Status/interrupt generating input, general-purpose output, or operation with H3 in the interlocked or pulsed output handshake protocols

Figure 6-42 (a) PACR and PBCR formats; (b) Mode 0 I/O configurations; (c) Mode 1 I/O configurations.

that it is ready to receive new data. Moreover, the H_4 line can be configured to operate in a number of different ways using other bits in PBCR.

I/O configurations and pin function descriptions for mode 1, mode 2, and mode 3 and their corresponding submodes are given in Fig. 6.42(c), (d), and (e), respectively.

Let us now look at the functions served by other control bits in PACR and PBCR. From the format of PACR in Fig. 6.42(a), we find that the next three bits, bits 5, 4, and 3, form a 3-bit code that selects a mode of operation for the H_2 control line. However, the type of operation depends on the mode and submode of operation selected for the port. The allowed configuration for all submodes of mode 0 operation

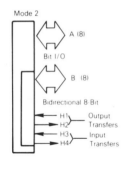

Mode 2

A (8)

Bit I/O

B (8)

Bidirectional 8-Bit

H1 ⎱ Output
H2 ⎰ Transfers
H3 ⎱ Input
H4 ⎰ Transfers

Mode 2 (Bidirectional 8-Bit Mode)
Port A — Bit I/O (with no handshaking pins)
  Submode XX (not used)
Port B — Bidirectional 8-Bit Data (Double-Buffered)
  Submode XX (not used)
  H1 — Indicates output data received by peripheral
  H2 — Operation with H1 in the interlocked or pulsed output
       handshake protocols
  H3 — Latches input data
  H4 — Operation with H3 in the interlocked or pulsed input
       handshake protocols

(d)

Mode 3

A and B (16)

Bidirectional 16-Bit

H1 ⎱ Output
H2 ⎰ Transfers
H3 ⎱ Input
H4 ⎰ Transfers

Mode 3 (Bidirectional 16-Bit Mode)
Port A — Double-Buffered Data (Most significant)
  Submode XX (not used)
Port B — Double-Buffered Data (Least significant)
  Submode XX (not used)
H1 — Indicates output data received by peripheral
H2 — Operation with H1 in the interlocked or pulsed output
     handshake protocols
H3 — Latches input data
H4 — Operation with H3 in the interlocked or pulsed input
     handshake protocols

(e)

PACR Mode 0 Port a Submode 01

PACR

2	**H2 Interrupt Enable**
0	The H2 interrupt is disabled.
1	The H2 interrupt is enabled.

PACR

1	**H1 SVCRQ Enable**
0	The H1 interrupt and DMA request are disabled.
1	The H1 interrupt and DMA request are enabled.

PACR Mode 0 Port A Submode 00

PACR

5	4	3	**H2 Control**
0	X	X	Input pin — status only.
1	0	0	Output pin — always negated.
1	0	1	Output pin — always asserted.
1	1	0	Output pin — interlocked input handshake protocol.
1	1	1	Output pin — pulsed input handshake protocol.

PACR

0	**H1 Status Control**
X	Not Used

PACR

5	4	3	**H2 Control**
0	X	X	Input pin — status only.
1	0	0	Output pin — always negated.
1	0	1	Output pin — always asserted.
1	1	0	Output pin — interlocked output handshake protocol.
1	1	1	Output pin — pulsed output handshake protocol.

PACR

0	**H1 Status Control**
0	The H1S status bit is 1 when either the Port A initial or final output latch can accept new data. It is 0 when both latches are full and cannot accept new data.
1	The H1S status bit is 1 when both of the Port A output latches are empty. It is 0 when at least one latch is full.

PACR Mode 0 Port A Submode 1X

PCR

5	4	3	**H2 Control**
0	X	X	Input pin — status only.
1	X	0	Output pin — always negated.
1	X	1	Output pin — always asserted.

PACR

0	**H1 Status Control**
X	Not used.

(f)

Figure 6-42 *(cont.)* (d) Mode 2 I/O configuration; (e) Mode 3 I/O configuration; (f) Mode 0 control bit functions.

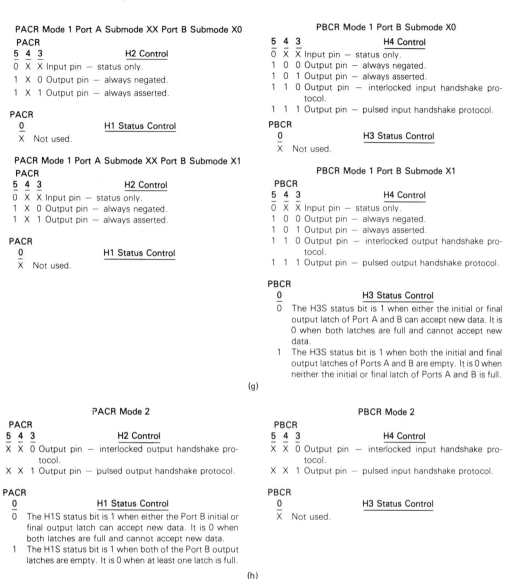

PACR Mode 1 Port A Submode XX Port B Submode X0

PACR

5	4	3	H2 Control
0	X	X	Input pin − status only.
1	X	0	Output pin − always negated.
1	X	1	Output pin − always asserted.

PACR

0	H1 Status Control
X	Not used.

PACR Mode 1 Port A Submode XX Port B Submode X1

PACR

5	4	3	H2 Control
0	X	X	Input pin − status only.
1	X	0	Output pin − always negated.
1	X	1	Output pin − always asserted.

PACR

0	H1 Status Control
X	Not used.

PBCR Mode 1 Port B Submode X0

5	4	3	H4 Control
0	X	X	Input pin − status only.
1	0	0	Output pin − always negated.
1	0	1	Output pin − always asserted.
1	1	0	Output pin − interlocked input handshake protocol.
1	1	1	Output pin − pulsed input handshake protocol.

PBCR

0	H3 Status Control
X	Not used.

PBCR Mode 1 Port B Submode X1

PBCR

5	4	3	H4 Control
0	X	X	Input pin − status only.
1	0	0	Output pin − always negated.
1	0	1	Output pin − always asserted.
1	1	0	Output pin − interlocked output handshake protocol.
1	1	1	Output pin − pulsed output handshake protocol.

PBCR

0	H3 Status Control
0	The H3S status bit is 1 when either the initial or final output latch of Port A and B can accept new data. It is 0 when both latches are full and cannot accept new data.
1	The H3S status bit is 1 when both the initial and final output latches of Ports A and B are empty. It is 0 when neither the initial or final latch of Ports A and B is full.

(g)

PACR Mode 2

PACR

5	4	3	H2 Control
X	X	0	Output pin − interlocked output handshake protocol.
X	X	1	Output pin − pulsed output handshake protocol.

PACR

0	H1 Status Control
0	The H1S status bit is 1 when either the Port B initial or final output latch can accept new data. It is 0 when both latches are full and cannot accept new data.
1	The H1S status bit is 1 when both of the Port B output latches are empty. It is 0 when at least one latch is full.

PBCR Mode 2

PBCR

5	4	3	H4 Control
X	X	0	Output pin − interlocked input handshake protocol.
X	X	1	Output pin − pulsed input handshake protocol.

PBCR

0	H3 Status Control
X	Not used.

(h)

Figure 6-42 *(cont.)* (g) Mode 1 control bit functions; (h) Mode 2 control bit functions.

are given in Fig. 6.42(f). Although this information is represented relative to port A's handshake signals, it also is valid for programming port B's handshake signals, H_3 and H_4, through the port B control register. Notice that for our earlier mode 0 submode 00 example H_2 can be configured in five different ways. For instance, if these three bits are set to

$$B_5 B_4 B_3 = 110$$

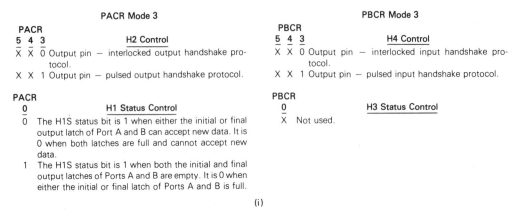

PACR Mode 3

PACR
5 4 3   H2 Control
X X 0 Output pin — interlocked output handshake protocol.
X X 1 Output pin — pulsed output handshake protocol.

PACR
0   H1 Status Control
0 The H1S status bit is 1 when either the initial or final output latch of Port A and B can accept new data. It is 0 when both latches are full and cannot accept new data.
1 The H1S status bit is 1 when both the initial and final output latches of Ports A and B are empty. It is 0 when either the initial or final latch of Ports A and B is full.

PBCR Mode 3

PBCR
5 4 3   H4 Control
X X 0 Output pin — interlocked input handshake protocol.
X X 1 Output pin — pulsed input handshake protocol.

PBCR
0   H3 Status Control
X Not used.

(i)

Figure 6-42 *(cont.)* (i) Mode 3 control bit functions (Motorola, Inc.).

H_2 is set up as an output and implements what is called the interlock input handshake protocol.

In this case, its operation is interlocked with that of the H_1 pin. In fact, the H_2 output will be at its active logic level whenever the port A data register is ready to accept new data. In this way, it can signal the input device that supplies PA_0 through PA_7 that the 68230 is ready to accept data from this port. The active logic level (sense) of H_2 is defined by a bit in PGCR. Therefore, the input device can apply a byte of data to the PA lines and then switches H_1 to its active logic level. In response to an active H_1, the 68230 latches the data at PA_0–PA_7 into PADR and then switches H_2 to its inactive logic level. This signals the input device that the 68230 is no longer ready to accept data. The port remains in this state until the MPU reads the byte of data from PADR.

In practical applications, H_4 can be used in conjunction with H_3 to implement an interlocked output handshake protocol for port B. Let us look just briefly at how this can be done when port B is configured for mode 0 submode 01 operation. In Fig. 6.42(f), we find that the kinds of operations that can be performed by H_2 for mode 0 submode 01 output ports are similar to those available for mode 0 submode 00 input ports. We will now describe the output operation for H_4 control code

$$B_5B_4B_3 = 110$$

In this case, H_3 and H_4 again operate in an interlocked mode of operation, but this time the MPU sends data to the output port by writing it into PBDR. When PBDR is loaded, the H_4 output switches to its active logic level. This signal line can be used to tell the output device attached to port B that a new byte of data is available at PB_0–PB_7. In response, the output device can read the byte of data from the port and then signal the 68230 that it is ready to accept new data by switching the H_3 input to its active logic level. The occurrence of the active logic level at H_3 causes H_4 to return to its inactive logic level. H_4 remains at its inactive level until the MPU writes another byte of data into PBDR.

A question that may arise from our description of the interlocked output handshake protocol is, How does the MPU know that new data needs to be sent to the output port's data register. It turns out that there are status bits for H_1 through H_4 in a register within the 68230. Therefore, the MPU can poll these bits through software to determine when data are to be output. Alternately, the 68230 can be configured to operate in an interrupt-driven mode of operation. When operated in this way, the 68230 automatically produces the $\overline{PIREQ}$ signal whenever the MPU needs to output new data to the port. This mode of operation eliminates the need for the software polling routine.

Bit 0 of PACR and PBCR are control bits for the H_1 and H_3 status bits, H_{1S} and H_{3S}, respectively. As shown in Fig. 6.42(f) for mode 0 submode 01 operation at port A, this bit can configure the operation of H_{1S} two different ways. For instance, if bit 0 is set to logic 1, H_{1S} will be logic 0 unless both of the port B data latches are empty.

The functions of the control bits of PACR and PBCR for mode 1, mode 2, and mode 3 operation at port A and port B are given in Figs. 6.42(g), (h), and (i), respectively. For these modes, separate bit functions are given for port A and port B.

We just mentioned that a register exists inside the 68230 that contains the status of the handshake lines. This is register R_{13}, the port status register (PSR). As shown in Fig. 6.43, the logic levels of the bits of this register represent the handshake pin signal's current logic levels and handshake status information. The four most significant bits in PSR are labeled H_4, H_3, H_2, and H_1, and if read by the MPU they represent the current logic levels at the respective handshake line. The 68000 can examine the state of the handshake lines through software by reading the values in these bits. The other four bits, H_{1S}, H_{2S}, H_{3S}, H_{4S}, are also handshake status bits. However, their logic levels are set or reset differently based on the port A and port B mode and submode and handshake signal activity.

7	6	5	4	3	2	1	0
H4 Level	H3 Level	H2 Level	H1 Level	H4S	H3S	H2S	H1S

Figure 6-43 Port status register (PSR) format (Motorola, Inc.).

Example 6.9

How is port A configured if the value in PACR is 78_{16}? Assume that mode 0 operation was selected for ports A and B in PGCR.

Solution.   In binary form, the control byte is

$$PACR = 01111000_2$$

From Fig. 6.42(b), we find that the port is configured for mode 0 submode 01 operation.

$$B_7B_6 = 01 = \text{Submode 0}$$

The next three bits in the register set the mode of operation for H_2. In Fig. 6.42(f) we find that the code 111 sets up H_2 for pulsed output handshake protocol.

$$B_5B_4B_3 = 111 = \text{Pulsed output handshake protocol}$$

The next two bits are both 0 and disable the H_2 interrupt request and H_1 interrupt and DMA service request functions, respectively.

$$B_2 = 0 = H_2 \text{ interrupt request disabled}$$

$$B_1 = 0 = H_1 \text{ interrupt and DMA request disabled}$$

Finally, bit 0 sets the operation of the H_{1S} status bit such that it is logic 0 if both the port A initial and final output latches are full and logic 1 if either latch is empty.

$$B_0 = H_{1S} \text{ is 0 if both port A output latches are full}$$
$$\text{and 1 if either is empty}$$

ASSIGNMENT

Section 6.2

1. Does the 68000 employ separate memory and I/O address spaces?

Section 6.3

2. Can an instruction access word data that starts at an odd memory address?

3. Write a sequence of instructions to store the long-word contents of D_0 in memory starting at address $A001.

Section 6.4

4. In which address range can interrupt service routine vectors be stored?

Section 6.5

5. What function code would be anticipated on the FC lines when the result of an ADD instruction is being written to the destination location in memory? Assume that the 68000 is in the user state.

6. Why would a user/supervisor system environment be employed?

7. Draw a circuit similar to the one in Fig. 6.9 in which a 16M-byte memory address space is implemented as four 4M-byte blocks: the user program memory, user data memory, supervisor program memory, and supervisor data memory. The supervisor is to have access to all memory areas.

Section 6.6

8. Give an overview of the sequence of events that occur when an instruction word is read from address $A000.

Section 6.7

9. Give an overview of the sequence of events that occur when a byte of data is written to address $A001.

Section 6.8

10. Write a single instruction to push the long-word contents of registers A_0, A_1, and A_2 onto the supervisor stack.

11. Restore the contents of the registers saved in problem 10 by individually popping them from the stack.

Section 6.9

12. Give an overview of the operation of the circuit in Fig. 6.13 for an upper byte access from the group 2 RAMs.

Section 6.10

13. Write an instruction sequence that will output the long-word contents of D_0 to four-byte-wide output ports starting at address \$16000. The output ports are located at consecutive even addresses.

14. Write an instruction that will input a word of data from two byte-wide input ports and store it in D_1. Assume that the input ports are located at consecutive odd addresses which are displaced by 10 bytes in the positive direction from an input address pointer held in register A_1.

Section 6.11

15. Referring to the table in Fig. 6.15, give an overview of each of the different modes of I/O operation for which a byte-wide port on the 6821 can be configured.

Section 6.12

16. For the circuit in Fig. 6.17 and the address map in Fig. 6.18(a), write instructions that do the following:
  (a) Configure the B port of both U_{14} and U_{15} as output ports.
  (b) Configure the A port of both U_{14} and U_{15} as input ports.
  (c) Configure the B output ports such that they produce a fixed duration strobe pulse at their CB_2 output and select its data output register.
  (d) Configure the A input ports such that they initiate an interrupt request through their CA_1 inputs; the interrupt is to be initiated by a high-to-low transition at CA_1; and the output register is to be selected.

17. Write a program that moves five bytes of data from a table in memory starting at address \$A000 to the B port of U_{14} in the circuit of Fig. 6.17. Assume that the B port is configured as defined in problem 16(c).

Section 6.13

18. What is meant by synchronous bus operation for the 68000?

19. How does the synchronous bus cycle of Fig. 6.20(a) differ from the asynchronous bus cycle in Fig. 6.10(a)?

Section 6.14

20. Name a signal line that distinguishes an asynchronous communication interface from that of a synchronous communication interface.

21. Describe the sequence of signals that become active in Fig. 6.5 when the microcomputer transfers a character to the terminal.

22. Define a simplex, a half-duplex, and a full-duplex communication link.

Section 6.15

23. If the control inputs of a 6850 are RS = 1 and R/$\overline{W}$ = 1, what type of operation is taking place over the microprocessor bus?

24. Describe the internal operation of the receiver section of the 6850 as a serial data character is read from the Rx_{DATA} input. How does the 6850 signal the microprocessor that a valid character has been received?

25. Overview the operation of the 6850 as it accepts a byte of character data from the microprocessor and then transmits it over the Tx_{DATA} line.

26. If the control register of the 6850 contains BE_{16}, how is the device configured for operation?

27. Write an instruction sequence that will reset the 6850. Assume that the device resides at address $Q0ABCD_{16}$.

28. If the contents of the 6850's status register are read as 00000010_{16}, in which state of data communications is the device?

Section 6.16

29. If RS_5 RS_4 RS_3 RS_2 RS_1 = 8_{16} is applied to the 68230, which of its internal registers is selected?

30. The PGCR register of a 68230 is found to contain 00010010_2. What mode of operation is selected for the I/O ports, which handshake lines are enabled, and what active logic levels are selected for the enabled handshake lines?

31. Write a sequence of instructions to load PGCR with 60_{16}. Assume that the 68230 is located at address $A001_{16}$.

32. The contents of the 68230's PSRR are 03_{16}. What functions are selected for the PC_4, PC_5, and PC_6 lines? How is interrupt priority assigned to the handshake lines?

33. Write a sequence of instructions to configure ports A, B, and C as input, output, and input ports, respectively. Assume that register PADDR is located at address $A005_{16}$; PBDDR is at address $A007_{16}$; and PCDDR is at address $A009_{16}$.

34. Specify the mode bits in PGCR and the submode bits in PBCR that are needed to configure the B port as a 16-bit input port and so that H_3 is used to latch the input data.

7

EXCEPTION PROCESSING OF THE 68000 MICROPROCESSOR

7.1 INTRODUCTION

In the last chapter, we covered the memory and input/output interfaces for the 68000-based microcomputer. Here we will consider the exception processing capability of the 68000 and a special input interface, the *external hardware interrupt interface*. The topics covered are as follows:

1. Types of exceptions
2. Exception vector table
3. Exception group priorities
4. External hardware interrupt interface
5. External interrupt priorities and the interrupt mask
6. General interrupt processing sequence
7. General interrupt interface circuit
8. Autovector interrupt mechanism
9. Autovector interrupt interface circuit
10. Exception instructions
11. Bus error
12. Reset
13. Internal exception functions

7.2 TYPES OF EXCEPTIONS

For the 68000 microcomputer system, Motorola, Inc., has defined the concept of *exception processing.* Exception processing is similar to what is more generally known as interrupt processing. Just like the interrupt capabilities of other microprocessors, the exception mechanism allows the 68000 to respond quickly to special internal or external events. Based on the occurrence of this type of event, the main program is terminated and a context switch is initiated to a new program environment. This new program environment, the exception service routine, is a segment of program designed to service the requesting condition. At completion of exception processing, program control can be returned to the point at which the exception occurred in the main program.

The 68000 has a broad variety of methods by which exception processing can be initiated. They include the *external exception functions, hardware reset, bus error,* and *user defined interrupts.* Furthermore, the 68000 has a number of instructions that can initiate exception processing. Some examples of these instructions are TRAP, TRAPV, and CHK. The 68000 also has extensive internal exception capability. It includes exceptions for internal error conditions (*address error, illegal/unimplemented opcodes,* and *privilege violation*) and internal functions (*trace* and *spurious interrupt*).

7.3 EXCEPTION VECTOR TABLE

Each of the exception functions that is performed by the 68000 has a number called the *vector number* assigned to it. For external interrupts, the interrupting device supplies the vector number to the 68000. On the other hand, for other types of interrupts, the vector number is generated within the microprocessor. The 68000 converts the vector number to the address of a corresponding long-word storage location in memory. Held at this memory location is a 24-bit address known as the *vector address* of the exception. It defines the starting point of the service routine in program storage memory. Figure 7.1 shows the format in which the address vector is stored in memory. As shown, it takes up two word locations. The lower addressed word is the high word of the new program counter and the higher addressed word is the low word of PC. Only the 8 LSBs of the high word are used.

The vector addresses are stored in a part of the 68000's memory system known as the *exception vector table.* As shown in Fig. 7.2, the vector table contains up to 256 vectors, which are labeled with vector numbers 0 through 255. Notice that the table must reside in the address range 000000_{16} through $0003FF_{16}$, which is the first

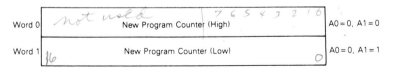

Figure 7-1 Exception vector organization (Motorola, Inc.).

Vector Number(s)	Address			Assignment
	Dec	Hex	Space	
0	0	000	SP	Reset: Initial SSP
–	4	004	SP	Reset: Initial PC
2	8	008	SD	Bus Error
3	12	00C	SD	Address Error
4	16	010	SD	Illegal Instruction
5	20	014	SD	Zero Divide
6	24	018	SD	CHK Instruction
7	28	01C	SD	TRAPV Instruction
8	32	020	SD	Privilege Violation
9	36	024	SD	Trace
10	40	028	SD	Line 1010 Emulator
11	44	02C	SD	Line 1111 Emulator
12*	48	030	SD	(Unassigned, reserved)
13*	52	034	SD	(Unassigned, reserved)
14*	56	038	SD	(Unassigned, reserved)
15	60	03C	SD	Uninitialized Interrupt Vector
16-23*	64	04C	SD	(Unassigned, reserved)
	95	05F		–
24	96	060	SD	Spurious Interrupt
25	100	064	SD	Level 1 Interrupt Autovector
26	104	068	SD	Level 2 Interrupt Autovector
27	108	06C	SD	Level 3 Interrupt Autovector
28	112	070	SD	Level 4 Interrupt Autovector
29	116	074	SD	Level 5 Interrupt Autovector
30	120	078	SD	Level 6 Interrupt Autovector
31	124	07C	SD	Level 7 Interrupt Autovector
32-47	128	080	SD	TRAP Instruction Vectors
	191	0BF		–
48-63*	192	0C0	SD	(Unassigned, reserved)
	255	0FF		–
64-255	256	100	SD	User Interrupt Vectors
	1023	3FF		–

Figure 7-2 Vector table (Motorola, Inc.).

1024 bytes of the 68000's 16M-byte address space. All vectors other than vector 0 must reside in supervisor data memory. Vector 0, which is assigned to the hardware reset function, must be stored in supervisor program memory.

The hexadecimal address at which each vector is located in memory is also provided in the table of Fig. 7.2. The address of the most significant word of any vector can be determined by multiplying its vector number by 4. For instance, vector 8 is stored starting at address $4_{10} \times 8_{10} = 32_{10} = 000020_{16}$.

All of the low-numbered vectors serve special functions of the 68000 microcomputer system. Examples are the *bus error exception vector* at address 000008_{16}, *address error exception vector* at $00000C_{16}$, *CHK instruction vector* at 000018_{16}, and *spurious interrupt vector* at 000060_{16}. Within this group we also find a small number of reserved vector locations. For instance, vectors 12 through 14 are unassigned and reserved for future use.

The next group, vectors 25 through 31 at addresses 000064_{16} through $00007C_{16}$, is dedicated to what are known as the *autovector interrupts*. They are followed by the *trap instruction vectors* in the address range 000080_{16} through $0000BF_{16}$ and some more reserved vector locations. The last 192 vectors, which are said to be user definable, are used for the external hardware interrupts.

Since the addresses that are held in this table are defined by the programmer, the corresponding exception service routines can reside anywhere in the 68000's 16M-byte address space.

Example 7.1

At what address is the vector for TRAP #5 stored in the memory? If the service routine for this exception is to start at address 010200_{16}, what will be the stored vector?

Solution. The TRAP #5 instruction corresponds to vector number 37. Therefore, its address is calculated as

$$4_{10} \times 37_{10} = 148_{10} = 000094_{16}$$

The vector address 010200_{16} is broken into two words for storage in memory. These words are

$$\text{Most significant word} = 0001_{16}$$

$$\text{Least significant word} = 0200_{16}$$

They get stored as

$$0001_{16} \quad \text{at address } 000094_{16}$$

$$0200_{16} \quad \text{at address } 000096_{16}$$

7.4 EXCEPTION PRIORITIES

The exception processing of the 68000 is handled on a *priority* basis. The *priority level* of an exception or interrupt function determines whether or not its operation can be interrupted by another exception. In general, the 68000 will acknowledge a request for service by an exception only if there is no other exception already in progress or if the requesting function is at a higher-priority level then the currently active exception.

Figure 7.3 shows that the exception functions are divided into three basic priority groups and then assigned additional priority levels within these groups. Here *group 0* represents the highest-priority group. It includes the exception functions of external events such as reset and bus error, as well as the internal address error detection

Group	Exception	Processing
0	*level 1.* Reset *level 2.* Bus Error *level 3* Address Error	Exception processing begins within two clock cycles.
1	Trace Interrupt Illegal Privilege	Exception processing begins before the next instruction
2	TRAP, TRAPV, CHK, Zero Divide	Exception processing is started by normal instruction execution

Figure 7-3 Exception priority groups (Motorola, Inc.).

condition. Within group 0, reset has the highest priority. It is followed by bus error and address error in that order.

Exception functions from group 0 always override an active exception from *group 1* or *group 2*. Moreover, a group 0 function does not wait for completion of execution of the current instruction; instead, it is initiated at the completion of the bus cycle that is in progress.

The next-to-highest priority group, group 1, includes the external hardware interrupts and internal functions: trace, illegal/unimplemented opcode, and privilege violation. In this group, trace has the highest priority and it is followed in order of descending priority by external interrupts, illegal/unimplemented instruction, and privilege violation.   *hardware*

In all four cases in group 1, exception processing is initiated with the completion of the current instruction. If a group 1 exception is in progress, its service routine can be interrupted only by a group 0 exception or another exception from group 1 with higher priority. For instance, if an interrupt service routine is in progress when an illegal instruction is detected, the interrupt service routine will run to completion before service is initiated for the illegal opcode.

Group 2 is the lowest-priority group and its exceptions will be interrupted by any group 0 or group 1 exception request. This group includes the software exception functions, TRAP, TRAPV, CHK, and divide by zero. These exceptions differ from those in the other groups in that they are initiated through execution of an instruction. Therefore, there are no individual priority levels within group 2.

Let us assume that a TRAP exception is in progress when an external device requests service using an interrupt input. In this case the hardware interrupt is of higher priority. Therefore, the trap routine is suspended and execution resumes with the first instruction of the interrupt service routine.

7.5 EXTERNAL HARDWARE INTERRUPTS   *Group 1*

The first type of 68000 exception that we shall consider in detail is the *external hardware interrupts*. The external hardware interrupt interface can be considered to be a special-purpose input interface. It allows the 68000 to respond quickly and efficiently to events that occur in its external hardware. Through it, external devices can signal the 68000 whenever they need to be serviced. For this reason, the processor does not have to dedicate any of its processing time for checking to determine which of the external devices needs service. For example, the occurrence of a power failure is typically detected by an external power failure detection circuit and signaled to the microprocessor as an interrupt.

The General Interrupt Interface

Figure 7.4 shows the *general interrupt interface* of the 68000. Here we have shown the signals that are involved in the interface and see that some circuitry is required to interface external devices to the interrupt request inputs of the 68000. Notice that as many as 192 unique devices could apply interrupt requests to the 68000. However, few applications require this many.

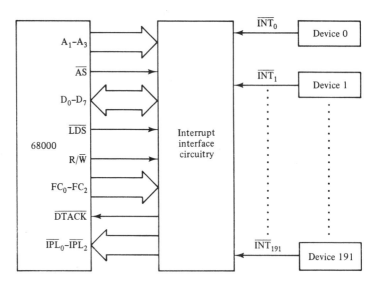

Figure 7-4 General interrupt interface.

Let us now look just briefly at the function of each of the signals involved in the interrupt interface. First we find that three address lines, A_1 through A_3, are in use. They carry an interrupt priority number that is output during the interrupt acknowledge bus cycle. The logic level of $\overline{AS}$ signals external circuitry when this code is available at $A_3A_2A_1$. Accompanying this priority-level number is the *interrupt acknowledge* (IACK) *function code* at outputs FC_2 through FC_0.

During the interrupt acknowledge bus cycle, external circuitry must return an 8-bit vector number to the 68000. Data bus lines D_0 through D_7 are used to input this vector number. The external device signals that the vector number is available on the bus with the data transfer acknowledge ($\overline{DTACK}$) signal. $R/\overline{W}$ and $\overline{LDS}$ control the direction and timing of data transfer over the bus.

External devices must issue a request for service to the 68000. The external *interrupt request inputs* of the 68000 are labeled $\overline{IPL}_2$, $\overline{IPL}_1$, and $\overline{IPL}_0$. The code 000_2 at these inputs represents no interrupt request. On the other hand, a nonzero input represents an active interrupt request.

External Hardware Interrupt Priorities

The external hardware interrupts of the 68000 have another priority scheme within their group 1 priority assignment. The number of priority levels that can be assigned is determined by the number of interrupt inputs. As shown in Fig. 7.5, for three interrupt inputs we get seven independent priority levels. They are identified as 1 through 7 and correspond to interrupt codes $\overline{IPL}_2\overline{IPL}_1\overline{IPL}_0$ equal 001_2 through 111_2, respectively. Here 7 represents the highest priority level and 1 the lowest priority level.

Priority Level	Interrupt Code		
	$\overline{IPL}_2$	$\overline{IPL}_1$	$\overline{IPL}_0$
None	0	0	0
1	0	0	1
2	0	1	0
3	0	1	1
4	1	0	0
5	1	0	1
6	1	1	0
7	1	1	1

no interr. req. but all interr's enabled

interr disable

Figure 7-5 External interrput priorities.

The external interrupt circuitry can be designed to allow a large number of devices to respond at each of these interrupt levels. It is for this reason that we have identified 192 external devices in Fig. 7.4. Any number of these 192 devices can be assigned to any one of the interrupt levels. Moreover, additional external priority logic circuitry can be added to prioritize the interrupts into 192 unique priority levels.

Interrupt Mask

Bits 8 through 10 in the system byte of the status register are used as a mask for the external hardware interrupts. Figure 7.6 shows that these bits are labeled I_0 through I_2, respectively. Only active interrupts with a priority level higher than the current value of the mask are enabled for operation. Those of equal or lower priority level are masked out.

When the 68000 is reset at power-up, the mask is automatically set to 111_2. This disables interrupts from occurring. For the interrupt interface to be enabled, the mask must be modified to a lower priority level through software. For instance, it could be set to 000_2. This would enable all interrupts for operation.

Whenever a higher-priority interrupt occurs, the mask is automatically changed so that equal- or lower-priority interrupts are masked out. For instance, with initiation of a level 5 interrupt it is changed to 101_2. This masks out from level 5 down through level 1.

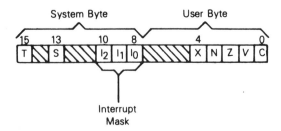

Figure 7-6 Interrput mask bits in the status register (Motorola, Inc.).

The level 7 interrupt request code is not actually masked out with the interrupt mask. Even if the mask is set to 111_2, it remains enabled. For this reason, it can be used to implement a nonmaskable interrupt for the 68000 microcomputer system.

7.6 GENERAL INTERRUPT PROCESSING SEQUENCE

Whenever the code at interrupt inputs $\overline{IPL_2}\,\overline{IPL_1}\,\overline{IPL_0}$ is nonzero, an external device is requesting service. It is said that an interrupt is *pending*. At the completion of the current instruction, the 68000 compares this code to the contents of the interrupt mask, $I_2I_1I_0$ in bits 10 through 8 of the status register. If the priority level of the active request is higher than that already in the mask, the request for service is accepted. Otherwise, execution continues with the next instruction in the currently active exception processing service routine.

Upon accepting the exception service request, the 68000 initiates a sequence by which it passes control to the service routine located at the address specified by the interrupt's vector. First, the contents of the status register are temporarily saved. Next, the S-bit, bit 13, of the status register is set to 1 and the T-bit, bit 15, is cleared to 0. They enable the supervisor mode of operation and disable the trace function, respectively. Then interrupt mask $I_2I_1I_0$ is set to the priority level of the interrupt request just granted.

Now the 68000 initiates an *interrupt acknowledge (IACK) bus cycle*. The sequence of events that occur during this bus cycle are summarized in Fig. 7.7(a) and are shown by waveforms in Fig. 7.7(b). Here we see that it first signals external devices that service has been granted. It does this by outputting the interrupt code of the device to which service was granted on address bus lines A_1 through A_3 and then makes control signals $R/\overline{W} = 1$, $\overline{AS} = 0$, and $\overline{LDS} = 0$. When $R/\overline{W} = 1$ and $\overline{LDS} = 0$, a byte of data will be transferred over data bus lines D_0 through D_7. At the same time, it outputs the interrupt acknowledge function code. This code is $FC_2FC_1FC_0$ equal to 111. In this way, it tells the external circuitry which priority-level interrupt is being processed.

In response to the interrupt acknowledge function code, the external device that corresponds to the interrupt code on A_1 through A_3 must put an 8-bit vector number on data bus lines D_0 through D_7. Then it must switch $\overline{DTACK}$ to logic 0 to signal the 68000 that the vector number is available on the bus. The 68000 reads the vector number off the bus and then returns both $\overline{LDS}$ and $\overline{AS}$ to logic 1.

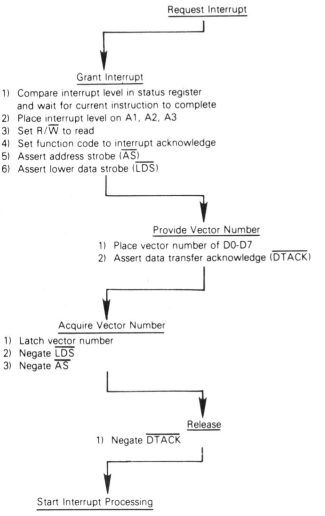

Request Interrupt

Grant Interrupt
1) Compare interrupt level in status register
   and wait for current instruction to complete
2) Place interrupt level on A1, A2, A3
3) Set R/$\overline{W}$ to read
4) Set function code to interrupt acknowledge
5) Assert address strobe ($\overline{AS}$)
6) Assert lower data strobe ($\overline{LDS}$)

Provide Vector Number
1) Place vector number of D0-D7
2) Assert data transfer acknowledge ($\overline{DTACK}$)

Acquire Vector Number
1) Latch vector number
2) Negate $\overline{LDS}$
3) Negate $\overline{AS}$

Release
1) Negate $\overline{DTACK}$

Start Interrupt Processing

(a)

Figure 7-7(a)   IACK bus cycle flowchart
(Motorola, Inc.).

It is this 8-bit code that tells the 68000 which of the devices associated with the active interrupt level is requesting service. Notice in Fig. 7.2 that not all of the 256 vectors in the table are to be used with the user-defined external hardware interrupts. Only the 192 vectors from vector 64 through 255 should be used for this purpose.

Finally, the interrupt knowledge bus cycle is completed when the external device returns $\overline{DTACK}$ to the 1 logic level.

Next, the 68000 pushes the current contents of its program counter onto the top of the supervisor stack. Since PC is 24 bits long, it requires two words of stack and takes two write bus cycles. Then the contents of the old status register, which

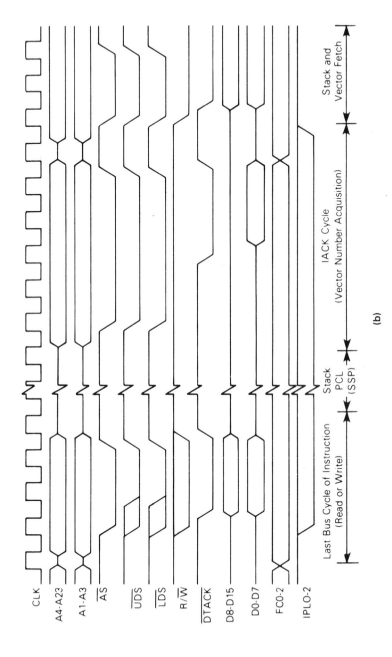

Figure 7-7 *(cont.)* (b) IACK bus cycle waveforms (Motorola, Inc.).

(b)

were saved earlier, are also pushed to the supervisor stack. It takes just one word of memory and is accomplished with one write cycle.

Now the address of the interrupt's vector, which the 68000 calculates from the interrupt vector number, is put on the address bus. The value at this address in the vector table is read over the data bus and loaded into PC. It takes two read bus cycles to fetch the complete vector. During the first bus cycle, the most significant word is carried over the bus and during the second bus cycle, the least significant word. The 68000 now has the new address at which it begins executing the routine that services the interrupt.

A return from exception (RTE) instruction must be included at the end of the service routine. Its execution initiates return of software control to the original program environment.

Figure 7.8 shows how the 68000 internally generates a *vector address* from an 8-bit *vector number*. As shown in Fig. 7.8(a), the vector number was read off of the lower eight data bus lines, D_0 through D_7. First, the 68000 multiples the vector number by 4. This is done by performing a shift left by two bit positions. Then it fills the upper 14 bits with 0s to form a 24-bit address. This gives the address shown in Fig. 7.8(b), which points to the vector in the table.

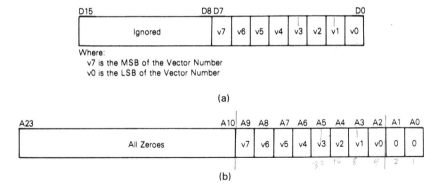

Figure 7-8   (a) Vector for address generation (Motorola, Inc.); (b) generated address (Motorola, Inc.).

7.7 GENERAL INTERRUPT INTERFACE OF THE 68000

The block diagram of Fig. 7.9 illustrates the type of circuitry needed to support a general interrupt interface for the 68000 microcomputer system. This circuit has 192 interrupt request inputs, which are labeled IRQ_0 through IRQ_{191}. These inputs are synchronized by latching them into an *interrupt latch circuit.*

The 192 outputs of the interrupt latch circuit are applied to inputs of the *interrupt absolute priority encoder circuit.* Here they are prioritized and encoded to produce an 8-bit output code which identifies the highest-priority active interrupt request. These codes are in the range IRQ_0 equal to $00000000_2 = 0_{10}$ to IRQ_{191} equal to $10111111_{16} = 191_{10}$.

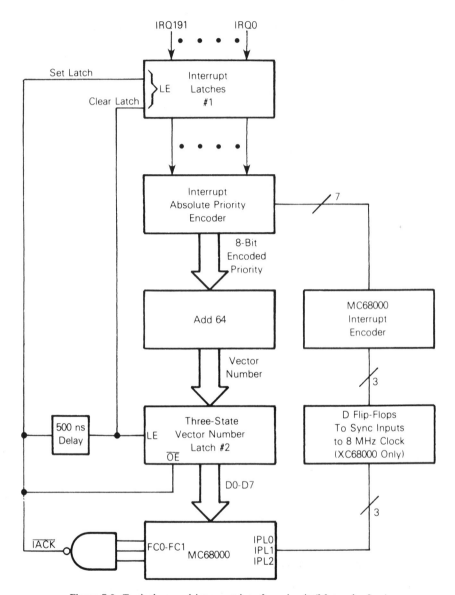

Figure 7-9 Typical general interrput interface circuit (Motorola, Inc.).

Remember that in the vector table of Fig. 7.2, the vectors assigned to the user-defined external interrupts are in the range 64 through 255, not 0 to 191. For this reason, the priority codes that are produced by the *encoder circuit* must be displaced by 64 before they are applied to the data bus of the 68000 during the IACK bus cycle. The circuit labeled *add 64* is provided for this purpose. It simply adds 64 to the 8-bit code at its input.

The output of the add 64 circuit, which is the correct vector number, is latched into the *three-state output vector number latch circuit*. Notice that the outputs of this latch are enabled by $\overline{IACK}$. In this way, the vector number is put on data bus lines D_0 through D_7 only during the interrupt acknowledge bus cycle. At all other times, the outputs of the latch are in the high-Z state.

Up to this point, we have just described the part of the interrupt interface circuit that is used to generate the vector number. But at the same time, another circuit path, which includes the *interrupt encoder* and *synchronization flip-flops*, must produce an interrupt request to the 68000.

Notice that the *interrupt absolute priority encoder circuit* outputs a 7-bit code in addition to the 8-bit priority code. The 7-bit code is input to the interrupt encoder circuit. In this code, just one bit is set to 0 and it identifies the priority level of the interrupt request. In response, the encoder produces a 3-bit request code for this priority level at its output. This code is latched onto the $\overline{IPL_2}$ through $\overline{IPL_0}$ inputs of the 68000, where it represents an interrupt request.

7.8 AUTOVECTOR INTERRUPT MECHANISM

In 68000 microcomputer systems that do not require more than seven interrupt inputs, a modified interrupt interface configuration can be used. This interface decreases the amount of external support circuits and at the same time shortens the response time from interrupt request to initiation of the service routine. This simplified interrupt mechanism uses what is known as the *autovector mode* of operation.

The *autovector interrupt interface* is shown in Fig. 7.10. It simplifies the interface requirements between external devices and the 68000. In this case, external hardware

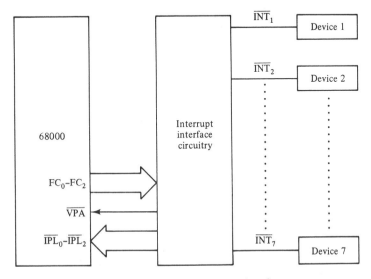

Figure 7-10 Autovector interrput interface.

need just recognize the IACK function code at $FC_2FC_1FC_0$ and respond by switching $\overline{VPA}$ to logic 0. This signals the 68000 to follow its *autovector interrupt sequence*.

When using autovector exception processing, the source of the interrupt vector is determined in a different way. Instead of external circuitry supplying an 8-bit vector number on D_7 through D_0, the 68000 generates the vector address internally from the interrupt request code $\overline{IPL_2}\overline{IPL_1}\overline{IPL_0}$ and the address of the service routine is fetched from the autovector section of the vector table in Fig. 7.2. In this way, we see that the interrupt acknowledge sequence is shortened. This is the reason that the response time between interrupt request and entry of the service routine is decreased.

As an example, assume that autovector interrupt request code 101_2 is applied to $\overline{IPL_2}$ through $\overline{IPL_0}$. Looking at the table in Fig. 7.2, we see that vector 29 is fetched from addresses 000074_{16} and 000076_{16} and loaded into the PC of the 68000.

7.9 AUTOVECTOR INTERFACE SUPPORT CIRCUIT

Now that we have introduced the autovector interrupt mechanism of the 68000, let us look at a simple circuit that can be used to implement the external hardware interface.

The circuit of Fig. 7.11 can be used to implement the autovector interface in a 68000 microcomputer system. Here we find the seven interrupt request inputs identified as level 1 through level 7. The logic levels at these inputs are latched into the 74LS273 octal latch synchronously with the CLK signal from the 68000. This latch is provided to synchronize the application of interrupt inputs to the priority encoder.

Interrupt requests must be prioritized and encoded into a 3-bit interrupt request code for input to the 68000. This is done by the 74LS348 8-line to 3-line priority encoder. Notice that the inputs of this device are active low, with input 7 corresponding to the highest-priority input and 0 to the lowest-priority input. The binary code corresponding to the highest-priority active input is output at $A_2A_1A_0$. This interrupt code is latched in a 74LS175 latch and its outputs applied to the $\overline{IPL_2}$ through $\overline{IPL_0}$ inputs of the 68000.

In addition to this interrupt request code interface circuit, another circuit is required to support the autovector interrupt interface. This circuit is required to detect the IACK code when it is output by the 68000 and in response assert the $\overline{VPA}$ signal. Typically, this is done by the function decoder circuit of the 68000 microcomputer system. Alternatively, a single three-input NAND gate can be used.

7.10 EXCEPTION INSTRUCTIONS

The instruction set of the 68000 includes a number of instructions that use the exception processing mechanism. They differ from the hardware-initiated exceptions that we have covered up to this point in that they are initiated as the result of the

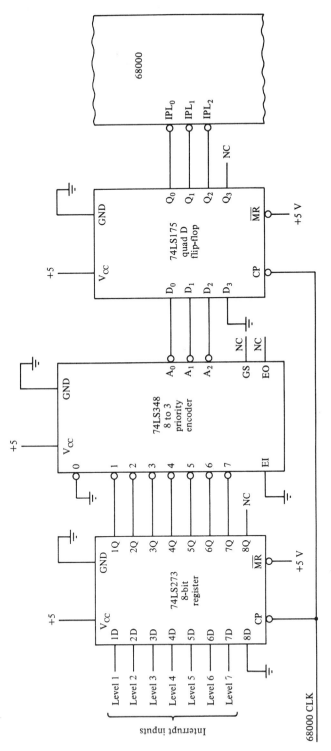

Figure 7-11 Typical autovector interrupt interface circuit (Motorola, Inc.).

68000 executing an instruction. Some of these instructions make a conditional test to determine whether or not to initiate exception processing.

There are five such instructions. They are *trap* (TRAP), *trap on overflow* (TRAPV), *check register against bounds* (CHK), *signed divide* (DIVS), and *unsigned divide* (DIVU). The operation of these instructions is summarized in Fig. 7.12. Let us now look at the exception processing for each of these instructions in more detail.

Instruction	Condition	Operation
TRAP #n	None	Trap sequence using trap vector n
TRAPV	V = 1	Trap sequence using TRAPV vector
CHK EA,Dn	Dn < 0 or Dn > (EA)	Trap sequence using CHK vector
DIVS EA,Dn DIVU EA,Dn	(EA) = 0	Trap sequence using zero divide vector
RTE		Return from exception routine to the program in which exception occurred

Figure 7-12 Exception instructions.

Trap Instruction—TRAP

The TRAP instruction can be considered to be the software interrupt instruction of the 68000. It permits the programmer to perform a vectored call of an exception service routine. We can call this routine the trap service routine and it is typically used to perform vectored subroutine calls such as *supervisory calls*.

The trap instruction is simply written as

$$\text{TRAP} \quad \#n$$

Here n represents the *trap vector number* that is to be used to locate the starting point of the exception processing routine in program memory. Looking at the vector table in Fig. 7.2, we see that the 24-bit starting addresses for the trap instructions are located at addresses in the range 000080_{16} through $0000BF_{16}$. This gives a total of 32 words of memory allocated to storage of trap vectors. Since each vector requires two words of memory, there is room for 16 vectors, which correspond to instructions TRAP #0 through TRAP #15.

For instance, the most significant word of the vector for TRAP #0 is held at 000080_{16} and its least significant word at 000082_{16}. Execution of the TRAP #0 instruction causes the 24-bit value stored at these locations to be loaded into the PC of the 68000. Therefore, program execution resumes with the first instruction of the TRAP #0 service routine.

Let us look more closely at the series of events that takes place to pass control to the exception service routine of a trap instruction. After the 68000 executes the trap instruction, it first saves the current contents of its status register in a temporary holding register. Then the S-bit of SR is set. This enables the supervisor system environment. Next, bit T of SR is cleared to disable the trace mode of operation.

Now the 68000 preserves the current program environment such that it can be reentered at completion of exception processing. It does this by pushing the current contents of PC onto the supervisor stack. This value of PC points to the instruction following the TRAP instruction that just initiated exception processing. Then the status word is pushed onto the supervisor stack.

We are now ready to enter the exception service routine. The address of the trap vector is automatically calculated by the 68000 from the trap number. The trap vector is read from this location and loaded into PC. Execution picks up with the first instruction of the service routine.

Notice that just the old PC and SR are automatically saved on the supervisor stack by the exception-processing mechanism. Frequently, the exception service routine will require use of the 68000's data or address registers. For this reason, their contents may also be saved on the stack. The 68000 does not have PUSH or POP instructions for this purpose. Instead, its MOVE instruction is used to perform these types of operations. For example, the instruction

$$\text{MOVE.L}\quad D0, -(SP)$$

will effectively push the 32-bit contents of D_0 onto the top of the supervisor stack. Typically, this is done with the first few instructions of the service routine.

Just as for interrupts, the return mechanism of the TRAP instruction is the return from exception (RTE) instruction. Execution of this instruction at the end of the service routine causes the saved values of PC and SR to be popped from the supervisor stack. Prior to executing the RTE instruction, the contents of any additional registers saved on the stack must also be popped back into the 68000. Again, this can be done with the MOVE instruction. For example,

$$\text{MOVE.L}\quad (SP)+,D0$$

causes the 32-bit value at the top of the stack to effectively be popped into register D_0.

TRAPV, CHK, and DIVU/DIVS Instructions

The rest of the exception instructions initiate a trap to an exception service routine only upon detection of an abnormal processing condition. For instance, the trap on overflow (TRAPV) instruction checks overflow bit V, bit 1 of the status register, to determine whether or not an overflow has resulted from execution of the previous instruction. If V is found to be set, an overflow has occurred and exception processing is initiated with an overflow service routine. In this case control is passed to the overflow service routine pointed to by the TRAPV vector at addresses $00001C_{16}$ and $00001E_{16}$ of the vector table. On the other hand, if V is not set, execution continues with the next sequential instruction in the program.

The check register against boundaries (CHK) instruction, as its name implies, can determine if the contents of a register lie within a set of minimum/maximum values. The minimum value (boundary) is always 0000_{16}. On the other hand, the maximum value (boundary), $MMMM_{16}$, is specified as a source operand and can reside in an internal register or a location in external memory.

An example is the instruction

$$CHK \quad \#\$5A,D0$$

Here register D_0 contains the parameter under test and $5A is the maximum boundary. If during execution of the instruction, the contents of D_0 are found to be within the range 0000_{16} to the value $5A_{16}$, the parameter is within bounds and exception processing is not initiated. On the other hand, if it is negative or greater than $5A_{16}$, it is out of bounds and exception processing is initiated. The change in program environment is to the address defined by vector 6 at addresses 000018_{16} and $00001A_{16}$ in the vector table.

The last two exception instructions, DIVU and DIVS, cause a trap to a service routine if the division they perform involves a divisor equal to zero. This divide-by-zero exception is initiated through the vector at addresses 000014_{16} and 000016_{16}.

7.11 BUS ERROR

It is possible with the asynchronous bus of the 68000 to get into a situation where a bus cycle is not completed. This would be due to the fact that the data acknowledge (DTACK) signal is not received by the 68000. If this happens, execution of the current instruction would not be completed; instead, the MPU would be hung up at the instruction. This represents what is known as a *bus error* condition.

To resolve this problem, bus error exception capability is provided on the 68000. This exception provides a way of assuring that bus cycles initiated by the 68000 are carried through to completion. The bus error condition is not detected automatically by the 68000 itself; instead, it must be detected with external circuitry and signaled to the 68000. External logic would do this by switching the BERR (bus error) input of the 68000 to logic 0. In fact, BERR and HALT can be used together to automatically rerun bus cycles that result in a bus error.

Remember that earlier we indicated that the only exception with higher-priority than the bus error function is reset. Therefore, the bus error exception takes precedence and occurs as long as the reset exception is not already in progress. Moreover, we found that it does not wait for the completion of the current instruction before it is initiated. This is also important because when a bus error occurs, execution of the instruction that is in progress will not be completed.

When BERR is switched to the 0 level, the MPU aborts the current bus cycle and initiates exception processing. A change in program environment is initiated to a service routine for the bus error condition. The location of this service routine is defined by vector 2 in the table of Fig. 7.2. Execution of this service routine can attempt to correct the bus error by rerunning the bus cycle or signal its occurrence by displaying or printing information such as the address at which the error occurred and the type of bus cycle that was in progress.

An example of a type of circuit that can be used to determine whether or not bus cycles are completed is a *watchdog timer*. This timer can be started as each bus cycle is initiated and then the 68000's bus control signals observed to assure that the cycle is completed before a maximum period of time has elapsed. If the timer times out before the bus cycle is finished, the circuit sets BERR to logic 0 signaling the 68000 of the bus error condition.

The sequence of events by which the 68000 passes control to the bus error exception service routine is almost the same as that described earlier for the TRAP instruction. For this reason, we will just look at how they differ.

The only difference between the two exception-processing control transfer sequences is that several additional parameters are pushed to the supervisor stack in the case of a bus error. Figure 7.13 shows this information and the order in which they are put onto the stack. Notice that, again, SR and PC are pushed to the stack. But this time they are followed by the first word of the instruction that was in progress when the bus error occurred, the address used in the bus cycle that resulted in the bus error, and a special *access-type error word*.

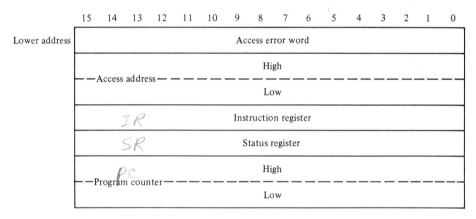

Figure 7-13 Information pushed to the stack during a bus error exception (Motorola, Inc.).

In Fig. 7.14 we have shown the implemented bits of the error word and their meanings. Just 5 bits are in use. Bit 4 identifies whether the bus cycle that was aborted due to the bus error condition was a read or a write cycle. It is reset if the bus cycle was for a write operation and is set if it was for a read operation.

15	14	13	12	11	10	9	8	7	6	5	4	3	2	1	0
											R/W	I/N		Function code	

Figure 7-14 Access error word (Motorola, Inc.).

The next bit, bit 3, indicates whether the bus cycle was related to normal instruction execution or exception processing. Logic 0 represents instruction execution and logic 1 means exception processing. The 68000 considers the occurrence of a bus error for any group 2 exception, that is, during the execution of an exception instruction, to be a normal instruction execution bus error. For this reason, bit 3 is set to logic 0 for this type of occurrence.

The last 3 bits are used to store the code, $FC_2FC_1FC_0$, that was output on the function code bus during the bus error cycle. This code tells what type of memory reference was in process when the bus error took place, that is, whether user or supervisor memory was being accessed or if it was an interrupt acknowledge reference.

The bus error service routine can access this bus error information in the stack. In this way, it can identify the type of error made and initiate an appropriate response in an attempt to recover from the condition or simply signal that the error condition has occurred.

Example 7.2

If the access-type error word pushed to the stack as the result of a bus error condition is 0005_{16}, what type of bus cycle was in progress when the error occurred?

Solution. To identify how the bus error bits are set, let us first express the error word in binary form. This gives

$$0005_{16} = 0000000000000101_2$$

Looking at bit 4, we see that it is set to 0. This stands for a write cycle. Bit 3 is also 0 and means that a normal instruction was being executed when the error took place. Finally, the function code that was output for the bus cycle was 101_2 or 5_{10}. This represents an access of supervisor data memory. Thus the bus error occurred when the 68000 was writing to supervisor data memory.

7.12 RESET EXCEPTION

Typically, a microcomputer system must be reset either at power-up or to recover from a system failure condition. An example of a system failure that may require a reset to be performed is the bus error condition we discussed in the preceding section. A reset will cause the microcomputer to be initialized.

The $\overline{RESET}$ line is provided on the 68000 for initiating initialization. Actually, $\overline{RESET}$ is a bidirectional line that provides for 68000 initialization when a reset signal is applied to it by the external hardware, and system initialization when the 68000 applies a reset signal to external hardware. Let us look first at its operation for 68000 initialization.

A reset exception at power-up is initiated by switching the $\overline{RESET}$ input of the 68000 to the 0 logic level. It must be maintained at this level for a minimum of 100 ms. Earlier we indicated that reset is the highest-priority exception function. Therefore, its exception processing sequence is always initiated and cannot be interrupted by any of the other exception functions.

The reset exception processing sequence begins just like other exception processing sequences, with the S-bit of the status register being set and the T-bit being cleared. This puts the 68000 in the supervisor mode and disables its trace function. But this is where the similarity ends. Next, the interrupt mask bits of the status register, bits 8 through 10, are all set to 1. This makes the interrupt mask equal to 7, which is the highest-priority level, and masks out all external interrupts other than level 7 (nonmaskable interrupt), preventing them from being serviced.

It is at this point in the control transfer sequence of an exception that the contents of the status register and program counter should be pushed to the stack. However, when the MPU is being reinitialized, control would never be returned to the program environment that existed prior to the reset. Therefore, the reset sequence does not save these values on the stack. Instead, it initiates automatic loading of the internal supervisor stack pointer (SSP) register and program counter from supervisor program memory and supervisor data memory, respectively.

First, the SSP register is loaded with vector 0 at addresses 000000_{16} and 000002_{16}. This defines a supervisor stack in supervisor data memory. Next, PC is loaded with vector 1 at addresses 000004_{16} and 000006_{16} and then execution begins with the first instruction of the reset exception service routine.

The reset exception service routine is normally a power-up routine for the microcomputer system. It is used to initialize all of the system's resources. For instance, it could clear the MPU's internal data and address registers, load its user stack pointer (USP) register, and modify the contents of the system byte of the status register to enable interrupts.

The output function of $\overline{\text{RESET}}$ is initiated through software by the RESET instruction. When a RESET instruction is executed by the 68000, its internal registers are not affected; instead, the $\overline{\text{RESET}}$ line is set to act as an output and a pulse is generated. The pulse produced at $\overline{\text{RESET}}$ is to the 0 logic level and has a duration of 124 clock periods. This pulse can be applied to the reset, clear, or preset inputs of external devices, such as LSI peripherals or flip-flops, to initialize their operation.

The reset instruction can be included as part of the power-up service routine. In this way, external devices can be initialized and then their internal registers loaded to configure their mode of operation.

7.13 INTERNAL EXCEPTION FUNCTIONS

The 68000 also has a number of internally initiated exception functions. In fact, it has four such functions: address error, privilege violation, trace, and illegal/unimplemented opcode detection. We will look next at each of these internal exception functions in detail.

Address Error Exception

In Chapter 6 we discussed how data are organized in the memory of a 68000 microcomputer system. At that time, we pointed out that instructions, words of data, and long words of data all must always reside at even-address boundaries. However, software can be written that incorrectly attempts to access one of these types of information from an odd-address boundary. It is to detect and correct for this error condition that the address error feature is provided on the 68000.

Address error detection does not have to be done with external circuitry as we saw earlier for bus error detection. Instead, this capability is built within the 68000 as an internal exception function. Whenever an attempt is made to read or write word-wide data from an odd-address boundary, the 68000 automatically recognizes the memory access as an address error condition. Upon detection, the exception processing sequence is initiated and control is passed to the address error exception service routine. This routine can attempt to correct the error condition, or if correction is not possible, its occurrence can be signaled in some way. For instance, the address and type of access could be displayed on a panel of LEDs.

The control transfer sequence that takes place for address error exceptions is identical to that performed for the bus error condition. As mentioned in Section 7.11, the information pushed to the stack includes the contents of SR and PC, the first word of the current instruction, the address that was in error, and an access-type error word. The format of the access-type error word saved on the stack during an address error exception is identical to that shown for the bus error in Fig. 7.14. One difference is that vector 3 instead of vector 2 is used to locate the service routine. As shown in Fig. 7.2, this vector resides at addresses $00000C_{16}$ and $00000E_{16}$ of the vector table.

Privilege Violation Exception

In earlier chapters, we found that the 68000 has the ability to easily implement a *user/supervisor microcomputer system environment* and that the state of operation can be selected under software control. The importance of this capability lies in that it permits certain system resources to be accessible only by the supervisor. In this way, it provides a level of security in the system design.

Another internal exception feature of the 68000 that we have not yet considered gives it the ability to identify when a user attempts to use a supervisor resource. These illegal accesses are referred to as *privilege state violations*.

Remember that the S-bit in the system byte of the status register determines whether the 68000 is in the user state or the supervisor state. For instance, when S is set to logic 0, the user state of operation is selected. The user state is the lower security level. Switching S to logic 1 under software control puts the microprocessor at the higher security level or supervisor state.

When in the supervisor state, the 68000 can execute all of the instructions of its instruction set. However, when in the user mode, certain instructions are considered privileged and cannot be executed. For example, instructions that AND, OR, or exclusive-OR an immediate word operand with the contents of the status register are not permitted. Any attempt to execute one of these privileged instructions, while in the user state, results in a privileged state violation exception. The privilege violation exception service routine can signal the occurrence of the violation and provide a means of recovery.

Figure 7.2 shows that the privilege mode violation uses vector 8 at addresses 000020_{16} and 000022_{16} of the vector table.

Trace Exception

The 68000 has a trace option that allows for implementation of the single-step mode of operation. Just like the privileged state, this option can be enabled or disabled under software control by toggling a bit in the status register. Trace is controlled by the T-bit in the system byte of SR. Trace is turned on by setting T to logic 1 and turned off by clearing it to 0.

When *trace mode* is enabled, the 68000 initiates a trace exception through vector 9 at completion of execution of each instruction. This exception routine can pass control to a monitor that allows examination of the MPU's internal registers or external memory. This type of information is necessary for debugging software. The monitor can also be used to initiate execution of the next instruction. In this way, the instructions of the program can be stepped through one after the other and their operations verified.

Illegal/Unimplemented Instructions

The last internal exception function of the 68000 is its *illegal/unimplemented instruction detection* capability. This feature of the 68000 permits it to detect automatically whether or not the opcode fetched as an instruction corresponds to one of the instructions in the instruction set. If it does not, execution is not attempted; instead, the opcode is identified as being illegal and exception processing is initiated. This *illegal opcode detection mechanism* permits the 68000 to detect errors in its instruction stream.

Occurrence of an illegal opcode initiates a change of program context through the illegal instruction vector, vector 4 in the table of Fig. 7.2. The exception service routine that gets initiated can signal the occurrence of the error condition.

The *unimplemented instruction* concept is an extension of the illegal instruction detection mechanism by which the instruction set of the 68000 can be expanded. It lets us use two ranges of unused opcodes to define new instructions. They correspond to all opcodes of the form $FXXX_{16}$ and $AXXX_{16}$. Here the X's stand for don't-care digits and can be any hexadecimal numbers.

Whenever an opcode of the form $FXXX_{16}$ is detected by the 68000, control is passed to an exception-processing routine through vector 11 at addresses $00002C_{16}$ and $00002E_{16}$ of the exception vector table. The service routine pointed to by this vector should be a *macroinstruction emulation routine* for the new instruction. For example, floating-point arithmetic or double-precision arithmetic emulation routines could be implemented. The emulation routine is written and debugged in assembly language and then stored in main memory as machine code. To use the new instruction in a program, we just insert this opcode, $FXXX_{16}$, as an instruction statement.

As shown in Fig. 7.2, the other unimplemented instruction opcode, $AXXX_{16}$, vectors out of addresses 000028_{16} and $00002A_{16}$.

ASSIGNMENT

Section 7.2

1. What are the different types of exceptions available on the 68000?

Section 7.3

2. Where in memory must the exception vector table be stored?

3. The illegal instruction exception service routine starts at address $B000. Show where and how its vector will be stored in the exception vector table.

Section 7.4

4. If the service routine for TRAPV is in progress when an external interrupt occurs, what happens?

Section 7.5

5. What is the highest priority level for external hardware interrupts?

6. If the interrupt mask value is 5 when the 68000 receives an external hardware interrupt request with code 100_2, will the request be acknowledged or ignored?

7. Write an instruction to load the interrupt mask with the value 011_2 without changing any of the other bits in the status register. Assume that the 68000 is in the supervisor state.

Section 7.6

8. Give an overview of the events that take place during the IACK bus cycle.

Section 7.7

9. Overview the response of the circuit in Fig. 7.9 to an active IRQ_{60} input.

Sections 7.8 and 7.9

10. Overview the operation of the autovector interrupt interface circuit in Fig. 7.11 when a level 2 request for service is received.

Section 7.10

11. Show the general structure of a TRAP service routine. Assume that the service routine uses registers D_0, D_1, and A_2.

12. Write an instruction sequence that will check the index of an array. The index is stored in memory location INDEX and the upper bound of the array is stored at UBD.

Section 7.11

13. What is a bus error in the 68000 microcomputer system?

14. Explain how a bus error condition is handled by the 68000.

Section 7.12

15. Write a reset service routine that will clear the data registers, address registers, and set the supervisor stack pointer to $FFFFFE. Then branch to $A000, where the application program begins.

Section 7.13

16. What internal exceptions are implemented in the 68000?

17. Explain what is meant by an address error exception.

18. What happens when the unused opcode $F100_{16}$ is encountered during instruction execution?

8 The Hardware of the MC68000 Educational Microcomputer

8.1 INTRODUCTION

In the previous two chapters, we presented in detail the memory, I/O, and interrupt interfaces of the 68000 microprocessor and its microcomputer system. In this chapter, we will examine how these interfaces are implemented in a simple microcomputer system. The microcomputer used for this purpose is that employed in Motorola's *MC68000 educational microcomputer board*. The topics presented in the chapter are:

1. The microcomputer of the MC68000 educational microcomputer board
2. Clock generator circuitry
3. Interrupt interface
4. Program storage memory
5. Data storage memory
6. Parallel I/O—the 68230
7. Serial I/O—the 6850

8.2 THE MICROCOMPUTER OF THE MC68000 EDUCATIONAL MICROCOMPUTER BOARD

The circuitry of the MC68000 educational microcomputer board represents the implementation of a complete 68000-based microcomputer system. A block diagram of this microcomputer is shown in Fig. 8.1. The heart of the microcomputer, the

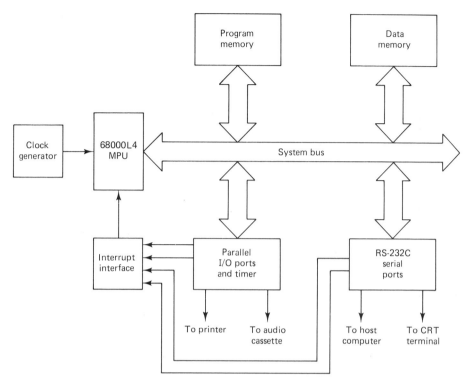

Figure 8-1 Block diagram of the MC68000 educational microcomputer.

MPU, is an 68000L4 microprocessor. It is this device that performs the arithmetic, logic, and control operations.

The operation of the microprocessor and other devices in the microcomputer system are synchronized by the clock signals produced by the *clock generator* section. The 68000 microprocessor in this microcomputer is set up to operate at a frequency of 4 MHz.

The *program memory* section stores the instructions of the monitor program. Program memory in the MC68000 educational microcomputer is implemented with PROMs and has a total storage capacity of 16K bytes. Use of PROMs makes the program storage *nonvolatile.* That is, the monitor program is maintained within the PROMs even when power is removed from the system. The program that is run on the MC68000 educational microcomputer is called the *Tutor monitor.* The 68000 fetches the instructions of the monitor program over the system bus and executes them.

Data that is being processed by the microcomputer are stored in the *data memory* section. For instance, during the execution of an instruction, the 68000 accesses source or destination operands that reside in data memory over the system's bus. This section of memory is implemented with 4116 dynamic RAMs and is 64K bytes in size. This part of the memory subsystem is actually *volatile;* therefore, any information stored in it is lost when power is turned off.

NOTES:

1. FOR REFERENCE DRAWINGS REFER TO BILL OF MATERIAL Ø1-W3111BØ1
2. UNLESS OTHERWISE SPECIFIED:
   - ALL RESISTORS ARE IN OHMS, ±5 PCT, 1/4 WATT.
   - ALL CAPACITORS ARE IN UF.
   - ALL VOLTAGES ARE DC.
3. INTERRUPTED LINES CODED WITH THE SAME LETTER OR LETTER COMBINATIONS ARE ELECTRICALLY CONNECTED.
4. DEVICE TYPE NUMBER IS FOR REFERENCE ONLY. THE NUMBER VARIES WITH THE MANUFACTURER.
5. J16 CUSTOMER USE OPTION (5Ø PINS). DEVICE TYPE NUMBERS AND CONNECTIONS NOT SHOWN ON SYMBOL ARE LISTED BELOW. UNDERLINED PORTION OF TYPE NUMBER IS USED AS A CODE TO IDENTIFY DEVICES ON DIAGRAM.

REF DES	TYPE △	GND	+5V	-5V	+12V	-12V
U1	74 S32	7	14			
U2	74LS32	7	14			
U3	74LS32	7	14			
U4	MC33Ø2	12	3			
U5	MC1488	7			14	1
U6	MC1489A	7	14			
U7	MC1488	7			14	1
U8	74LSØØ	7	14			
U9	MC6823Ø	38	12			
U10	MCM68764	12	24			
U11	MCM68764	12	24			
U12	MC685Ø	1	12			
U13	MC685Ø	1	12			
U14	MC14411	12	24			
U15	74LS93	10	5			
U16		7	14			
U17	74LS2Ø	7	14			
U18	74LSØ4	7	14			
U19	74LS21	7	14			
U20	MC68000L4	16,53	14,49			
U21	74LS175	8	16			
U22	74LS175	8	16			
U23	74LSØ8	7	14			
U24	74LS11	7	14			
U25	74LSØØ	7	14			
U26	74LS393	7	14			
U27	74LS153	8	16			
U28	74LS153	8	16			
U29	74LS26Ø	7	14			
U30	74LS138	8	16			
U31	74LS27	7	14			
U32	74LSØ4	7	14			
U33	74LSØ2	7	14			
U34	74LS32	7	14			
U35	74LS153	8	16			
U36	74LS153	8	16			
U37	74LS26Ø	7	14			
U38	74LS1Ø	7	14			
U39	74LS175	8	16			
U4Ø	74LS148	8	16			
U41	74LS273	10	20			
U42	MC3456	7	14			
U43	MC74Ø5	7	14			
U44	74LSØØ	7	14			
U45	74LS11	7	14			
U46	74LS74	7	14			

POWER/GROUND TABLE CONT'D

REF DES	TYPE △	GND	+5V	-5V	+12V	-12V
U47	MCM4116	16	9	1	8	
U48	MCM4116	16	9	1	8	
U49	MCM4116	16	9	1	8	
U5Ø	MCM4116	16	9	1	8	
U51	MCM4116	16	9	1	8	
U52	MCM4116	16	9	1	8	
U53	MCM4116	16	9	1	8	
U54	MCM4116	16	9	1	8	
U55	MCM4116	16	9	1	8	
U56	MCM4116	16	9	1	8	
U57	MCM4116	16	9	1	8	
U58	MCM4116	16	9	1	8	
U59	MCM4116	16	9	1	8	
U6Ø	MCM4116	16	9	1	8	
U61	MCM4116	16	9	1	8	
U62	MCM4116	16	9	1	8	

Y1	
VR1	
U62	
S2	
R38	
J17	
E7	
CR3	
C62	
HIGHEST NUMBER USED	NOT USED
REFERENCE DESIGNATIONS	

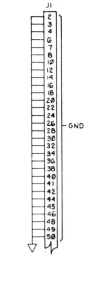

PART OF J1

2 3 4 6 7 8 10 12 14 16 18 20 22 24 26 28 30 32 34 36 38 40 41 42 44 45 46 48 49 50 — GND

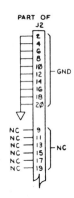

PART OF J2

2 4 6 8 10 12 14 16 18 20 — GND

NC — 9
NC — 11
NC — 13
NC — 15
NC — 17
NC — 19
— NC

Figure 8-2 68000 Educational Microcomputer Board Schematic Diagram (Motorola, Inc.). SH 1 of 3

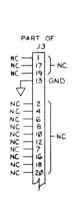

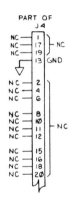

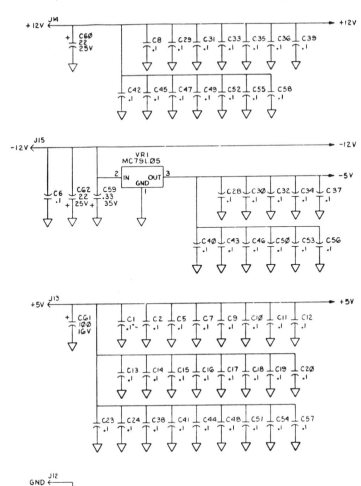

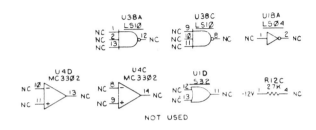

Figure 8-2 *(cont.)*   SH 1 of 3

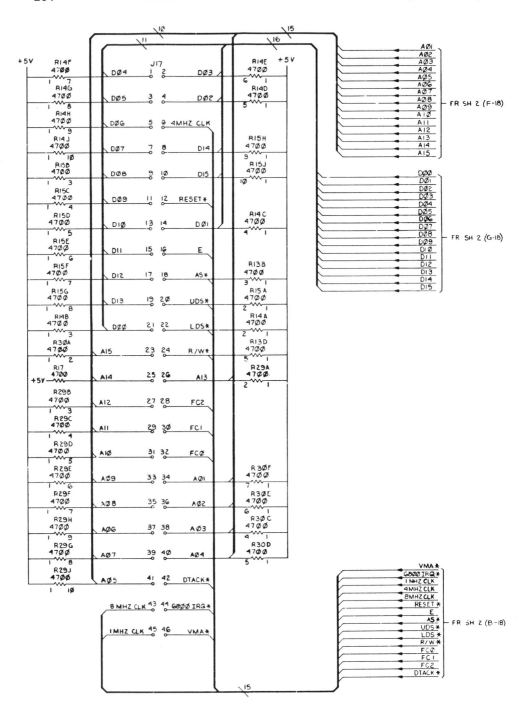

Figure 8-2 *(cont.)* Sh 1 of 3 *(cont.)*

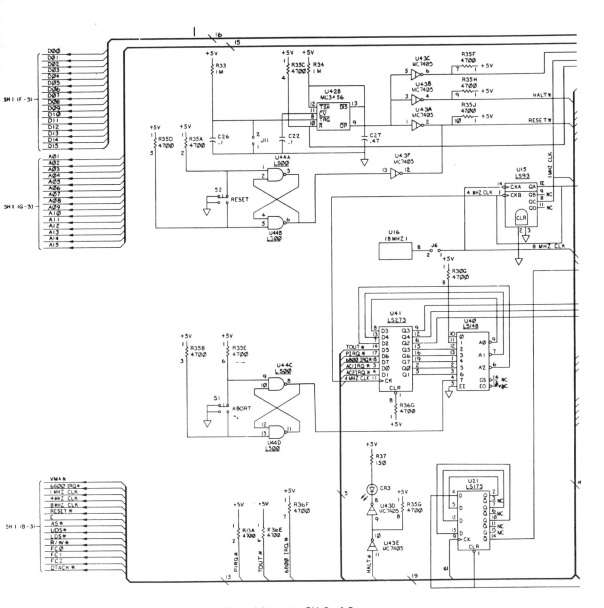

Figure 8-2 *(cont.)* SH 2 of 3

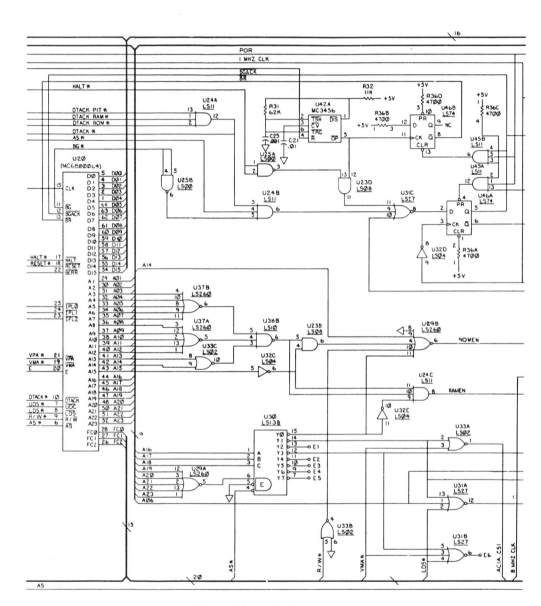

Figure 8-2 *(cont.)* SH 2 of 3 *(cont.)*

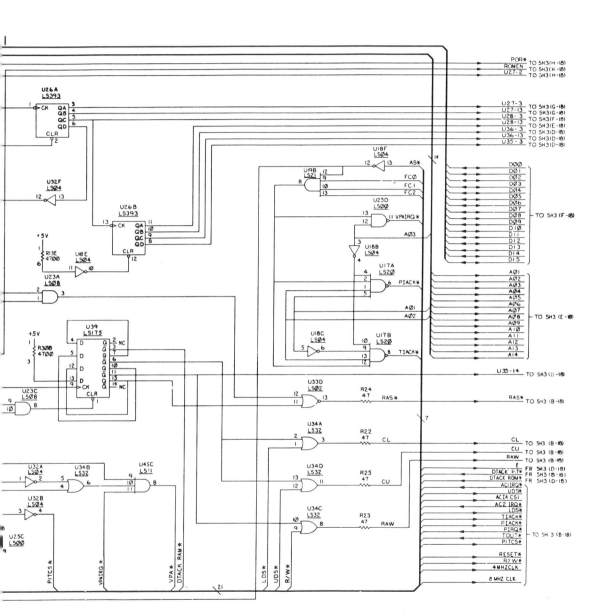

Figure 8-2 *(cont.)* SH 2 of 3 *(cont.)*

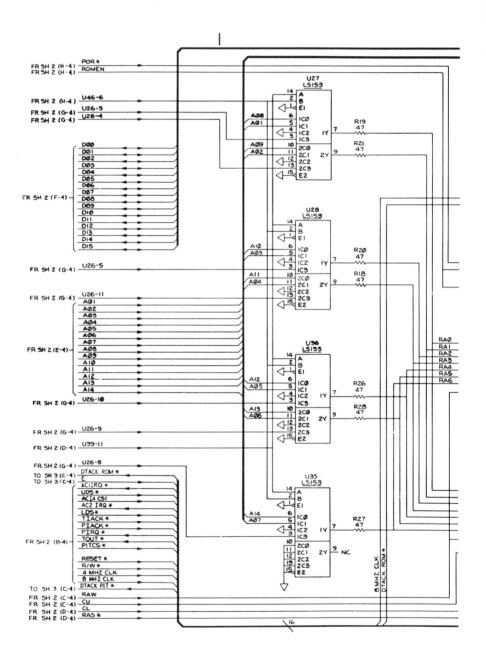

Figure 8-2 *(cont.)* SH 3 of 3

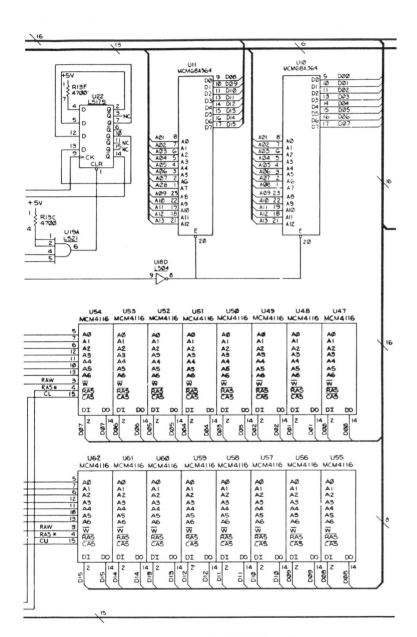

Figure 8-2 *(cont.)* Sh 3 of 3 *(cont.)*

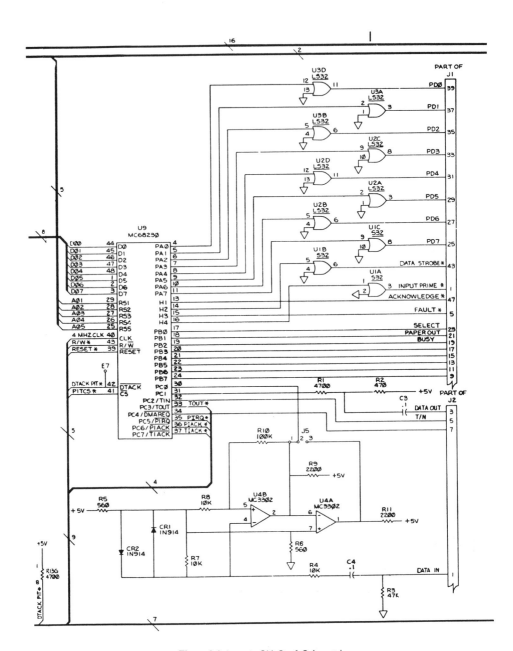

Figure 8-2 *(cont.)* SH 3 of 3 *(cont.)*

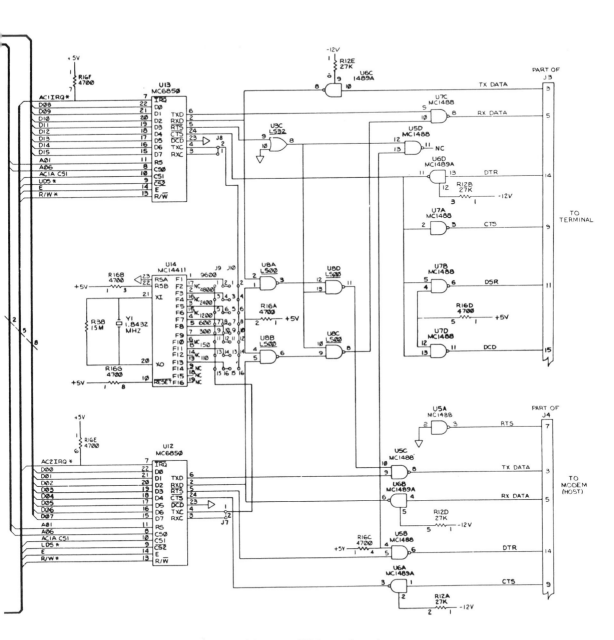

Figure 8-2 *(cont.)*   SH 3 of 3 *(cont.)*

When using the educational microcomputer to enter, execute, and debug 68000 assembly language programs, the instructions of the program are stored and executed from data storage memory, not from program memory. This permits the program to be loaded and modified by the user from the keyboard. Only the Tutor monitor program resides in program storage memory.

The microcomputer in the educational microcomputer also has a number of *I/O resources*. Looking at the block diagram in Fig. 8.1, we see that there is a *parallel I/O* section and *RS-232C serial communication ports*.

The parallel I/O section of the microcomputer provides 24 individual I/O lines. This part of the I/O interface is implemented with the 68230 parallel interface/timer device and can be configured under software control to work as inputs or outputs and with a variety of different modes of operation. These parallel I/O ports are designed to interface to a parallel printer (Centronics interface) and a tape recorder.

The serial communication ports permit a CRT terminal to be connected to the microcomputer and also provide for connection to a host computer. The serial ports are implemented with 6850 asynchronous communications interface adapters.

The keyboard of the terminal allows the user to input information to the microcomputer. For example, in Chapter 5, we showed that monitor commands such as DU or DF are issued from the keyboard. Commands like these allow the programmer to modify the contents of data memory, single step executive programs, and implement program debug operations by giving the ability to examine the contents of registers or memory.

The terminal, which connects to one of the RS-232C ports, is also an output device. On the screen, it provides the user with a visual representation of data related to the monitor commands that are entered through the keyboard. For instance, as the MM command is used to enter a byte of data, the current contents of the memory location are first displayed and then the new value is displayed digit by digit as it is entered from the keyboard. Similarly, when a DF command is issued to examine the contents of the 68000's internal registers, their descriptors and contents are displayed.

Figure 8.2 shows schematic diagrams that detail the circuits used to implement each of the functional blocks of the microcomputer in the MC68000 educational microcomputer board.

8.3 CLOCK GENERATOR CIRCUITRY

Now that we have introduced the architecture and functions of the fundamental blocks in the MC68000 educational microcomputer, let us continue by examining the operation of the circuitry used to implement these blocks. We will begin in this section with the clock generator circuit. Figure 8.3 shows this segment of circuitry.

Looking at Fig. 8.3, we find that clock signals are generated by an 8-MHz crystal controlled oscillator and a 74LS93 binary counter IC. This circuit produces three different frequency clock signals—8 MHz, 4 MHz, and 1 MHz.

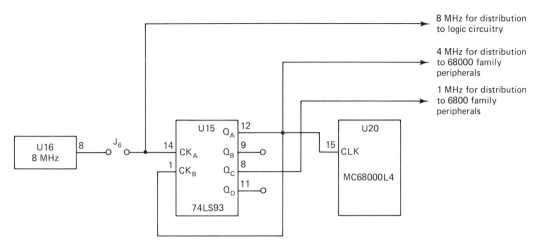

Figure 8-3 Clock generator circuitry.

The 8-MHz clock is directly produced by the crystal controlled oscillator U_{16}. One use of the 8-MHz output at pin 8 of this oscillator is that it is distributed to control logic circuitry within the microcomputer. Notice that the 8-MHz clock is also applied to the $\widehat{CKA}$ input of 74LS93 counter. Here it is divided by 2 to produce a 4-MHz clock at the $\widehat{QA}$ output. This is the clock signal that is applied to the CLK input at pin 15 of the 68000 microprocessor. In Fig. 8.3, we see that the 4-MHz clock is also distributed to other parts of the microcomputer system. For instance, it is required to synchronize the operation of all 68000 family LSI peripherals. For this reason, one place that it is supplied is to the 68230 PI/T device.

The 4-MHz clock signal is also supplied to the $\widehat{CKB}$ input of the 74LS93. $CK\widehat{B}$ is the input to the other three stages of the counter. It is divided by 2 to produce the $\widehat{QB}$ output, by 4 to give the $Q\widetilde{C}$ output, and by 8 to give the $\widehat{QD}$ output. Notice that just the divide-by-4 output (1 MHz) at pin 8 of U_{15} is in use. This 1-MHz clock is required by 6800 family LSI peripherals within the microcomputer system, such as the 6850 ACIA.

8.4 INTERRUPT INTERFACE

The interrupts of the MC68000 educational microcomputer can be categorized into three groups: the reset interrupt, the nonmaskable interrupt, and the maskable hardware interrupts. The circuitry needed to support these three parts of the 68000's interrupt interface is shown in Fig. 8.4. In this section, we will examine the operation of the interrupt interface circuits for each of these interrupts.

Reset Interrupt

The reset interrupt is used to initialize the operation of the 68000 microcomputer at power-up. This section of circuitry is located in the upper left corner of the circuit

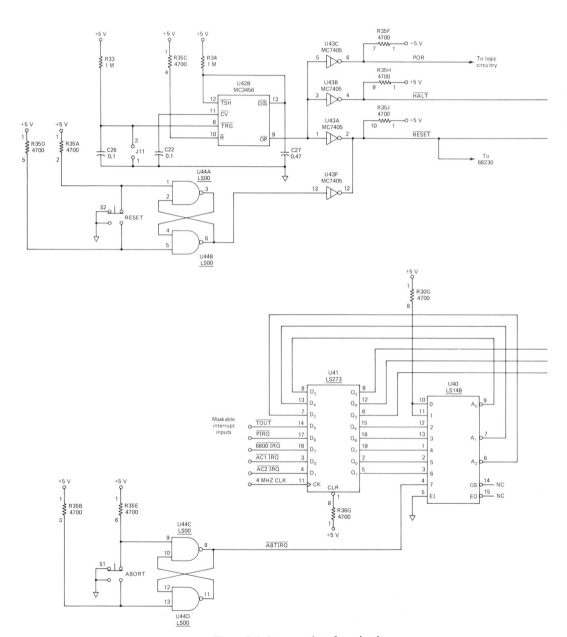

Figure 8-4 Interrupt interface circuitry.

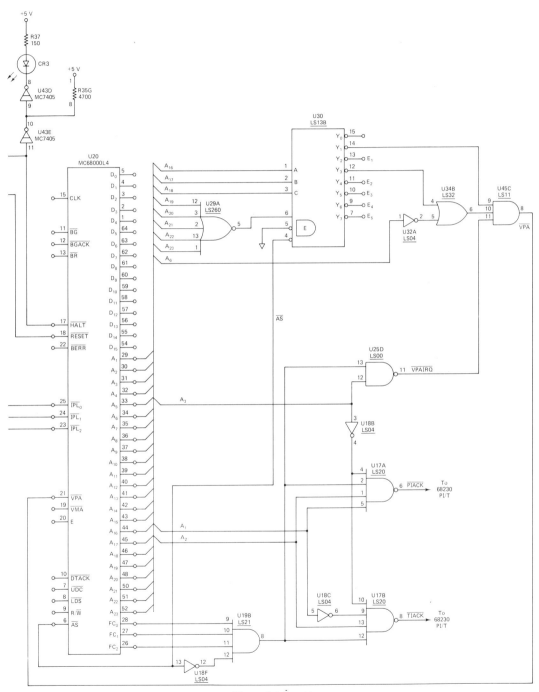

Figure 8-4 *(cont.)*

diagram of Fig. 8.4 and consists of a reset flip-flop constructed from two of the AND gates on the 74LS00 IC U_{44} and a monostable and multivibrator formed with the MC3456 timer IC U_{42}.

The monostable multivibrator circuit is used to initialize the complete microcomputer system at power on. When the power switch is turned on, capacitor C_{26}, which is connected from pin 8 of U_{42} to ground, acts like a short circuit to ground and forces the trigger. ($\overline{\text{TRG}}$) input of the MC3456 timer to logic 0. This causes the $\overline{\text{OP}}$ output at pin 9 to switch to the 1 logic level. As time elapses, C_{26} charges toward the 1 logic level threshold of the $\overline{\text{TRG}}$ input. As it exceeds this value, the $\overline{\text{OP}}$ output returns to the 0 logic level. In this way, we see that a single pulse to the 1 logic level is produced at the timer's $\overline{\text{OP}}$ output.

The pulse output at $\overline{\text{OP}}$ is buffered with 7405 inverts to give signals: power on reset (POR), halt ($\overline{\text{HALT}}$), and reset ($\overline{\text{RESET}}$). $\overline{\text{RESET}}$ is applied to both the 68000 microprocessor and the 68230 parallel interface/timer IC. As it switches to logic 0, the operation of these devices is initialized. Initialization causes the S bit in the 68000's status register to be set and the T bit to be cleared. In this way, it is put into the supervisor mode and the trace mode of operation is disabled. Then the interrupt mask, which is also in the status register of the 68000, is set to 7. This masks out all external hardware interrupts. Moreover, the supervisor stack pointer register is loaded with vector 0 from addresses 000000_{16} and 000002_{16}. This creates a supervisor stack in data memory. Next the program counter is loaded with vector 1 (actually the second half of vector 0) from addresses 000004_{16} and 000006_{16}. The new value of PC points to the beginning of the Tutor firmware package in program memory.

At the same time, the pulse at $\overline{\text{OP}}$ produces a pulse to logic 0 at POR. This stands for power on reset and is used to initialize some of the on-board logic circuits. For instance, it is used to clear or preset a number of flip-flop circuits.

Notice that the $\overline{\text{HALT}}$ signal is also generated from $\overline{\text{OP}}$ at power-on. It is applied to the $\overline{\text{HALT}}$ input at pin 17 of the 68000. This halts the operation of the MPU and lights the LED labeled CR_3 to indicate this fact. As the reset pulse is completed, the $\overline{\text{HALT}}$ line of the MPU is also released. Therefore, the 68000 begins execution of the Tutor program. The early part of this program is an initialization routine for the microcomputer's resources. For instance, it causes initial values to be loaded into the internal registers of the 68000 MPU as well as the 68230 and 6850 LSI peripherals. Besides this, it causes all storage locations in the microcomputer's data storage memory to be initialized.

The microcomputer can also be reset without turning off the main power. This is done by depressing the reset switch on the microcomputer board. Looking at Fig. 8.4, we find that the reset switch is the input of the reset flip-flop. Notice that this flip-flop is formed from two NAND gates of IC U_{44}. When the switch is depressed, the output of the flip-flop at pin 6 of U_{44} is set to 1 and as it is released the output is reset to 0. The reset pulse output at pin 6 is inverted by U_{43F} and applied to the reset inputs of the 68000 and 68230. This reset mechanism represents what is called a *warm start* and does not cause the POR or $\overline{\text{HALT}}$ outputs to be produced.

Maskable Hardware Interrupts

The next part of the interrupt interface that we will look at is the part that provides what are called maskable hardware interrupts. By hardware interrupt, we mean that it represents a device external to the 68000 microprocessor that requests service by the MPU by asserting a hardware signal called an interrupt request. By maskable interrupt, we mean that the interrupt input is accepted on a priority basis. That is, when a device issues a request for service to the MPU by issuing an interrupt request, the 68000 first compares its priority to the setting of the interrupt mask in the status register. If the value already in the mask is that of an equal or higher priority interrupt, the request for service is ignored. Otherwise, the request for service is granted.

In Fig. 8.4, the 74LS148 priority encoder U_{40} and 74LS273 interrupt latch U_{41}, which are located just to the left of the MPU, as well as all of the circuitry located to the right of the MPU are used to implement the maskable interrupt interface. The circuitry on the left is for input of interrupt requests. Notice that there are five maskable hardware interrupt inputs: $\overline{TOUT}$, $\overline{PIRQ}$, $\overline{6800IRQ}$, $\overline{AC1IRQ}$, and $\overline{AC2IRQ}$. Figure 8.5 lists the priority level, function, and autovector number for each of these interrupts. For instance, $\overline{AC2IRQ}$ stands for asynchronous communications controller 2 interrupt request. It has a priority level of 6 and uses autovector 30 at address 000078_{16} to define the starting point of its service routine.

Signal Mnemonic	Priority Level	Function	AutoVector Number
ABORT	7	Abort logic request	31
$\overline{AC2IRQ}$	6	Asynchronous communication controller 2 request	30
$\overline{AC1IRQ}$	5	Asynchronous communication controller 1 request	29
$\overline{6800IRQ}$	4	6800 device request	28
$\overline{PIRQ}$	3	PI/T parallel ports request	Not used
$\overline{TOUT}$	2	PI/T timer request	Not used
——	1	Not used	Not used

Figure 8-5 Maskable interrupts.

Also notice in Fig. 8.5 that the $\overline{TOUT}$ and $\overline{PIRQ}$ interrupt requests are for the timer and parallel ports of the 68230 PI/T device, respectively, and that they do not use autovector interrupt levels. Instead, their interrupt vectors are stored in registers within the PI/T device and are output to the 68000 over the data bus during an interrupt acknowledge bus cycle.

Let us now look at what happens when an interrupt request becomes active. Assume that the $\overline{AC1IRQ}$ input at pin 3 of U_{41} has been switched to logic 0. This means that the 6850 device U_{13} in Fig. 8.2(b) is requesting service. On the next pulse of 4MHZCLK (pin 11 of U_{41}), the logic levels of the interrupt request inputs are latched at the outputs of the 74LS273 interrupt latch. The latched interrupt requests are applied to inputs 2 through 6 of the 74LS148 priority encoder. Since just $\overline{AC1IRQ}$ is active, only the 5 input at pin 2 of the priority encoder (U_{40}) is at logic 0. This input makes the encoder output equal to $A_2A_1A_0 = 101$. This output is returned to inputs D_2 through D_4 of the interrupt latch. On the next pulse at 4MHZCLK, the code is latched at outputs Q_2 through Q_4 and is applied to the interrupt request inputs ($\overline{IPL_2}\,\overline{IPL_1}\,\overline{IPL_0}$) of the microprocessor.

Earlier we pointed out that interrupt requests, ABORT, $\overline{AC2IRQ}$, $\overline{AC1IRQ}$, and $\overline{6800IRQ}$, are serviced as autovector interrupts. For this reason, when one of them is acknowledged for service by the 68000, the external logic circuitry must switch the $\overline{VPA}$ input of the 68000 to logic 0. This signals the MPU that an autovector operation is in progress. In this case, it internally generates the vector addresses and fetches the vector from external memory. The circuitry that produces the $\overline{VPA}$ signal is located to the right of the 68000 in Fig. 8.4.

Let us now look in more detail at how $\overline{VPA}$ is generated. For our earlier example, $\overline{AC1IRQ}$, the interrupt code is $\overline{IPL_2}\,\overline{IPL_1}\,\overline{IPL_0} = 101$. During the interrupt acknowledge bus cycle, the interrupt acknowledge function code 111 is output on function code lines $FC_2FC_1FC_0$. At the same time, the interrupt code 101 is output on address lines $A_2A_1A_0$. Looking at the circuits in Fig. 8.4, we see that the function code is gated together with $\overline{AS}$ by the 74LS21 AND gate U_{19B}. Since all of its inputs are logic 1, the output at pin 8 of the AND gate switches to logic 1. This output is an enable input to the 74LS00 NAND gate U_{25D}. Here it is gated with the logic level on the A_3 address line. This signal is also 1; therefore, output $\overline{VPAIRQ}$ switches to logic 0 to indicate that the current interrupt bus cycle is to use autovectoring. The logic 0 at $\overline{VPAIRQ}$ is input to the 74LS11 AND gate U_{45C} at pin 11 and causes the $\overline{VPA}$ input of the 68000 to switch to logic 0. This completes the signaling sequence required to initiate an autovector interrupt response.

Earlier we pointed out that the parallel I/O ports and timer within the 68230 device are not serviced using autovector interrupts. This is because it has internal vector registers that can be programmed by the user with a vector number. During the interrupt acknowledge bus cycle, the 68230 supplies the vector number to the 68000 by outputting it on data bus lines D_0 through D_7. For instance, let us assume that the $\overline{TOUT}$ interrupt request input is active. This causes the code 010 to be applied to the $\overline{IPL}$ inputs of the 68000. As the interrupt acknowledge bus cycle is initiated, the function code $FC_2FC_1FC_0 = 111$ is again output and the output at pin 8 of AND gate U_{19B} switches to logic 0. However, this time the code output on address lines A_3 through A_1 is 010. This makes all inputs on NAND gate U_{17B} 1 and its output, $\overline{TIACK}$ at pin 8, switches to logic 0. $\overline{TIACK}$ signals the 68230 that the timer's request for service has been granted and that it should put the timer's interrupt vector on the bus. Later in the bus cycle, the 68000 reads the vector number off the data bus and then passes control to the address held in this vector location.

Nonmaskable Interrupt—ABORT

The ABORT switch, which is located by the RESET switch on the microcomputer board, when depressed causes software to be returned to the monitor program. For instance, if the microcomputer became hung up during execution of a user-written program, control can be returned to the monitor by simply depressing the ABORT switch. The ABORT service routine does not reinitialize the MPU, it just returns control to the monitor without changing the contents of internal registers or data memory.

The abort request signal ($\overline{\text{ABTIRQ}}$) is generated by a flip-flop similar to the one described earlier in this section for the reset switch. In fact, as shown in Fig. 8.4, this flip-flop is made with the other two AND gates of IC U_{44}.

When the ABORT switch is depressed, the $\overline{\text{ABTIRQ}}$, which is output at pin 8 of U_{44}, switches to logic 0 and as it is released, this output returns to logic 1. The pulse to logic 0 at $\overline{\text{ABTIRQ}}$ is applied to the 7 input at pin 4 of the 74LS148 priority encoder. This is the highest-priority input and causes the code 111 to be output on $A_2A_1A_0$. This code is latched into the 74LS273 latch U_{41} synchronously with 4MHZCLK. From the output of the latch, it is supplied to interrupt request inputs $\overline{\text{IPL}_2}\overline{\text{IPL}_1}\overline{\text{IPL}_0}$ of the 68000. Here code 111 represents a nonmaskable interrupt request and is serviced by the routine pointed to by autovector interrupt vector 31 at address 000070_{16}. When executed, this routine returns software control to the monitor program.

8.5 PROGRAM AND DATA STORAGE MEMORY

In Section 8.4, we covered the interrupt interface of the MC68000 educational microcomputer. Here we will continue with the circuitry used to implement the memory interfaces. This represents three separate sections of circuitry, the program storage memory, data storage memory, and the watchdog timer.

Program Storage Memory

Figure 8.6 shows the 68000 MPU and the program storage part the MC68000 educational microcomputer's memory subsystem. Notice that it involves three key elements of circuitry: the ROM address decoder, the read-only memories, and the ROM DTACK circuit. The storage array is formed from two MC68A364 ROMs. These devices are organized as 8K × 8-bits and are connected together to give an 8K × 16 bank of memory for a total of 16K bytes of program storage memory. Notice that the MPU supplies address information to both ROMs in parallel over address lines A_1 through A_{13}. Device U_{10} supplies the lower bits of the instruction word to the MPU over data bus lines D_0 through D_7, while U_{11} supplies it with the upper byte over D_8 through D_{15}.

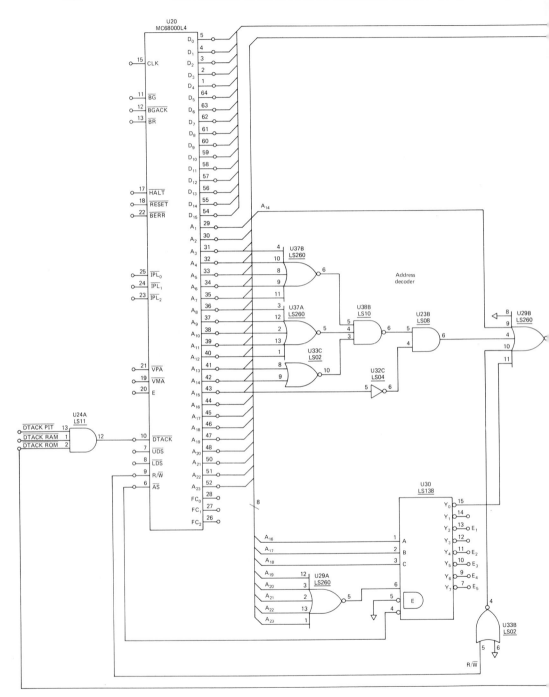

Figure 8-6 Program storage memory.

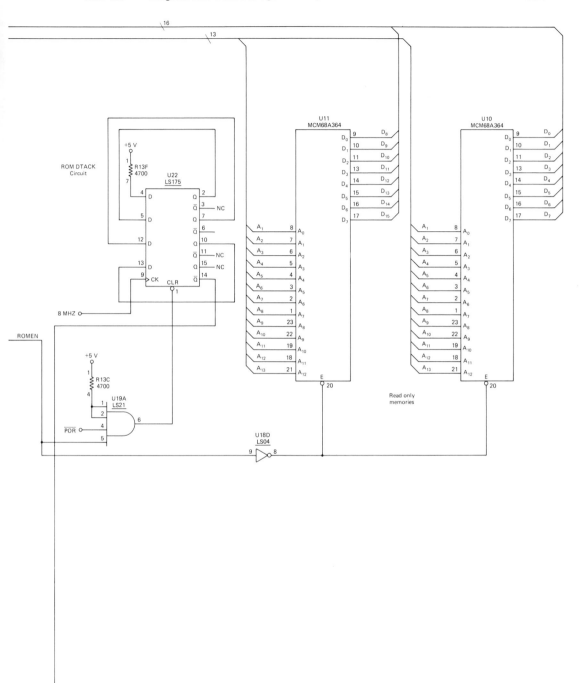

Figure 8-6 *(cont.)*

The address map in Fig. 8.7 shows that ROM resides in two pages of the 68000's address space. One part is the page in the address range from 008000_{16} to $00BFFF_{16}$. It is in this section of memory that the instructions of the Tutor monitor program are stored. The other part of the ROM address space is the eight bytes from address 000000_{16} through 000007_{16}. This part of memory stores the reset interrupt vector.

Function	Type	Address
Exception vector table	ROM	000000_{16} to 000007_{16}
	RAM	000008_{16} to $0003FF_{16}$
Tutor scratchpad	RAM	000400_{16} to $0008FF_{16}$
User memory	RAM	000900_{16} to $007FFF_{16}$
Tutor firmware	ROM	008000_{16} to $00BFFF_{16}$
Not used		$00C000_{16}$ to $00FFFF_{16}$
PI/T	I/O	010000_{16} to $01003F_{16}$
ACIA2 (lower byte)	I/O	010040_{16} to 010043_{16}
ACIA1 (upper byte)		
Redundant mapping	I/O	010044_{16} to $01FFFF_{16}$
Not used		020000_{16} to $02FFFF_{16}$
6800 page (E6)		030000_{16} to $03FFFF_{16}$
Not used		040000_{16} to $FFFFFF_{16}$

Figure 8-7 Memory address map (Motorola, Inc.).

Whenever an address in these ranges is output on address bus lines A_1 through A_{23}, the address decoder circuit detects its occurrence and produces the ROM enable (ROMEN) signal. ROMEN is supplied by the output of the 74LS260 NOR gate U_{29B}. For this output to be logic 1, all of its inputs must be logic 0. Notice in Fig. 8.6 that switching ROMEN to logic 1 enables both the ROM DTACK circuit and the two ROM ICs.

The ROM DTACK circuit is used to produce the $\overline{\text{DTACK ROM}}$ signal that tells the MPU to complete asynchronous bus cycles that are performed to the program memory. This circuit is actually a counter constructed from the D-type flip-flops of the 74LS175 IC U_{22}. The flip-flops on this IC are connected to form a 4-bit binary counter. The CK input at pin 5 of this counter is supplied by the 8-MHz clock signal. Whenever a ROM bus cycle is not in progress, the output of the 74LS21 AND gate U_{19A} is logic 0 and the output of the counter is cleared. As a memory bus cycle is initiated to program memory, ROMEN is switched to 1 and the counter increments toward a count of 1000. When this count is reached, the $\overline{Q}$ output at pin 14 switches to the 0 logic level. This makes the signal $\overline{\text{DTACK ROM}}$ logic 0 and the output of the 74LS11 AND gate U_{24A} signals the 68000 that the bus cycle can be completed by switching $\overline{\text{DTACK}}$ to logic 0.

Let us now look more closely at the address decoding that takes place at the address decoder to produce the ROMEN signal. Assume that the address output on the address bus during an instruction acquisition bus cycle is 008000_{16}. Expressing this address in binary form, we get

$$A_{23}A_{22}\ldots\ldots A_1 = 00000000100000000000000_2$$

To make ROMEN equal to 1, this address must cause all inputs to the 74LS260 NOR gate U_{29B} logic 0. Looking at this gate, we see that its first input is A_{14} and that this bit is at logic 0 in the address. The next input of the gate is supplied by the random logic section of the address decoder. The address inputs to this section of circuitry are:

$$A_7A_6A_5A_4 = 0000_2$$

which makes the output at pin 6 of the 74LS260 NOR gate U_{37B} equal to 1,

$$A_{12}A_{11}A_{10}A_9 = 0000_2$$

which makes the output at pin 5 of NOR gate U_{37A} equal to 1, and

$$A_{14}A_{13} = 00_2$$

which makes the output at pin 10 of NOR gate U_{33C} equal to 1. These three outputs are inputs from the 74LS10 NAND gate U_{38B}. Since all of its inputs are logic 1, the output at pin 6 is logic 0. This signal is combined with $\overline{A_{15}}$, which is logic 0, by the 74LS08 AND gate U_{23B}. This output, which is at pin 6, gives a second input of NOR gate U_{29B}, which is also 0. Next, $R/\overline{W}$, which is at logic 1 during read bus cycles of program memory, is inverted by U_{33B} to give logic 0 at output pin 4 and applied to the third input of NOR gate U_{29B}. Finally

$$A_{18}A_{17}A_{16} = 000_2$$

selects the Y_0 output at pin 15 of the 74LS138 three-line to 8-line decoder.

$$A_{23}A_{22}A_{21}A_{20}A_{19} = 00000_2$$

causes the output at pin 5 of U_{29A} to switch to logic 1 and supplies one of the enable inputs at pin 6 of U_{30}. $\overline{AS} = 0$ at pin 4 supplies the last signal needed to enable the decoder for operation. Therefore, Y_0 switches to logic 0 to produce the last input of NOR gate U_{29B}. Since all inputs of U_{29B} are now at logic 0, this address causes the ROMEN output to switch to the 1 logic level.

Data Storage Memory

The data storage memory interface of the MC68000 educational microcomputer is quite different than that just described for program storage memory. Looking at Fig. 8.8, we see that it includes the address decoder, the RAM timing/DTACK circuit, the address multiplexer, the RAM storage array, and the RAM refresh control circuit.

The RAM storage array is 32K bytes in size and is organized as 16K words. In Fig. 8.8, we find that it is formed with sixteen 4116 dynamic RAM ICs. Each of these devices is organized 16K × 1-bit. It is this part of the memory subsystem that is used as a scratchpad memory for the Tutor program and to store data and programs that are keyed in for execution and debugging.

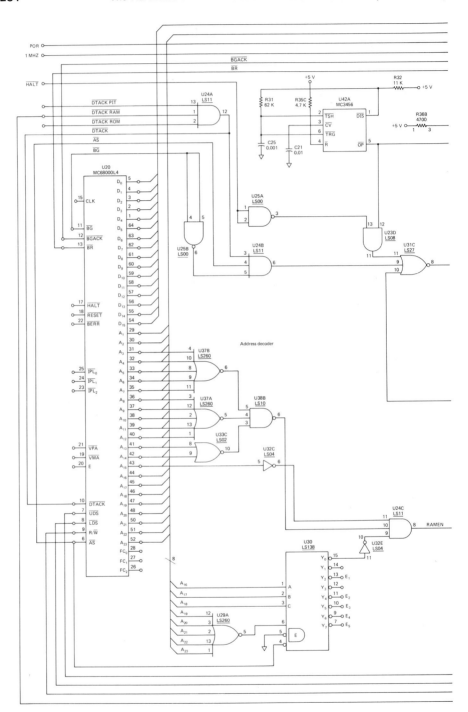

Figure 8-8 Data storage memory.

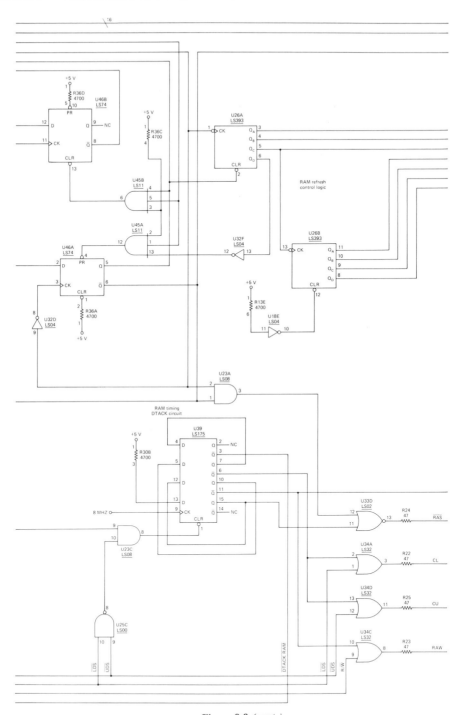

Figure 8-8 *(cont.)*

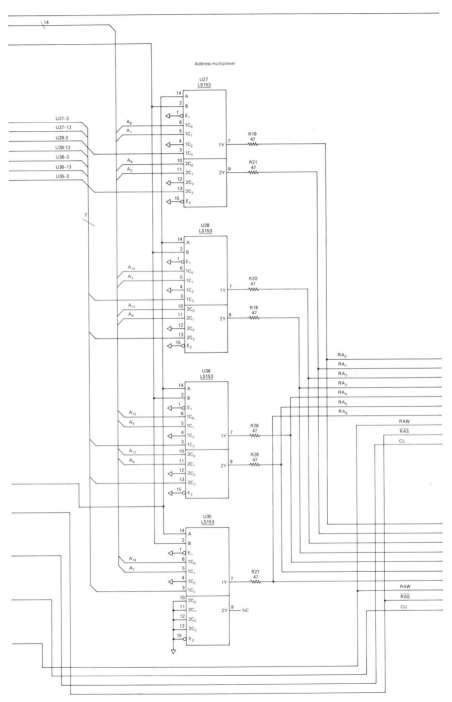

Figure 8-8 *(cont.)*

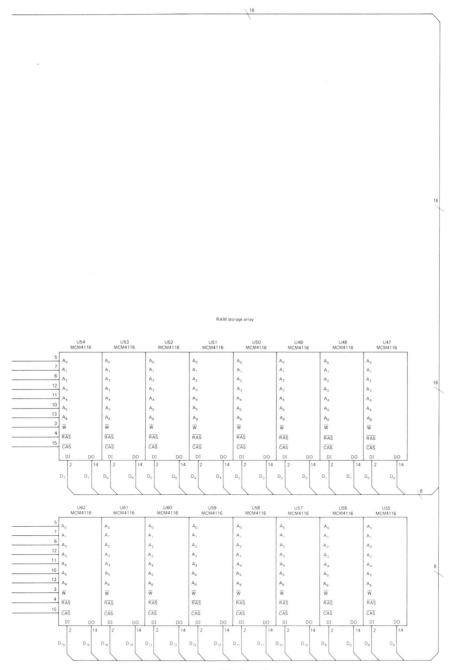

Figure 8-8 *(cont.)*

The data input (DI) leads and data output (DO) leads of the individual RAMs are wired together and then tied to the corresponding data bus lines of the 68000. For instance, DI and DO from IC U_{47} are connected together and supplied to the D_0 line of the data bus.

Unlike the ROMs used in the program storage part of the memory subsystem, these DRAMs require a multiplexed address. That is, a 14-bit address is input to the address multiplexer circuit over address lines A_1 through A_{14} and under control of the RAM timing/DTACK circuit, it is multiplexed into a 7-bit row select address (RAS) and 7-bit column select address (CAS). These two parts of the address are output one after the other in time on the RA_0 through RA_6 lines and applied to address inputs A_0 through A_6 of all memory devices in parallel.

The application of these two addresses are synchronized with the ROW address select ($\overline{RAS}$) signal and column address select signal, column upper (CU) and column lower (CL). Looking at Fig. 8.8, we find that these signals are applied to the $\overline{RAS}$ and $\overline{CAS}$ inputs of the RAMs, respectively.

The last control signal that is applied to the memory devices in the RAM storage array is RAW. Note that it is applied to the $\overline{W}$ input of all RAM ICs in parallel. This line is used to signal to the data storage memory subsystem whether a read or write bus cycle is in progress.

The same address decoder that we discussed relative to program storage memory is shown in Fig. 8.8 to decode the 68000's address to give the RAM enable (RAMEN) signal. Again address bits A_3 through A_{14} must all be logic 0 to make the output at pin 6 of U_{38B} switch to logic 0; A_{15} must be logic 0, instead of 1, to make the output at pin 6 of U_{32C} logic 1; and finally A_{16} through A_{23} must equal 0 to make the Y_0 output at pin 15 of U_{30} equal to 0. This output is inverted by U_{32E} to give logic 1 at the output at pin 11. Therefore, all three inputs of AND gate U_{24C} are logic 1 and RAMEN switches to the active 1 logic level.

RAMEN does not directly enable the memory array. Instead, it is applied along with the output of NAND gate U_{25C} to inputs of AND gate U_{23C}. The output of U_{25C} is generated from lower data select ($\overline{LDS}$) and upper data select ($\overline{UDS}$). If either or both of these signals are logic 0, the output at pin 8 of U_{25C} is logic 1. This condition makes both inputs of U_{23C} logic 1 and its output at pin 8 switches to the 1 level, thereby releasing the clear input of the 74LS175 device (U_{39}). U_{39} contains four D-type flip-flops that are interconnected to form a 4-bit binary counter. Therefore, as CLR is released, the output of the counter begins to increment through its count sequence synchronously with the 8-MHz clock signal that is applied to its CK input.

After the first clock pulse, output Q at pin 15 is logic 1. This makes the $\overline{RAS}$ output at pin 13 of U_{33D} switch to logic 0. $\overline{RAS}$ signals the devices in the memory array that a row address is available at address inputs A_0 through A_6. On the next clock pulse, the $\overline{Q}$ output at pin 11 of U_{39} switches to logic 0 and enables the R/$\overline{W}$ signal to the RAW output at pin 8 of U_{34C} and signals the memory array whether data will be read from or written into data memory during the current bus cycle. The fourth clock pulse causes $\overline{Q}$ at pin 6 of U_{39} to switch to the 0 logic level and enables $\overline{LDS}$ and $\overline{UDS}$ to the CL and CU outputs, respectively. This tells the RAMs in the memory array that a column address is applied at inputs A_0 through A_6. In this way, we find that the counter controls the timing of memory bus control signals $\overline{RAS}$, CU, CL, and RAW.

As the fifth clock pulse occurs, $\overline{Q}$ at pin 3 of U_{39} switches to logic 0. This produces the signal $\overline{DTACK\ RAM}$, which is returned by way of AND gate U_{24A} to the $\overline{DTACK}$ input of the 68000. When the $\overline{DTACK\ RAM}$ input at pin 1 of this gate switches to logic 0, the output at pin 12 and $\overline{DTACK}$ input of the 68000 are also switched to logic 0. This signals the 68000 that the current data memory bus cycle can be completed.

From the memory map of Fig. 8.7 we see that RAM is located from address 000008_{16} through $007FFF_{16}$. Notice that the addresses in the range from 000008_{16} through $0003FF_{16}$ are used to store exception vectors. This area of memory is followed by a 2K-byte segment of RAM at addresses 000400_{16} through $0008FF_{16}$, which is used as a scratchpad by the Tutor program. The rest of the RAM, which resides from address 000900_{16} through $007FFF_{16}$, provides user memory for storage of programs and data. In this way, we see that RAM is located at the lower part of the 68000's address space.

Now that we know how the $\overline{W}$, $\overline{RAS}$, and $\overline{CAS}$ signals are generated for the RAMs, let us look more closely at how the address on A_1 through A_{14} is multiplexed to the A_0 through A_6 inputs of the RAMs in the RAM storage array. The address multiplexer is formed with four dual 4-line to 1-line mutliplexer ICs. These are devices U_{27}, U_{28}, U_{35}, and U_{36} in Fig. 8.8. Notice that address bits A_1, A_3, A_5, and A_7 are applied to the $1C_0$ inputs of the multiplexer devices and A_9, A_{11}, and A_{13} are applied to their $2C_1$ inputs. These seven address bits form the row address (RAS) part of the memory address. Moreover, we find that address bits A_8, A_{10}, A_{12}, and A_{14} are applied to the $1C_0$ inputs of the multiplexer devices and A_9, A_{11}, and A_{13} are applied to their $2C_0$ input. This is the 7-bit column address (CAS) part of the memory address. The two bit code applied to the BA select inputs of the multiplexer determines whether the RAS or CAS part of the address is passed to the RA lines at the outputs of the multiplexers. These outputs are supplied to address inputs A_0 through A_6 of all RAMs in parallel. For instance, when BA = 01, address bits A_1 through A_7 are output on lines RA_0 through RA_7, respectively. This address is accompanied by a logic 0 at the $\overline{RAS}$ input.

Now that we have described the operation of the circuits involved in the memory interface, let us trace through their operation as the 68000 writes a word of data to memory. The write bus cycle that is performed to write data to the data storage memory begins with the 68000 outputting the address of the storage location that is to be accessed on address bus lines A_1 through A_{23}. Then it switches the $\overline{AS}$ output to its active 0 logic level. This signal tells external circuitry that a valid address is available on the bus. We will assume that this address is for a storage location in the data storage memory part of the memory subsystem.

At the same time, the 68000 sets $R/\overline{W}$ to logic 0 to signal that a write bus cycle is in progress. Morever, it sets both $\overline{UDS}$ and $\overline{LDS}$ to their active 0 logic level to signal that a word data transfer is to take place over the data bus. Finally, the word of data that is to be written into memory is output on data bus lines D_0 through D_{15}.

Address bits A_3 through A_{15} and A_{16} through A_{23} are decoded by the address decoder circuit. Since we have assumed that the address on the bus corresponds to a storage location in data memory, the RAMEN output of AND gate U_{24C} becomes active (logic 1). This makes the pin 9 input of AND gate U_{23C} logic 1. At the same moment, both inputs ($\overline{LDS}$ and $\overline{UDS}$) of NAND gate U_{25C} are logic 0; therefore, its output switches to logic 1. This makes the other input (pin 10) of U_{23C} logic 1 and its output switches to the 1 level. As the output switches to 1, the CLR input of the RAM timing/DTACK counter circuit is released.

Now the counter begins to increment at a rate set by the 8 MHz clock and as it increments through its counting sequence, signals $\overline{RAS}$, RAW, CL, CU, and $\overline{DTACK\ RAM}$ are generated in that order. When $\overline{RAS}$ is switched to logic 0, the control input of the address multiplexer is logic 1 and B is logic 0. This causes the RAS part of the address, A_1 through A_7, to be multiplexed to RA_0 through RA_7 and then applied to the A_0 through A_6 inputs of the RAMs.

As the counter continues to increment, the A multiplexer control signal is switched to logic 0, while B remains at logic 0. This causes the CAS part of the address, A_8 through A_{14}, to be output on RA_0 through RA_6. Then memory control signals CL and CU are switched to logic 0 to signal the memory devices that the CAS address is available at their A_0 through A_6 inputs.

Each RAM IC inputs the bit of the data word that is applied to its data input (DI) line and stores the corresponding logic level into the storage location selected by the RAS and CAS address.

At this point, the data has already been written into memory. However, the 68000 does not yet know that the bus cycle can be completed. But as the RAM timing/DTACK circuit continues to count it next switches $\overline{DTACK\ RAM}$ to logic 0. This signal is returned to one input of AND gate U_{24A} and makes the output at pin 12 switch to logic 0. This output is applied directly to the $\overline{DTACK}$ input of the 68000. Switching $\overline{DTACK}$ to logic 0 signals the 68000 that it can terminate the current bus cycle. In response to $\overline{DTACK}$, it returns outputs $\overline{UDS}$, $\overline{LDS}$, and $\overline{AS}$ to their inactive 1 logic level; $R/\overline{W}$ is returned to the 1 logic level; and the data word is removed from bus lines D_0 through D_{15}. As the counter continues to increment, $\overline{DTACK\ RAM}$ is returned to logic 1. This represents the end of the write bus cycle.

Example 8.1

Write an instruction sequence that can be used to clear Tutor's scratchpad memory.

Solution.   As shown in Fig. 8.7, the Tutor's scratchpad RAM resides in the address range from 000400_{16} to $0008FF_{16}$. This range is

$$0008FF_{16} - 000400_{16} + 1 = 500_{16} \text{ bytes}$$

$$= 280_{16} \text{ words}$$

$$= 140_{16} \text{ long words}$$

in length.

Let us use A_1 as an address pointer to the scratchpad RAM and D_0 as a counter of the number of word addresses to be initialized. Furthermore, D_1 will be loaded with the value 0_{16}. This is the value that will be written to each word storage location in the scratchpad RAM. To initialize these three registers, the following sequence of instructions can be executed

> MOVE.L   #$400,A1
>
> MOVE.L   #$280,D0
>
> MOVE.L   #0,D1

Next we need to execute instructions that write the word contents of D_1 (0000_{16}) to the memory location pointed to by A_1; increment the address in A_1; decrement the count in D_0, and test the count in D_0 to determine if it is 0. If the value in D_0 is not 0, the data write, address increment, count decrement, and zero test operations must be repeated. However, when the count in D_0 becomes equal to 0, all storage locations in the scratchpad RAM have been cleared and initialization is done. These operations are performed with the instruction sequence that follows

> NXT   MOVE.W   D1,(A1)+
>
>   SUBQ.L   #1,D0
>
>   BNZ   NXT
>
> DONE   B   DONE

The complete program is repeated in Fig. 8.9.

>   MOVE.L   #$400,A1
>
>   MOVE.L   #$280,D0
>
>   MOVE.L   #0,D1
>
> NXT   MOVE.W   D1,(A1)+
>
>   SUBQ.L   #1,D0
>
>   BNZ   NXT
>
> DONE   B   DONE

Figure 8-9 Scratchpad memory initialization routine.

Watchdog Timer Circuit

The 68000 system bus is asynchronous. That is, once a bus cycle is started, the data transfer is not complete until the external circuitry indicates that the bus cycle is to be finished. We have found in our description of the program and data storage

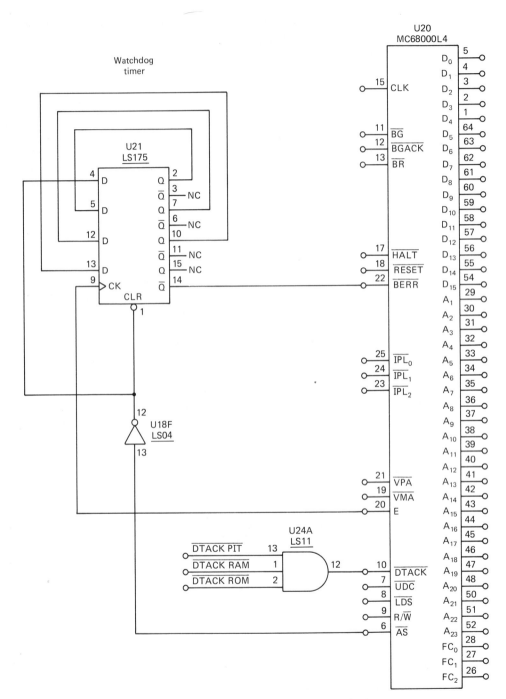

Figure 8-10 WATCHDOG timer circuit.

memory subsystems that external circuitry is provided to switch the $\overline{\text{DTACK}}$ input of the 68000 to logic 0. Notice in Fig. 8.10 that three different signals drive the $\overline{\text{DTACK}}$ input through the 74LS11 AND gate U_{24A}. These signals, $\overline{\text{DTACK PIT}}$, $\overline{\text{DTACK RAM}}$, and $\overline{\text{DTACK ROM}}$, correspond to bus cycles initiated to the 68230 PI/T device, data memory (RAM), and program memory (ROM), respectively. If none of these signals is received to indicate that the bus cycle is to be completed, a bus error condition exists.

A watchdog timer circuit is provided in the MC68000 educational microcomputer to detect a bus error condition. This circuit, as shown in Fig. 8.10, is constructed with U_{21}, a 74LS175 D-type flip-flop IC. Looking at the circuit diagram, we see that the flip-flops in this device are cascaded to form a 4-bit binary counter. When a bus cycle is not in progress, the data input D at pin 4 and CLR input at pin 1 are at logic 0. Therefore, the flip-flops are all reset and the $\overline{Q}$ output at pin 14 is at logic 1. This output is applied to the bus error $\overline{(\text{BERR})}$ input of the 68000 and signals that a bus error has not occurred.

When a bus cycle is initiated, the $\overline{\text{AS}}$ output of the MPU is switched to logic 0 and maintained at that level throughout the bus cycle. $\overline{\text{AS}}$ is inverted by U_{18F} and supplies logic 1 to the CLR and D inputs. The counter is now released and begins to count through its binary sequence at a rate set by the clock pulse at the E output of the 68000. As long as $\overline{\text{DTACK}}$ becomes active before this count reaches 1000_2 no bus error occurs; however, if $\overline{\text{DTACK}}$ is not received, the $\overline{\text{BERR}}$ input is switched to logic 0 and a bus error exception has occurred. In this way, we see that the watchdog timer observes all bus activities and assures that all bus cycles that are initiated are also completed.

8.6 PARALLEL AND SERIAL I/O INTERFACES

There are four I/O interfaces provided in the MC68000 educational microcomputer. Looking at the block diagram in Fig. 8.1, we find that there are two *RS-232C serial ports,* one for connection to the terminal and the other for connection to a host computer, and two *parallel I/O interfaces,* one for connection to a printer and the other for connection of an audio cassette. Let us now look at how each of these interfaces is implemented in the microcomputer system.

Parallel I/O Interfaces

The parallel I/O circuitry of the MC68000 educational microcomputer is shown in Fig. 8.11. Here we see that a single 68230 parallel interface/timer (PI/T) IC has been used to implement the printer and audio cassette interfaces. This device has three byte-wide I/O ports, port A (PA_0–PA_7), port B (PB_0–PB_7), and port C (PC_0–PC_7) and four programmable handshake lines, H_1 through H_4. This gives a total of 28 I/O lines for implementation of the printer and audio cassette interfaces.

Input or output data transfers between the 68000 and the A, B, and C ports are performed by reading from or writing to a corresponding data register within

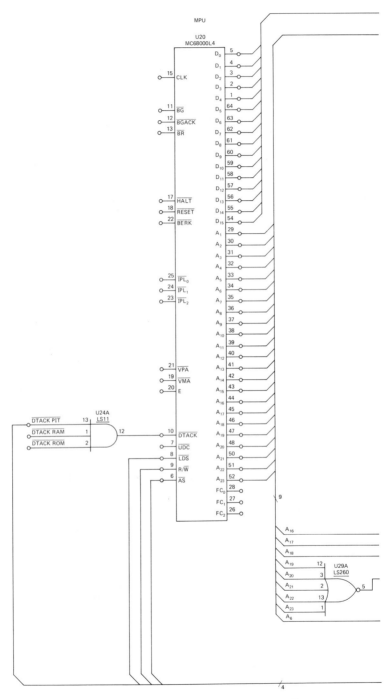

Figure 8-11 Parallel I/O interface—printer and audio cassette.

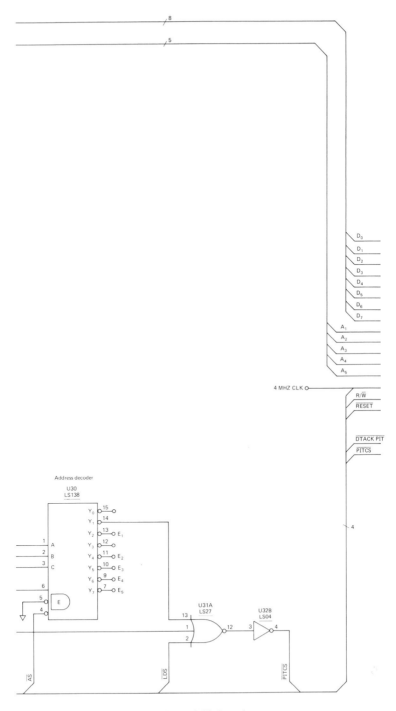

Figure 8-11 *(cont.)*

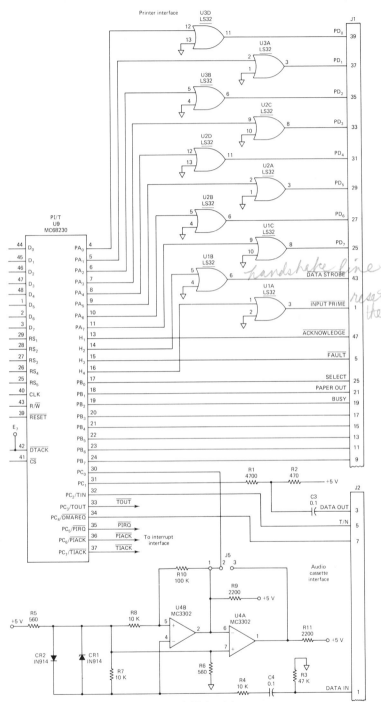

Figure 8-11 *(cont.)*

the 68230. Figure 8.12 lists the location of all of the 68230's registers in the microcomputer's address space. For example, the port A I/O lines are accessed through the port A data register (PADR) at address 010011_{16}.

Remember that the I/O lines on a 68230 can be configured for many different modes of operation. In general, they can be set up to work as bit addressable inputs or outputs, byte-wide unidirectional inputs or outputs, or byte-wide bidirectional inputs/outputs. Moreover, the A and B ports can be configured to work together as a word-wide unidirectional or bidirectional port. In Chapter 6, we found that four control registers must be loaded with appropriate control bytes to configure the I/O lines of the A port as inputs or outputs, select between mode 0, mode 1, mode 2, or mode 3 operation, select the submode of operation, define the operation of the handshake signals, and assign handshake pin interrupt priorities. These registers are called the port general control register (PGCR), the port service request register (PSRR), and port A data direction register (PADDR), and the port A control register (PACR). From Fig. 8.12, we find that they are located at addresses 010001_{16}, 010003_{16}, 010005_{16}, and $01000D_{16}$, respectively, of the 68000's address space.

Let us continue by looking at how the 68000 is interfaced to the PI/T device. The microprocessor interface is shown to the left of the PI/T device (U$_9$) in Fig. 8.11. Looking at the circuit diagram, we find that the 68230 is located on the lower eight

Address	Register
010001_{16}	Port general control register (PGCR)
010003_{16}	Port service request register (PSRR)
010005_{16}	Port A data direction register (PADDR)
010007_{16}	Port B data direction register (PBDDR)
010009_{16}	Port C data direction register (PCDDR)
$01000B_{16}$	Port interrupt vector register (PIVR)
$01000D_{16}$	Port A control register (PACR)
$01000F_{16}$	Port B control register (PBCR)
010011_{16}	Port A data register (PADR)
010013_{16}	Port B data register (PBDR)
010015_{16}	Port A alternate register (PAAR)
010017_{16}	Port B alternate register (PBAR)
010019_{16}	Port C data register (PCDR)
$01001B_{16}$	Port status register (PSR)
010021_{16}	Timer control register (TCR)
010023_{16}	Timer interrupt vector register (TIVR)
010027_{16}	Counter preload register high (CPRH)
010029_{16}	Counter preload register middle (CPRM)
$01002B_{16}$	Counter preload register low (CPRL)
$01002F_{16}$	Count register high (CNTRH)
010031_{16}	Count register middle (CNTRM)
010033_{16}	Count register low (CNTRL)
010035_{16}	Timer status register (TSR)

Figure 8-12 Addresses of the 68230's internal registers.

data bus lines D_0 through D_7. It is over these lines that the 68000 accesses the internal registers of the PI/T to input or output data, load or read configuration information, or read status information.

The next group of inputs at the microprocessor interface is the register select lines RS_1 through RS_5. The binary code applied at these inputs determines which of the 68230's 23 internal registers is accessed. They are supplied directly by address bus lines A_1 through A_5. Other bits of the address are decoded by the 74LS138 address decoder (U_{30}) to produce the PI/T chip select signal $\overline{PITCS}$. This signal is applied to the $\overline{CS}$ input of the PI/T and when it is switched to logic 0, the 68230's microprocessor interface is enabled for operation.

The PI/T is a 68000 family peripheral. For this reason, it is designed so that its internal registers are to be accessed with asynchronous bus cycles. A data transfer acknowledge ($\overline{DTACK}$) output is provided on the 68230 for this purpose. During write cycles, the logic level of $\overline{DTACK}$ is switched to logic 0 just after the 68230 has accepted the data off the bus. In this way, it tells the 68000 to complete the current bus cycle. On the other hand, when data is being read from within the 68230, $\overline{DTACK}$ is switched to 0 when valid data is available at D_0 through D_7. This time it signals the 68000 to first read the data off the bus and then complete the bus cycle.

Now that we have introduced the parallel I/O interface let us trace through the operation of the circuitry in Fig. 8.11 as the 68000 writes a byte of data to the port A data register. Since the 68230 is located in the memory address space, this represents a write bus cycle and could be initiated by executing a MOVE instruction.

As the write bus cycle begins, the address of the port A data register, which is 010011_{16}, is output on address bus lines A_1 through A_{23} and lower data strobe $\overline{LDS}$ is switched to its active (logic 0) level. This gives the binary address

$$A_{23}A_{22}\ldots\ldots A_1 = 00000010000000000010001_2$$

and

$$\overline{LDS} = 0$$

At the same time, address strobe ($\overline{AS}$) is asserted (logic 0) and $R/\overline{W}$ is set to logic 0 to signal that a write operation is to take place.

Address lines A_6 and A_{16} through A_{23} are inputs to the address decoder circuit. From the binary form of the address, we find that bits A_{19} through A_{23} are all logic 0; therefore, the output of the 74LS260 NOR gate U_{29A} is logic 1. At the same time, $\overline{AS}$ is at the 0 logic level. These two signals enable the 74LS138 3-line to 8-line decoder (U_{30}) for operation. Now that the decoder is enabled address lines A_{16} through A_{18} at the A through C inputs, which are 001, causes the Y_1 output to switch to logic 0. A logic 0 on this line signals that an I/O operation is in progress.

Next, the logic 0 at Y_1 is combined with the logic 0 at $\overline{LDS}$ and the logic 0 at A_6 by the 74LS27 NOR gate on IC U_{31A}. Since all three inputs are logic 0, the output of the NOR gate switches to the 1 logic level. This output is inverted by U_{32B} to give an 0 logic level at $\overline{PITCS}$. This logic 0 is applied to the $\overline{CS}$ input of the 68230, thereby enabling it for operation.

The 68230 is now enabled for operation and the logic 0 at R/$\overline{\text{W}}$ has signaled that the 68000 is going to write data into one of its registers. Moreover, this data also has already been output on data bus lines D_0 through D_7 and the register select code of 01000 on A_1 through A_5 has selected the port A data register. The 68230 reads the data off the bus; enters it into PADR; and then switches the $\overline{\text{DTACK}}$ output to logic 0. $\overline{\text{DTACK}}$ is carried over the $\overline{\text{DTACK PIT}}$ line to one input of AND gate U_{24A} and causes the output at pin 12 to switch to logic 0. This output is connected to the $\overline{\text{DTACK}}$ input of the 68000 and signals it to complete the current write cycle. In response, the MPU returns $\overline{\text{LDS}}$, $\overline{\text{AS}}$, D_0 through D_7, and R/$\overline{\text{W}}$ to their inactive logic levels.

Having examined the microprocessor interface in detail, let us now look at the circuitry on the I/O port side of the 68230. Here we find that all of port A and B and the handshake lines are used to implement a parallel (Centronics) printer interface at connector J_1. Notice that the port A lines, PA_0 through PA_7 are buffered to produce printer data lines PD_0 through PD_7. It is on these lines that the microcomputer outputs character data to the printer. The handshake lines H_1 through H_4 at PB_0 through PB_2 are used to implement control signals for the Centronics interface. For instance, H_2 is buffered by IC U_{18} and then output to the printer as the $\overline{\text{DATA STROBE}}$ signal. This line signals the printer that there is data available to it on data lines PD_0 through PD_7. Moreover, H_1 is supplied by an input signal called $\overline{\text{ACKNOWLEDGE}}$, with which the printer can tell the microcomputer that it has read the character data from the PD lines.

Looking at port C of the 68230 in Fig. 8.11, we find that lines PC_0 through PC_2 are used to implement the interface to the audio cassette at connector J_2. Data or other information that is to be recorded are output in bit serial form to the audio cassette recorder over line PC_1. Notice that the voltage at PC_1 is first divided between resistors R_1 and R_2 and then A.C. coupled to the DATA line at pin 3 of J_2 through capacitor C_3. The 0 and 1 logic levels output at DATA OUT are encoded as a 1-kHz 50 percent-duty cycle square wave and a 2-kHz 50 percent-duty cycle square wave, respectively.

When loading information such as programs from the tape player, data are input to the microcomputer from the DATA IN line at pin 1 of J_2. Diodes CR_1 and CR_2 and the MC3302 comparator IC (U_{48}) square and clip the analog signal input from the tape. The microprocessor reads this signal at PC_0 and by evaluating its frequency through software determines whether the input data is at logic 0 or logic 1.

Example 8.2

Write a sequence of instructions that will set up the 68230 in the MC68000 educational microcomputer to work as follows:
(a) Unidirectional 8-bit ports operate with active handshake lines
(b) DMA and interrupts not used
(c) Port A is an 8-bit output port
(d) Port B is an 8-bit input port
(e) Initialize the printer

Solution. In Chapter 6, we studied the 68230 and how the bits in its internal registers are used to configure various modes of operation. Here we will just list the registers and the values with which they must be loaded to achieve the modes of operation described in steps a through e.

To configure the 68230 as described in step a, the PGCR register must be loaded with

$$PGCR = 00000000_2 = 00_{16}$$

followed by

$$PGCR = 00110000_2 = 30_{16}$$

Next to configure the 68230 for no DMA or interrupts as described in step b, PSRR must be loaded with

$$PSRR = 00000000_2 = 00_{16}$$

To configure port A as described in step c, PADDR is loaded with

$$PADDR = 11111111_2 = FF_{16}$$

and PACR must be initialized with

$$PACR = 01100000_2 = 60_{16}$$

Now port B is configured as described in step d by loading PBDDR with the value

$$PBDDR = 00000000_2 = 00_{16}$$

and PBCR with

$$PBCR = 10100000_2 = A0_{16}$$

Finally, to initialize the printer for step e, bit 3 of PBCR is first set and then reset. This sends out an initialization pulse to the printer. To do this, we must first load PBCR with

$$PBCR = 10101000_2 = A8_{16}$$

and then reload it with

$$PBCR = 10100000_2 = A0_{16}$$

To initialize the 68230, we must write the values just given into the identified registers. Figure 8.13(a) lists the initialization parameters as a block of data. Notice that the parameter table begins in memory at address X and has one parameter stored at each word address up through $X + 16$. Notice that the value of each parameter, the mnemonic for the register to which it is to be written, and the address of the register are listed in the table.

Let us now write the sequence of instructions that are needed to load the 68230's registers. We begin by loading address register A_1 with the address X. In this way, it acts as a pointer to the beginning of the table in memory. This is done by executing the instruction

$$MOVE.L \quad \#X,A1$$

Address	Contents	Register	Register address
X	00_{16}	PGCR	10001_{16}
X + 2	00_{16}	PSRR	10003_{16}
X + 4	FF_{16}	PADDR	10005_{16}
X + 6	00_{16}	PBDDR	10007_{16}
X + 8	60_{16}	PACR	$1000D_{16}$
X + 10	$A0_{16}$	PBCR	$1000F_{16}$
X + 12	30_{16}	PGCR	10001_{16}
X + 14	$A8_{16}$	PBCR	$1000F_{16}$
X + 16	$A0_{16}$	PBCR	$1000F_{16}$

(a)

```
MOVE.L   #X,A1
MOVEP    (A1),D0
MOVE.L   #$10001,A2
MOVEP    D0,(A2)
MOVE.B   #$00,D0
MOVE.B   D0,$7(A2)
MOVE.B   #$60,D0
MOVE.B   D0,$D(A2)
MOVE.B   #$A0,D0
MOVE.B   D0,$F(A2)
MOVE.B   #$30,D0
MOVE.B   D0,$1(A2)
MOVE.B   #$A8,D0
MOVE.B   D0,$F(A2)
MOVE.B   #$A0,D0
MOVE.B   D0,$F(A2)
```
(b)

Figure 8-13 (a) Parameter table for initializing the 68230; (b) initialization instruction sequence.

Next we read the first four byte wide parameters in the table as a long word into data register D_0. To do this we use the instruction

MOVEP   (A1),D0

Now we load a pointer to the first of the four registers into A_2 and then write them into the registers of the 68230 with the instruction

MOVE.L   #$10001,A2

MOVEP   D0,(A2)

The rest of the parameters in the table are written to their respective register within the 68230 with the instructions that follow:

```
MOVE.B    #$00,D0
MOVE.B    D0,$7(A2)
MOVE.B    #$60,D0
MOVE.B    D0,$D(A2)
MOVE.B    #$A0,D0
MOVE.B    D0,$F(A2)
MOVE.B    #$30,D0
MOVE.B    D0,$1(A2)
MOVE.B    #$A8,D0
MOVE.B    D0,$F(A2)
MOVE.B    #$A0,D0
MOVE.B    D0,$F(A2)
```

The complete sequence of instructions is repeated in Fig. 8.13(b).

RS-232C Communications Interface

Another important I/O interface in the MC68000 educational microcomputer is its RS-232C serial I/O ports. In Fig. 8.1, we find that the microcomputer has two serial ports. One of these ports permits a CRT terminal to be connected to the microcomputer. In this way, the user can input information to the microcomputer from the keyboard of the terminal and the microcomputer outputs results on the display for the user to read. The other serial port is provided for a modem communication link to a host computer.

The circuitry involved in implementing the serial ports is shown in detail in Fig. 8.14. Here we will concentrate on the port 1 UART, which is the one that is used to connect the terminal to the microcomputer. Looking at the circuit diagram, we find that this port is implemented at connector J_3. Notice that the 6850 ACIA device is the communications controller that is used. In Chapter 6 we introduced this LSI device.

At power up, the control register within the port 1 ACIA (U_{13}) is loaded by the Tutor software to configure the serial port to operate as follows: 8-bit character length, even parity, and one stop bit. Moreover, it sets up the internal clock divider circuitry such that the externally generated baud clock signal that is applied to the receiver and transmitter clock inputs is divided by 16 within the device; $\overline{RTS}$ is set for an active low logic level; and the transmitter interrupt is disabled.

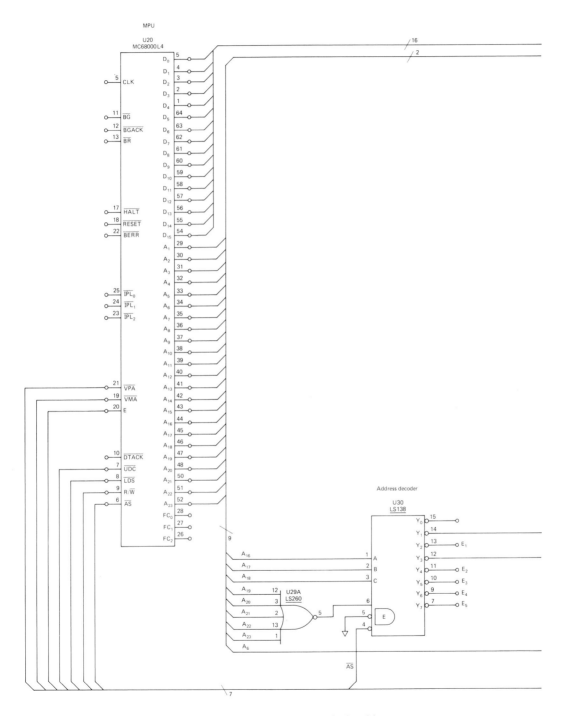

Figure 8-14 Serial I/O interface—the terminal and host computer ports.

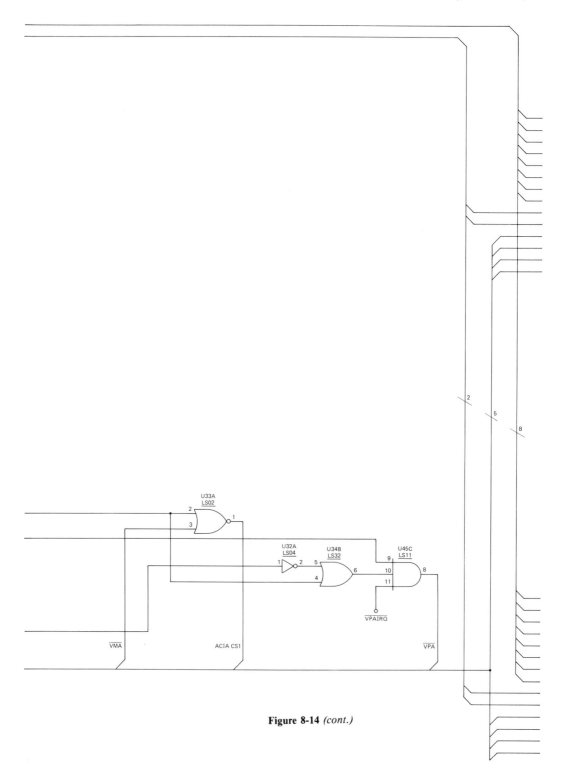

Figure 8-14 *(cont.)*

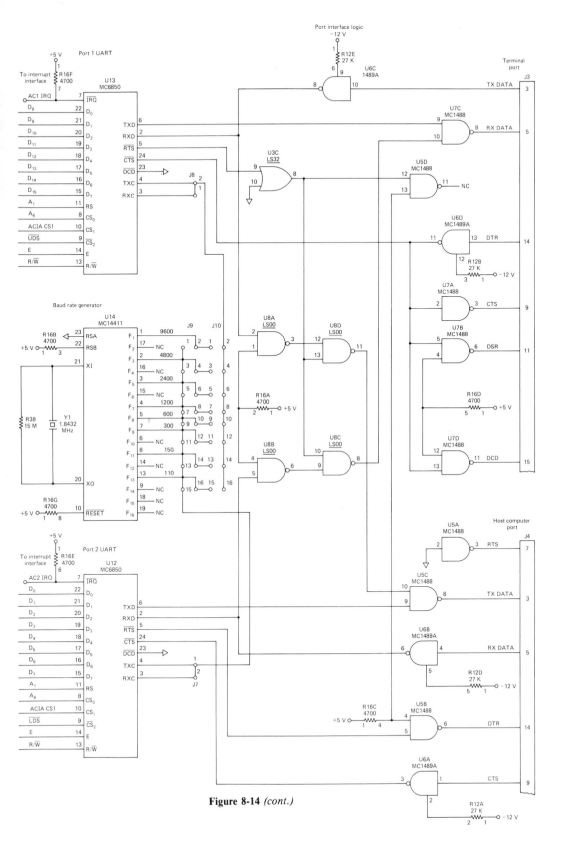

Figure 8-14 *(cont.)*

The table in Fig. 8.15 shows that the registers within the 6850 that implements RS-232C port 1 in the MC68000 educational microcomputer are located on even byte address boundaries starting at address 010040_{16}. For instance, execution of a MOVE instruction with a source operand at address 010040_{16} lets the 68000 read the contents of the 6850's status register. Executing a similar instruction with the destination operand at address 010040_{16} would let us write a byte of control information into its control register. Moreover, executing a MOVE instruction to address 010042_{16} permits either reading of a byte of data from the receive data register or loading of a byte of data into the transmit data register.

Address	R/W	Register
010040_{16}	Write	ACIA1 control register
	Read	ACIA1 status register
010041_{16}	Write	ACIA2 control register
	Read	ACIA2 status register
010042_{16}	Write	ACIA1 transmit data register
	Read	ACIA1 receive data register
010043_{16}	Write	ACIA2 transmit data register
	Read	ACIA2 receive data register

Figure 8-15 Addresses of the 6850's internal registers (Motorola, Inc.).

Now that we know where the registers of the 6850 are located in the 68000's address space, let us trace through the operation of the circuitry as the 68000 reads a byte of data from the receive data register of ACIA1 (U_{13}).

Looking at Fig. 8.14, we find that chip select inputs, CS_0, CS_1, and $\overline{CS_2}$, of the 6850 are driven by the signals A_6, ACIA CS1, and $\overline{UDS}$, respectively. These inputs must be set to the 1, 1, and 0 logic levels, respectively, to enable the 6850 for operation. Let us assume that the instruction

$$\text{MOVE.B   ACIA1\_DATA,D0}$$

which is correctly written to access the receiver data register of the ACIA for serial port 1, is executed by the 68000. When the instruction is executed, it initiates a memory read bus cycle. During the bus cycle, the 68000 sets $\overline{UDS}$ to logic 0 to signal external circuitry that a byte of data is to be transferred over the upper part of the data bus, D_8 through D_{15}. In the circuit diagram, we see that $\overline{UDS}$ is applied directly to the $\overline{CS_2}$ input of U_{13}. At the same time, the logic level applied to the CS_0 input of the ACIA is bit A_6 of the address. Since we are accessing the receive data register within $ACIA_1$, the address is

$$\text{ACIA\_DATA} = 0100042_{16}$$

and in binary form it is

$$A_{23}A_{22}.\,.\,.\,.\,.A_1 = 000000100000000000001000010_2$$

Notice that in the binary form of the address A_6 is at the 1 logic level. This is the level needed at CS_0 to enable the 6850 for operation.

The third chip select input, CS_1, of 6850 U_{13} is supplied by signal ACIA CS1. This signal is produced by decoding address bits A_{16} through A_{23} in the 3-line to 8-line decoder U_{30}. From the binary form of the address, we see that bits A_{19} through A_{23} are all at logic 0. Therefore, all inputs of the 74LS260 NOR gate U_{29A} are logic 0. This makes its output, which is applied to pin 6 of U_{30}, logic 1. This signal and the logic 0 that is output at $\overline{AS}$ whenever an address is on the system bus are used to enable decoder U_{30} for operation. Again looking at the binary form of the address, we see that bits A_{16} through A_{18} are 001. Applying this binary combination to the inputs of the decoder causes output Y_1 to be switched to the 0 logic level.

The 6850 is one of the LSI peripherals produced by Motorola for use with its older 6800 family of microprocessors. For this reason, read/write transfers that take place to it must be performed using synchronous instead of asynchronous memory bus cycles. Notice in Fig. 8.14 that the logic 1 at bit A_6 of the address is inverted to logic 0 and then gated with the logic 0 at the Y_1 output of the decoder by the 74LS32 NOR gate U_{34B}. Since both inputs are at the 0 logic level, the output of the gate switches to logic 0 and forces the $\overline{VPA}$ output of the 74LS11 AND gate U_{45C} to the 0 level. This signal is returned to pin 2 of the 68000, which is the valid peripheral address ($\overline{VPA}$) input. Logic 0 at $\overline{VPA}$ signals the 68000 that the current bus cycle is to be synchronous, instead of asynchronous.

In response to the logic 0 at $\overline{VPA}$, the 68000 switches its valid memory address ($\overline{VMA}$) output to the 0 logic level. In Fig. 8.14 we see that $\overline{VMA}$ is input along with Y_1 to the 74LS02 NOR gate U_{33A}. Both of these signals are now logic 0; therefore, output ACIA CS1 switches to logic 1. Now the chip select inputs of U_{13} are:

$$CS_0 = A_6 = 1$$
$$CS_1 = \text{ACIA CS1} = 1$$

and

$$\overline{CS_2} = \overline{UDS} = 0$$

Therefore, ACIA device U_{13} is enabled for operation.

The 68000 sets memory control signal $R/\overline{W}$ to logic 1 to tell the 6850 that a read bus cycle is in progress. At the same time, the register select (RS) input of the 6850 is supplied by bit A_1 of the address and in our example it is logic 1. This tells the 6850 that the receive data register, not the status register, is to be accessed. Next, the 68000 switches its enable (E) output to logic 0. This signals the 6850 to put the byte of data held in the receive data register onto the data bus lines D_8 through D_{15}. Then the 68000 completes the bus cycle by reading the data off the bus and returning the $\overline{VMA}$, $\overline{AS}$, and $\overline{UDS}$ signal lines to their inactive logic levels.

Now that we have examined the operation of the microprocessor's interface to the 6850 let us continue by looking at how the clock signal that sets the baud rate of the receiver and transmitter sections of the UART is generated. In Fig. 8.14, we see that the baud rate generator is formed by a MC14411 oscillator/clock generator device. The clock rate of this oscillator is set by the 1.8432-MHz crystal Y_1 that is connected between pins XI and XO. Once power is applied to the MC14411, the oscillator circuit begins to run and the counters within the device generate sixteen different clock signals at parallel outputs F_1 through F_{16}. To select the baud for port 1, we simply install a jumper between one set of the terminal pairs at J_{10}. For instance, putting the jumper in position 5-6 selects clock output F_5 and sets the data communication rate at 2,400 baud. Figure 8.16 summarizes all of the jumper settings and their corresponding baud rates.

Jumper pins	Baud rate
1–2	9600
3–4	4800
5–6	2400
7–8	1200
9–10	600
11–12	300
13–14	150
15–16	110

Figure 8-16 Baud rate selection table (Motorola, Inc.).

In the circuit of Fig. 8.14, both the receiver and transmitter are run at the same baud rate; therefore, the Tx_C and Rx_C inputs of U_{13} are connected together by jumper J_8. This common baud rate input is connected through the jumper at 5-6 to the F_5 output of the baud rate generator.

Example 8.3

If a jumper is installed in position 15-16 of J_{10}, what baud rate is selected for ACIA U_{12}?

Solution. Looking at Fig. 8.14, we see that installing a jumper at position 15-16 of J_{10} selects a baud rate of 110 baud for U_{12}.

The last part of the port 1 serial communications interface in Fig. 8.14 is the RS-232C port interface itself. Here we see that this part of the circuit involves the receive data (Rx_D) and transmit data (Tx_D) lines of the 6850 and interface control signals request-to-send ($\overline{RTS}$) and clear-to-send ($\overline{CTS}$). The logic included at this interface sets the transmission and reception voltage levels for signals Tx_{DATA} and Rx_{DATA}; gates data from the Tx_D output of the 6850 onto the Rx_{DATA} output; and creates three additional communication interface signals, data terminal ready (DTR), data set ready (DSR), and data carrier detect (DCD), from $\overline{CTS}$.

The microcomputer receives character data from the terminal over the Tx_{DATA} line and sends character data to it over the Rx_{DATA} line. Moreover, the handshake control for these data transfers is provided by control lines DTR, CTS, DSR, and DCD. For instance, to write data to the terminal, the port 1 ACIA produces the CTS, DSR, and DCD signals by outputting logic 0 at $\overline{CTS}$. All of these signals are available to the terminal through its RS-232C interface. Therefore, any of them can be tested by the terminal to determine if it needs to read data from the Rx_{DATA} line.

ASSIGNMENT

Section 8.2

1. What is the capacity of the program storage memory in the MC68000 educational microcomputer system? What is its function?

2. How much RAM is supplied in the data storage part of the MC68000 educational microcomputer's memory?

3. What happens to the contents of program storage memory when power is turned off? What would happen to the contents of the data storage memory?

4. Where are user-written programs that are typed in at the keyboard of the terminal stored by the microcomputer?

5. What I/O resources are supplied on the MC68000 educational microcomputer?

6. What LSI device is used to interface the terminal to the 68000 microprocessor?

7. What does the 68230 device implement in the MC68000 educational microcomputer?

Section 8.3

8. At what frequency is the microprocessor in the MC68000 educational microcomputer run?

9. Name a peripheral device in the educational microcomputer that is operated with the 1-MHz clock.

10. What clock frequency is output at $Q\hat{B}$ and $Q\hat{D}$ of U_{15} in Fig. 8.3?

Section 8.4

11. Which devices in the educational microcomputer are initialized with the $\overline{\text{RESET}}$ signal?

12. What happens within the 68000 microprocessor when a reset pulse is applied to its $\overline{\text{RESET}}$ input?

13. What purpose is served by the POR signal?

14. Why is a $\overline{\text{HALT}}$ pulse generated along with the $\overline{\text{RESET}}$ pulse when the microcomputer's power is turned on?

15. What is meant by a *warm start*?

16. What interrupt priority code ($\overline{\text{IPL}_2}\overline{\text{IPL}_1}\overline{\text{IPL}_0}$) is applied to the 68000 in Fig. 8.4 if the maskable interrupt signal $\overline{\text{6800IRQ}}$ becomes active?

17. Assuming that the request for service by the $\overline{\text{6800IRQ}}$ interrupt signal is granted by the 68000 in Fig. 8.4, specify the logic states produced at $FC_2FC_1FC_0$, $A_3A_2A_1$, $\overline{\text{VPAIRQ}}$, $\overline{\text{PIACK}}$, $\overline{\text{TIACK}}$, and $\overline{\text{VPA}}$ during the interrupt acknowledge sequence. How is the exception vector produced?

18. What is the difference between the response of the 68000 to the closure of the ABORT switch in Fig. 8.4 and closure of the RESET switch?

Section 8.5

19. What time elapses between the occurrence of a valid ROM address on the bus and the return of the $\overline{\text{DTACK}}$ signal to the MPU in Fig. 8.6?

20. In Fig. 8.6 what will be the logic state of signals ROMEN, $\overline{\text{DTACK}}$, and R/$\overline{\text{W}}$ in response to an instruction fetch from address 9000_{16}?

21. What signals are generated by the timing/RAM DTACK circuit in Fig. 8.8? In what order are they produced during a read cycle to a valid RAM address?

22. Trace the operation of the circuit in Fig. 8.8 for a bus cycle in which data are read from an address in RAM.

23. What is the function of the watchdog timer in Fig. 8.10?

Section 8.6

24. Trace the sequence of events that take place as a bus cycle is performed to read the contents of the 68230's port B data register in Fig. 8.11.

25. Describe the functions of the $\overline{\text{DATA STROBE}}$ and $\overline{\text{ACKNOWLEDGE}}$ control signals of the printer interface in Fig 8.11.

26. What frequency signals are used to record logic 0 and logic 1 on cassette tape?

27. What is the maximum baud rate for the terminal port of the educational microcomputer? The minimum baud rate?

28. What is the difference between the terminal and host computer ports?

BIBLIOGRAPHY

BRYCE, HEATHER, Microprogramming Makes the MC68000 a Processor for the Future, *Electronic Design 22,* Oct. 25, 1979.

DAVIS, REX, *Prioritized Individually Vectored Interrupts for Multiple Peripheral Systems with the 68000.* Austin, Tex.: Motorola Inc., 1981.

GRADEN, DUANE, *Software Refreshed Memory Card for the MC68000 (AN-816).* Austin, Tex.: Motorola Inc., 1981.

KANE, GERRY, DOUG HAWKINS, AND LANCE LEVENTHAL, *68000 Assembly Language Programming.* Berkeley, Calif.: Osborne/McGraw-Hill, 1981.

MCKENZIE, JAMES, *Dual 16-Bit Ports for the MC68000 Using Two MC6821s (AN-810).* Austin, Tex.: Motorola Inc., 1981.

MOTOROLA INC., *MC68000 16-Bit Microprocessor User's Manual,* 3rd ed. Englewood Cliffs, N.J.: Prentice-Hall, Inc., 1982.

MOTOROLA INC., *MC68000 Educational Computer Board User's Manual.* Austin, Tex.: Motorola Inc., 1982.

MOTOROLA INC., *Motorola Microprocessors Data Manual.* Austin, Tex.: Motorola Inc., 1981.

SCANLON, LEO J., *The 68000: Principles and Programming.* Indianapolis, Ind.: Howard W. Sams & Company, Inc., Publishers, 1981.

STARNES, THOMAS W., Compact Instructions Give the MC68000 Power While Simplifying Its Operation, *Electronic Design 20,* Sept. 27, 1979.

STARNES, THOMAS W., Handling Exceptions Gracefully Enhances Software Reliability, *Electronics,* Sept. 11, 1980.

STARNES, THOMAS W., Powerful Instructions and Flexible Registers of the MC68000 Make Programming Easy, *Electronic Design 9,* Apr. 26, 1980.

STRITTNER, SKIP, AND TOM GUNTER, A Microprocessor Architecture for a Changing World: The Motorola 68000, *Computer,* Feb. 1979.

STRITTNER, SKIP, AND NICK TREDENNICK, Microprogrammed Implementation of a Single Chip Microprocessor, *Proceedings, 11th Annual Microprogramming Workshop,* Dec. 1978.

TRIEBEL, WALTER A., *Integrated Digital Electronics* 2nd ed. Englewood Cliffs, N.J.: Prentice-Hall, Inc., 1985.

TRIEBEL, WALTER A., AND ALFRED E. CHU, *Handbook of Semiconductor and Bubble Memories.* Englewood Cliffs, N.J.: Prentice-Hall, Inc., 1982.

ANSWERS
TO SELECTED PROBLEMS

Chapter 1

Section 1.2

1. Computer program.

Section 1.3

5. A computer that has been tailored to meet the needs of a specific application.

Section 1.4

7. Secondary storage is for long-term storage of data that are not in use. On the other hand, the data that are currently being processed are held temporarily in primary storage memory.

Section 1.5

9. Program storage memory is the part of the memory subsystem that contains the program that is executed by the microcomputer. On the other hand, the data that are processed during execution of the program are held in the data storage part of memory.

Section 1.6

11. 4-bit, 8-bit, 16-bit, and 32-bit.

Chapter 2

Section 2.2

1. High-density N-channel MOS (HMOS).

3. 16 general-purpose registers, 8 data registers D_0 through D_7 and 8 address registers A_0 through A_7, and all are 32 bits in length.

Section 2.3

5. 23 address lines A_1 through A_{23}, 2^{23} unique addresses.

7. For an asynchronous bus, once the bus cycle is initiated, it is not completed until external circuitry returns a signal to the processor.

9. The address lines A_1 through A_{23} present a word address and the upper and lower bytes of that word are accessed using the $\overline{UDS}$ and $\overline{LDS}$ signals.

11. $FC_2FC_1FC_1 = 110$.

13. The code value applied at the interrupt priority inputs is compared to the internal mask. If its value is more than that in the mask, the interrupt is serviced; otherwise, it is ignored.

15. To provide interface signals so that low-speed 6800 synchronous peripheral devices can be used with the high-speed 68000 CPU.

Section 2.5

17. In general, the address registers are meant for use in storing memory addresses such as pointers, while the data registers are to be used to store data that are to be processed by the CPU. However, their functions can be interchanged according to the need.

19. The program counter provides the address of the next instruction to be executed.

Section 2.6

21. Macroinstructions are the basic assembly language instructions defined by the instruction set of the 68000. Microinstructions are the internal machine instructions which are executed by the CPU in order to perform the function defined by a macroinstruction.

Chapter 3

Section 3.2

1. No, all words of data must be at even-address boundaries.

3. Bit, byte, word, long word, and BCD.

Section 3.4

7.

Instruction	Source Addressing Mode	Destination Addressing Mode
(a) MOVE.W D3,D2	Data register direct	Data register direct
(b) MOVE.B D3,A2	Data register direct	Address register direct
(c) MOVE.B D3,$ABCD	Data register direct	Absolute short
(d) MOVE.L XYZ,D2	Immediate/absolute	Data register direct
(e) MOVE.W XYZ(A0.L),D2	Register indirect with offset	Data register direct
(f) MOVE.B D3,(A2)	Data register direct	Register indirect
(g) MOVE.L A1,(A2)+	Address register direct	Postincrement register indirect
(h) MOVE.L −(A2),D3	Predecrement register indirect	Data register direct

(i)	MOVE.W	10(A2),D3	Register indirect with offset	Data register direct
(j)	MOVE.B	10(A2,A3.L),$A123	Indexed register indirect with offset	Absolute short
(k)	MOVE.W	#$ABCD,$1122	Immediate	Absolute short

9. $ABCD = $10 + A1 = $100 + A2 + D1 = A3.

Section 3.6

11. MOVEM $B000,D5/D6/D7

Section 3.7

13.
MOVE.L	#$C000,A1
MOVE.L	$A000,D0
ADD.L	$B000,D0
MOVE.L	D0,(A1)
MOVE.L	$A000,D0
SUB.L	$B000,D0
MOVE.L	D0,4(A1)
MOVE.L	$A000,D0
MULU	$B000,D0
MOVE.L	D0,8(A1)
MOVE.L	$A000,D0
DIVU	$B000,D0
MOVE.W	D0,12(A1) ;QUOTIENT

Section 3.9

15.
MOVE.B	D0,D7
AND.B	NUM1,D7
MOVE.B	NUM2,D6
NOT.B	D6
AND.B	D0,D6
OR.B	D1,D6
OR.B	D6,D7
MOVE.B	D7,RESULT

Section 3.10

17.
MOVE.B	D0,$B001
ROR.L	#8,D0
MOVE.W	D0,$B002
ROR.L	#8,D0
ROR.L	#8,D0
MOVE.B	D0,$B004
ROR.L	#8,D0

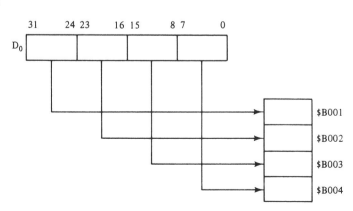

Chapter 4

Section 4.2

1.

Instruction	N	Z	V	C
Initial value	0	0	0	0
SUB.L A0,A0	0	1	0	0
CMPI.W #$A000,A0	0	0	0	1
TST A0	0	1	0	0

Section 4.3

3. The JMP instruction encodes the address of the location to which the jump is to take place into the instruction. On the other hand, the BRA instruction encodes the displacement, the number of bytes, of the "branch to address" from the BRA instruction, into the instruction word. Therefore, BRA both encodes in fewer bytes and executes faster than JMP.

Section 4.4

5.
```
        MOVEQ    #1,D7
        CLR.W    D6
LOOP    CMP.B    N,D6
        BEQ      DONE
        ADDQ.W   #1,D6
        MULU     D6,D7
        BRA      LOOP
DONE    MOVE.L   D7,FACT
```

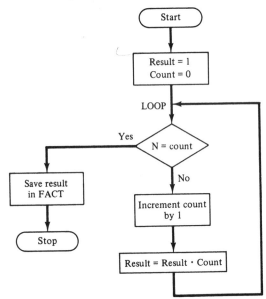

```
7.           MOVE.B      #100,D7
             MOVE.L      $A000,A6
             MOVE.L      $B000,A5
             MOVE.L      $C000,A4
   LOOP      CMPI.W      #0,(A6)
             BMI         NEGTV
   POSTV     MOVE.W      (A6) + ,(A5) +
             BRA         NXT
   NEGTV     MOVE.W      (A6) + ,(A4) +
   NXT       SUBI        #1,D7
             BNE         LOOP
   DONE      BRA         DONE
```

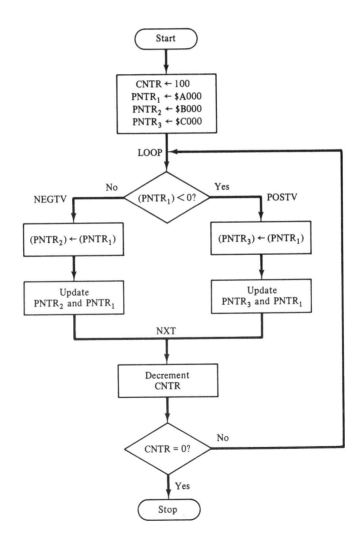

Section 4.6

11. AGAIN   BTST.B   #0,D0
            BNE   SUBA
            BTST.B   #1,D0
            BNE   SUBB
            BTST.B   #2,D0
            BNE   SUBC
            BRA   AGAIN
   SUBA   •   •
             •   •
             •   •
            EORI.B   #1,D0
            RTS
   SUBB   •   •
             •   •
             •   •
            EORI.B   #2,D0
   SUBC   •   •
             •   •
             •   •
            EORI.B   #4,D0
            RTS

Chapter 5

Section 5.2

1. Software and hardware development and debugging for a project involving one of the microprocessors that the development system supports.

3. Four ports: one each for the cassette player/recorder, printer, CRT terminal, and a host computer communications link.

Section 5.3

5. A monitor program provides the programmer with the ability to enter (assemble), store, execute, and debug assembly language programs. It is stored in PROMs on the MC68000 educational microcomputer board.

7. 32K bytes

Section 5.4

9. Command field.

11. (a) $100_{16} + R0 = 1100_{16}$
     (b) $100_{16} + R3 = 2100_{16}$
     (c) $A0 + R0 = 1100_{16}$
     (d) $A0 + D0 + R0 = 1300_{16}$

Section 5.5

13. (a) R5 $= 1000_{16}$ + R0 $= 2000_{16}$
    (b) R5 $= 1000_{16}$ + 0 $= 1000_{16}$

Section 5.6

15. TUTOR 1.3 > BF 1000 10FE 'ABCD'   (cr)
     TUTOR 1.3 > BF 2000 20FE 5555   (cr)
     TUTOR 1.3 > MD 1000 FE   (cr)
     TUTOR 1.3 > MD 2000 FE   (cr)
     TUTOR 1.3 > BM 1000 100F 3000   (cr)

Section 5.7

17. TUTOR 1.3 > TM   (cr)

Section 5.8

19. TUTOR 1.3 > MM 1000;DI
     001000 DC.W $ABCD   (cr)
     001002 DC.W $1234 .   (cr)

Section 5.9

21. To execute a single instruction in a program the command is TR (T); to execute the entire program the command is GD; and to execute a block of instructions in a program the commands are TT, GO, or GT.

23. TUTOR 1.3 > BR 1150 10   (cr)

Section 5.11

27. TUTOR supports debugging of programs by providing commands that give the programmer the ability to display/modify registers, display/modify memory locations, control program execution (trace, breakpoint, etc.), and assemble/disassemble instructions.

Chapter 6

Section 6.2

  1. No, both memory and I/O are located in the same address space.

Section 6.3

  3. See Problem 17, Section 3.10.

Section 6.5

  5. $FC_2FC_1FC_0 = 001$.

7.

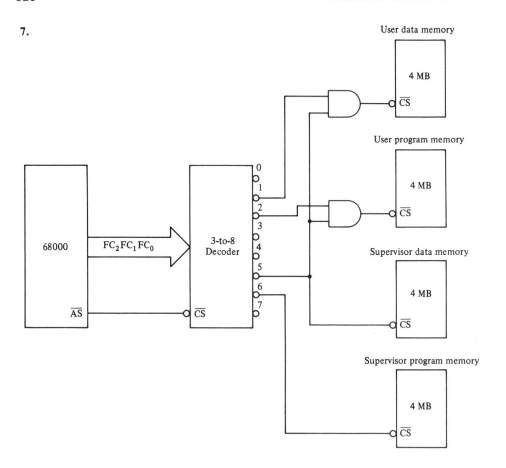

Section 6.7

9. **(a)** 68000 outputs $FC_2FC_1FC_0 = 001$ in user mode or 101 in supervisor mode.
 (b) 68000 places address \$A001 on A_{23} through A_1.
 (c) 68000 asserts $\overline{AS}$ (logic 0).
 (d) 68000 sets $R/\overline{W}$ to logic 0.
 (e) 68000 places the byte of data on D_7 through D_0.
 (f) 68000 asserts $\overline{LDS}$ (logic 0).
 (g) Memory interface decodes the address and enables memory devices.
 (h) Memory stores data available at D_7 through D_0 in \$A001 using $\overline{LDS}$.
 (i) Memory interface asserts $\overline{DTACK}$ (logic 0).
 (j) 68000 negates $\overline{LDS}$ and $\overline{AS}$ (logic 1).
 (k) 68000 removes data from D_7 through D_0.
 (l) 68000 returns $R/\overline{W}$ to logic 1.
 (m) Memory interface negates $\overline{DTACK}$ (logic 1).

Section 6.8

11. MOVE.L   (SSP)+,A2
    MOVE.L   (SSP)+,A1
    MOVE.L   (SSP)+,A0

Section 6.10

13. MOVE.L   #$16000,A0
    MOVEP.L   D0,0(A0)

Section 6.12

17.
	MOVE.L	#$A000,A1
	MOVE.L	#$18007,A2
	MOVE.L	#5,D0
NXT	MOVE.B	(A1),D1
	MOVE.B	D1,(A2)
	SUBQ.L	#1,D0
	BNZ	NXT
DONE	B	DONE

Section 6.13

19. In a synchronous bus cycle, the data transfers are synchronized with the enable (E) clock signal. In an asynchronous bus cycle, the microprocessor waits for the $\overline{\text{DTACK}}$ to be returned by the peripheral device to terminate the write bus cycle or to read data off the bus and then terminate the read bus cycle.

Section 6.15

23. These inputs represent the control state identified as RS · R/$\overline{\text{W}}$ in Fig. 6.29. From the table, we find that character data is being read from the 6850 over the bus.

25. **(a)** The MPU outputs the address of the 6850 on the address bus. This address is decoded in external circuitry to select the 6850 for operation.
    (b) At the same time, the MPU puts a byte of character data on the data bus and signals the 6850 that a write bus cycle is in progress with R/$\overline{\text{W}}$.
    (c) The 6850 accepts the data off the bus.
    (d) The 6850 frames the byte of character data with a start bit, parity bit, and stop bits and then loads it into the transmit data register.
    (e) The framed character is converted to serial form by shifting it through the transmit shift register and output over the Tx$_{\text{DATA}}$ line.
    (f) When the transmit data register becomes empty, the 6850 sets the transmit data register empty (TDRE) flag in the status register.
    (g) If the interrupt on TDRE function is enabled, the $\overline{\text{IRQ}}$ output becomes active. This signal can be applied to an interrupt input of the 68000 to tell it that the character has been transmitted.
    (h) The MPU must next output another character to the 6850.

27. MOVE.B   #3,D0
    MOVE.L   #$0ABCD,A0
    MOVE.B   D0,(A0)

Section 6.16

29. $RS_5RS_4RS_3RS_2RS_1 = 8_{16} = 01000_2$
Looking at the table in Fig. 6.35, we see that register R_8 (PADR) is selected.

31. MOVE.L   #$0A001,A1
    MOVE.B   #$40,(A1)
    MOVE.B   #$60,(A1)

33. MOVE.L   #$0A001,A1
    MOVE.B   #0,(A1)
    MOVE.B   #$FF,2(A1)
    MOVE.B   #0,4(A1)

Chapter 7

Section 7.2

1. External exceptions: reset, interrupts, and bus error.
   Internal exceptions: instructions (TRAP, TRAPV, CHK, DIVS, DIVU), privilege violation, trace, illegal address, illegal instruction, and unimplemented instruction.

Section 7.3

3.

Vector Address	Contents
$10	$0
$12	$B000

Section 7.5

5. 7

7. ORI #$0300,SR

Section 7.10

11.

Save registers D_0, D_1, and A_2
Service routine body
Restore registers D_0, D_1, and A_2
Return to calling program

Section 7.11

13. "Bus error" means that an error has occurred during the execution of a bus cycle. For instance, external circuitry has detected a parity error or a watchdog timer has timed out before $\overline{\text{DTACK}}$ was asserted.

Section 7.12

15. CLR.L   D0
    CLR.L   D1
    •   •
    •   •
    •   •
    CLR.L   D7
    CLR.L   A0
    CLR.L   A1
    •   •
    •   •
    •   •
    CLR.L   A6
    MOVE.L $FFFFFE,SSP
    BRA $A000

Section 7.13

17. An attempt is made to access a word or long word that resides at an odd-numbered address.

Chapter 8

Section 8.2

1. 16K bytes; stores the Tutor monitor.

3. Program storage memory is nonvolatile; therefore, its contents remain intact even when power is turned off. Data storage memory is volatile and if power is turned off its contents are lost.

5. Parallel I/O—24 I/O lines that are used to implement the parallel printer (Centronics) and cassette player/recorder interfaces.
RS-232C serial communication ports—2: one for connection of a CRT terminal and the second for implementing a communication link to a host computer.

7. Parallel I/O interfaces for the printer and cassette player/recorder.

Section 8.3

9. 6850 ACIA.

Section 8.4

11. 68000 microprocessor and 68230 parallel interface/timer.

13. POR is used to reset on-board logic circuits such as flip-flops.

15. When the microcomputer is reset by pressing the reset button, it is called a warm reset. In this case, only the 68000 and 68230 devices receive pulses at their reset inputs. Furthermore, the $\overline{\text{HALT}}$ and POR signals are not produced as they are when power is turned on.

17. $FC_2FC_1FC_0 = 111$, $A_3A_2A_1 = 100$, $\overline{\text{VPAIRQ}} = 0$, $\overline{\text{PIACK}} = 1$, $\overline{\text{TIACK}} = 1$, and $\overline{\text{VPA}} = 0$. In this case, the 68000 uses its autovector capability to generate an interrupt vector from the code $IPL_2 IPL_1 IPL_0$. As shown in Fig. 8.5, the autovector number is 28.

19. $T = (\frac{1}{8\text{MHz}} \times 8 = 1 \text{ us}$

21. $\overline{\text{RAS}}$, $\overline{\text{RAW}}$, $\overline{\text{CL}}$, $\overline{\text{CU}}$, and $\overline{\text{DTACK RAM}}$.

23. If the data transfer acknowledge ($\overline{\text{DTACK}}$) signal is not received by the 68000 during a read or write bus cycle prior to the watchdog timer timing out, the watchdog timer circuit outputs the $\overline{\text{BERR}}$ signal. $\overline{\text{BERR}}$ is returned to the 68000 to tell it that a bus error condition has occurred.

Section 8.6

25. $\overline{\text{DATA STROBE}}$ is an output by which the PI/T tells the printer that valid character data is available on data lines PD_0 through PD_7; $\overline{\text{ACKNOWLEDGE}}$ is an input by which the printer tells the PI/T that it has read the character data from the data lines.

27. Maximum baud rate = 9,600, minimum baud rate = 110.

Appendix:
68230 Data Sheet*

*Data Sheets Courtesy of Motorola, Inc.

MOTOROLA
SEMICONDUCTORS
3501 ED BLUESTEIN BLVD., AUSTIN, TEXAS 78721

MC68230L8
MC68230L10

Advance Information

MC68230 PARALLEL INTERFACE/TIMER

The MC68230 Parallel Interface/Timer provides versatile double buffered parallel interfaces and an operating system oriented timer to MC68000 systems. The parallel interfaces operate in unidirectional or bidirectional modes, either 8 or 16 bits wide. In the unidirectional modes, an associated data direction register determines whether the port pins are inputs or outputs. In the bidirectional modes the data direction registers are ignored and the direction is determined dynamically by the state of four handshake pins. These programmable handshake pins provide an interface flexible enough for connection to a wide variety of low, medium, or high speed peripherals or other computer systems. The PI/T ports allow use of vectored or autovectored interrupts, and also provide a DMA Request pin for connection to the MC68450 Direct Memory Access Controller or a similar circuit. The PI/T timer contains a 24-bit wide counter and a 5-bit prescaler. The timer may be clocked by the system clock (PI/T CLK pin) or by an external clock (TIN pin), and a 5-bit prescaler can be used. It can generate periodic interrupts, a square wave, or a single interrupt after a programmed time period. Also it can be used for elapsed time measurement or as a device watchdog.

- MC68000 Bus Compatible
- Port Modes Include:
  - Bit I/O
  - Unidirectonal 8-Bit and 16-Bit
  - Bidirectional 8-Bit and 16-Bit
- Selectable Handshaking Options
- 24-Bit Programmable Timer
- Software Programmable Timer Modes
- Contains Interrupt Vector Generation Logic
- Separate Port and Timer Interrupt Service Requests
- Registers are Read/Write and Directly Addressable
- Registers are Addressed for MOVEP (Move Peripheral) and DMAC Compatibility

HMOS
(HIGH-DENSITY N-CHANNEL SILICON-GATE)

PARALLEL INTERFACE/TIMER

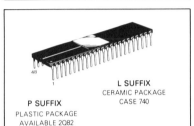

L SUFFIX
CERAMIC PACKAGE
CASE 740

P SUFFIX
PLASTIC PACKAGE
AVAILABLE 2Q82

PIN ASSIGNMENT

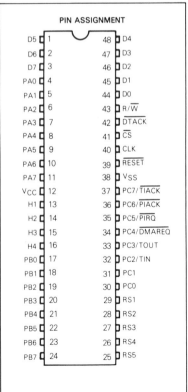

D5	1	48	D4
D6	2	47	D3
D7	3	46	D2
PA0	4	45	D1
PA1	5	44	D0
PA2	6	43	R/$\overline{W}$
PA3	7	42	$\overline{DTACK}$
PA4	8	41	$\overline{CS}$
PA5	9	40	CLK
PA6	10	39	$\overline{RESET}$
PA7	11	38	VSS
VCC	12	37	PC7/$\overline{TIACK}$
H1	13	36	PC6/$\overline{PIACK}$
H2	14	35	PC5/$\overline{PIRQ}$
H3	15	34	PC4/$\overline{DMAREQ}$
H4	16	33	PC3/TOUT
PB0	17	32	PC2/TIN
PB1	18	31	PC1
PB2	19	30	PC0
PB3	20	29	RS1
PB4	21	28	RS2
PB5	22	27	RS3
PB6	23	26	RS4
PB7	24	25	RS5

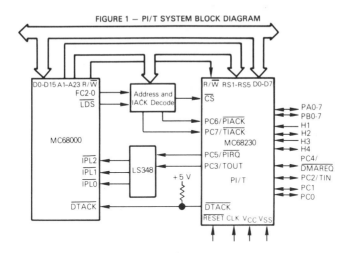

FIGURE 1 — PI/T SYSTEM BLOCK DIAGRAM

POWER CONSIDERATIONS

The average chip-junction temperature, T_J, in °C can be obtained from:

$$T_J = T_A + (P_D \bullet \theta_{JA}) \qquad (1)$$

Where:

$T_A \equiv$ Ambient Temperature, °C

$\theta_{JA} \equiv$ Package Thermal Resistance, Junction-to-Ambient, °C/W

$P_D \equiv P_{INT} + P_{PORT}$

$P_{INT} \equiv I_{CC} \times V_{CC}$, Watts — Chip Internal Power

$P_{PORT} \equiv$ Port Power Dissipation, Watts — User Determined

For most applications $P_{PORT} \blacktriangleleft P_{INT}$ and can be neglected. P_{PORT} may become significant if the device is configured to drive Darlington bases or sink LED loads.

An approximate relationship between P_D and T_J (if P_{PORT} is neglected) is:

$$P_D = K \div (T_J + 273°C) \qquad (2)$$

Solving equations 1 and 2 for K gives:

$$K = P_D \bullet (T_A + 273°C) + \theta_{JA} \bullet P_D^2 \qquad (3)$$

Where K is a constant pertaining to the particular part. K can be determined from equation 3 by measuring P_D (at equilibrium) for a known T_A. Using this value of K the values of P_D and T_J can be obtained by solving equations (1) and (2) iteratively for any value of T_A.

 MOTOROLA *Semiconductor Products Inc.*

MAXIMUM RATINGS

Characteristics	Symbol	Value	Unit
Supply Voltage	V_{CC}	−0.3 to +7.0	V
Input Voltage	V_{in}	−0.3 to +7.0	V
Operating Temperature Range	T_A	0 to 70	°C
Storage Temperature	T_{stg}	−55 to +150	°C

This device contains circuitry to protect the inputs against damage due to high static voltages or electric fields; however, it is advised that normal precuations be taken to avoid application of any voltage higher than maximum-rated voltages to this high-impedance circuit. Reliability of operation is enhanced if unused inputs are tied to an appropriate logic voltage level (e.g., either V_{SS} or V_{CC}).

THERMAL CHARACTERISTICS

Characteristics	Symbol	Value	Rating
Thermal Resistance Ceramic	θ_{JA}	50	°C/W

DC ELECTRICAL CHARACTERISTICS (V_{CC} = 5.0 Vdc ±5%, T_A = 0 to 70°C unless otherwise noted)

Characteristics		Symbol	Min	Max	Unit
Input High Voltage	All Inputs	V_{IH}	V_{SS} + 2.0	V_{CC}	V
Input Low Voltage	All Inputs	V_{IL}	V_{SS} − 0.3	V_{SS} + 0.8	V
Input Leakage Current (V_{in} = 0 to 5.25 V)	H1, H3, R/$\overline{W}$, $\overline{RESET}$, CLK, RS1-RS5, $\overline{CS}$	I_{in}	−	10.0	μA
Three-State (Off State) Input Current (V_{in} = 0.4 to 2.4)	$\overline{DTACK}$, PC0-PC7, D0-D7 H2, H4, PA0-PA7, PB0-PB7	I_{TSI}	− −0.1	20 −1.0	μA mA
Output High Voltage (I_{Load} = −400 μA, V_{CC} = min) (I_{Load} = −150 μA, V_{CC} = min) (I_{Load} = −100 μA, V_{CC} = min)	$\overline{DTACK}$, D0-D7 H2, H4, PB0-PB7, PA0-PA7 PC0-PC7	V_{OH}	V_{SS} + 2.4	−	V
Output Low Voltage (I_{Load} = 8.8 mA, V_{CC} = min) (I_{Load} = 5.3 mA, V_{CC} = min) (I_{Load} = 2.4 mA, V_{CC} = min)	PC3/TOUT, PC5/$\overline{PIRQ}$ D0-D7, $\overline{DTACK}$ PA0-PA7, PB0-PB7, H2, H4, PC0-PC2, PC4, PC6, PC7	V_{OL}	−	0.5	V
Internal Power Dissipation (Measured at T_A = 0°C)		P_{INT}	−	500	mW
Input Capacitance (V_{in} = 0, T_A = 25°C, f = 1 MHz)		C_{in}	−	15	pF

CLOCK TIMING (See Figure 2)

Characteristic	Symbol	8 MHz MC68230L8		10 MHz MC68230L10		Unit
		Min	Max	Min	Max	
Frequency of Operation	f	2.0	8.0	2.0	10.0	MHz
Cycle Time	t_{cyc}	125	500	100	500	ns
Clock Pulse Width	t_{CL} t_{CH}	55 55	250 250	45 45	250 250	ns
Clock Rise and Fall Times	t_{Cr} t_{Cf}	− −	10 10	− −	10 10	ns

FIGURE 2 — INPUT CLOCK WAVEFORM

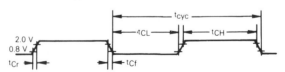

 MOTOROLA *Semiconductor Products Inc.*

AC ELECTRICAL CHARACTERISTICS ($V_{CC} = 5.0$ Vdc $\pm 5\%$, $V_S = 0$ Vdc, $T_A = 0°C$ to $70°C$)

Number	Characteristic	8 MHz MC68230L8 Min	8 MHz MC68230L8 Max	10 MHz MC68230L10 Min	10 MHz MC68230L10 Max	Unit
1	R/$\overline{W}$, RS1-RS5 Valid to $\overline{CS}$ Low (Setup Time)	0	—	0	—	ns
2(10)	$\overline{CS}$ Low to R/$\overline{W}$ and RS1-RS5 Invalid (Hold Time)	100	—	65	—	ns
3(1)	$\overline{CS}$ Low to CLK Low (Setup Time)	30	—	20	—	ns
4(2)	$\overline{CS}$ Low to data Out Valid (Delay)	—	75	—	60	ns
5	RS1-RS5 Valid to Data Out Valid (Delay)	—	140	—	100	ns
6	CLK Low to $\overline{DTACK}$ Low (Read/Write Cycle) (Delay)	0	70	0	60	ns
7(3)	DTACK Low to $\overline{CS}$ High (Hold Time)	0	—	0	—	ns
8	$\overline{CS}$ or $\overline{PIACK}$ or $\overline{TIACK}$ High to Data Out Invalid (Hold Time)	0	—	0	—	ns
9	$\overline{CS}$ or $\overline{PIACK}$ or $\overline{TIACK}$ High to D0-D7 High-Impedance (Delay)	—	50	—	45	ns
10	$\overline{CS}$ or $\overline{PIACK}$ or $\overline{TIACK}$ High to DTACK High (Delay)	—	50	—	30	ns
11	$\overline{CS}$ or $\overline{PIACK}$ or $\overline{TIACK}$ High to $\overline{DTACK}$ High Impedance (Delay)	—	100	—	55	ns
12	Data Invalid to $\overline{CS}$ Low (Setup Time)	0	—	0	—	ns
13	$\overline{CS}$ Low to Data In INvalid (Hold Time)	100	—	65	—	ns
14	Input Data Valid to H1(H3) Asserted (Setup Time)	100	—	60	—	ns
15	H1(H3) Asserted to Input Data Invalid (Hold Time)	20	—	20	—	ns
16	Handshake Input H1(H4) Pulse Width Asserted	40	—	40	—	ns
17	Handshake Input (H1-H4) Pulse Width Negated	40	—	40	—	ns
18	H1(H3) Asserted to H2(H4) Negated (Delay)	—	150	—	120	ns
19	CLK Low to H2(H4) Asserted (Delay)	—	100	—	100	ns
20(4)	H2(H4) Asserted to H1(H3) Asserted	0	—	0	—	ns
21(5)	CLK Low to H2(H4) Pulse Negated (Delay)	—	125	—	125	ns
22(9, 11)	Synchronized H1(H3) to CLK Low on which $\overline{DMAREQ}$ is Asserted (See Figures 13 and 14)	2.5	3.5	2.5	3.5	CLK Per
23	CLK Low $\overline{DMAREQ}$ is Asserted to CLK Low on which $\overline{DMAREQ}$ is Negated	3	3	3	3	CLK Per
24	CLK Low to Output Data Valid (Delay) (Modes 0, 1)	—	150	—	120	ns
25(9, 11)	Synchronized H1(H3) to Output Data Invalid (Modes 0, 1)	1.5	2.5	1.5	2.5	CLK Per
26	H1 Negated to Output Data Valid (Modes 2, 3)	—	70	—	50	ns
27	H1 Asserted to Output Data High Impedance (Modes 2, 3)	0	70	0	70	ns
28	Read Data Valid to $\overline{DTACK}$ Low (Setup Time)	0	—	0	—	ns
29	CLK Low to Data Output Valid (Interrupt Acknowledge Cycle)	—	120	—	100	ns
30(7)	H1(H3) Asserted to CLK High (Setup Time)	50	—	40	—	ns
31	$\overline{PIACK}$ or $\overline{TIACK}$ Low to CLK Low (Setup Time)	50	—	40	—	ns
32(11)	Synchronized $\overline{CS}$ to CLK Low on which $\overline{DMAREQ}$ is Asserted (See Figures 13 and 14)	3	3	3	3	CLK Per
33(9, 11)	Synchronized H1(H3) to CLK Low on which H2(H4) is Asserted	3.5	4.5	3.5	4.5	CLK Per
34	CLK Low to $\overline{DTACK}$ Low (Interrupt Acknowledge Cycle (Delay)	—	75	—	60	ns
35	CLK Low to $\overline{DMAREQ}$ Low (Delay)	0	120	0	100	ns
36	CLK Low to $\overline{DMAREQ}$ High (Delay)	0	120	0	100	ns
—	CLK Low to $\overline{PIRQ}$ Low or High Impedance	—	200	—	150	ns
— (8)	TIN Frequency (External Clock) — Prescaler Used	0	1	0	1	Fclk(Hz)(6)
—	TIN Frequency (External Clock) — Prescaler Not used	0	1/32	0	1/32	Fclk(Hz)(6)
—	TIN Pulse Width High or Low (External Clock)	55	—	45	—	ns
—	TIN Pulse Width Low (Run/Halt Control)	1	—	1	—	CLK
—	CLK Low to TOUT High, Low, or High Impedance	0	200	0	150	ns
—	$\overline{CS}$, $\overline{PIACK}$, or $\overline{TIACK}$ High to $\overline{CS}$, $\overline{PIACK}$, or $\overline{TIACK}$ Low	50	—	30	—	ns

NOTES:

1. This specification only applies if the PI/T had completed all operations initiated by the previous bus cycle when $\overline{CS}$ was asserted. Following a normal read or write bus cycle, all operations are complete within three CLKs after the falling edge of the CLK pin on which $\overline{DTACK}$ was asserted. If $\overline{CS}$ is asserted prior to completion of these operations, the new bus cycle, and hence, $\overline{DTACK}$ is postponed.

   If all operations of the previous bus cycle were complete when $\overline{CS}$ was asserted, this specification is made only to insure that $\overline{DTACK}$ is asserted with respect to the falling edge of the CLK pin as shown in the timing diagram, not to guarantee operation of the part. If the $\overline{CS}$ setup time is violated, $\overline{DTACK}$ may be asserted as shown, or may be asserted one clock cycle later.

2. Assuming the RS1-RS5 to Data Valid time has also expired.

 MOTOROLA *Semiconductor Products Inc.*

3. This specification imposes a lower bound on $\overline{CS}$ low time, guaranteeing that $\overline{CS}$ will be low for at least 1 CLK period.

4. This specification assures recognition of the asserted edge of H1(H3).

5. This specification applies only when a pulsed handshake option is chosen and the pulse is not shortened due to an early asserted edge of H1(H3).

6. CLK refers to the actual frequency of the CLK pin, not the maximum allowable CLK frequency.

7. If the setup time on the rising edge of the clock is violated, H1(H3) may not be recognized until the next rising of the clock.

8. This limit applies to the frequency of the signal at TIN compared to the frequency of the CLK signal during each clock cycle. If any period of the waveform at TIN is smaller than the period of the CLK signal at that instant, then it is likely that the timer circuit will completely ignore one cycle of the TIN signal.

    If these two signals are derived from different sources they will have different instantaneous frequency variations. In this case the frequency applied to the TIN pin must be distinctly less than the frequency at the CLK pin to avoid lost cycles of the TIN signal. With signals derived from different crystal oscillators applied to the TIN and CLK pins with fast rise and fall times, the TIN frequency can approach 80 to 90% of the frequency of the CLK signal without a loss of a cycle of the TIN signal.

    If these two signals are derived from the same frequency source then the frequency of the signal applied to TIN can be 100% of the frequency at the CLK pin. They may be generated by different buffers from the same signal or one may be an inverted version of the other. The TIN signal may be generated by an 'AND' function of the clock and a control signal.

9. The maximum value is caused by a peripheral access (H1(H3) asserted) and bus access ($\overline{CS}$ asserted) occurring at the same time.

10. See BUS INTERFACE CONNECTION section for exception.

11. Synchronized means that the input signal has been seen by the PI/T on the appropriate edge of the clock (rising edge for H1(H3) and falling edge for $\overline{CS}$). (Refer to the BUS INTERFACE CONNECTION section for the exception concerning $\overline{CS}$.)

FIGURE 3 — BUS READ CYCLE TIMING

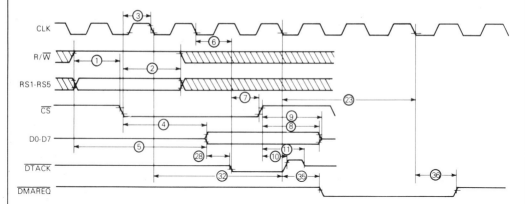

NOTE: Timing measurements are referenced to and from a low voltage of 0.8 volts and a high voltage of 2.0 volts, unless otherwise noted.

 MOTOROLA *Semiconductor Products Inc.*

FIGURE 4 — BUS WRITE CYCLE TIMING

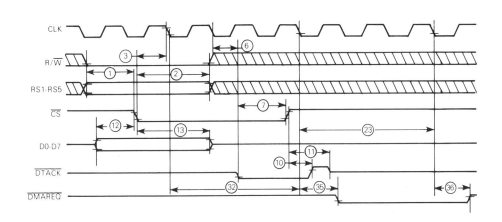

FIGURE 5 — INTERRUPT ACKNOWLEDGE
FUNCTIONAL TIMING DIAGRAM

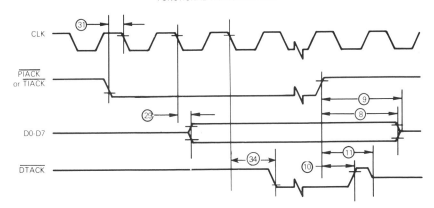

Note: Timing measurements are referenced to and from a low voltage of 0.8 volts and a high voltage of 2.0 volts, unless otherwise noted.

 MOTOROLA *Semiconductor Products Inc.*

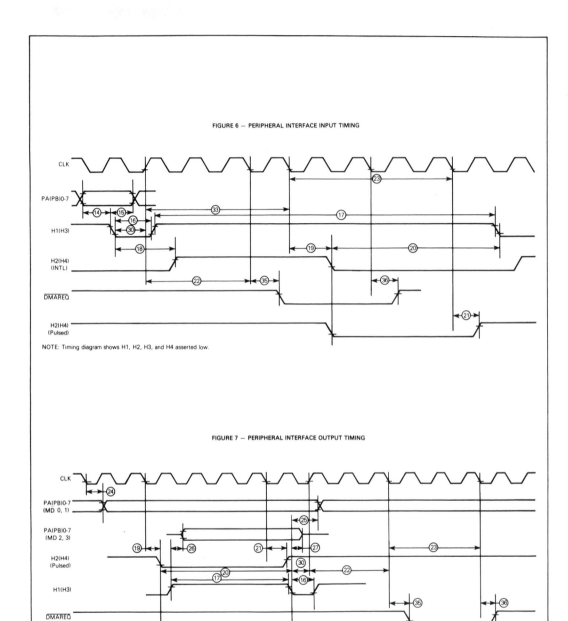

FIGURE 6 — PERIPHERAL INTERFACE INPUT TIMING

NOTE: Timing diagram shows H1, H2, H3, and H4 asserted low.

FIGURE 7 — PERIPHERAL INTERFACE OUTPUT TIMING

NOTE: Timing diagram shows H1, H2, H3, and H4 asserted low.

GENERAL DESCRIPTION

The PI/T consists of two logically independent sections: the ports and the timer. The port section consists of Port A (PA0-7), Port B (PB0-7), four handshake pins (H1, H2, H3, and H4), two general I/O pins, and six dual-function pins. The dual-function pins can individually operate as a third port (Port C) or an alternate function related to either Ports A and B, or the timer. The four programmable handshake pins, depending on the mode, can control data transfer to and from the ports, or can be used as interrupt generating inputs, or I/O pins.

The timer consists of a 24-bit counter, optionally clocked by a 5-bit prescaler. Three pins provide complete timer I/O: PC2/TIN, PC3/TOUT, and PC7/TIACK. Of course, only the ones needed for the given configuration perform the timer function, while the others remain Port C I/O.

The system bus interface provides for asynchronous transfer of data from the PI/T to a bus master over the data bus (D0-D7). Data transfer acknowledge (DTACK), register selects (RS1-RS5), chip select, the read/write line (R/W), and Port Interrup Acknowledge (PIACK) or Timer Interrupt Acknowledge (TIACK) control data transfer between the PI/T and the MC68000.

FIGURE 8 — MC68230 BLOCK DIAGRAM

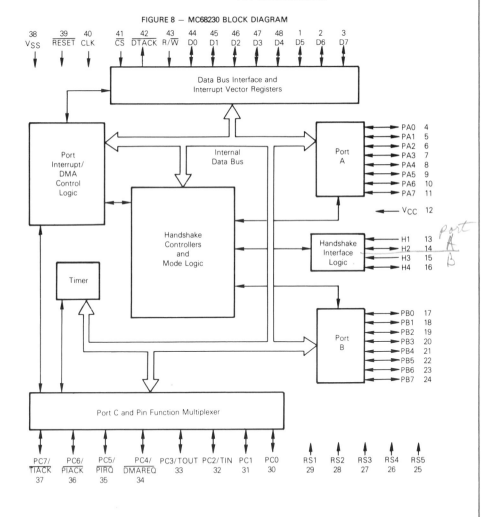

PI/T PIN DESCRIPTION

Throughout the data sheet, signals are presented using the terms active and inactive or asserted and negated independent of whether the signal is active in the high-voltage state or low-voltage state. (The active state of each logic pin is given below.) Active low signals are denoted by a superscript bar. R/$\overline{W}$ indicates a write is active low and a read active high.

FIGURE 9 — LOGICAL PIN ASSIGNMENT

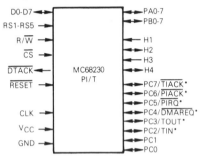

*Individually Programmable Dual-Function Pin

D0-D7 — Bidirectional Data Bus. The data bus pins D0-D7 form an 8-bit bidirectional data bus to/from the MC68000 or other bus master. These pins are active high.

RS1-RS5 — Register Selects. RS1-RS5 are active high high-impedance inputs that determine which of the 25 possible registers is being addressed. They are provided by the MC68000 or other bus master.

R/$\overline{W}$ — Read/Write Input — R/$\overline{W}$ is the high-impedance Read/Write signal from the MC68000 or bus master, indicating whether the current bus cycle is a read (high) or write (low) cycle.

$\overline{CS}$ — Chip Select Input. $\overline{CS}$ is a high-impedance input that selects the PI/T registers for the current bus cycle. Address strobe and the data strobe (upper or lower) of the bus master, along with the appropriate address bits, must be included in the chip select equation. A low level corresponds to an asserted chip select.

$\overline{DTACK}$ — Data Transfer Acknowledge Output. $\overline{DTACK}$ is an active low output that signals the completion of the bus cycle. During read or interrupt acknowledge cycles, $\overline{DTACK}$ is asserted by the MC68230 after data has been provided on the data bus; during write cycles it is asserted after data has been accepted at the data bus. Data transfer acknowledge is compatible with the MC68000 and with other Motorola bus masters such as the MC68450 DMA controller. A holding resistor is required to maintain $\overline{DTACK}$ high between bus cycles.

$\overline{RESET}$ — Reset Input. $\overline{RESET}$ is a high-impedance input used to initialize all PI/T functions. All control and data direction registers are cleared and most internal operations are disabled by the assertion of $\overline{RESET}$ (low).

CLK — Clock Input. The clock pin is a high-impedance TTL-compatible signal with the same specifications as the MC68000. The PI/T contains dynamic logic throughout, and hence this clock must not be gated off at any time. It is not necessary that this clock maintain any particular phase relationship with the MC68000 clock. It may be connected to an independent frequency source (faster or slower) as long as all bus specifications are met.

PA0-PA7 and PB0-PB7 — Port A and Port B. Ports A and B are 8-bit ports that may be concatenated to form a 16-bit port in certain modes. The ports may be controlled in conjunction with the handshake pins H1-H4. For stabilization during system power-up, Ports A and B have internal pullup resistors to V$_{CC}$. All port pins are active high.

H1-H4 — Handshake pins (I/O depending on the Mode and Submode). Handshake pins H1-H4 are multi-purpose pins that (depending on the operational mode) may provide an interlocked handshake, a pulsed handshake, an interrupt input (independent of data transfers), or simple I/O pins. For stabilization during system power-up, H2 and H4 have internal pullup resistors to V$_{CC}$. Their sense (active high or low) may be programmed in the Port General Control Register bits 3-0. Independent of the mode, the instantaneous level of the handshake pins can be read from the Port Status Register.

Port C — (PC0-PC7/Alternate function). This port can be used as eight general purpose I/O pins (PC0-PC7) or any combination of six special function pins and two general purpose I/O pins (PC0-PC1). (Each dual function pin can be standard I/O or a special function independent of the other port C pins.) The dual function pins are defined in the following paragraphs. When used as a port C pin, these pins are active high. They may be individually programmed as inputs or outputs by the Port C Data Direction Register.

The alternate functions (TIN, TOUT, and $\overline{TIACK}$) are timer I/O pins. TIN may be used as a rising-edge triggered external clock input or an external run/halt control pin (the timer is in the run state if run/halt is high and in the halt state if run/halt is low). TOUT may provide an active low timer interrupt request output or a general-purpose square-wave output, initially high. $\overline{TIACK}$ is an active low high-impedance input used for timer interrupt acknowledge.

Port A and B functions have an independent pair of active low interrupt request ($\overline{PIRQ}$) and interrupt acknowledge ($\overline{PIACK}$) pins.

The $\overline{DMAREQ}$ (Direct Memory Access Request) pin provides an active low Direct Memory Access Controller (DMAC) request pulse of 3 clock cycles, completely compatible with the MC68450 DMAC.

REGISTER MODEL

A register model that includes the corresponding Register Selects is shown in Table 1.

MOTOROLA *Semiconductor Products Inc.*

TABLE 1 — REGISTER MODEL

Register Select Bits 5	4	3	2	1	7	6	5	4	3	2	1	0	Register
0	0	0	0	0	Port Mode Control		H34 Enable	H12 Enable	H4 Sense	H3 Sense	H2 Sense	H1 Sense	Port General Control Register
0	0	0	0	1	*	SVCRQ Select		Interrupt PFS		Port Interrupt Priority Control			Port Service Request Register
0	0	0	1	0	Bit 7	Bit 6	Bit 5	Bit 4	Bit 3	Bit 2	Bit 1	Bit 0	Port A Data Direction Register
0	0	0	1	1	Bit 7	Bit 6	Bit 5	Bit 4	Bit 3	Bit 2	Bit 1	Bit 0	Port B Data Direction Register
0	0	1	0	0	Bit 7	Bit 6	Bit 5	Bit 4	Bit 3	Bit 2	Bit 1	Bit 0	Port C Data Direction Register
0	0	1	0	1	Interrupt Vector Number						*	*	Port Interrupt Vector Register
0	0	1	1	0	Port A Submode		H2 Control			H2 Int Enable	H1 SVCRQ Enable	H1 Stat Ctrl.	Port A Control Register
0	0	1	1	1	Port B Submode		H4 Control			H4 Int Enable	H3 SVCRQ Enable	H3 Stat Ctrl.	Port B Control Register
0	1	0	0	0	Bit 7	Bit 6	Bit 5	Bit 4	Bit 3	Bit 2	Bit 1	Bit 0	Port A Data Register
0	1	0	0	1	Bit 7	Bit 6	Bit 5	Bit 4	Bit 3	Bit 2	Bit 1	Bit 0	Port B Data Register
0	1	0	1	0	Bit 7	Bit 6	Bit 5	Bit 4	Bit 3	Bit 2	Bit 1	Bit 0	Port A Alternate Register
0	1	0	1	1	Bit 7	Bit 6	Bit 5	Bit 4	Bit 3	Bit 2	Bit 1	Bit 0	Port B Alternate Register
0	1	1	0	0	Bit 7	Bit 6	Bit 5	Bit 4	Bit 3	Bit 2	Bit 1	Bit 0	Port C Data Register
0	1	1	0	1	H4 Level	H3 Level	H2 Level	H1 Level	H4S	H3S	H2S	H1S	Port Status Register
0	1	1	1	0	*	*	*	*	*	*	*	*	(null)
0	1	1	1	1	*	*	*	*	*	*	*	*	(null)
1	0	0	0	0	TOUT/TIACK Control		Z D Ctrl.	*	Clock Control			Timer Enable	Timer Control Register
1	0	0	0	1	Bit 7	Bit 6	Bit 5	Bit 4	Bit 3	Bit 2	Bit 1	Bit 0	Timer Interrupt Vector Register
1	0	0	1	0	*	*	*	*	*	*	*	*	(null)
1	0	0	1	1	Bit 23	Bit 22	Bit 21	Bit 20	Bit 19	Bit 18	Bit 17	Bit 16	Counter Preload Register (High)
1	0	1	0	0	Bit 15	Bit 14	Bit 13	Bit 12	Bit 11	Bit 10	Bit 9	Bit 8	(Mid)
1	0	1	0	1	Bit 7	Bit 6	Bit 5	Bit 4	Bit 3	Bit 2	Bit 1	Bit 0	(Low)
1	0	1	1	0	*	*	*	*	*	*	*	*	(null)
1	0	1	1	1	Bit 23	Bit 22	Bit 21	Bit 20	Bit 19	Bit 18	Bit 17	Bit 16	Count Register (High)
1	1	0	0	0	Bit 15	Bit 14	Bit 13	Bit 12	Bit 11	Bit 10	Bit 9	Bit 8	(Mid)
1	1	0	0	1	Bit 7	Bit 6	Bit 5	Bit 4	Bit 3	Bit 2	Bit 1	Bit 0	(Low)
1	1	0	1	0	*	*	*	*	*	*	*	ZDS	Timer Status Register
1	1	0	1	1	*	*	*	*	*	*	*	*	(null)
1	1	1	0	0	*	*	*	*	*	*	*	*	(null)
1	1	1	0	1	*	*	*	*	*	*	*	*	(null)
1	1	1	1	0	*	*	*	*	*	*	*	*	(null)
1	1	1	1	1	*	*	*	*	*	*	*	*	(null)

*Unused, read as zero.

 MOTOROLA *Semiconductor Products Inc.*

PORT CONTROL STRUCTURE

The primary focus of most applications will be on Ports A and B, the handshake pins, the port interrupt pins, and the DMA request pin. They are controlled in the following way: the Port General Control Register contains a 2-bit field that specifies a set of four operation modes. These govern the overall operation of the ports and determine their interrelationships. Some modes require additional information from each port's control register to further define its operation. In each port control register, there is a 2-bit submode field that serves this purpose. Each port mode/submode combination specifies a set of programmable characteristics that fully define the behavior of that port and two of the handshake pins. This structure is summarized in Table 2 and Figure 10.

FIGURE 10 — PORT MODE LAYOUT

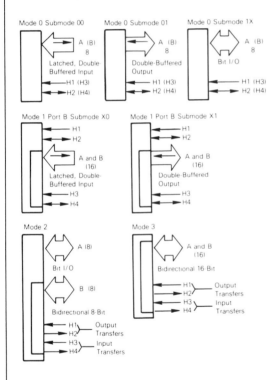

TABLE 2 — PORT MODE CONTROL SUMMARY

Mode 0 (Unidirectional 8-Bit Mode)
 Port A
  Submode 00 — Double-Buffered Input
   H1 — Latches input data
   H2 — Status/interrupt generating input, general-purpose output, or operation with H1 in the interlocked or pulsed input handshake protocols
  Submode 01 — Double-Buffered Output
   H1 — Indicates data received by peripheral
   H2 — Status/interrupt generating input, general-purpose output, or operation with H1 in the interlocked or pulsed output handshake protocols
  Submode 1X — Bit I/O
   H1 — Status/interrupt generating input
   H2 — Status/interrupt generating input or general-purpose output
 Port B, H3 and H4 — Identical to Port A, H1 and H2

Mode 1 (Unidirectional 16-Bit Mode)
 Port A — Double-Buffered Data (Most significant)
  Submode XX (not used)
   H1 — Status/interrupt generating input
   H2 — Status/interrupt generating input or general-purpose output
 Port B — Double-Buffered Data (Least significant)
  Submode X0 — Unidirectional 16-Bit Input
   H3 — Latches input data
   H4 — Status/interrupt generating input, general-purpose output, or operation with H3 in the interlocked or pulsed input handshake protocols
  Submode X1 — Unidirectional 16-Bit Output
   H3 — Indicates data received by peripheral
   H4 — Status/interrupt generating input, general-purpose output, or operation with H3 in the interlocked or pulsed output handshake protocols

Mode 2 (Bidirectional 8-Bit Mode)
 Port A — Bit I/O (with no handshaking pins)
  Submode XX (not used)
 Port B — Bidirectional 8-Bit Data (Double-Buffered)
  Submode XX (not used)
   H1 — Indicates output data received by peripheral
   H2 — Operation with H1 in the interlocked or pulsed output handshake protocols
   H3 — Latches input data
   H4 — Operation with H3 in the interlocked or pulsed input handshake protocols

Mode 3 (Bidirectional 16-Bit Mode)
 Port A — Double-Buffered Data (Most significant)
  Submode XX (not used)
 Port B — Double-Buffered Data (Least significant)
  Submode XX (not used)
   H1 — Indicates output data received by peripheral
   H2 — Operation with H1 in the interlocked or pulsed output handshake protocols
   H3 — Latches input data
   H4 — Operation with H3 in the interlocked or pulsed input handshake protocols

 MOTOROLA *Semiconductor Products Inc.*

PORT GENERAL INFORMATION AND CONVENTIONS

The following paragraphs introduce concepts that are generally applicable to the PI/T ports independent of the chosen mode and submode. For this reason, no particular port or handshake pins are mentioned; the notation H1 (H3) indicates that, depending on the chosen mode and submode, the statement given may be true for either the H1 or H3 handshake pin.

Unidirectional vs Bidirectional — Figure 10 shows the configuration of Ports A and B and each of the handshake pins in each port mode and submode. In Modes 0 and 1, a data direction register is associated with each of the ports. These registers contain one bit for each port pin to determine whether that pin is an input or an output. Modes 0 and 1 are, thus, called unidirectional modes because each pin assumes a constant direction, changeable only by a reset condition or a programming change. These modes allow double-buffered data transfers in one direction. This direction, determined by the mode and submode definition, is known as the primary direction. Data transfers in the primary direction are controlled by the handshake pins. Data transfers not in the primary direction are generally unrelated, and single or unbuffered data paths exist.

In Modes 2 and 3 there is no concept of primary direction as in Modes 0 and 1. Except for Port A in Mode 2 (Bit I/O), the data direction registers have no effect. These modes are bidirectional, in that the direction of each transfer (always 8 or 16 bits, double-buffered) is determined dynamically by the state of the handshake pins. Thus, for example, data may be transferred out of the ports, followed very shortly by a transfer into the same port pins. Transfers to and from the ports are independent and may occur in any sequence. Since the instantaneous direction is always determined by the external system, a small amount of arbitration logic may be required.

Control of Double-Buffered Data Paths — Generally speaking, the PI/T is a double-buffered device. In the primary direction, double-buffering allows orderly transfers by using the handshake pins in any of several programmable protocols. (When Bit I/O is used, double-buffering is not available and the handshake pins are used as outputs or status/interrupt inputs.)

Use of double-buffering is most beneficial in situations where a peripheral device and the computer system are capable of transferring data at roughly the same speed. Double-buffering allows the fetch operation of the data transmitter to be overlapped with the store operation of the data receiver. Thus, throughput measured in bytes or words-per-second may be greatly enhanced. if there is a large mismatch in transfer capability between the computer and the peripheral, little or no benefit is obtained. In these cases there is no penalty in using double-buffering.

Double-Buffered Input Transfers — In all modes, the PI/T supports double-buffered input transfers. Data that meets the port setup and hold times is latched on the asserted edge of H1(H3). H1(H3) is edge-sensitive, and may assume any duty-cycle as long as both high and low minimum times are observed. The PI/T contains a Port Status Register whose H1S(H3S) status bit is set anytime any input data is present in the double-buffered latches that has not been read by the bus master. The action of H2(H4) is programmable; it may indicate whether there is room for more data in the PI/T latches or it may serve other purposes. The following options are available, depending on the mode.

1. H2(H4) may be an edge-sensitive input that is independent of H1(H3) and the transfer of port data. On the asserted edge of H2(H4), the H2S(H4S) status bit is set. It is cleared by the direct method (refer to Direct Method of Resetting Status), the $\overline{\text{RESET}}$ pin being asserted, or when the H12 Enable (H34 Enable) bit of the Port General Control Register is 0.

2. H2(H4) may be a general purpose output pin that is always negated. The H2S(H4S) status bit is always 0.

3. H2(H4) may be a general purpose output pin that is always asserted. The H2S(H4S) status bit is always 0.

4. H2(H4) may be an output pin in the interlocked input handshake protocol. It is asserted when the port input latches are ready to accept new data. It is negated asynchronously following the asserted edge of the H1(H3) input. As soon as the input latches become ready, H2(H4) is again asserted. When the input double-buffered latches are full, H2(H4) remains negated until data is removed. Thus, anytime the H2(H4) output is asserted, new input data may be entered by asserting H1(H3). At other times transitions on H1(H3) are ignored. The H2S(H4S) status bit is always 0. When H12 Enable (H34 Enable) is 0, H2(H4) is held negated.

5. H2(H4) may be an output pin in the pulsed input handshake protocol. It is asserted exactly as in the interlocked input protocol, but never remains asserted longer than 4 clock cycles. Typically, a four clock cycle pulse is generated. But in the case that a subsequent H1(H3) asserted edge occurs before termination of the pulse, H2(H4) is negated asynchronously. Thus, anytime after the leading edge of the H2(H4) pulse, new data may be entered in the PI/T double-buffered input latches. The H2S(H4S) status bit is always 0. When H12 Enable (H34 Enable) is 0, H2(H4) is held negated.

A sample timing diagram is shown in Figure 11. The H2(H4) interlocked and pulsed input handshake protocols are shown. The $\overline{\text{DMAREQ}}$ pin is also shown assuming it is enabled. All handshake pin sense bits are assumed to be 0 (refer to Port General Control Register); thus, the pins are in the low state when asserted. Due to the great similarity between modes, this timing diagram is applicable to all double-buffered input transfers.

 MOTOROLA *Semiconductor Products Inc.*

FIGURE 11 — DOUBLE-BUFFERED INPUT TRANSFERS

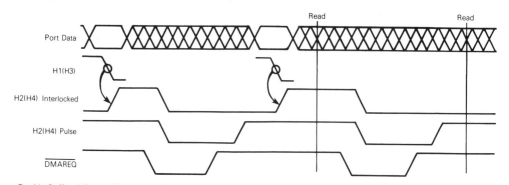

Double-Buffered Output Transfers — The PI/T supports double-buffered output transfers in all modes. Data, written by the bus master to the PI/T, is stored in the port's output latch. The peripheral accepts the data by asserting H1(H3), which causes the next data to be moved to the port's output latch as soon as it is available. The function of H2(H4) is programmable; it may indicate whether new data has been moved to the output latch or it may serve other purposes. The H1S(H3S) status bit may be programmed for two interpretations. Normally the status bit is a 1 when there is at least one latch in the double-buffered data path that can accept new data. After writing one byte/word of data to the ports, an interrupt service routine could check this bit to determine if it could store another byte/word; thus, filling both latches. When the bus master is finished, it is often useful to be able to check whether all of the data has been transferred to the peripheral. The H1S(H3S) Status Control bit of the Port A and B Control Registers provide this flexibility. The programmable options of the H2(H4) pin are given below, depending on the mode.

1. H2(H4) may be an edge-sensitive input pin independent of H1(H3) and the transfer of port data. On the asserted edge of H2(H4), the H2S(H4S) status bit is set. It is reset by the direct method (refer to Direct Method of Resetting Status), the RESET pin being asserted, or when the H12 Enable (H34 Enable) bit of the Port General Control Register is 0.

2. H2(H4) may be a general-purpose output pin that is always negated. The H2S(H4S) status bit is always 0.

3. H2(H4) may be a general-purpose output pin that is always asserted. The H2S(H4S) status bit is always 0.

4. H2(H4) may be an output pin in the interlocked output handshake protocol. H2(H4) is asserted two clock cycles after data is transferred to the double-buffered output latches. The data remains stable and H2(H4) remains asserted until the next asserted edge of the H1(H3) input. At that time, H2(H4) is asynchronously negated. As soon as the next data is available, it is transferred to the output latches. When H2(H4) is negated, asserted transitions on H1(H3) have no effect on the data paths. As is explained later, however, in Modes 2 and 3 they do control the three-state output buffers of the bidirectional port(s). The H2S(H4S) status bit is always 0. When H12 Enable (H34 Enable) is 0, H2(H4) is held negated.

5. H2(H4) may be an output pin in the pulsed output handshake protocol. It is asserted exactly as in the interlocked output protocol above, but never remains asserted longer than four clock cycles. Typically, a four clock pulse is generated. But in the case that a subsequent H1(H3) asserted edge occurs before termination of the pulse, H2(H4) is negated asynchronously shortening the pulse. The H2S(H4S) status bit is always 0. When H12 Enable (H34 Enable) is 0 H2(H4) is held negated.

A sample timing diagram is shown in Figure 12. The H2(H4) interlocked and pulsed output handshake protocols are shown. The DMAREQ pin is also shown assuming it is enabled. All handshake pin sense bits are assumed to be 0; thus, the pins are in the low state when asserted. Due to the great similarity between modes, this timing diagram is applicable to all double-buffered output transfer.

FIGURE 12 — DOUBLE-BUFFERED OUTPUT TRANSFERS

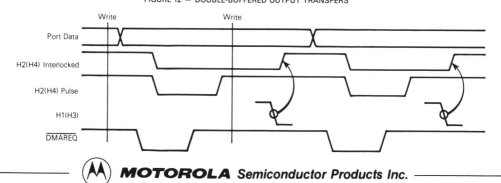

Ⓜ **MOTOROLA** *Semiconductor Products Inc.*

Requesting Bus Master Service — The PI/T has several means of indicating a need for service by a bus master. First, the processor may poll the Port Status Register. It contains a status bit for each handshake pin, plus a level bit that always reflects the instantaneous state of that handshake pin. A status bit is 1 when the PI/T needs servicing, i.e., generally when the bus master needs to read or write data to the ports, or when a handshake pin used as a simple status input has been asserted. The interpretation of these bits is dependent on the chosen mode and submode.

Second, the PI/T may be placed in the processor's interrupt structure. As mentioned previously, the PI/T contains Port A and B Control Registers that configure the handshake pins. Other bits in these registers enable an interrupt associated with each handshake pin. This interrupt is made available through the PC5/$\overline{PIRQ}$ pin, if the $\overline{PIRQ}$ function is selected. Three additional conditions are required for $\overline{PIRQ}$ to be asserted: (1) the handshake pin status bit set, (2) the corresponding interrupt (service request) enable bit is set, (3) and DMA requests are not associated with that data transfer (H1 and H3 only). The conditions from each of the four handshake pins and corresponding status bits are ORed to determine $\overline{PIRQ}$.

The third method of requesting service is via the PC4/$\overline{DMAREQ}$ pin. This pin can be associated with double-buffered transfers in each mode. If it is used as a DMA controller request, it can initiate requests to keep the PI/T's input/output double-buffering empty/full as much as possi-

ble. It will not overrun the DMA controller. The pin is compatible with the MC68450 Direct Memory Access Controller (DMAC).

Vectored, Prioritized Port Interrupts — Use of MC68000-compatible vectored interrupts with the PI/T requires the $\overline{PIRQ}$ and $\overline{PIACK}$ pins. When $\overline{PIACK}$ is asserted, the PI/T places an 8-bit vector on the data pins D0-D7. Under normal conditions, this vector corresponds to highest priority, enabled, active port interrupt source with which the $\overline{DMAREQ}$ pin is not currently associated. The most-significant six bits are provided by the Port Interrupt Vector Register (PIVR), with the lower two bits supplied by prioritization logic according to conditions present when $\overline{PIACK}$ is asserted. It is important to note that the only affect on the PI/T caused by interrupt acknowledge cycles is that the vector is placed on the data bus. Specifically, no registers, data, status, or other internal states of the PI/T are affected by the cycle.

Several conditions may be present when the $\overline{PIACK}$ input is asserted to the PI/T. These conditions affect the PI/T's response and the termination of the bus cycle. If the PI/T has no interrupt function selected, or is not asserting $\overline{PIRQ}$, the PI/T will make no response to $\overline{PIACK}$ ($\overline{DTACK}$ will not be asserted). If the PI/T is asserting $\overline{PIRQ}$ when $\overline{PIACK}$ is received, the PI/T will output the contents of the Port Interrupt Vector Register and the prioritization bits. If the PIVR has not been initialized, $0F will be read from this register. These conditions are summarized in Table 3.

TABLE 3 — RESPONSE TO PORT INTERRUPT ACKNOWLEDGE

Conditions	$\overline{PIRQ}$ negated OR interrupt request function not selected	$\overline{PIRQ}$ asserted
PIVR has not been initialized since $\overline{RESET}$	No response from PI/T. No $\overline{DTACK}$.	PI/T provides $0F, the Uninitialized Vector.*
PIVR has been initialized since $\overline{RESET}$	No response from PI/T. No $\overline{DTACK}$.	PI/T provides PIVR contents with prioritization bits.

*The uninitialized vector is the value returned from an interrupt vector register before it has been initialized.

The vector table entries for the PI/T appear as a contiguous block of four vector numbers whose common upper six bits are programmed in the PIVR. The following table pairs each interrupt source with the 2-bit value provided by the prioritization logic, when interrupt acknowledge is asserted.

H1 source — 00
H2 source — 01
H3 source — 10
H4 source — 11

Autovectored Port Interrupts — Autovecored interrupts use only the $\overline{PIRQ}$ pin. The operation of the PI/T with vectored and autovectored interrupts is identical except that no vectors are supplied and the PC6/$\overline{PIACK}$ pin can be used as a Port C pin.

Direct Method of Resetting Status — In certain modes one or more handshake pins can be used as edge-sensitive inputs for sole purpose of setting bits in the Port Status Register. These bits consist of simple flip-flops. They are set (to 1) by the occurrence of the asserted edge of the hand-

shake pin input. Resetting a handshake status bit can be done by writing an 8-bit mask to the Port Status Register. This is called the direct method of resetting. To reset a status bit that is resettable by the direct method, the mask must contain a 1 in the bit position of the Port Status Register corresponding to the desired bit. Other positions must contain 0's. For status bits that are not resettable by the direct method in the chosen mode, the data written to the port status register has no effect. For status bits that are resettable by the direct method in the chosen mode, a 0 in the mask has no effect.

Handshake Pin Sense Control — The PI/T contains exclusive-OR gates to control the sense of each of the handshake pins, whether used as inputs or outputs. Four bits in the Port General Control Register may be programmed to determine whether the pins are asserted in the low or high voltage state. As with other control registers, these bits are reset to 0 when the $\overline{RESET}$ pin is asserted, defaulting the asserted level to be low.

Enabling Ports A and B — Certain functions involved with double-buffered data transfers, the handshake pins, and the status bits, may be disabled by the external system or by the

 MOTOROLA *Semiconductor Products Inc.*

programmer during initialization. The Port General Control Register contains two bits, H12 Enable and H34 Enable, which control these functions. These bits are cleared to the o state when the RESET pin is asserted, and the functions are disabled. The functions are the following:

1. Independent of other actions by the bus master or peripheral (via the handshake pins), the PI/T's disabled handshake controller is held to the ''empty'' state, i.e., no data is present in the double-buffered data path.

2. When any handshake pin is used to set a simple status flip-flop, unrelated to double-buffered transfers, these flip-flops are held reset to 0. (See Table 2.)

3. When H2(H4) is used in an interlocked or pulsed handshake with H1(H3), H2(H4) is held negated, regardless of the chosen mode, submode, and primary direction. Thus, for double-buffered input transfers, the programmer may signal a peripheral when the PI/T is ready to begin transfers by setting the associated handshake enable bit to 1.

The Port A and B Alternate Registers — In addition to the Port A and B Data Registers, the PI/T contains Port A and B Alternate Registers. These registers are read-only, and simply provide the instantaneous level of each port pin. They have no effect on the operation of the handshake pins, double-buffered transfers, status bits, or any other aspect of the PI/T, and they are mode/submode independent.

PORT MODES

This section contains information that distinguishes the various port modes and submodes. General characteristics, common to all modes, have been defined previously.

MODE 0 — UNIDIRECTIONAL 8-BIT MODE

In Mode 0, Ports A and B operate independently. Each may be configured in any of its three possible submodes:

Submode 00 — Double-Buffered Input
Submode 01 — Double-Buffered Output
Submode 1X — Bit I/O

Handshake pins H1 and H2 are associated with Port A and configured by programming the Port A Control Register. (The H12 Enable bit of the Port General Control Register enables Port A transfers.) Handshake pins H3 and H4 are associated with Port B and configured by programming the Port B Control Register. (The H34 Enable bit of the Port General Control Register enables Port B transfers.) The Port A and B Data Direction Registers operate in all three submodes. Along with the submode, they affect the data read and written at the associated data register according to Table 4. They also enable the output buffer associated with each port pin. The DMAREQ pin may be associated with either (not both) Port A or Port B, but does not function if the Bit I/O submode is programmed for the chosen port.

TABLE 4 — MODE 0 PORT DATA PATHS

Mode	Read Port A/B Data Register		Write Port A/B Data Register	
	DDR = 0	DDR = 1	DDR = X	
0 Submode 00	FIL, D.B.	FOL Note 3	FOL, S.B.	Note 1
0 Submode 01	Pin	FOL Note 3	IOL/FOL, D.B.	Note 2
0 Submode 1X	Pin	FOL Note 3	FOL, S.B.	Note 1

Abbreviations:
IOL — Initial Output Latch   S.B. — Single Buffered
FOL — Final Output Latch   D.B. — Double Buffered
FIL — Final Input Latch   DDR — Data Direction Register

Note 1: Data is latched in the output data registers (final output latch) and will be single buffered at the pin if the DDR is 1. The output buffers will be turned off if the DDR is 0.

Note 2: Data is latched in the double-buffered output data registers. The data in the final output latch will appear on the port pin if the DDR is a 1.

Note 3: The output drivers that connect the final output latch to the pins are turned on.

 MOTOROLA *Semiconductor Products Inc.*

Port A or B Submode 00 (8-Bit Double-Buffered Input) —

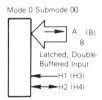

Mode 0 Submode 00

A (B)
8

Latched, Double-
Buffered Input

H1 (H3)
H2 (H4)

In Mode 0, double-buffered input transfers of up to 8-bits are available by programming Submode 00 in the desired port's control register. The operation of H2 and H4 may be selected by programming the Port A and Port B Control Registers, respectively. All five double-buffered input handshake options, previously mentioned in the Port General Information and Conventions section, are available.

For pins used as outputs, the data path consists of a single latch driving the output buffer. Data written to the port's data register does not affect the operation of any handshake pin, status bit, or any other aspect of the PI/T. Output pins may be used independently of the input transfer. However, read bus cycles to the data register do remove data from the port. Therefore, care should be taken to avoid processor instructions that perform unwanted read cycles.

Refer to PARALLEL PORTS Double-Buffered Input Transfers for a sample timing diagram (Figure 11).

Port A or B Submode 01 (8-Bit Double-Buffered Output) —

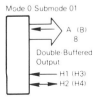

Mode 0 Submode 01

A (B)
8

Double-Buffered
Output

H1 (H3)
H2 (H4)

In Mode 0, double-buffered output transfers of up to 8 bits are available by programming submode 01 in the desired port's control register. The operation of H2 and H4 may be selected by programming the Port A and Port B Control Registers, respectively. All five double-buffered output handshake options, previously mentioned in the Port General Information and Conventions section, are available.

For pins used as inputs, data written to the associated data register is double-buffered and passed to the initial or final output latch, as usual, but the output buffer is disabled.

Refer to PARALLEL PORTS Double-Buffered Output Transfers for a sample timing diagram (Figure 12).

Port A or B Submode 1X (Bit I/O) —

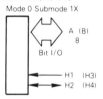

Mode 0 Submode 1X

A (B)
8

Bit I/O

H1 (H3)
H2 (H4)

In Mode 0, simple Bit I/O is available by programming Submode 1X in the desired port's control register. This submode is intended for applications in which several independent devices must be controlled or monitored. Data written to the associated data register is single-buffered. If the data direction register bit for that pin is a 1 (output), the output buffer is enabled. If it is 0 (input), data written is still latched, but is not available at the pin. Data read from the data register is the instantaneous value of the pin or what was written to the data register, depending on the contents of the data direction register. H1(H3) is an edge-sensitive status input pin only and it controls no data-related function. The H1S(H3S) status bit is set following the asserted edge of the input waveform. It is reset by the direct method, the RESET pin being asserted, or when the H12 Enable (H34 Enable) bit is 0.

H2(H4) can be programmed as a simple status input (identical to H1(H3)), or as an asserted or negated output. The interlocked or pulsed handshake configurations are not available.

MODE 1 — UNIDIRECTIONAL 16-BIT MODE

In Mode 1, Ports A and B are concatenated to form a single 16-bit port. The Port B Submode field controls the configuration of both ports. The possible submodes are:

Port B Submode X0 — Double-Buffered Input
Port B Submode X1 — Double-Buffered Output

Handshake pins H3 and H4, configured by programming the Port B Control Register, are associated with the 16-bit double-buffered transfer. These 16-bit transfers, are enabled by the H34 Enable bit of the Port General Control Register. Handshake pins H1 and H2 may be used as simple inputs not related to the 16-bit data transfer or H2 may be an output. Enabling of the H1 and H2 handshake pins is done by the H12 Enable bit of the Port General Control Register. The Port A and B Data Direction Registers operate in each submode. Along with the submode, they affect the data read and written at the data register according to Table 5. They also enable the output buffer associated with each port pin. The DMAREQ pin may be associated only with H3.

Mode 1 can provide convenient, high-speed 16-bit transfers. The Port A and B data registers are addressed for compatibility with the MC68000 Move Peripheral (MOVEP) instruction and with the MC68450 DMAC. To take advantage of this, Port A should contain the most-significant byte of data and always be read or written by the bus master first. The interlocked and pulsed handshake protocols are keyed to accesses to the Port B Data Register in Mode 1. If it is accessed last, the 16-bit double-buffered transfers proceed smoothly.

TABLE 5 — MODE 1 PORT DATA PATHS

Mode	Read Port A/B Register		Write Port A/B Register	
	DDR = 0	DDR = 1	DDR = 0	DDR = 1
1, Port B Submode X0	FIL, D.B.	FOL Note 3	FOL, S.B. Note 2	FOL, S.B. Note 2
1, Port B Submode X1	Pin	FOL Note 3	IOL/FOL, D.B., Note 1	IOL/FOL, D.B., Note 1

Note 1: Data written to Port A goes to a temporary latch. When the Port B data register is later written, Port A data is transferred to IOL/FOL.

Note 2: Data is latched in the output data registers (final output latch) and will be single buffered at the pin if the DDR is 1. The output buffers will be turned off if the DDR is 0.

Note 3: The output drivers that connect the final output latch to the pins are turned on.

Abbreviations:
IOL — Initial Output Latch   S.B. — Single Buffered
FOL — Final Output Latch   D.B. — Double Buffered
FIL — Final Input Latch   DDR — Data Direction Register

Port B Submode X0 (16-Bit Double-Buffered Input) —

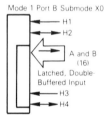

Mode 1 Port B Submode X0

H1
H2
A and B (16)
Latched, Double-Buffered Input
H3
H4

Port B Submode X1 (16-Bit Double-Buffered Output) —

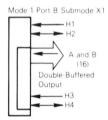

Mode 1 Port B Submode X1

H1
H2
A and B (16)
Double-Buffered Output
H3
H4

In Mode 1 Port B Submode X0, double-buffered input transfers of up to 16 bits may be obtained. The level of all 16 pins is asynchronously latched with the asserted edge of H3. The processor may check H3S status bit to determine if new data is present. The $\overline{\text{DMAREQ}}$ pin may be used to signal a DMA controller to empty the input buffers. Regardless of the bus master, Port A data should be read first. (Actually, Port A data need not be read at all.) Port B data should be read last. The operation of the internal handshake controller, the H3S bit, and $\overline{\text{DMAREQ}}$ are keyed to the reading of the Port B data register. (The MC68450 DMAC can be programmed to perform the exact transfers needed for compatibility with the PI/T.) H4 may be programmed for all five of the handshake options mentioned in the Port General Information and Conventions section.

For pins used as outputs, the data path consists of a single latch driving the output buffer. Data written to the port's data register does not affect the operation of any handshake pin, status bit, or any other aspect of the PI/T. Thus, output pins may be used independently of the input transfer. However, read bus cycles to the Port B Data Register do remove data, so care should be taken to avoid unwanted read cycles.

Refer to PARALLEL PORTS Double-Buffered Input Transfers for a sample timing diagram (Figure 11).

In Mode 1 Port B Submode X1, double-buffered output transfers of up to 16 bits may be obtained. Data is written by the bus master (processor or DMA controller) in two bytes. The first byte (most-significant) is written to the Port A Data Register. It is stored in a temporary latch until the next byte is written to the Port B Data Register. Then all 16 bits are transferred to the final output latches of Ports A and B. Both options for interpretation of the H3S status bit, mentioned in Port General Information and Comments section, are available and apply to the 16-bit port as a whole. The $\overline{\text{DMAREQ}}$ pin may be used to signal a DMA controller to transfer another word to the port output latches. (The MC68450 DMAC can be programmed to perform the exact transfers needed for compatibility with the PI/T.) H4 may be programmed for all five of the handshake options mentioned in the Port General Information and Comments section.

For pins used as inputs, data written to either data register is double-buffered and passed to the initial or final output latch, as usual, but the output buffer is disabled.

Refer to PARALLEL PORTS Double-Buffered Input/Output Transfer for a sample timing diagram (Figure 12).

 MOTOROLA *Semiconductor Products Inc.*

MODE 2 — BIDIRECTIONAL 8-BIT MODE

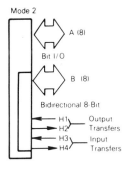

Mode 2

A (8)

Bit I/O

B (8)

Bidirectional 8-Bit

H1 — Output
H2 — Transfers
H3 — Input
H4 — Transfers

In Mode 2, Port A is used for simple bit I/O with no associated handshake pins. Port B is used for bidirectional 8-bit double-buffered transfers. H1 and H2, enabled by the H12 Enable bit in the Port General Control Register, control output transfers, while H3 and H4, enabled by the Port General Control Register bit H34 Enable, control input transfers. The instantaneous direction of the data is determined by the H1 handshake pin. The Port B Data Direction Register is not used. The Port A and Port B submode fields do not affect PI/T operation in Mode 2.

Double-Buffered I/O (Port B) — The only aspect of bidirectional double-buffered transfers that differs from the unidirectional modes lies in controlling the Port B output buffers. They are controlled by the level of H1. When H1 is negated, the Port B output buffers (all 8) are enabled and the pins drive the bidirectional bus. Generally, H1 is negated in response to an asserted H2, which indicates that new output data is present in the double-buffered latches. Following acceptance of the data, the peripheral asserts H1, disabling the Port B output buffers. Other than controlling the output buffer, H1 is edge-sensitive as in other modes. Input transfers proceed identically to the double-buffered input protocol described in the Port General Information and Conventions Section. In Mode 2, only the interlocked and pulsed handshake pin options are available on H2 and H4. The $\overline{\text{DMAREQ}}$

pin may be associated with either input transfers (H3) or output transfers (H1), but not both. Refer to Table 6 for a summary of the Port B Data Register responses in Mode 2.

Bit I/O (Port A) — Mode 2, Port A performs simple bit I/O with no associated handshake pins. This configuration is intended for applications in which several independent devices must be controlled or monitored. Data written to the Port A data register is single-buffered. If the Port A Data Direction Register bit for that pin is 1 (output), the output buffer is enabled. If it is 0, data written is still latched but not available at the pin. Data read from the data register is either the instantaneous value of the pin or what was written to the data register, depending on the contents of the Port A Data Direction Register. This is summarized in Table 7.

MODE 3 — BIDIRECTIONAL 16-BIT DOUBLE-BUFFERED I/O

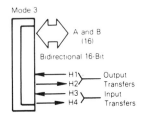

Mode 3

A and B
(16)

Bidirectional 16-Bit

H1 — Output
H2 — Transfers
H3 — Input
H4 — Transfers

In Mode 3, Ports A and B are used for bidirectional 16-bit double-buffered transfers. H1 and H2 control output transfers, while H3 and H4 control input transfers. (H1 and H2 are enabled by the H12 Enable bit while H3 and H4 are enabled by the H34 Enable bit of the Port General Control Register.) The instantaneous direction of the data is determined by the H1 handshake pin, and thus, the data direction registers are not used. The Port A and Port B submode fields do not affect PI/T operation in Mode 3.

The only aspect of bidirectional double-buffered transfers that differs from the unidirectional modes lies in controlling the Port A and B output buffers. They are controlled by the level of H1. When H1 is negated, the output buffers (all 16) are enabled and the pins drive the bidirectional bus. General-

TABLE 6 — MODE 2 PORT B DATA PATHS

Mode	Read Port B Data Register	Write Port B Data Register
2	FIL, D.B.	IOL/FOL, D.B.
Abbreviations: IOL — Initial Output Latch FOL — Final Output Latch FIL — Final Input Latch	D.B. — Double Buffered	

TABLE 7 — MODE 2 PORT A DATA PATHS

Mode	Read Port A Data Register		Write Port A Data Register	
	DDR = 0	DDR = 1	DDR = 0	DDR = 1
2	Pin	FOL	FOL	FOL, S.B.
Abbreviations: S.B. — Single Buffered FOL — Final Output Latch DDR — Data Direction Register				

MOTOROLA *Semiconductor Products Inc.*

ly, H1 is negated in response to an asserted H2, which indicates that new output data is present in the double-buffered latches. Following acceptance of the data, the peripheral asserts H1, disabling the output buffers. Other than controlling the output buffers, H1 is edge-sensitive as in other modes. Input transfers proceed identically to the double-buffered input protocol described in the Port General Information and Conventions section. Port A and B data is latched with the asserted edge of H3. In Mode 3, only the interlocked and pulsed handshake pin options are available to H2 and H4. The $\overline{\text{DMAREQ}}$ pin may be associated with either input transfers (H3) or output transfers (H1), but not both. H2 indicates when new data is available in the Port B (and implicitly Port A) output latches, but unless the buffer is enabled by H1, the data is not driving the pins.

Mode 3 can provide convenient high-speed 16-bit transfers. The Port A and B Data Registers are addressed for compatibility with the MC68000's Move Peripheral (MOVEP) instruction and with the MC68450 DMAC. To take advantage of this, Port A should contain the most-significant data and always be read or written by the bus master first. The interlocked and pulsed handshake protocols are keyed to accesses to the Port B Data Register in Mode 3. If it is accessed last, the 16-bit double-buffered transfer proceed smoothly. Refer to Table 8 for a summary of the Port A and B data paths in Mode 3.

DMA REQUEST OPERATION

The Direct Memory Access Request ($\overline{\text{DMAREQ}}$) pulse (when enabled) is associated with output or input transfers to keep the initial and final output latches full or initial and final input latches empty, respectively. Figures 13 and 14 show all the possible paths in generating DMA requests.

$\overline{\text{DMAREQ}}$ is generated on the bus side of the MC68230 by the synchronized* Chip Select. If the conditions of Figures 13 and 14 are met, an access of the bus (assertion of $\overline{\text{CS}}$) will cause $\overline{\text{DMAREQ}}$ to be asserted 3 PI/T clocks (plus the delay time from the clock edge) after $\overline{\text{CS}}$ is synchronized.* $\overline{\text{DMAREQ}}$ remains asserted 3 clock cycles (plus the delay time from the clock edge) and is then negated.

The $\overline{\text{DMAREQ}}$ pulse associated with a peripheral or port side of the PI/T is caused by the synchronized* H1(H3) input. If the conditions of Figures 13 and 14 are met, a port access (assertion of the H1(H3) input) will cause $\overline{\text{DMAREQ}}$ to be asserted 2.5 PI/T clock cycles (plus the delay time from clock edge) after H1(H3) is synchronized.* $\overline{\text{DMAREQ}}$ remains asserted 3 clock cycles (plus the delay time from the clock edge) and is then negated.

TABLE 8 — MODE 3 PORT A AND B DATA PATHS

Mode	Read Port A and B Data Register	Write Port A and B Data Register
3	FIL, D.B.	IOL/FOL, D.B., Note 1

Note 1: Data written to Port A goes to a temporary latch. When the Port B data register is later written, Port A data is transferred to IOL/FOL.

Abbreviations:
IOL — Initial Output Latch	S.B. — Single Buffered
FOL — Final Output Latch	D.B. — Double Buffered
FIL — Final Input Latch	

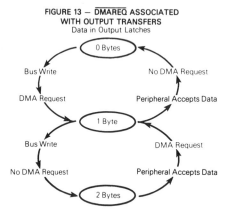

FIGURE 13 — $\overline{\text{DMAREQ}}$ ASSOCIATED
WITH OUTPUT TRANSFERS
Data in Output Latches

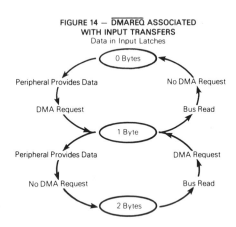

FIGURE 14 — $\overline{\text{DMAREQ}}$ ASSOCIATED
WITH INPUT TRANSFERS
Data in Input Latches

*Synchronized means that the input signal has been seen by the PI/T on the appropriate edge of the clock (rising edge for H1(H3) and falling edge for $\overline{\text{CS}}$). (Refer to the BUS INTERFACE CONNECTION section for the exception concerning $\overline{\text{CS}}$.) If a bus access (assertion of $\overline{\text{CS}}$) and a port access (assertion of H1(H3)) occur at the same time, $\overline{\text{CS}}$ will be recognized without any delay. H1(H3) will be recognized one clock cycle later.

 MOTOROLA *Semiconductor Products Inc.*

TIMER

The MC68230 timer can provide several facilities needed by MC68000 operating systems. It can generate periodic interrupts, a square wave, or a single interrupt after a programmed time period. Also, it can be used for elapsed time measurement or as a device watchdog. This section describes the programmable options available, capabilities, and restrictions that apply to the timer.

The PI/T timer contains a 24-bit synchronous down counter that is loaded from three 8-bit Counter Preload Registers. The 24-bit counter may be clocked by the output of a 5-bit (divide-by-32) prescaler or by an external timer input TIN. If the prescaler is used, it may be clocked by the system clock (CLK pin) or by the TIN external input. The counter signals the occurrence of an event primarily through zero detection. (A zero is when the counter of the 24-bit timer is equal to zero.) This sets the zero detect status (ZDS) bit in the Timer Status Register. It may be checked by the processor or may be used to generate a timer interrupt. The ZDS bit is reset by writing a 1 to the Timer Status Register in that bit position.

The general operation of the timer is flexible and easily programmable. The timer is fully configured and controlled by programming the 8-bit Timer Control Register. It controls: (1) the choice between the Port C operation and the timer operation of three timer pins, (2) whether the counter is loaded from the Counter Preload Register or rolls over when zero detect is reach, (3) the clock input, (4) whether the prescaler is used, and (5) whether the timer is enabled.

RUN/HALT DEFINITION

The overall operation of the timer is described in terms of the run or halt states. The control of the current state is determined by programming the Timer Control Register. When in the halt state, all of the following occur:

1. The prior contents of the counter is not altered and is reliably readable via the Count Registers.
2. The prescaler is forced to $1F whether or not it is used.
3. The ZDS status bit is forced to 0, regardless of the possible zero contents of the 24-bit counter.

The run state is characterized by:

1. The counter is clocked by the source programmed in the Timer Control Register.
2. The counter is not reliably readable.
3. The prescaler is allowed to decrement if programmed for use.
4. The ZDS status bit is set when the 24-bit counter transitions from $000001 to $000000.

TIMER RULES

This section provides a set of rules that allow easy application of the timer.

1. Refer to the Run/Halt Definition above.
2. When the RESET pin is asserted, all bits of the Timer Control Register go to 0, configuring the dual function pins as Port C inputs.
3. The contents of the Counter Preload Registers and counter are not affected by the RESET pin.
4. The Count Registers provide a direct read data path from each portion of the 24-bit counter, but data written to their addresses is ignored. (This results in a normal bus cycle.) These registers are readable at any time, but their contents are never latched. Unreliable data may be read when the timer is in the run state.

5. The Counter Preload Registers are readable and writable at any time and this occurs independently of any timer operation. No protection mechanisms are provided against ill-timed writes.
6. The input frequency to the 24-bit counter from the TIN pin or prescaler output, must be between 0 and the input frequency at CLK pin divided by 32 regardless of the configuration chosen.
7. For configurations in which the prescaler is used (with the CLK pin or TIN pin as an input), the contents of the Counter Preload Register (CPR) is transferred to the counter the first time that the prescaler passes from $00 to $1F (rolls over) after entering the run state. Thereafter, the counter decrements or is loaded from the Counter Preload Register when the prescaler rolls over.
8. For configurations in which the prescaler is not used, the contents of the Counter Preload Registers are transferred to the counter on the first asserted edge of the TIN input after entering the run state. On subsequent asserted edges the counter decrements or is loaded from the Counter Preload Registers.
9. The lowest value allowed in the Counter Preload Register for use with the counter is $000001.

TIMER INTERRUPT ACKNOWLEDGE CYCLES

Several conditions may be present when the timer interrupt acknowledge pin (TIACK) is asserted. These conditions affect the PI/T's response and the termination of the bus cycle. (See Table 9.)

TABLE 9 — RESPONSE TO TIMER INTERRUPT ACKNOWLEDGE

PC3/TOUT Function	Response to Asserted TIACK
PC3 — Port C Pin	No response. No DTACK.
TOUT — Square Wave	No response. No DTACK.
TOUT — Negated Timer Interrupt Request	No response. No DTACK.
TOUT — Asserted Timer Interrupt Request	Timer Interrupt Vector Contents. DTACK Asserted.

PROGRAMMER'S MODEL

The internal accessible register organization is represented in Table 10. Address space within the address map is reserved for future expansion. Throughout the PI/T data sheet the following conventions are maintained:

1. A read from a reserved location in the map results in a read from the "null register." The null register returns all zeros for data and results in a normal bus cycle. A write to one of these locations results in a normal bus cycle but no write occurs.
2. Unused bits of a defined register are denoted by "*" and are read as zeroes.
3. Bits that are unused in the chosen mode/submode but are used in others, are denoted by "X", and are readable and writeable. Their content, however, is ignored in the chosen mode/submode.
4. All registers are addressable as 8-bit quantities. To facilitate operation with the MOVEP instruction and the DMAC, addresses are ordered such that certain sets of registers may also be accessed as words (2 bytes) or long words (4 bytes).

MOTOROLA *Semiconductor Products Inc.*

TABLE 10 — PI/T REGISTER ADDRESSING ASSIGNMENTS

Register	Register Select Bits					Accessible	Affected by Reset	Affected by Read Cycle
	5	4	3	2	1			
Port General Control Register (PGCR)	0	0	0	0	0	R W	Yes	No
Port Service Request Register (PSRR)	0	0	0	0	1	R W	Yes	No
Port A Data Direction Register (PADDR)	0	0	0	1	0	R W	Yes	No
Port B Data Direction Register (PBDDR)	0	0	0	1	1	R W	Yes	No
Port C Data Direction Register (PCDDR)	0	0	1	0	0	R W	Yes	No
Port Interrupt Vector Register (PIVR)	0	0	1	0	1	R W	Yes	No
Port A Control Register (PACR)	0	0	1	1	0	R W	Yes	No
Port B Control Register (PBCR)	0	0	1	1	1	R W	Yes	No
Port A Data Register (PADR)	0	1	0	0	0	R W	No	* *
Port B Data Register (PBDR)	0	1	0	0	1	R W	No	* *
Port A Alternate Register (PAAR)	0	1	0	1	0	R	No	No
Port B Alternate Register (PBAR)	0	1	0	1	1	R	No	No
Port C Data Register (PCDR)	0	1	1	0	0	R W	No	No
Port Status Register (PSR)	0	1	1	0	1	R W*	Yes	No
Timer Control Register (TCR)	1	0	0	0	0	R W	Yes	No
Timer Interrupt Vector Register (TIVR)	1	0	0	0	1	R W	Yes	No
Counter Preload Register High (CPRH)	1	0	0	1	1	R W	No	No
Counter Preload Register Middle (CPRM)	1	0	1	0	0	R W	No	No
Counter Preload Register Low (CPRL)	1	0	1	0	1	R W	No	No
Count Register High (CNTRH)	1	0	1	1	1	R	No	No
Count Register Middle (CNTRM)	1	1	0	0	0	R	No	No
Count Register Low (CNTRL)	1	1	0	0	1	R	No	No
Timer Status Register (TSR)	1	1	0	1	0	R W*	Yes	No

* A write to this register may perform a special status resetting operation.   R = Read
** Mode dependent.   W = Write

Port General Control Register (PGCR) —

7	6	5	4	3	2	1	0
Port Mode Control		H34 Enable	H12 Enable	H4 Sense	H3 Sense	H2 Sense	H1 Sense

The Port General Control Register controls many of the functions that are common to the overall operation of the ports. The PGCR is composed of three major fields: bits 7 and 6 define the operational mode of Ports A and B and affect operation of the handshake pins and status bits; bits 5 and 4 allow a software controlled disabling of particular hardware associated with the handshake pins of each port; and bits 3-0 define the sense of the handshake pins. The PGCR is always readable and writeable.

All bits are reset to 0 when the RESET pin is asserted.

The Port Mode Control field should be altered only when the H12 Enable and H34 Enable bits are 0. Except when Mode 0 is desired, the Port General Control register must be written once to establish the mode, and again to enable the respective operation(s).

PGCR

7	6	Port Mode Control
0	0	Mode 0 (Unidirectional 8-Bit Mode)
0	1	Mode 1 (Unidirectional 16-Bit Mode)
1	0	Mode 2 (Bidirectional 8-Bit Mode)
1	1	Mode 3 (Bidirectional 16-Bit Mode)

PGCR

5	H34 Enable
0	Disabled
1	Enabled

PGCR

4	H12 Enable
0	Disabled
1	Enabled

PGCR

3-0	Handshake Pin Sense
0	The associated pin is at the high-voltage level when negated and at the low-voltage level when asserted.
1	The associated pin is at the low-voltage level when negated and at the high-voltage level when asserted.

 MOTOROLA *Semiconductor Products Inc.*

Port Service Request Register (PSRR) —

7	6	5	4	3	2	1	0
*	SVCRQ Select		Interrupt PFS		Port Interrupt Priority Control		

The Port Service Request Register controls other functions that are common to the overall operation to the ports. It is composed of four major fields: bit 7 is unused and is always read as 0; bits 6 and 5 define whether interrupt or DMA requests are generated from activity on the H1 and H3 handshake pins; bits 4 and 3 determine whether two dual function pins operate as Port C or port interrupt request/-acknowledge pins; and bits 2, 1, and 0 control the priority among all port interrupt sources. Since bits 2, 1, and 0 affect interrupt operation, it is recommended that they be changed only when the affected interrupt(s) is (are) disabled or known to remain inactive. The PSRR is always readable and writeable.

All bits are reset to 0 when the $\overline{RESET}$ pin is asserted.

PSRR

6	5	SVCRQ Select
0	X	The PC4/$\overline{DMAREQ}$ pin carries the PC4 function; DMA is not used.
1	0	The PC4/$\overline{DMAREQ}$ pin carries the $\overline{DMAREQ}$ function and is associated with double-buffered transfers controlled by H1. H1 is removed from the PI/T's interrupt structure, and thus, does not cause interrupt requests to be generated. To obtain $\overline{DMAREQ}$ pulses, Port A Control Register bit 1 (H1 SVCRQ Enable) must be a 1.
1	1	The PC4/$\overline{DMAREQ}$ pin carries the $\overline{DMAREQ}$ function and is associated with double-buffered transfers controlled by H3. H3 is removed from the PI/T's interrupt structure, and thus, does not cause interrupt requests to be generated. To obtain $\overline{DMAREQ}$ pulses, Port B Control Register bit 1 (H3 SVCRQ Enable) must be 1.

PSRR

4	3	Interrupt Pin Function Select
0	0	The PC5/$\overline{PIRQ}$ pin carries the PC5 function. The PC6/$\overline{PIACK}$ pin carries the PC6 function.
0	1	The PC5/$\overline{PIRQ}$ pin carries the $\overline{PIRQ}$ function. The PC6/$\overline{PIACK}$ pin carries the PC6 function.
1	0	The PC5/$\overline{PIRQ}$ pin carries the PC5 function. The PC6/$\overline{PIACK}$ pin carries the $\overline{PIACK}$ function.
1	1	The PC5/$\overline{PIRQ}$ pin carries the $\overline{PIRQ}$ function. The PC6/$\overline{PIACK}$ pin carries the $\overline{PIACK}$ function.

Bits 2, 1, and 0 determine port interrupt priority. The priority is shown in descending order left to right.

PSRR			Port Interrupt Priority Control			
2	1	0	Highest			............Lowest
0	0	0	H1S	H2S	H3S	H4S
0	0	1	H2S	H1S	H3S	H4S
0	1	0	H1S	H2S	H4S	H3S
0	1	1	H2S	H1S	H4S	H3S
1	0	0	H3S	H4S	H1S	H2S
1	0	1	H3S	H4S	H2S	H1S
1	1	0	H4S	H3S	H1S	H2S
1	1	1	H4S	H3S	H2S	H1S

Port A Data Direction Register (PADDR) — The Port A Data Direction Register determines the direction and buffering characteristics of each of the Port A pins. One bit in the PADDR is assigned to each pin. A 0 indicates that the pin is used as an input, while a 1 indicates it is used as an output. The PADDR is always readable and writeable. This register is ignored in Mode 3.

All bits are reset to the 0 (input) state when the $\overline{RESET}$ pin is asserted.

Port B Data Direction Register (PBDDR) — The PBDDR is identical to the PADDR for the Port B pins and the Port B Data Register, except that this register is ignored in Modes 2 and 3.

Port C Data Direction Register (PCDDR) — The Port C Data Direction Register specifies whether each dual-function pin that is chosen for Port C operation is an input (0) or an output (1) pin. The PCDDR, along with bits that determine the respective pin's function, also specify the exact hardware to be accessed at the Port C Data Register address. (See the Port C Data Register description for more details.) The PCDDR is an 8-bit register that is readable and writeable at all times. Its operation is independent of the chosen PI/T mode.

These bits are cleared to 0 when the $\overline{RESET}$ pin is asserted.

Port Interrupt Vector Register (PIVR) —

7	6	5	4	3	2	1	0
Interrupt Vector Number						*	*

The Port Interrupt Vector Register contains the upper order six bits of the four port interrupt vectors. The contents of this register may be read two ways: by an ordinary read cycle, or by a port interrupt acknowledge bus cycle. The exact data read depends on how the cycle was initiated and other factors. Behavior during a port interrupt acknowledge cycle is summarized above in Table 3.

 MOTOROLA *Semiconductor Products Inc.*

From a normal read cycle (CS), there is never a consequence to reading this register. Following negation of the RESET pin, but prior to writing to the PIVR, a $0F will be read. After writing to the register, the upper 6 bits may be read and the lower 2 bits are forced to 0. No prioritization computation is performed.

Port A Control Register (PACR) —

7	6	5	4	3	2	1	0
Port A Submode		H2 Control			H2 Int. Enable	H1 SVCRQ Enable	H1 Stat. Ctrl.

The Port A Control Register, in conjunction with the programmed mode and the Port B submode, control the operation of Port A and the handshake pins H1 and H2. The Port A Control Register contains five fields: bits 7 and 6 specify the Port A submode; bits 5, 4, and 3 control the operation of the H2 handshake pin and H2S status bit; bit 2 determines whether an interrupt will be generated when the H2S status bit goes to 1; bit 1 determines whether a service request (interrupt request or DMA request) will occur; bit 0 controls the operation of the H1S status bit. The PACR is always readable and writeable.

All bits are cleared to 0 when the RESET pin is asserted.

When the Port A submode field is relevant in a mode/submode definition, it must not be altered unless the H12 Enable bit in the Port General Control Register is 0. (See Table 2.)

The operation of H1 and H2 and their related status bits is given below, for each of the modes specified by Port General Control Register bits 7 and 6. This description is organized such that for each mode/submode all programmable options of each pin and status bit are given.

Bits 2 and 1 carry the same meaning in each mode/submode, and thus are specified only once.

PACR

2	H2 Interrupt Enable
0	The H2 interrupt is disabled.
1	The H2 interrupt is enabled.

PACR

1	H1 SVCRQ Enable
0	The H1 interrupt and DMA request are disabled.
1	The H1 interrupt and DMA request are enabled.

PACR Mode 0 Port A Submode 00

PACR

5	4	3	H2 Control
0	X	X	Input pin — status only.
1	0	0	Output pin — always negated.
1	0	1	Output pin — always asserted.
1	1	0	Output pin — interlocked input handshake protocol.
1	1	1	Output pin — pulsed input handshake protocol.

PACR

0	H1 Status Control
X	Not Used

PACR Mode 0 Port a Submode 01

PACR

5	4	3	H2 Control
0	X	X	Input pin — status only.
1	0	0	Output pin — always negated.
1	0	1	Output pin — always asserted.
1	1	0	Output pin — interlocked output handshake protocol.
1	1	1	Output pin — pulsed output handshake protocol.

PACR

0	H1 Status Control
0	The H1S status bit is 1 when either the Port A initial or final output latch can accept new data. It is 0 when both latches are full and cannot accept new data.
1	The H1S status bit is 1 when both of the Port A output latches are empty. It is 0 when at least one latch is full.

PACR Mode 0 Port A Submode 1X

PCR

5	4	3	H2 Control
0	X	X	Input pin — status only.
1	X	0	Output pin — always negated.
1	X	1	Output pin — always asserted.

PACR

0	H1 Status Control
X	Not used.

PACR Mode 1 Port A Submode XX Port B Submode X0

PACR

5	4	3	H2 Control
0	X	X	Input pin — status only.
1	X	0	Output pin — always negated.
1	X	1	Output pin — always asserted.

PACR

0	H1 Status Control
X	Not used.

PACR Mode 1 Port A Submode XX Port B Submode X1

PACR

5	4	3	H2 Control
0	X	X	Input pin — status only.
1	X	0	Output pin — always negated.
1	X	1	Output pin — always asserted.

PACR

0	H1 Status Control
X	Not used.

 MOTOROLA *Semiconductor Products Inc.*

PACR Mode 2

PACR

5	4	3	H2 Control

X X 0 Output pin — interlocked output handshake protocol.

X X 1 Output pin — pulsed output handshake protocol.

PACR

0	H1 Status Control

0 The H1S status bit is 1 when either the Port B initial or final output latch can accept new data. It is 0 when both latches are full and cannot accept new data.

1 The H1S status bit is 1 when both of the Port B output latches are empty. It is 0 when at least one latch is full.

PACR Mode 3

PACR

5	4	3	H2 Control

X X 0 Output pin — interlocked output handshake protocol.

X X 1 Output pin — pulsed output handshake protocol.

PACR

0	H1 Status Control

0 The H1S status bit is 1 when either the initial or final output latch of Port A and B can accept new data. It is 0 when both latches are full and cannot accept new data.

1 The H1S status bit is 1 when both the initial and final output latches of Ports A and B are empty. It is 0 when either the initial or final latch of Ports A and B is full.

Port B Control Register (PBCR) —

7	6	5	4	3	2	1	0
Port B Submode		H4 Control			H4 Int. Enable	H3 SVCRQ Enable	H3 Stat. Ctrl.

The Port B Control Register specifies the operation of Port B and the handshake pins H3 and H4. The Port B control register contains five fields: bits 7 and 6 specify the Port B submode; bits 5, 4, and 3 control the operation of the H4 handshake pin and H4S status bit; bit 2 determines whether an interrupt will be generated when the H4S status bit goes to 1; bit 1 determines whether a service request (interrupt request or DMA request) will occur; bit 0 controls the operation of the H3S status bit. The PACR is always readable and writeable. There is never a consequence to reading the register.

All bits are cleared to 0 when the RESET pin is asserted. When the Port B submode field is relevant in a mode/submode definition, it must not be altered unless the H34 Enable bit in the Port General Control Register is 0. (See Table 2.)

The operation of H3 and H4 and their related status bits is given below, for each of the modes specified by Port General Control Register bits 7 and 6. This description is organized such that for each mode/submode all programmable options of each pin and status bit are given.

Bits 2 and 1 carry the same meaning in each mode/submode, and thus are specified only once.

PBCR

2	H4 Interrupt Enable

0 The H4 interrupt is disabled.

1 The H4 interrupt is enabled.

PBCR

1	H3 SVCRQ Enable

0 The H3 interrupt and DMA request are disabled.

1 The H3 interrupt and DMA request are enabled.

PBCR Mode 0 Port B Submode 00

PBCR

5	4	3	H4 Control

0 X X Input pin — status only.

1 0 0 Output pin — always negated.

1 0 1 Output pin — always asserted.

1 1 0 Output pin — interlocked input handshake protocol.

1 1 1 Output pin — pulsed input handshake protocol.

PBCR

0	H3 Status Control

X Not used.

PBCR Mode 0 Port B Submode 01

PBCR

5	4	3	H4 Control

0 X X Input pin — status only.

1 0 0 Output pin — always negated.

1 0 1 Output pin — always asserted.

1 1 0 Output pin — interlocked output handshake protocol.

1 1 1 Output pin — pulsed output handshake protocol.

PBCR

0	H3 Status Control

0 The H3S status bit is 1 when either the Port B initial or final output latch can accept new data. It is 0 when both latches are full and cannot accept new data.

1 The H3S status bit is 1 when both of the Port B output latches are empty. It is 0 when at least one latch is full.

PBCR Mode 0 Port B Submode 1X

PBCR

5	4	3	H4 Control

0 X X Input Pin — status only.

1 X 0 Output pin — always negated.

1 X 1 Output pin — always asserted.

PBCR

0	H3 Status Control

X Not used.

PBCR Mode 1 Port B Submode X0

5	4	3	H4 Control

0 X X Input pin — status only.

1 0 0 Output pin — always negated.

1 0 1 Output pin — always asserted.

1 1 0 Output pin — interlocked input handshake protocol.

1 1 1 Output pin — pulsed input handshake protocol.

 MOTOROLA *Semiconductor Products Inc.*

PBCR

0	H3 Status Control
X̲	Not used.

PBCR Mode 1 Port B Submode X1

PBCR

5	4	3	H4 Control
0̲	X	X	Input pin — status only.
1	0	0	Output pin — always negated.
1	0	1	Output pin — always asserted.
1	1	0	Output pin — interlocked output handshake protocol.
1	1	1	Output pin — pulsed output handshake protocol.

PBCR

0	H3 Status Control
0̲	The H3S status bit is 1 when either the initial or final output latch of Port A and B can accept new data. It is 0 when both latches are full and cannot accept new data.
1	The H3S status bit is 1 when both the initial and final output latches of Ports A and B are empty. It is 0 when neither the initial or final latch of Ports A and B is full.

PBCR Mode 2

PBCR

5	4	3	H4 Control
X̲	X	0	Output pin — interlocked input handshake protocol.
X	X	1	Output pin — pulsed input handshake protocol.

PBCR

0	H3 Status Control
X̲	Not used.

PBCR Mode 3

PBCR

5	4	3	H4 Control
X	X̲	0	Output pin — interlocked input handshake protocol.
X	X	1	Output pin — pulsed input handshake protocol.

PBCR

0	H3 Status Control
X̲	Not used.

Port A Data Register (PADR) — The Port A Data Register is an address for moving data to and from the Port A pins. The Port A Data Direction Register determines whether each pin is an input (0) or an output (1), and is used in configuring the actual data paths. This is mode dependent and is described with the modes above.

This register is readable and writeable at all times. Depending on the chosen mode/submode, reading or writing may affect the double-buffered handshake mechanism. The Port A Data Register is not affected by the assertion of the $\overline{\text{RESET}}$ pin.

Port B Data Register (PBDR) — The Port B Data Register is an address for moving data to and from the Port B pins. The Port B Data Direction Register determines whether each pin is an input (0) or an output (1), and is used in configuring the actual data paths. This is mode dependent and is described with the modes, above.

This register is readable and writeable at all times. Depending on the chosen mode/submode, reading or writing may affect the double-buffered handshake mechanism. The Port B Data Register is not affected by the assertion of the $\overline{\text{RESET}}$ pin.

Port A Alternate Register (PAAR) — The Port A Alternate Register is an alternate address for reading the Port A pins. It is a read-only address and no other PI/T condition is affected. In all modes the instantaneous pin level is read and no input latching is performed except at the data bus interface (see Bus Interface Connection). Writes to this address are answered with $\overline{\text{DTACK}}$, but the data is ignored.

Port B Alternate Register (PBAR) — The Port B Alternate Register is an alternate address for reading the Port B pins. It is a read-only address and no other PI/T condition is affected. In all modes the instantaneous pin level is read and no input latching is performed except at the data bus interface (see Bus Interface Connection). Writes to this address are answered with $\overline{\text{DTACK}}$, but the data is ignored.

Port C Data Register (PCDR) — The Port C Data Register is an address for moving data to and from each of the eight Port C/alternate-function pins. The exact hardware accessed is determined by the type of bus cycle (read or write) and individual conditions affecting each pin. These conditions are (1) whether the pin is used for the Port C or alternate function, and (2) whether the Port C Data Direction Register indicates the input or output direction. The Port C Data Register is single buffered for output pins and not buffered for input pins. These conditions are summarized in Table 11.

The Port C Data Register is not affected by the assertion of the $\overline{\text{RESET}}$ pin.

The operation of the PCDR is independent of the chosen PI/T mode.

TABLE 11 — PCDR HARDWARE ACCESSES

Read Port C Data Register			
Port C function PCDDR = 0	Port C function PCDDR = 1	Alternate function PCDDR = 0	Alternate function PCDDR = 1
pin	Port C output register	pin	Port C output register
Write Port C Data Register			
Port C Function PCDDR = 0	Port C Function PCDDR = 1	Alternate function PCDDR = 0	Alternate function PCDDR = 1
Port C output register, buffer disabled	Port C output register, buffer enabled	Port C output register	Port C output register

 MOTOROLA *Semiconductor Products Inc.*

Note that two additional useful benefits result from this structure. First, it is possible to directly read the state of a dual-function pin while used for the non-Port C function. Second, it is possible to generate program controlled transitions on alternate-function pins by switching back to the Port C function, and writing to the PCDR.

This register is readable and writeable at all times.

Port Status Register (PSR) —

7	6	5	4	3	2	1	0
H4 Level	H3 Level	H2 Level	H1 Level	H4S	H3S	H2S	H1S

The Port Status Register contains information about handshake pin activity. Bits 7-4 show the instantaneous level of the respective handshake pin, and is independent of the handshake pin sense bits in the Port General Control Register. Bit 3-0 are the respective status bits referred to throughout this data sheet. Their interpretation depends on the programmed mode/submode of the PI/T. For Bits 3-0 a 1 is the active or asserted state.

Timer Control Register (TCR) —

7	6	5	4	3	2	1	0
TOUT/$\overline{\text{TIACK}}$ Control			Z.D. Ctrl.	*	Clock Control		Timer Enable

The Timer Control Register (TCR) determines all operations of the timer. Bits 7-5 configure the PC3/TOUT and PC7/$\overline{\text{TIACK}}$ pins for Port C, square wave, vectored interrupt, or autovectored interrupt operation; bit 4 specifies whether the counter receives data from the Counter Preload Register or continues counting when zero detect is reached; bit 3 is unused and is read as 0; bits 2 and 1 configure the path from the CLK and TIN pins to the counter controller; bit 0 enables the timer. This register is readable and writeable at all times.

All bits are cleared to 0 when the $\overline{\text{RESET}}$ pin is asserted.

TCR
7 6 5   **TOUT/$\overline{\text{TIACK}}$ Control**

0 0 X The dual-function pins PC3/TOUT and PC7/$\overline{\text{TIACK}}$ carry the Port C function.

0 1 X The dual-function pin PC3/TOUT carries the TOUT function. In the run state it is used as a square wave output and is toggled on zero detect. The TOUT pin is high while in the halt state. The dual-function pin PC7/$\overline{\text{TIACK}}$ carries the PC7 function.

1 0 0 The dual-function pin PC3/TOUT carries the TOUT function. In the run or halt state it is used as a timer interrupt request output. The timer interrupt is disabled; thus, the pin is always three-stated. The dual-function pin PC7/$\overline{\text{TIACK}}$ carries the $\overline{\text{TIACK}}$ function; however, since interrupt request is negated, the PI/T produces no response, i.e., no data or $\overline{\text{DTACK}}$, to an asserted $\overline{\text{TIACK}}$. Refer to Timer Interrupt Cycle section for details. This combination and the 101 state below support vectored timer interrupts.

1 0 1 The dual-function pin PC3/TOUT carries the TOUT function and is used as a timer interrupt request output. The timer interrupt is enabled; thus, the pin is low when the timer ZDS status bit is 1. The dual function pin PC7/$\overline{\text{TIACK}}$ carries the $\overline{\text{TIACK}}$ function and is used as a timer interrupt acknowledge input. Refer to the Timer Interrupt Acknowledge Cycle section for details. This combination and the 100 state above support vectored timer interrupts.

1 1 0 The dual-function pin PC3/TOUT carries the TOUT function. In the run or halt state it is used as a timer interrupt request output. The timer interrupt is disabled; thus, the pin is always three-stated. The dual-function pin PC7/$\overline{\text{TIACK}}$ carries the PC7 function.

1 1 1 The dual-function pin PC3/TOUT carries the TOUT function and is used as a timer interrupt request output. The timer interrupt is enabled; thus, the pin is low when the timer ZDS status bit is 1. The dual-function pin PC7/$\overline{\text{TIACK}}$ carries the PC7 function and autovectored interrupts are supported.

TCR
4   **Zero Detect Control**

0 The counter is loaded from the Counter Preload Register on the first clock to the 24-bit counter after zero detect, and resumes counting.

1 The counter rolls over on zero detect, then continues counting.

Bit 3 is unused and is always read as 0.

TCR
2 1   **Clock Control**

0 0 The PC2/TIN input pin carries the Port C function and the CLK pin and prescaler are used. The prescaler is decremented on the falling transition of the CLK pin; the 24-bit counter is decremented or loaded from the Counter Preload Registers when the prescaler rolls over from $00 to $1F. The Timer Enable bit determines whether the timer is in the run or halt state.

0 1 The PC2/TIN pin serves as a timer input and the CLK pin and prescaler are used. The prescaler is decremented on the falling transition of the CLK pin; the 24-bit counter is decremented or loaded from the Counter Preload Registers when the prescaler rolls over from $00 to $1F. The timer is in the run state when the Timer Enable bit is 1 and the TIN pin is high; otherwise the timer is in the halt state.

1 0 The PC2/TIN pin serves as a timer input and the prescaler is used. The prescaler is decremented following the rising transition of the TIN pin after syncing with the internal clock. The 24-bit counter is decremented or loaded from the counter preload registers when the prescaler rolls over from $00 to $1F. The Timer Enable bit determines whether the timer is in the run or halt state.

1 1 The PC2/TIN pin serves as a timer input and the prescaler is unused. The 24-bit counter is decremented or loaded from the Counter Preload Registers following the rising edge of the TIN pin after syncing with the internal clock. The Timer Enable bit determines whether the timer is in the run or halt state.

 MOTOROLA *Semiconductor Products Inc.*

TCR

0		Timer Enable
0	Disabled.	
1	Enabled.	

Timer Interrupt Vector Register (TIVR) — The timer interrupt vector register contains the 8-bit vector supplied when the timer interrupt acknowledge pin TIACK is asserted. The register is readable and writeable at all times, and the same value is always obtained from a normal read cycle and a timer interrupt acknowledge bus cycle (TIACK). When the RESET pin is asserted the value of $0F is automatically loaded into the register. Refer to Timer Interrupt Acknowledge Cycle section for more details.

Counter Preload Register H, M, L (CPRH-L)

7	6	5	4	3	2	1	0	
Bit 23	Bit 22	Bit 21	Bit 20	Bit 19	Bit 18	Bit 17	Bit 16	CPRH
Bit 15	Bit 14	Bit 13	Bit 12	Bit 11	Bit 10	Bit 9	Bit 8	CPRM
Bit 7	Bit 6	Bit 5	Bir 4	Bit 3	Bit 2	Bit 1	Bit 0	CPRL

The Counter Preload Registers are a group of three 8-bit registers used for storing data to be transferred to the counter. Each of the registers is individually addressable, or the group may be accessed with the MOVEP .L or the MOVEP.W instructions. The address one less than the address of CPRH is the null register, and is reserved so that zeros are read in the upper 8 bits of the destination data register when a MOVEP.L is used. Data written to this address is ignored.

The registers are readable and writeable at all times. A read cycle proceeds independently of any transfer to the counter, which may be occuring simultaneously.

To insure proper operation of the PI/T Timer, a value of $000000 may not be stored in the Counter Preload Registers for use with the counter.

The RESET pin does not affect the contents of these registers.

Count Register H, M, L (CNTRH-L) —

7	6	5	4	3	2	1	0	
Bit 23	Bit 22	Bit 21	Bit 20	Bit 19	Bit 18	Bit 17	Bit 16	CNTRH
Bit 15	Bit 14	Bit 13	Bit 12	Bit 11	Bit 10	Bit 9	Bit 8	CNTRM
Bit 7	Bit 6	Bit 5	Bit 4	Bit 3	Bit 2	Bit 1	Bit 0	CNTRL

The count registers are a group of three 8-bit addresses at which the counter can be read. The contents of the counter are not latched during a read bus cycle; thus, the data read at these addresses is not guaranteed if the timer is in the run

state. (Bits 2, 1, and 0 of the Timer Control Register specify the state.) Write operations to these addresses result in a normal bus cycle but the data is ignored.

Each of the registers is individually addressable, or the group may be accessed with the MOVEP.L or the MOVEP.W instructions. The address one less than the address of CNTRH is the null register, and is reserved so that zeros are read in the upper 8 bits of the destination data register when a MOVEP.L is used. Data written to this address is ignored.

Timer Status Register (TSR) —

7	6	5	4	3	2	1	0
*	*	*	*	*	*	*	ZDS

The Timer Status Register contains one bit from which the zero detect status can be determined. The ZDS status bit (bit 0) is an edge-sensitive flip-flop that is set to 1 when the 24-bit counter decrements from $000001 to $000000. The ZDS status bit is cleared to 0 following the direct clear operation (similar to that of the ports), or when the timer is halted. Note also that when the RESET pin is asserted the timer is disabled, and thus enters the halt state.

This register is always readable without consequence. A write access performs a direct clear operation if bit 0 in the written data is 1. Following that, the ZDS bit is 0.

This register is constructed with a reset dominant S-R flip-flop so that all clearing conditions prevail over the possible zero detect condition.

Bits 7-1 are unused and are read as 0.

TIMER APPLICATIONS SUMMARY

This section outlines programming of the Timer Control Register for several typical examples.

Periodic Interrupt Generator

7	6	5	4	3	2	1	0
TOUT/TIACK Control			Z D Ctrl	*	Clock Control		Timer Enable
1	X	1	0	0	00 or 1X		changed

In this configuration the timer generates a periodic interrupt. The TOUT pin is connected to the system's interrupt request circuitry and the TIACK pin may be used as an interrupt acknowledge input to the timer. The TIN pin may be used as a clock input.

The processor loads the Counter Preload Registers and Timer Control Register, and then enables the timer. When the 24-bit counter passes from $000001 to $000000 the ZDS status bit is set and the TOUT (interrupt request) pin is asserted. At the next clock to the 24-bit counter it is again loaded with the contents of the CPR's, and thereafter decrements. In normal operation, the processor must direct clear the status bit to negate the interrupt request (see Figure 15).

MOTOROLA *Semiconductor Products Inc.*

FIGURE 15 — PERIODIC INTERRUPT GENERATOR

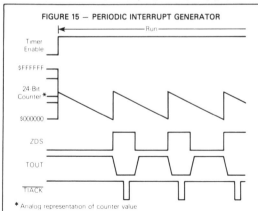

* Analog representation of counter value

Square Wave Generator

7	6	5	4	3	2	1	0
TOUT/TIACK Control			Z.D Ctrl.	*	Clock Control		Timer Enable
0	1	X	0	0	00 or 1X		changed

In this configuration the timer produces a square wave at the TOUT pin. The TOUT pin is connected to the user's circuitry and the TIACK pin is not used. The TIN pin may be used as a clock input.

The processor loads the Counter Preload Registers and Timer Control Register, and then enables the timer. When the 24-bit counter passes from $000001 to $000000 the ZDS status bit is set and the TOUT (square wave output) pin is toggled. At the next clock to the 24-bit counter it is again loaded with the contents of the CPRs, and thereafter decrements. In this application there is no need for the processor to direct clear the ZDS status bit; however, it is possible for the processor to sync itself with the square wave by clearing the ZDS status bit, then polling it. The processor may also read the TOUT level at the Port C address.

Note that the PC3/TOUT pin functions as PC3 following the negation of RESET. If used in the square wave configuration a pullup resistor may be required to keep a known level prior to programming. Prior to enabling the timer, TOUT is high (see Figure 16).

FIGURE 16 — SQUARE WAVE GENERATOR

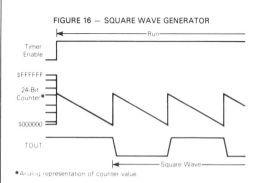

* Analog representation of counter value.

Interrupt After Timeout

7	6	5	4	3	2	1	0
TOUT/TIACK Control			Z.D Ctrl.	*	Clock Control		Timer En.
1	X	1	1	0	00 or 1X		changed

In this configuration the timer generates an interrupt after a programmed time period has expired. The TOUT pin is connected to the system's interrupt request circuitry and the TIACK pin may be an interrupt acknowledge input to the timer. The TIN pin may be used as a clock input.

This configuration is similar to the periodic interrupt generator except that the Zero Detect Control bit is set. This forces the counter roll over after Zero Detect is reached, rather than reloading from the CPRs. When the processor takes the interrupt it can halt the timer and read the counter. This allows the processor to measure the delay time from Zero Detect (interrupt request) to entering the service routine. Accurate knowledge of the interrupt latency may be useful in some applications (see Figure 17).

FIGURE 17 — SINGLE INTERRUPT AFTER TIMEOUT

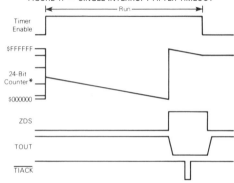

* Analog representation of counter value.

Elapsed Time Measurement

Elapsed time measurement takes several forms; two are described below.

System Clock

7	6	5	4	3	2	1	0
TOUT/TIACK Control			Z.D Ctrl.	*	Clock Control		Timer Enable
0	0	X	1	0	0		changed

This configuration allows time interval measurement by software. No timer pins are used.

The processor loads the Counter Preload Registers (generally with all 1s) and Timer Control Register, and then enables the timer. The counter decrements until the ending event takes place. When it is desired to read the time interval, the processor must halt the timer, then read the counter.

For applications in which the interval could have exceeded that programmable in this timer, interrupts can be counted to provide the equivalent of additional timer bits. At the end, the timer can be halted and read (see Figure 18).

 MOTOROLA Semiconductor Products Inc.

FIGURE 18 — ELAPSED TIME MEASUREMENT

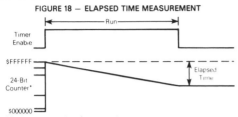

*Analog representation of counter values.

External Clock

7	6	5	4	3	2	1	0
TOUT/TIACK Control			Z. D. Ctrl.	*	Clock Control		Timer Enable
0	0	X	1	0	1	X	changed

This configuration allows measurement (counting) of the number of input pulses occurring in an interval in which the counter is enabled. The TIN input pin provides the input pulses. Generally the TOUT and TIACK pins are not used.

This configuration is identical to the Elapsed Time Measurement/System Clock configuration except that the TIN pin is used to provide the input frequency. It can be connected to a simple oscillator, and the same methods could be used. Alternately, it could be gated off and on externally and the number of cycles occurring while in the run state can be counted. However, minimum pulse width high and low specifications must be met.

Device Watchdog

7	6	5	4	3	2	1	0
TOUT/TIACK Control			Z. D. Ctrl.	*	Clock Control		Timer Enable
1	X	1	1	0	0	1	changed

This configuration provides the watchdog function needed in many systems. The TIN pin is the timer input whose period at the high (1) level is to be checked. Once allowed by the processor, the TIN input pin controls the run/halt mode. The TOUT pin is connected to external circuitry requiring notification when the TIN pin has been asserted longer than the programmed time. The TIACK pin (interrupt acknowledge) is only needed if the TOUT pin is connected to interrupt circuitry.

The processor loads the Counter Preload Register and Timer Control Register, and then enables the timer. When the TIN input is asserted (1, high) the timer transfers the contents of the Counter Preload Register to the counter and begins counting. If the TIN input is negated before Zero Detect is reached, the TOUT output and the ZDS status bit remain negated. If Zero Detect is reached while the TIN input is still asserted the ZDS status bit is set and the TOUT output is asserted. (The counter rolls over and keeps on counting.)

In either case, when the TIN input is negated the ZDS status bit is 0, the TOUT output is negated, the counting stops, and the prescaler is forced to all 1s (see Figure 19).

FIGURE 19 — DEVICE WATCHDOG

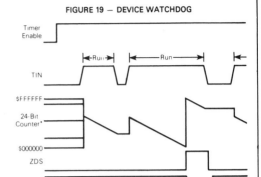

*Analog representation of counter value.

BUS INTERFACE CONNECTION

The PI/T has an asynchronous bus interface, primarily designed for use with the MC68000 microprocessor. With care, however, it can be connected to synchronous microprocessor buses. This section completely describes the PI/T's bus interface, and is intended for the asynchronous bus designer unless otherwise mentioned.

In an asynchronous system the PI/T CLK may operate at a significantly different frequency, either higher or lower, than the bus master and other system components, as long as all bus specifications are met. The MC68230 CLK pin has the same specifications as the MC68000 CLK, and must not be gated off at any time.

The following signals generate normal read and write cycles to the PI/T: CS (Chip Select), R/W (Read/Write), RS1-RS5 (five Register Select bits), D0-D7 (the 8-bit bidirectional data bus), and DTACK (Data Transfer Acknowledge). To generate interrupt acknowledge cycles PC6/PIACK or PC7/TIACK is used instead of CS, and the Register Select pins are ignored. No combination of the following pins may be asserted simultaneously: CS, PIACK, or TIACK.

READ CYCLES VIA CHIP SELECT

This catagory includes all register reads, except port or timer interrupt acknowledge cycles. When CS is asserted, the Register Select and R/W inputs are latched internallly. They must meet small setup and hold time requirements with respect to the asserted edge of CS. (See the AC ELECTRICAL CHARACTERISTICS table.) The PI/T is *not* protected against aborted (shortened) bus cycles generated by an Address Error or Bus Error exception in which it is addressed.

Certain operations triggered by normal read (or write) bus cycles are not complete within the time allotted to the bus cycle. One example is transfers to/from the double-buffered latches that occur as a result of the bus cycle. If the bus master's CLK is significantly faster than the PI/T's the possibility exists that, following the bus cycle, CS can be

 MOTOROLA *Semiconductor Products Inc.*

negated then re-asserted before completion of these internal operations. In this situation the PI/T does not recognize the re-assertion of $\overline{CS}$ until these operations are complete. Only at that time does it begin the internal sequencing necessary to react to the asserted $\overline{CS}$. Since $\overline{CS}$ also controls the $\overline{DTACK}$ response, this "bus cycle recovery time" can be related to the CLK edge on which $\overline{DTACK}$ is asserted for that cycle. The PI/T will recognize the subsequent assertion of $\overline{CS}$ three (3) CLK periods after the CLK edge on which $\overline{DTACK}$ was previously asserted.

The Register Select and R/$\overline{W}$ inputs pass through an internal latch that is transparent when the PI/T can recognize a new $\overline{CS}$ pulse (see above paragraph). Since the internal data bus of the PI/T is continuously enabled for read transfers, the read access time (to the data bus buffers) begins when the Register Selects are stabilized internally. Also, when the PI/T is ready to begin a new bus cycle, the assertion of $\overline{CS}$ enables the data bus buffers within a short propagation delay. This does not contribute to the overall read access time unless $\overline{CS}$ is asserted significantly after the Register Select and R/$\overline{W}$ inputs are stabilized (as may occur with synchronous bus microprocessors).

In addition to Chip Select's previously mentioned duties, it controls the assertion of $\overline{DTACK}$ and latching of read data at the data bus interface. Except for controlling input latches and enabling the data bus buffers, all of these functions occur only after $\overline{CS}$ has been recognized internally and synchronized with the internal clock. Chip Select is recognized on the falling edge of the CLK if the setup time is met, $\overline{DTACK}$ is asserted (low) on the next falling edge of the CLK. Read data is latched at the PI/T's data bus interface at the same time $\overline{DTACK}$ is asserted. It is stable as long as Chip Select remains asserted independent of other external conditions.

From the above discussion it is clear that if the $\overline{CS}$ setup time prior to the falling edge of the CLK is met, the PI/T can consistently respond to a new read or write bus cycle every four (4) CLK cycles. This fact is especially useful in designing the PI/T's clock in synchronous bus systems not using $\overline{DTACK}$. (An extra CLK period is required in interrupt acknowledge cycles, see Read Cycles via Interrupt Acknowledge.)

In asynchronous bus systems in which the PI/T's CLK differs from that of the bus master, generally there is no way to guarantee that the $\overline{CS}$ setup time with respect to the PI/T

CLK is met. Thus, the only way to determine that the PI/T recognized the assertion of $\overline{CS}$ is to wait for the assertion of $\overline{DTACK}$. In this situation, all latched bus inputs to the PI/T must be held stable until $\overline{DTACK}$ is asserted. These include Register Select, R/$\overline{W}$, and write data inputs (see below).

System specifications impose a maximum delay from the trailing (negated) edge of Chip Select to the negated edge of $\overline{DTACK}$. As system speeds increase this becomes more difficult to meet with a simple pullup resistor tied to the $\overline{DTACK}$ line. Therefore, the PI/T provides an internal active pullup device to reduce the rise time, and a level-sensitive circuit that later turns this device off. $\overline{DTACK}$ is negated asynchronously as fast as possible following the rising edge of Chip Select, then three-stated to avoid interference with the next bus cycle.

The system designer must take care that $\overline{DTACK}$ is negated and three-stated quickly enough after each bus cycle to avoid interference with the next one. With the MC68000 this necessitates a relatively fast external path from the data strobe to $\overline{CS}$ going negated.

WRITE CYCLES

In many ways write cycles are similar to normal read cycles (see above). On write cycles, data at the D0-D7 pins must meet the same setup specifications as the Register Select and R/$\overline{W}$ lines. Like these signals, write data is latched on the asserted edge of $\overline{CS}$, and must meet small setup and hold time requirements with respect to that edge. The same bus cycle recovery conditions exist as for normal read cycles. No other differences exist.

READ CYCLES VIA INTERRUPT ACKNOWLEDGE

Special internal operations take place on PI/T interrupt acknowledge cycles. The Port Interrupt Vector Register or the Timer Interrupt Vector Register are implicitly addressed by the assertion of PC6/$\overline{PIACK}$ or PC7/$\overline{TIACK}$, respectively. The signals are first synchronized with the falling edge of the CLK. One clock period after they are recognized the data bus buffers are enabled and the vector is driven onto the bus. $\overline{DTACK}$ is asserted after another clock period to allow the vector some setup time prior to $\overline{DTACK}$. $\overline{DTACK}$ is negated, then three-stated as with normal read or write cycle, when $\overline{PIACK}$ or $\overline{TIACK}$ is negated.

 MOTOROLA *Semiconductor Products Inc.*

INDEX